DITKA:

Monster of the Midway

Books by Armen Keteyian

DITKA: Monster of the Midway*

RAW RECRUITS: The High-Stakes Game Colleges Play to Get Their Basketball Stars—*And What It Costs to Win** (with Alexander Wolff)

BIG RED CONFIDENTIAL: Inside Nebraska Football

CATFISH: My Life in Baseball (with Jim "Catfish" Hunter)

CALLING THE SHOTS (with Mike Singletary)

ROD CAREW'S ART AND SCIENCE OF HITTING (with Rod Carew and Frank Pace)

*Published by POCKET BOOKS

DITKA:
Monster of the Midway

ARMEN KETEYIAN

POCKET BOOKS

New York   London   Toronto   Sydney   Tokyo   Singapore

POCKET BOOKS, a division of Simon & Schuster Inc.
1230 Avenue of the Americas, New York, NY 10020

ISBN: 0-671-74999-4

First Pocket Books hardcover printing September 1992

10 9 8 7 6 5 4 3 2 1

POCKET and colophon are registered trademarks of
Simon & Schuster Inc.

Printed in the U.S.A.

To my darling Dede, and the girls, Kristen and Kelly:
Patience, Kindness, and Love are your middle names . . .
It's great to be a family again.

1

IT WAS THE LAST PLACE HE WANTED TO BE. IN FRONT OF THE LAST PEOPLE HE wanted to see.

"This is the final, final," said Mike Ditka.

He was behind a podium in a subterranean classroom of Halas Hall, the hallowed home of the 1986 Super Bowl champion Chicago Bears, making it clear this was it—his last formal word on the maddening 1991 season. Not twenty-four hours earlier Ditka's Bears had been outhit, outhustled, and outcoached, and in the end, outscored by a brash bunch of Dallas Cowboys in a National Football League wild-card playoff game, a game that offered an unobstructed view of just how far the Bears had fallen since Super Bowl XX and the glory days of McMahon, Payton, Fencik, and The Fridge.

For the fourth time in five years the Bears had come apart at crunch time. Worse, three of those playoff losses were at Soldier Field, but none hurt quite like this one: losing 17–13 to a team whose regular-season record had been a god-awful 1–15 two years earlier.

It wasn't so much being inside the Cowboys 10-yard line four times and scoring just 10 points. It wasn't so much the stupid penalties, painfully obvious play-calling, blocked punt that fed a Cowboys touchdown, the Keystone Kops special teams, or even the ass-kicking along the line of scrimmage. All that could be balanced by the heart and hands of wide receiver Tom Waddle (9 catches, 104 yards), the folk hero of this football season; the breakout performance by forgotten fullback Darren Lewis; the gritty fire of quarterback Jim Harbaugh. No, it was something else. It was the *way* the team had lost. How flat,

1

listless, and scared so many players were. How Ditka stood so idly by, hands buried deep in the pockets of his groovy black leather jacket, the once–Master Motivator suddenly silent and serene. This wasn't Bears football; it was barely football.

After the game a fuming Kevin Butler, the team's clutch placekicker, sat naked in the corner of the locker room and spit out his disgust. "There are a lot of fucking gutless people in this locker room." Spit. "We played fucking scared." Spit. Of special teams coach Steve Kazor, he said, "The guy's a fucking joke."

Across the room defensive captain and nine-time All-Pro middle linebacker Mike Singletary, the heart and soul of the team, slowly shook his head and quietly questioned why "our two-million-dollar running back had run with his head down all afternoon," a reference to the team's enigmatic superback Neal Anderson. "I don't know what's wrong with Neal," Singletary said. Neither did anybody else.

The locker room was almost empty as Singletary spoke. The guilty rushing away from the scene of the crime, moving faster than they had all day. Left behind were wads of tape, wet towels, and lost hopes. Only the innocent remained: Singletary, defensive ends Trace Armstrong and Richard Dent, offensive linemen Tom Thayer, Jay Hilgenberg, and Keith Van Horne, and Harbaugh—men who, for better or worse, had left their part of themselves out on the field. They all dressed as if headed for a funeral, mulling over their miseries, reflecting back, peering forward, stressing the need for recommitment and discipline. "We need to weed out the guys who don't want to work," said Singletary. "That '85 team was crazy, but it paid the price to win. Down ten points in a game, you'd hear guys on the sidelines saying, 'Let's go, let's do it.'" He paused, grimacing as he raised his right arm, the one attached to the hyperextended elbow, to comb his hair. "I just didn't see that fire today with this team," he said.

"Everyone has to look at himself and say 'What can I do to get better?'" said Armstrong, the young defensive end Singletary had tabbed as the future leader on the team. "We have to ask ourselves, have we paid the price?"

Harbaugh certainly had. After taking a back-alley beating from a Dallas defense that was flying to the ball all day, he was dressing with the temerity of a bypass patient. Despite a courageous effort he had heard the taunts and boos. "Harbaugh, you piece of shit!" one local yokel had screamed just before Harbaugh entered a canopy leading to the locker room. The twenty-seven-year-old quarterback who, in his fifth year, had completely answered all the questions about his arm, heart, and head raised that head and told the guy to f-off. Then

2

Harbaugh flipped him off for good measure. "I'm proud of the way I played this year," Harbaugh said in the dead calm of the locker room. "But this is a miserable way to end it."

Yes, it was. The kind of game that made it oh so easy to forget how inspiring and courageous this Chicago Bear team had been early in the year. Who could forget that 19–13 Monday-night miracle against the Jets? Or Anderson's divine 42-yard TD sprint that sent the defending Super Bowl champion New York Giants home on the wrong end of a 20–17 score? Or how about Waddle's 13-Wing-Jet-and-a-prayer TD reception in a last-minute upset over undefeated New Orleans? In truth the Bears had been one bad back (the loss of future Hall of Fame left tackle Jim Covert) and one bad snap—the Miami game—away from a 13-3 or 12-4 season. As it was, they won eleven games and lost just five, despite playing without their starting backfield for half the year. Eleven wins squeezed out of a bunch of "overachievers" and a bitch of a schedule by the only coach in the NFL capable of doing it.

Ditka. Iron Mike. Da Coach . . .

Call him what you want. Whatever it is, he is, without question, the most charismatic, controversial, and compelling coach in sport. A man who wasn't so much born as forged from the raw materials of his beloved hometown of Aliquippa, Pennsylvania, a fierce, fiery monster of a man cast deep inside the earth. His self-esteem and temperament are forever tied to that one constant in his life, the one elixir that cured any ill—winning.

If ever a man was made for a game it was Ditka and football. With its primal pleasures and individual wars, football is a sport where you can physically beat a man into submission, watch the quit come to his eyes. Football is where you test your will, where you conquer and overpower your enemy. The kind of game given to putting a foot on a man's chest and beating your breast in triumph.

"I wasn't always the best," he once said, "but nobody worked harder. You and me. Let's see who's tougher. I lived for competition."

Today, despite some semblance of inner peace, he remains a complex and contradictory man. At times a volatile, vitriolic, and foreboding giant, greedy as a grizzly when it comes to money. "A frightening figure," in the words of one longtime business associate. Yet also, a softhearted teddy who cuddles and comforts disabled children, raises and donates millions of dollars for charities and scholarships, loyal as the day is long. "If he believes in something," says another longtime friend, "he'll go to the ends of the earth for you."

As every Bear fan knows, Ditka went to those ends as a football player, epitomizing the raw, survivalistic nature of his sport. He played in a molten fury, fighting, scrapping, scratching for every inch of turf. He was a high school star, a college All-American, rookie of the year for the Chicago Bears in 1961, a five-time All-Pro who revolutionized the position of tight end before becoming the first tight end ever inducted into the Pro Football Hall of Fame. His calling cards were head-rattling blocks, rampaging runs through the secondary, hits so violent you heard pads popping forty-five rows up into the stands. He coaches the same way, with a frenetic mix of volcanic rage and impassioned purpose, preaching Bear football like some old-time religion, ranting, raving, intimidating, motivating—the all-powerful spiritual and physical embodiment of a city and its team. "The perfect coach for the Chicago Bears," says Dent.

Today he's treated like some larger-than-life American icon, which in many ways he is. On the sidelines, cameras lock like lasers on his face, watching the endless chewing and spit, spit, spitting, waiting for him to throw a fit as he matches wits in his winner-take-all world. How many coaches—how many people—compare to Iron Mike Ditka? How many are that tough? That motivated? That glib and natural on the tube? Not many. Not in the homogenized, pasteurized National Football League.

"Mike Ditka *is* the National Football League," says Bears defensive tackle Steve McMichael.

But does Mike Ditka really need the NFL anymore? Have the heart scare in 1988 and the estimated $5 million-plus he makes a year off the field—in the same league with Palmer and Nicklaus—finally snuffed out his fire? Is he too busy banging out motivational speeches at $20,000 a pop, too busy telling his audiences "the American dream is alive and well if you're willing to pursue it," to make another Super Bowl dream come true?

And he is busy—far and away the most commercialized coach in sports, a man with a Q-rating (for nationwide public recognition) comparable to Magic and Michael (Jordan, not Jackson). A Fortune 500 coaching conglomerate with his restaurants, million-dollar endorsement deals, airplane charter companies, golf course construction, supermarket line of pork chops, and syndicated TV and radio shows. "With all due respect," says David Hynes, a Chicago marketing specialist who frequently works with Ditka, "we treat Mike like a quality-brand product."

Mike Ditka—Famous Tough Guy. Mike Ditka—All-American Hero. Mike Ditka—Everyman. Pick an image, any image. Ditka does. He switches effortlessly from Iron Mike to Corporate Coach selling everything from Toyotas to antifreeze to chewing gum, computer games, a bank, baby bibs, rustproofing, rental cars, even his own brand of cologne. Watch him tool around town in his antique cars or sip fine wines at gourmet restaurants. See him joke with Johnny Carson, star on "L.A. Law," spawn brilliant satire on "Saturday Night Live." (Who can forget "The Mike Ditka Type-A Christmas Special" and of course, "Da Bears"?) He's become a Claymation character, a real-life California Raisin, for goodness' sake, designed, shaped, and packaged to peddle his success story to middle America.

And if that's not enough (and with Ditka it's not), he has parlayed his fame and fortune into his own brand of motivational ministry; he has become a kind of Billy Graham of coaching, a modern-day football evangelist eager to preach his populist can-do message. In Chicago his "in life" phrase has become part of the city's lexicon, like the Loop and Lake Shore Drive. Time and time again, in TV or print, Ditka offers up personal sermons, parables, discourses on the ebb and flow of American life: Ditka on the candidacy of George Bush; Ditka on David Duke; Ditka on getting up in the morning; on overcoming adversity. Do we really need this? Some folks love it; others gag every time they see one of those "Believe and Achieve" buttons or "Whatever It Takes" T-shirts.

Judging by local reaction to the Dallas loss, the prevailing opinion in December 1991 was Ditka was better off in permanent hibernation; he no longer had whatever it took to coach Da Bears. Monday's papers were packed with stinging postmortems. "Bears DOA and O-U-T" blared the headline in the *Chicago Tribune*. One *Trib* columnist, Bernie Lincicome, a saber in Ditka's side for years, put the blame squarely on Ditka's shoulders and dared him to resign. For good measure Lincicome told the team to trade its $2-million All-Pro running back "before the secret is out that something is awfully wrong here, either in attitude or ability" and urged the Bears to fire their anything-but-special-teams coach Kazor. "Now," said Lincicome. Over at the *Sun-Times*, their star sports columnist Jay Mariotti honed in on the front office bickering between team president Mike McCaskey, player personnel director Bill Tobin, and "Rev. Ditka," who was suddenly, predictably, spreading the blame in other directions.

"We have overachievers, and sometimes you need people who are a little bit better than overachievers," Ditka had said after the loss, deflecting potential criticism, a habit since youth. "I'll play with them anytime because, hey, gang, it's the hand I'm dealt."

Yet there he was Monday afternoon hobbling toward that podium at Halas Hall, ready to deal with the media one last time. As always, the press snapped to attention. Cameras clicked on. Tape recorders rolled.

Shuffling like an eighty-year-old man barely able to put pressure on his degenerative left hip, he scanned a sea of familiar faces all squeezed into flip-top desks best suited for elementary school. Behind the reporters, like a crescent moon, were a battery of klieg lights and TV cameras. Nobody expected much. In less than twenty-four hours, Ditka had made his appointed media rounds: a postgame interview on CBS, his two radio shows, and his Sunday-night TV show. What more could he say?

After such a bitter loss most coaches would stonewall or bleat out the banal and be done with it. Not Ditka. He came out swinging. He took shots at the press, the front office, his players, even admitting this Mellow Mike business had gone too far: "I think I became so worried about the Mike Ditka image of getting excited and getting angry at times that I became this guy who didn't get excited and didn't get angry at the right times," he said. He acknowledged team discipline had dropped off the cliff. So he issued a series of ultimatums, warning the likes of William "the Refrigerator" Perry, the 380-pound blimp of a defensive tackle, to shape up or ship out. And, he said, either he and McCaskey and Tobin settled their differences "or else I'm out of here."

In the end it was not only a tableau for a team but an epitaph for an era. A decade in which Ditka's Bears won 101 regular-season games (against 51 losses) and made the playoffs seven out of the last eight seasons. That night in New Orleans on January 26, 1986 was probably his finest hour. The night he held that shimmering Vince Lombardi Trophy in his hands, moments after his team had mauled the New England Patriots 46–10 in Super Bowl XX. It was a bright shining moment, wiping away all the doubts and doubters, proving once and for all the Bears, his 18-1 Bears, deserved a spot in the pantheon of pro football's greatest teams. But there had been no return trip to a Super Bowl city since that week in New Orleans. No more Super Bowl Shuffles despite *averaging* better than twelve wins a year from 1986 through '88, a very sore statistic to the likes of Dent. "I'm supposed to be sitting here with three or four Super Bowl rings on my hand," he said one day not long before the final playoff game. "That's what we had."

What they had on Monday afternoon was the end of that era. A football obit written by the man born to coach the Chicago Bears, who "built this football team exactly the way I wanted it" then goaded it to greatness. Yet a man who, as we shall see, must also share—and often bear—the burden of its decline.

"I know who I am," Ditka says. "When I wake up in the morning and shave, I know who I am."

Is it the man who utters such statements as the "I don't have a temper" line found in his 1986 autobiography? Is it the man who boasts of being a "regular guy," a "Grabowski," while living the life of a Rockefeller? Is it the all-American man, son of a union president, who drives pricey foreign cars and makes $1.25 million a year selling Toyotas? Is it the man who routinely trashes fans who dare question his coaching as "$100-a-week guys, losers in life." Or the man who screamed, "I'm not going to sit here all night, *I don't give a fuck, clear the fucking place out!*" when a waitress at his downtown restaurant made the "mistake" of serving paying customers who sat down before Ditka did? Is it the man who wallowed in drink and depression in Philadelphia for two years? A man whose life is littered with failure as a father, husband, a businessman, *in life?* Is it the man whose life was changed not by the heart scare in 1988 but by a dramatic moment in a Minneapolis hotel meeting room one year later? Actually, it is each and every one of these men, all part of the puzzle of personalities named Ditka. Men and memories Mike Ditka made clear prior to the 1991 season he would rather not see made public. . . .

(Voice at full scream now:) "I don't want a book written about me! Who even cares about Mike Ditka! You're Kitty Kelley, that's who you are! I don't want it done on me.

"It's an unauthorized biography, that's what it is, and I don't want it done. You're gonna get information from idiots in this world. You have no right to write this book!"

No right?

"You're goddamn right, no right! If you want to write an article like the other clowns in this city—fine. You don't have the right to write a book. You're just like Kitty Kelley! She's an asshole and you're an asshole. . . . I don't want a book written about me!

"It's an unauthorized biography, that's what it is, and I don't want it done! You're gonna get information from idiots. . . . Why are you talking to sportswriters? I saw it. Why you're talking to those clowns I'll never know. You can get hearsay from anybody. Don't expect any cooperation from me. Nobody cares if I'm a bad guy or a good guy. There's no reason to write a book about me! Who can this help besides yourself?"

What about the millions of Bears fans who might be interested?

"People in Chicago don't care! You're not getting the time of day from me. I don't want a book written about me. When I'm done coaching I'll write my own book. I don't want to go through all the bullshit when it comes out, saying this, saying that. Is this true? Is that true? It's bullshit.

7

"Do whatever you got to do. As long as you know my feelings."

But he couldn't stop. The lava continued to flow.

"Who's going to read it! Who cares! Who are you gonna enlighten?"

The serious reporting effort gave me the right to yell back. The words "rise and fall of the Chicago Bears" were part of the package.

"What fucking fall? The Chicago Bears had the best record of any team in the 1980s. Check it out."

This was 1991, he was reminded.

"I don't want to talk about it, except for the fact if we get beat, we get beat by better people. But we're going to make it work. It's gonna work."

THE GOLF CART CAREENS UP THE PATH BEHIND HALAS HALL OFFICIALLY auguring the start of the 1991 Chicago Bears football season. It is now 10:26 A.M., April 25, 1991, the first day of minicamp, the NFL's version of Coming Attractions. The star of the show accelerates up the short, steep hill much like a fullback in full stride, narrowly missing some daydreaming free-agent linebacker. Minicams and motor drives whir, capturing the moment for posterity—or at least for the evening news. As Iron Mike Ditka flies by, he closes his right hand into a fighter's fist and pops the thumb toward the spectators cheering along the sidelines, charging across a practice field cut to PGA perfection. All over the field some eighty-five athletes mingle in helmets and shorts, laughing and stretching easily in the sun. Only one athlete, Singletary, the Bears' inspirational leader, seems unusually restrained; he jogs alone around the field, lost in thought, wondering, perhaps, about the incongruity of the day. It is hardly football weather: a picture-perfect seventy degrees, air scented with the smell of fresh-cut grass, the warm wind tickling his nose and cheeks. Chicago, a beguiling blend of multicultural mayhem, a city of the fit and the fitful, is at its springtime best. It is a day for sailing, tennis, or a stroll in Lincoln Park.

But like it or not, four minutes later, right on the dot, two sharp blasts of a coaching whistle—*Toot! Toot!*—signal the start of calisthenics. "How about a moment of silence for Ham?" asks outside linebacker Ron Rivera, offering an ode to dearly departed defensive star Dan Hampton, a fixture at tackle for twelve seasons.

"Fuck 'im, he's a civilian now," counters Steve McMichael, the lewd, long-haired Texan, Hampton's erstwhile pardner on the defensive line.

McMichael, in the last possible row, is sandwiched between the team's two notorious nontalkers, William "I got nothing to say" Perry and John "No comment" Roper. Forty yards away, finally dislodged from his personalized cart, is the head coach. He looks great for fifty-one, tanned and rested from his springtime regimen of golf, early-morning swims, and aerobic workouts. The granite-gray slacks blend beautifully with his orange, blue, and white Bears sweater, the word DEFENSE blocked across the back. But clothes don't make this man. He could be standing out there in his bathrobe and you would feel the power of his presence. It's the head that does it, huge and foreboding, swallowing up TV screens, out of proportion with the rest of his strapping 6'3", 220-pound frame. Combined with the slicked-back hair, brush mustache, and fire-hydrant neck, Ditka's face resembles a sea lion's or wet otter's, or perhaps as others have suggested, the emblem of the Chicago Bears.

Today his deep-set eyes, the color of summer sky, are hidden behind tinted aviator sunglasses. These eyes are much like the man, cold and callous one second, warm and comforting the next. The kind of eyes, a longtime friend swears, "that can look right into your soul."

Ditka rotates his hips a time or two and quits. His lower body was a mess, the price he paid for twelve years in the NFL. The right hip joint collapsed and was replaced back in 1984. The arduous rehab process— six months or more—had kept Ditka from having the left hip done (he did not want to give up golf). So instead he endured the pain of bone scraping against bone on every step, the right foot always leading, splayed out at an odd angle, relieving the pressure on the weakened joint. The right shoulder always following, dipping as the stiff left leg swings up and around, a bit like a peg-leg pirate. Splay, step, dip, lift,

9

step, hobble. Never a complaint or a grimace. "His pain threshold is off the charts," marvels Rick Telander, a senior writer for *Sports Illustrated,* who has stopped by minicamp, not a particularly taxing trip since his house sits just beyond the goalposts at the west end of the practice field. "In a way he's like Ali," Telander says. "Ali absolutely ignored body punches, the blows to the brain. He didn't accept it. He just ignored it. Ditka is very similar. People like that just don't let physical boundaries stop them."

Staring out at his players, Ditka had no way of knowing what this season's boundaries would be. No way of knowing the season would be touched by the collapse of communism, the demented doings of Jeffrey Dahmer, and the stunning news of Magic Johnson's retirement, just five months after Michael Jordan and his Chicago Bulls had defeated Magic and his Lakers for the NBA title.

Chicago was a Bulls, not Bears, market now. Jordan and Pippen and coach Phil Jackson had sport-crazed Chicago screaming like the banshees down at the Board of Trade. Memories of the 1985 team were best suited for the WGN late-night movie; only fifteen Bears from that team were on the minicamp roster. Payton and Fenick and Hampton and Suhey had retired, along with cornerbacks Leslie Frazier and Mike Richardson. McMahon was last sighted in Philadelphia, wearing a Darth Vader helmet, earrings, and a Willie Nelson ponytail. Wilber Marshall, Willie Gault, and Dave Duerson were making waves in Washington, Los Angeles, and Phoenix, respectively. Otis Wilson? Released. Quarterback Mike Tomczak, just pushed into Plan B free agency, could now be reached by dialing a Green Bay Packer area code. Some members of the media moaned the current team had the personality of a mayonnaise sandwich. "A nondescript team," said Mark Giangreco, the tart-tongued sports anchor for the local NBC affiliate for nine years. "I don't know what's worse, too many crazy things going on, like in '85, or God, how are we going to create a story? There's no conflict."

"Three eighty! Three eighty! Hut! Hut!"

Near midfield the team's biggest story barked out the first play of the year. It was Harbaugh, on the cusp of a make-or-break season, spinning and tossing the ball to Anderson, the team's biggest star. Ditka eyed the All-Pro halfback carefully as he swept easily around right end. Ditka knew full well Anderson, one of the top two all-purpose running backs in the league, was the only franchise player left on his roster. He knew age and injuries had weakened his team; so had poor draft position (the product of the Bears' success), a reluctance to enter the free-agent

10

market, and even tragedy (the death of defensive tackle Fred Washington a year earlier in a drunken-driving accident). Could the Bears match the Washington Redskins or Buffalo Bills or the rest of the league's upper echelon? Ditka didn't think so. "The best word is *resigned*," said former Bears general manager Jerry Vainisi, one of Ditka's closest friends. "He's resigned to the fact that's the way it is. He knows his team really doesn't have much of a chance."

The regular-season schedule, courtesy of Marquis de Sade, was certainly no help. Coming off the Bears' dismal 6-10 showing in '89, the NFL pooh-bahs had bumped the team off prime time in 1990. But now, realizing even a rebuilding Ditka club was better than none at all, the NFL had served up three Monday-night and two Thursday contests, plus one on Saturday afternoon. Ditka was not pleased. "They're the fuckers," he said privately of the league schedule, "and we're the fuckees."

After the morning minicamp Ditka drives over toward the assembled media horde, setting off a mad scramble for positioning around his cart, which carries the faint odor of cigar smoke and chewing tobacco. About twenty members of the press—cameras, microphones, tape recorders, or notebooks in hand—jockey for position. With good reason. "No one wants to miss a word he says in this town," explains Dan Pompei, the beat reporter for the *Chicago Sun-Times.*

Conventional wisdom suggests Ditka wouldn't lose a wink of sleep if Pompei and the rest of the Bears press corps disappeared right into the brackish waters of the Chicago River with some cronies of Capone's. To Ditka, reporters are often agents provocateurs, "clowns," "jerks," or "pontificators" eager to twist facts and distort the truth. "They just build you up to tear you down," he says. Yet two years ago during training camp a few Bear beat reporters saw a different side of Ditka . . . and vice versa, bringing some needed perspective to both parties.

It was dinnertime at the Timbers Supper Club in Platteville, Wisconsin, home of the Bears summer training camp, when Fred Mitchell of the *Chicago Tribune,* Pompei, and a few other beat reporters plopped down at the bar. Mitchell and Pompei are the acknowledged leaders on the Bears beat. Both are skilled, savvy reporters who have covered the team for years with distinction. As they sat down to order drinks, a voice a couple of stools away interrupted and said, "Put 'em on my tab." It was Ditka. Over drinks and later, dinner, he and the beat guys engaged in the kind of off-the-record, casual conversation baseball managers and reporters have almost every night in hotel bars. "That

11

was the first time it ever happened," says Mitchell, who has been on the Bears beat since 1988. "It was special." So special, when it came time for dinner, the reporters ate right at the bar, trading "in life" stories with the coach. Mitchell talked about growing up in Gary, Indiana, his career as a kicker at Wittenberg University, his days as a high school coach. Ditka reminisced about fights with his brother, Ashton, his feelings toward Halas and McCaskey. "I know he doesn't know about us, and the impression has always been he could care less," Mitchell says. "I think it made reporters into people rather than people with pens in hand." Four hours later the head coach picked up the entire food and bar tab and said good-night. Says Mitchell, "It was just a great time because it was such a rare thing to happen."

In public, when the mood strikes, Ditka can be as charming and candid as he was that night in Platteville. A voracious, eclectic reader (*The Wall Street Journal,* Thomas Jefferson, Benjamin Disraeli, Robert Schuler) he is unmatched at taking simple, sometimes inane questions and spinning strands of football gold, mixing incisive strategy with "in life" oration. "It's like the Ed Sullivan show," says Pompei, a weight-lifting buff who has covered the team since 1986. "He walks in and delivers sound bites. He doesn't even answer questions. He comes in, does his tap dance, and leaves. He's like an entertainer. Things happen wherever he is. That's why we love to cover him. Even though he's a prick at times, he's a joy to cover because he fills up your notebook."

Other times the neck is bulled, eyes raking the room, spoiling for a fight. "Okay, we don't have much time here, get to it," he'll bark. Or: "Red . . . Time-out. We lost a game. So what? That's your problem, not my problem. You are the one who is offended by all of that." Rage days when reporters know the first one to open his mouth is going to get tagged. "He wants it known he's in control," says Mitchell. "It seems to bother him that the media has a certain degree of control. That's why he feels it incumbent upon himself to try and correct us, unquote, and let us know what's really going on."

To try to keep the press in its place Ditka often bullies or belittles one or two members of the media, cutting them off in midsentence, mocking their manner. It serves as an explicit warning to others. "Brad," he'll shout at local TV reporter Brad Palmer, "don't give me all your pontificating!" Or at Pompei: "Dan, you're not going to write what I say anyway!" Because of that tactic, virtually every Ditka press conference features a sense of journalistic dread, as assembled report-ers play the "I Wonder What Ditka It Will Be Today?" game. Will it be Jekyll? Hyde? Or some Sybil in between? And when he does arrive, an uneasy silence settles in the air, a frozen moment before one hearty soul dips a toe into the water. The questions are always something innocuous in the beginning, to test the temperature—"Any update on the injuries, Mike?"—before deciding whether to jump right in.

Just how intimidating Ditka can be with the Chicago press is best spelled out in one story. It dates back to October 1985, the day Ditka had been arrested for drunken driving near O'Hare Airport. The Bears had just done a number (26–10) on San Francisco out on the coast. During the flight back, Ditka, who despises the 49ers, partied hard with his players. "He had some wine he had received as a gift and he was coming up to us saying, 'Try this,'" recalls former Bears star Gary Fencik. "And we were gladly drinking it." So was Ditka.

Two miles out of O'Hare the cruiser lights came on. Ditka refused a Breathalyzer test. After becoming what the police officer later called "abusive," Ditka was handcuffed and hauled away. The result was a driving-under-the-influence charge, speeding, and other traffic offenses. Front-page news.

But when Ditka met the press downstairs at Halas Hall later that day, nobody dared ask The Question. There was no way to dance around the news. No way to ask about injury or the upcoming opponent. Yet for several painful moments the room stood silent as a tomb. "People were afraid to ask the question," admits Giangreco. Finally, from the back, a strange voice: "Mr. Ditka, what do you think your arrest for drunk driving says to the youth of America?"

Every head in the room whipped around. Who said that? It was a woman, a black female reporter from a small FM radio station. Ditka didn't bite back or bark. He simply admitted his mistake and moved on.

Ditka doesn't always turn the page so quickly. He abhors criticism. Couldn't stand it as a child, hates it as an adult. Ditka didn't talk to Giangreco for two years after a series of rather hilarious put-downs that aired on WMAQ. "It's ancient history now," says Giangreco, "but back three or four years ago, we had a feud. I wasn't on the bandwagon. I was always taking shots just for fun, nothing malicious. But we'd come out of a sound bite and I'd say something like, 'You're out of control, Mike. You're not the mayor. You're not the president. You're not the pope. You're a football coach.' That's when Mike was giving his philosophy of life at every press conference." Giangreco responded with his "Ditkaism of the Week," a graphic illustration of Ditka's dumbest "in life" statement. Later on Giangreco bumped two "sound bites" together—Ditka totally contradicting himself from one day to the next. But most of the time Giangreco was taking shots at Ditka's seven-digit ego. "He was out of control," says the anchor. "People perceived him as a god and he just ran with it. He was drunk with power and celebrity status.

"There's still a lot of media in this town who just hang on his every word. All this nervous laughter. 'Oh, Mike, you're so funny. You're so great.' He's still intimidating to a lot of reporters; a lot of people still kiss his ass."

In the huddle around the golf cart, a radio reporter politely inquires about the killer schedule. "It leaves a lot to be desired, the way they did it," Ditka says. "At least they left out Tuesday, Wednesday, and Fridays," he says. A media laugh. "We weren't on TV a lot last year. We do have a lot of appeal across the country. It's nice to be appreciated . . . funny how they show it."

But, he says, "There is nothing I can do." Why?

"Philippians three, verse thirteen and fourteen," says Ditka. "Read it."

It's all about running toward the goal, not looking back. A religious reference perfectly suited for the moment and life:

Of course, brothers, I really do not think I have already won it; the one thing I do, however, is to forget what is behind me and do my best to reach what is ahead. So I run straight toward the goal in order to win the prize, which is God's call through Christ Jesus to the life above.

The press conference lasts exactly eight minutes. In that time Ditka dishes out more quotes than any ten NFL coaches combined. Not ten minutes later he dashes out the front door of Halas Hall, all slicked and showered, sporting a tuxedo, hustling past his stunning blue-gray Bentley, the one with the vanity plates (MKD-DSD) parked in the primo spot, right next to the door. (By comparison Chairman of the Board Ed McCaskey gets the Avis spot.) A beaming Diana Ditka waits as her husband steps into a waiting limo, and they drive off to yet another charity event. . . .

The next day, the sky is gray and gloomy, the drills sharp, despite an annoying drizzle and dampened field. Afterward Ditka brings his team together and maps out the "long journey" ahead. "We've got a tough, tough, rough road," he says. "There's no room for errors or mistakes." A few minutes later he's in the first-floor media room at Halas Hall, sporting a beautiful pullover sweater, a mosaic of purple and gray. He speaks passionately about the season, the need to throw the ball more, to not be so predictable. "Our mood is a carryover from last year," he says. "It's never fun to go out and get your butts kicked, and we got our butts kicked the last time out. Now we've got to prove we're better than that."

There's always something to prove. Thoughts go back to the words of *SI* writer Telander, who for all his savvy and insight (he has written several stories about the Bears), still hasn't grasped the essence of the man. "I'm not sure he is understandable," Telander says. "He's got that drive, that restlessness that can only come from . . ."

He stops.

Ten seconds pass.

"It would seem . . ."

He stops again. Shaking his head, he says, "He's compensating for something. What he is compensating *for* I just don't know."

THE MILL CITY INN HAS A HISTORY NOT UNLIKE THE CITY AND PEOPLE IT serves. It's a man's bar in a man's town, dark and forgiving, filled with the sound of slapped backs and clinking bottles of beer, and the smell of Lebanese food spiced with year-round chatter of high school football. The Mill City is part of Aliquippa, Pennsylvania, in the heart of western-Pennsylvania steel country, a place not unlike Carnegie, Duquesne, or Homestead, homes to the shot-and-a-beer steel crowd. Back in those good old days, back in the thirties and forties and fifties, right up until the mid-seventies, really, the steel mills and the Mill City Inn were made for each other. It didn't matter what shift—the seven

A.M. to three P.M., the eight A.M. to four P.M., the four to midnight, midnight to eight—steelworkers flowed in and out of the Mill City round the clock. Maybe a cup of coffee with a Seagram's 7 chaser to start the day. Certainly, after the shift, a shot of head-shaking whiskey and a beer—or two or three or four—to burn away the taste, and often the memory, of the misery of the mill. "A lot of guys had rough jobs, and they just wanted to come in and relax and wind down, take the edge off of everything," says Tommy Mowad, the owner and the man behind the bar at the Mill City for thirty-one years. "They would have a few drinks and bullshit a little bit with everybody, you know, with the guys."

The guys. That's what Mill City and Aliquippa have always had in common. The guys. Men whose motto in life can be reduced to three precious words: Pride. Tradition. Winning. Men who in the 1990s seem part of another time and place—solid everyday workers whose pride took a beating in the mid-1970s as they watched, piece by piece, their mill torn down, and steel imported cheaper from Japan. In 1960 less than 5 percent of the steel in this country was imported. By 1984, that number had increased to 26 percent. Today in Aliquippa there is so little left to hang on to, which is why men such as Frank Marocco and Mike Ditka mean so much, because they preserve the one image Aliquippa will never let die. "Winning is built into the kids around here," says Mowad. "Winning is most important."

And because he is such a "winner," no "Fighting Quip" is more welcome back home, more revered, than Ditka.

"Mike Ditka has more pull in this town than the Pope. He's the Pied Piper and the Wizard of Oz rolled into one," says Marocco, the stocky, handsome former high school All-American guard–turned–head football coach at Aliquippa High.

Marocco just happens to be standing in the Mill City Inn as he speaks. He points to a banner behind the bar. It reads, "America's High School Football Team—Home of Mike Ditka." Now Marocco nods to a back corner of the bar and says, "He could do this every day. He's home."

Indeed, Mike Ditka is *home* on this Thursday afternoon in June 1991, the opening day of his fifth annual Mike Ditka Celebrity Golf Tournament, a big, boozy two-day affair that raises about $30,000 for high school scholarships and other community causes. Earlier in the day he had jetted into town on one of the private planes he and a business partner lease, heading straight for the golf course. By late afternoon he was off the back nine and sitting in a back corner of the Mill City, locked in a high-stakes gin rummy game, putting a win-or-lose dot on the day, just the way he likes it.

He looked stylish, as usual, Chicago cool in his Ditka's/City Lights golf shirt, suntanned face, white Panama hat pulled tight toward his eyes. He drank nothing stronger than ice water, having cut way back on his drinking since the heart attack. Occasionally he pulled an unlit Castro-sized cigar off a plain black table and rolled it around his mouth. He cut the cards like a Vegas pro, eyes flickering first to his partner, Mike Lucci, a longtime friend and former Detroit Lions star, then back to their opponents, two well-heeled locals. "These guys," whispered somebody in the crowd, referring to Ditka's opponents, "are real heavy hitters. They play for big bucks."

So does Ditka. Gin games where individual losses can reach $400 an hour are not unusual for Ditka; neither are $2,500 rounds of golf with stakes sometimes pushing $10,000 or more a round. "He's a competitor," says an attendant at one of the many country clubs Ditka frequents. "If somebody wants to play, he'll play for a lot of money."

The reasons, as with many former athletes, are equal parts psychological and financial. During his playing days Ditka's competitive cravings were easily satisfied in any number of ways: on the football field, golf course, card table, racquetball and tennis courts, even charging down mountains on skis and up hills on a dirt bike. But his hip and heart can't take the abuse anymore. His most strenuous physical activity these days is swimming (first one to the other end wins?), so outside of the twenty or so Bears games he coaches a year, golf and gin rummy are it. They provide the almost-daily dose of competition Ditka needs in much the same manner a junkie needs drugs.

He's an inveterate golfer—eighteen holes or more, four or five times a week during the off-season, and late Friday afternoons in the fall. As with so many other golfaholics he is drawn to the humbling, emotional rhythms of the game, the continual challenge, the fresh competitive rush it affords. Ditka's love of the sport is such he lumped "Family and Golf" in the same chapter of his 1986 autobiography. "What does that say?" asks his daughter Megan. "The kids were an aside."

For those who doubt Ditka's addiction, consider this story courtesy of Dallas sportswriter Skip Bayless: "A friend invited me to a little country club called Los Rios in Plano [Texas] back in March of 1979," Bayless begins. "I arrived about noon and soon after what we in Texas call a 'norther' hit. The temperature dropped about forty degrees in an hour, the wind turned from the north. It got brutally cold. I was sitting in the men's grill, looking out the picture window to the ninth green and tenth tee. And even though I was addicted to golf, we had already bagged it. It was just miserable. Then, looking up the ninth fairway, I saw this large man in a golf cart, playing the hole in all this cold and wind. He got to the green and putted out. It was Ditka. I figured he would pull into the grill and wait out the storm. Not Mike. He made a little U-turn and went to the tenth tee all by himself."

With cards, Ditka can be just as obsessive. Some days he'll play golf in the morning, sit down at a card table at noon, and not get up until midnight—Ditka's ideal day, providing he's won, of course. "He'll play twelve, fourteen hours in a row; sometimes he'll play all night," says a longtime observer of Ditka's gin rummy games.

His home turf, so to speak, is the exclusive—critics would charge discriminatory—Bob 'O' Link Golf Club in Highland Park, Illinois, where real estate runs around $250,000 an acre and Mercedes is the name of the game. Bob 'O' Link is known as one of the classic so-called second membership clubs. It's a millionaires' retreat, one of only about a half dozen all-male golf clubs left in the U.S. Women are not allowed to so much as set foot in the clubhouse unless the offending member seeks a quick reason for dismissal. Possibly an apocryphal account of the club's attitude toward the opposite sex is reflected in a call it received a few years back. It seems a top-flight local amateur golfer, a woman of means, called the club and explained how a group of fifty Chicago women, all five-handicappers or less, would like to play one round of golf at the club. In exchange for this privilege, they would make a $100,000 donation to the American Cancer Society in the name of the club members, giving each member a personal deduction. "Madam," came the reply, "I believe the men of Bob 'O' Link would rather have cancer."

Bob 'O' Link has the look of a fine English manor. The countrified clubhouse, all warm and wood-paneled, is staffed by white-shirted attendants who bustle about bringing drinks, fresh decks of mono-grammed cards, or perhaps a bowl of peanuts. The golf course itself is among the finest in the state, a 6,700-yard layout featuring the signature rolling fairways of famed golf architect Donald Ross, lined with 150-year-old oak trees. Membership is limited to about 240 men and, when it is offered, runs about $45,000. The club directory is all white and primarily Catholic—$300-an-hour lawyers, traders, heavy-weights in the business and political community. The golf course and card room are their refuge—in Ditka's case, a welcome escape from the publicity and pressures of Halas Hall. His normal routine is a round of golf in the morning and, if he desires, cards in the afternoon and evening. His game of choice is either "California," "Hollywood," or "Bob 'O' Link" gin, fast-paced, hybrid formats using two decks and a third "call" deck that sets the boundary for scoring. In Ditka's crowd you also need deep pockets. His usual stakes at Bob 'O' Link are said to be $200 for the first game, $200 for the second, $400 for the third. Given these stakes, a two-man team could lose $800 every forty-five minutes, although it's unlikely, with swings of $2,000 or more per man common over the course of an afternoon or evening. "But Ditka is smart," says a source at the club. "He always golfs before he plays cards, and if you have to beat Mike Ditka in golf to make a living, you might as well try something else in life."

His regular gin partners rotate around eight men, all rich, all powerful, just like the coach. There are a couple of big-time attorneys, a trucking magnate, the cofounder of the Board of Options Exchange, two printing executives, owners of a restaurant and a brewery. Their games are often long, loud, and hotly contested, just the way Ditka likes it. "They play year around," says one club source. "They're always exchanging checks." Ditka is termed an excellent card player, aided by a remarkable memory and what one club source calls "tunnel vision," the ability to block out all distractions. He rarely drinks when he plays, sipping a little Coors Light over ice. He either smokes a cigar or chews tobacco. Ditka is so obsessive about gin and gambling that during the summer of 1990, according to club sources, he and the brewery president, a top-flight gin player named Fred Huber, went at it mano-a-mano for fourteen straight hours. Just the two of them. All alone in the card room, save one attendant. They sat down one Sunday night at seven P.M. and except for a pit stop or two, didn't quit until nine o'clock the next morning. Ditka, so the story goes, was not happy when he left.

Just how much does Ditka hate to lose? Certainly, given his titanic temper, there is a fairly obvious trail of broken putters, snapped shafts, and overturned tables. Former Philadelphia Eagles teammate Gary Ballman says he saw Ditka toss $600 worth of golf clubs and bag into a lake. Other teammates recall chairs flung into walls, doors ripped right off their hinges. "He was out of control," recalls Lee Roy Jordan, the great Dallas linebacker who played golf, cards, and football with Ditka in the early seventies. "He'd miss a shot or a putt and he'd break his club. There were unbelievable tirades; with Mike it was about once every three holes."

But those outbursts, all the vile and venom, say far less about Ditka's hell-bent hatred of loss than one simple line uttered several years ago down in Florida.

It was 1984 or '85 when Ron Kushner, president of an automotive supply company, invited Ditka and a couple of other buddies to his second home in Delray Beach, Florida, for some serious golf at Delaire Country Club. Kushner, who shoots in the mid-80s, was the worst player in the group. "We were beating Mike and his partner, who was really an excellent player, the first day, and of course Mike was unhappy about it," says Kushner. "And we beat them the second day and he was getting even more unhappy about it. He kept putting pressure on his partner, and his partner started to play worse and worse under this pressure."

On the third day, a very windy one, the score was tight as the foursome approached the seventeenth tee, a long par three over water. Dead into the wind, at least 240 yards long. Ditka's partner, whom we'll call Ned, was feeling the strain. He pulled an iron from his bag.

"What are you doing?" Ditka said.

"I'm going to lay up in front of the water because I can't get to the green," Ned replied.

"What the hell's going on here?" Ditka cried. "Play like a man. Go for the green!"

Ned went back to his bag and pulled out a driver. Swinging from his heels he shanked the ball straight out of bounds. The color drained from his face faster than Pippen runs the break.

That night, around four A.M. Kushner heard a knock at his door. "I hate to bother you, but I'm not feeling so good," said Ned. "I've kind of got pains in my chest."

Kushner rushed Ned over to a nearby hospital where he was immediately placed in intensive care and checked for signs of a heart attack. Kushner left the hospital around seven in the morning. By this time Ditka was up, drinking coffee and reading the newspaper at the kitchen table.

"You'll never believe what happened," Kushner gushed, reliving the harrowing night. "I just left the hospital and Ned's in intensive care."

Ditka barely glanced up from his paper.

"So," he inquired of Kushner, "what are we going to do for a fourth?"

In the past, during days when Ditka's ego far outweighed his wallet, he sometimes showed the same callous disregard for covering his bets as he did for Ned's chest pains. In his early days in Chicago, his obstreperous gambling habits led to debts that were not always immediately squared away. "He liked to gamble and didn't always have the money to back it up," says a source at Bob 'O' Link. "A couple of his buddies, the first year or so, had a hard time collecting."

Today in Mill City, Ditka's concentration on gin rummy is tested by a steady stream of well-wishers. A half dozen locals with golf-course tans crowd the game, peppering the coach with, "Hey, Mike, how you doing?" or, "Mike, Mike, you look great." One local presses closer than most.

"Mike, what's that line you used? Hard times make . . . ?"

Ditka ignores this query. The rebuffed local shows no concern, turning to an acquaintance and saying, "He had a beautiful phrase. He said, 'Hard times make . . .'"

Another pause. Another headshake. "Oh, hell, I loved it."

Turn of the head. "Tommy, what was that line Ditka used . . . ?"

Mowad, who happens to be up to his ears in requests for beer, doesn't answer either. The bar is humming along nicely with a late-afternoon buzz, fueled by the kind of drinking that hardly seems troublesome or abusive, just natural. Alcohol in Aliquippa is a way of life, the social cement that binds people together whether it be on the golf course, in social clubs, or here in the Mill City Inn, where the words "Hey, Tommy, get my buddy a beer" or "I've got this round" ring out time and time again, even though some friendships are less than ten minutes old, and maybe you're really a buddy of a buddy. Relax, Mowad says, that's Aliquippa. "My younger brother," he says, "used to bring guys in from Colorado, where he went to school. Guys would say why are you buying me a drink? Well, if you're a friend of Tommy's brother, you're a friend of mine. The guys from Colorado couldn't believe it."

Good people, people such as Bernie Strauss, a local businessman, who leans over and says something that belongs on a banner behind the bar, right next to the homage to Mike Ditka.

"People here want to know how much you care," says Strauss, "before they care how much you know."

Former Green Bay Packer and Detroit Lion tight end Ron Kramer, who used to raise hell with Ditka, is on the other side of the bar, in town for the tournament. A small army of empty Bud bottles—"dead soldiers," he says—stand before him. He's been here awhile. Kramer has a laugh befitting a man who stands 6' 3", 245 pounds. "Ditka?" he says. "Ha! We used to go out on Rush Street and drink them fucking

21

martinis! We both had the same problem—we didn't know when to stop!" For emphasis Kramer howls, then leans down and takes a bite out of a stray diet Coke can. He turns to the man beside him who just happens to be a high school administrator. "Okay," says Kramer, "your turn." In the resultant howl, a male voice cuts above the din.

"I remember it now! 'Hard times never last—good people do'!"

Back in the 1930s and '40s, Aliquippa was a boomtown—thirty thousand people, half of them steelworkers whose labor in the seven miles of mills along the banks of the Ohio River helped build the backbone of this nation: its cars, bridges, highways, and office buildings. All day, every day, six shifts punching the clock for Jones & Laughlin (J&L) Structural Steel, which later became part of LTV (Ling, Tempco & Vaught). During shift changes a bit of bedlam would break loose as thousands of workers passed in and out of "the tunnel" to and from work.

In a geographical quirk, virtually every single worker entered the mill through what was then known as the "Y"—a confluence of streets that pinched together at the main entrance of the mill. Once you walked through the tunnel a right turn led you toward the machine shop, then the car shop, home to A&S Railroad, the rail car company that moved coal and other raw materials throughout the mill. A left turn took you to the mills and ovens that stretched all along the Ohio. In his book *American Steel,* Richard Preston writes, "The making of steel is said to be the most spectacular manufacturing process on earth. Steel is the monster of heavy industry; steelmaking machines are the fiercest, largest, and heaviest engines on the planet." Steelworkers are known as "hot-metal" men, so named because steel in its natural state runs as hot as three thousand degrees Fahrenheit, painful to the eyes, fluid as a flag rippling in the breeze. Most men today wouldn't last ten minutes in a steel mill. Rocked by the sound of red-hot strips of steel being shaped . . . *ba-boom, ba-boom, ba-boom* . . . in rolling machines . . . standing a few feet from bubbling baths of live liquid . . . blinded by a blast furnace hot enough to fry your face in seconds. In Aliquippa sparks from those furnaces gave the town a glow all its own, one continuous Fourth of July firecracker lighting up the midnight sky. Inside the mill, immigrant men magically forged and fused everything from nails to pipes to tubes for the oil industry, to beams for bridges. Smelling the mix of vaporized iron ore, carbon, limestone, and coke is startling; as is inhaling the putrid mix of oxygen and celatin, the blue gassy fire spewing from an acetylene torch four or five hours a day.

Vapors are brought into the head and heart of a hot-metal man, never to be forgotten.

No wonder eyes watered and the throat screamed for relief. No wonder when that whistle blew, grown men charged through that tunnel like sinners out of hell storming up Franklin Avenue eager to wash the day away. "You were dying to have a shot and a cold beer," says Rudy LaGatta, who spent thirty-five years in the mills. Lord knows LaGatta and others didn't have far to go. Franklin Avenue was filled with beer gardens, bars, and social clubs. The back streets were even wilder; bars everywhere and alleys alive with illegal dice games. "It was just wide open," says Mowad, whose original Mill City Inn was on Franklin. To make matters worse (or better) the company paid in cash, leaving LaGatta to admit, "By the time they got up the avenue, most guys were half-broke." Then the wives stepped in. Soon they were standing right at the Y too, kids in one hand, pocketbook in the other, waiting for that little cash envelope. On Saturday, they took that money and headed downtown, strolling up and down Franklin, stopping by the beauty salons, the children's stores, the four movie theaters packed with patrons, smiles on everybody's face.

Today the tunnel is still there. But precious little else remains. Downtown Aliquippa is dead, "lost" in the words of Mowad. Franklin is not an active avenue anymore but a decaying stretch of boarded-up buildings, broken dreams, and drunken bums. The watch repair shop, the furniture stores, the beauty salons, and the movie theaters, all shuttered and empty. Drug dealers and the homeless loiter on the streets. The mills are gone, too. Ripped out and removed much like the heart of these people. It began in the 1970s when Japanese steel exports started shrinking the U.S.-made market share. First the nail section closed. Then Jones & Laughlin (J&L) merged with LTV. "That's when the real trouble started," says LaGatta. In 1981, thanks in part to the policies of the Reagan administration, the steel industry was brought to its knees. One mill after another—pipe, rods, tube, welded tube, and seamless tube—all gone. A&S closed up in 1972. J&L started tearing the mills down in 1983. In June 1991 only the 14" tin mill, repair shop, and one section of the seamless mill was operational; just 600 jobs out of the original 16,000.

So it was, in the summer of '91, the banks of the Ohio had the look of burned-out Beirut or of decaying dinosaurs rotting in the sun. Piles of scrap metal, all rusty and mishapen, sagged into empty shells. Twenty silent smokestacks sat, abandoned, like so many hopes and dreams. The closest thing to hope the people of Aliquippa have these days is about fifteen miles away: the $700-million expansion of Pittsburgh Greater International Airport has sparked talk of a spillover effect, a big new hotel nearby, more jobs. Hope. It's what Mike Ditka and his golf tournament are really all about.

About two hundred golfers who had paid $175 each for the privilege of rubbing shoulders with Ditka and some celebs over at Beaver Lakes Country Club were on hand. It was hardly a star-studded field, especially since only one current Bear, local boy Jim Covert, showed up despite promotional literature promising several others. But it didn't matter. Ditka was the show. Just like the night before at a three-hour cocktail party at the airport Ramada Inn, though on this night, he did little more than just sit between his parents and greet those who stopped by his table. There was Charlotte on one side, Mike Sr. on the other, and some of Ditka's regular Chicago crowd: Ed O'Bradovich, the ex-Bear great; Ted Roberts, a friend from back in Ditka's Dallas days and the manager of Ditka's O'Hare restaurant.

As for Ditka's parents, Charlotte is the outgoing, card-playing chatterbox. "A shrewd, sharp-tongued Irishwoman," in the words of longtime family friend Dan Sildra. A devout Roman Catholic, Charlotte Ditka rarely misses a Sunday in church. "A very pleasant woman," says Father Dan Sweeney of St. Titus Catholic Church.

On the other hand, Mike Sr. communicates with the turn of the head, the raise of a brow. And he wouldn't know one end of a religious service from another.

"Never spoken to the man," says Father Sweeney.

There is a wonderful little story about Charlotte and Mike Sr. that Charlotte herself likes to tell. It begins with Big Mike, with a bit of a buzz, driving like a madman with Charlotte and the kids in the car. "You son of a bitch," Charlotte screamed, "let me out of the car!" Mike pays her no mind, pedal to the metal, when suddenly Charlotte sees the flashing red light. "Thank God!" she cries. "You gonna get arrested. Who gives a shit about you now!"

Mike pulls over and the Aliquippa policeman is all ready to write him up, until, that is, he notices who's behind the wheel. "Hey, Mike, how you doing?" says the cop. Pretty good, says Mike.

"I couldn't even get the son of a bitch arrested," says Charlotte. "Worse, the cop escorted us home."

All during the cocktail party friends drop by to pay respects to the entire family. Most stay just a minute or two. The rest of the night the men of Aliquippa and beyond, about one hundred or so altogether, share Ditka stories among themselves. The Ditka talkfest picks up about halfway through the party when an impressive array of "Budweiser girls" arrive. There's Tamantha and April and Marcie and Michelle, nine in all. Only Ditka seems unfazed by their arrival. Part of the reason is, unknown to most people in the room, he's still recovering from minor surgery for kidney stones two days earlier. But mostly it's just the peace and joy of being home. "He did all the things he wanted to do today," says Marocco. "He played golf. He played gin. And now this. People back in Chicago don't understand this side of him."

Toward the end of the evening, one of the Budweiser girls, a knockout named Cathy, approaches the Ditka table. She leans in and asks a simple question; Ditka cracks his crooked smile. "This is America," he tells her quietly. "This is what it's all about. Friends. Relatives. I love this country." Five minutes later he walks out alone, but not before kissing his mother good-bye.

Friday morning. Beaver Lakes Country Club. Ditka is hugged and loved and mugs for cameras a dozen different times before stepping to the first tee. Once there he poses with his partners for a group shot, then takes control. "All right," he barks, "somebody hit it, let's go." His partners obey but offer rather humbling drives. The pressure is on. The home crowd of some two hundred people draws quiet, save for Charlotte, ever the mom, who clicks away with her camera.

Ditka's form is far from perfect—marred by a short backswing—but he more than compensates with extraordinary arm strength and hand-eye coordination. When Ditka is on, he plays to a solid five handicap; long and straight off the tee, deft around the greens, with the guts of a cat burglar.

He looks confident now, setting his stance in front of his Aliquippa fans, launching a big drive, 270 yards or more, right down the middle of the fairway. "The Hammer!" comes a cry from the crowd. "He put the hammer to it!" screams another.

The sixsome departs down the fairway, three groups of carts. It turns out to be a mixed bag of businessmen, three local golfers, two Chicago imports plus Ditka. Just one other player, an "Aliquippa boy" named Tom Stauffer, has a swing that says seventies. But it doesn't much matter. This is a best-ball format where each player hits a shot then the best shot becomes the group's next shot. On the first hole that second shot again belongs to Ditka, as he has wedged a short iron to within six feet of the pin. Strangely, after the huge gathering on the first tee, only one local photographer and one out-of-town writer follow along. They watch as one by one Ditka's partners miss the birdie putt. Again it's up to him. Win or lose. Do or die. Just the way he likes it. He lumbers up, sights his line, and smoothly strokes the ball. It falls right into the middle of the cup.

The group manages just two birdies in the next four holes, thanks largely to the putting stroke of Stauffer, but it's quite obvious nobody is having much fun. Ditka is in pain. Between his hip problems and kidney stones it's an ordeal just getting in and out of the cart. Ditka is repeatedly reduced to pulling and pushing on the cart's frame for leverage and relief. The pain keeps Ditka in his cart, off his feet, but even on the tee or after shots, he keeps small talk with his partners to an absolute minimum, intense, content to work on his chewing tobacco and to stare straight ahead. Even the Chicago businessman who shares Ditka's cart is shut out to some degree. Strange since they've known each other for years, and chances are, Marv Fiocchi wouldn't be alive today if it weren't for Ditka.

Fiocchi, in many respects, represents the good Mike Ditka, the softhearted, humanitarian Dr. Jekyll known for charity drives and good deeds. Fiocchi owns a popular restaurant called Night 'n Gale in the far north Chicago suburb of Highwood, a small, white-collar community famous for its fine food. Night 'n Gale is among the finest, a fixture for Bears players and coaches for more than thirty years. Formerly a hot college pitching prospect in Oklahoma, Fiocchi saw his career cut short after an early heart attack. He returned to Highwood and opened the restaurant where he and Ditka became friends and golf partners. But then Fiocchi's heart began to fail. By the summer of 1990 he not only needed a transplant but was in trouble financially given all the medical bills. It didn't look good. Until, that is, Ditka spearheaded a benefit dinner at a local country club that drew about a thousand people and raised around $75,000. A few months later, at the last minute, Fiocchi got the donor heart. He and Ditka later teamed up for a public service spot supporting the donor program. (That's Marv tooling around on the bicycle.)

Many of Ditka's charities deeds are just as public, the most visible, perhaps, his unstinting efforts on the behalf of the Misericordia Home for developmentally disabled children and adults. There is the Mike Ditka Golf Classic in Chicago and Mike Ditka Foundation dinner, annual events which have raised several hundred thousand dollars for the home; there is his heavily promoted Candy Days campaign, which, in the last six years, has drawn ten thousand volunteers to Chicago street corners and collected some $750,000 annually; there's his willingness to be roasted, as he was in Las Vegas in 1990, raising another $115,000 for Misericordia. But there are far less public efforts as well. Just ask Jerry Lyne, director of development for the Misericordia. Lyne spent four and a half months in the hospital in late 1989 and early '90 with cancer of the esophagus and colon. As Lyne readily admits, "a lot of people had me buried," but not Ditka. He showed at the hospital almost every Wednesday night just before taping his TV show. He and Lyne were business associates but hardly close. "We never went out socially," says Lyne. "He could have been a hundred different places. As I say to you today, I don't understand it." Every week, after all the doctors and nurses had left, Ditka would slide a little closer to the bed and ask, "Are you still fighting?" Then he would exhort Lyne to get up and do things, not lie there and die. Did he inspire you? "You bet your sweet ass he did," Lyne said. "Just his presence there in front of you. I was a basket case. You look forward to him coming to see you. You wonder why? Why me? I guess he just felt he had to do it."

Evidently Ditka felt the exact same way with one of the old boys over at Bob 'O' Link. As the story goes it involved some former millionare who hit rock bottom after a divorce. Around the club, the guy was known as kind of a goof, the type who in '85, at the height of the Bears undefeated run, handed Ditka a six-page critique of the team. Ditka just smiled and thanked the guy. A month later he was selling encyclopedias. Ditka, according to a source at the club, bought a full set, $6,000 worth, and never said boo.

He has done similar good deeds in his hometown. In 1986, a thousand seats sold in one day for a testimonial dinner that raised thousands for the football team; then there are the $5,000 annual donations to the high school in the name of his former high school coach; and the quiet $10,000 gift to St. Titus Catholic Church. "I've never met the man," says Father Sweeney. "We sent a letter in 1989 to all our alumni for our endowment fund. He called and said, 'What are you looking for?' I shot for the moon and said five thousand. He gave ten."

It's gifts such as these that make him "The Pride of Aliquippa," as so many of the signs and banners attest. It's the reason total strangers seek him out and shake his hand, as they did just before he reached the sixth tee at his golf tournament. "Thanks for keeping on coming back," says a pretty blonde leaving her husband's hand to shake Ditka's.

"That's what life is all about," Ditka says.

The homecoming continues as he cruises down the fairway, a plug of chewing tobacco bobbing in his cheek. Shouts echo from an adjacent condo. He looks. Hanging from the balcony is a huge computer-generated sign: THANKS, MIKE, FOR SUPPORTING TEACHERS. (Some St. Titus instructors perhaps?) Next to that is a life-size cardboard cutout of The Coach. Ditka whips the cart around, stops and chats for a minute or two. He signs autographs. The cheers and clapping echo in the hot morning air.

Two holes later, Charlotte shows up. She's commandeered a cart and driver. But her boy isn't happy. Missed birdie putts at eight, nine, and ten leave him quiet and cold. The eleventh is another showcase hole, bending back toward the entrance of the club, with the largest gallery of the day. By the time they reach the eleventh green, at least two hundred spectators stand around. "His hip gets worse every year," whispers one local to another as Ditka struggles across the green to read a snakey six-footer for birdie. The scene unfolds just as it should. Tom misses. Marv misses. "Be a hero, Rudy," screams one local to LaGatta, the mill man. Not today. Ron Mueller, a shoe executive from Chicago, putts next. His try slides by on the right. Another partner comes up short.

Leaving it up to the hometown hero.

"C'mon, Mike!"

"You can do it, Mike!"

Another hush. For a moment it seems more than a putt, a harbinger instead of where this proud yet poor city is headed. Make it and all this talk of airport expansion and Aliquippa getting a piece of the progress makes sense. Miss it and they go home and grumble about days gone by. Ditka checks his line, draws back his blade, . . . nobody breathes.

"Thataway, Mike!"

"Way to go, Hammer!"

A few holes later the original Hammer streams down the sixteenth fairway in a golf cart, riding shotgun, a cold Coors Light in his hand. The tournament is, by now, several hours old, and this is the first time today he's seen his son play. But so what? The old man can do what he wants. Always has. Always will.

The golf cart slows to a stop near the seventeenth tee. Mike Ditka, Sr., takes another long pull on his beer and stares ahead. Straight at his son, not fifteen feet away, resting in his cart waiting to tee off. Father and son, separated all day, now sit in silence. Not one word passes between the two. Not "Hello." Not "How are you?" Not "Good to see you." Not one single, solitary word.

God created me, and my parents raised me a certain way, and evidently some of the qualities and some of this drive that I have were achieved back home when I was a kid.
　　—*Mike Ditka, "PrimeTime Live" interview, July 9, 1990*

As far as father and son being close, real close, it was never there. The father liked Mike a lot, but there was no communication.

　　　　　　　　　　　　　　—*Mike Dzvonar, family friend*

HE SITS SHIRTLESS IN THE MORNING SUN. HIS BARE CHEST, THE COLOR OF copper, sags slightly. The voice is low and raspy. He is now seventy-four years old but hardly feeble. No, the strength of Mike Ditka, Sr., is found in other places. The iron grip. The lines that crisscross his hardened face; the steel gray eyes that generally do far more talking than he does. But break the silence of the famous father, and as the locals say, you'll begin to understand the famous son.

A baby cries. The plaintive whine floats across a quiet, grassy courtyard from a white, two-story town house not unlike his own. The Ditkas have lived in the Linmar Plan, unit No. 14, for fifty-one years. "Nineteen forty-one," he says, remembering move-in day as if it were yesterday. "December twenty-seventh, 1941." They could have left the area a thousand times by now, set up in Florida comfort by their millionaire son. But Aliquippa is what they know, what they love. This small but tidy town house—one of hundreds of government-subsidized co-ops built specifically for the steelworkers—is their anchor. There is no need to pull up stakes.

Mike Ditka, Sr., may be the toughest man in what may be the toughest city in this country. He was the original "Hammer" and "Iron Mike," earning those nicknames and respect on the clay fields in nearby Carnegie, Pennsylvania. He played football without a helmet, smashing into dirt, rocks—and an occasional parked car. As president of his railroad union for thirty-four years, he bargained with the best of them, building an international reputation as a negotiator. "Mike was the toughest labor leader of any local [railroad] union in the country," says Milo Shimrak, former assistant director of the Railroad Division of the Transport Workers Union of America and a close friend and ally for forty years.

How tough?

One story spells it out. A story that seems borrowed from a Hollywood script starring Bogart or Cagney or Edward G. Robinson. A story that begins in the mid-1950s with Ditka, then president of Local 1432, set to start another round of bitter contract talks with the Aliquippa & Southern Railroad. His union numbers were chicken feed (some 250 men) compared to the 15,000 steelworkers who passed in and out of the tunnel every day. But Ditka's union had never blindly ratified the steelworkers' contract; his reputation was built on bettering it, pushing A&S management as far as he could. In one three-year contract, for example, steelworkers were given fifteen weeks vacation. Local 1432 negotiated eight weeks *every year*. "He had the best labor contract of any railroad union in the United States," says Shimrak. "The most money, the most fringes, the most benefits."

But in the midfifties A&S started playing hardball. No more sweetheart contracts. No more concessions. They offered *less* than the steelworkers were getting, like it or not, not a nickel more.

Mike Ditka gave them the only answer he could:

"We're gonna shut it down."

Riiiight, management laughed. A couple hundred men shut down a steel mill? Hah! Stop 15,000 men, union buddies or not, from coming to work. Hah! Hah! Keep laughing, thought Iron Mike. He knew exactly what he would do; he knew the only way in or out of that mill was through the mouth of that tunnel, and that night over beers in the back room at Savin's Bar, he sketched out his plan. This isn't about money, he told other union reps. Or fringes. Or benefits. It's about principle. If the company wins now, they'll win again, and again and again. "We got to shut the goddamn place down to save our self-respect!" he stormed.

So at five A.M., before the sun came up, Mike Ditka took a stand.

Steelworkers stumbling off the buses and leaving the bars on Franklin, warmed by their whiskey and coffee, saw a chilling, inspiring sight: one man, alone, on top of the tunnel, a bullhorn in his hand. Below him, stretched across the mouth of the tunnel, were a hundred and fifty men, *his* men, stacked five deep into the dark of the tunnel. Some were holding bats or sticks. All were taking a stand. The mouth had been closed. "He stood there on top of the tunnel and just dared fifteen thousand steelworkers to come through," says Shimrak. "Just stood on top of that tunnel and dared them."

He stood there all day and all night. Iron Mike and his band of merry men tying up traffic for miles, standing on principle. That first night, the company reopened negotiations; by the next morning, the strike was over. A new contract was signed. Mike Ditka had won. "He even got more than he asked for before the strike," says Shimrak.

Mike Ditka, Sr., was born on June 23, 1918, in the Roslyn area of Carnegie, Pennsylvania, the son of Waysl and Bertha Dyzcko, immigrants from the Ukraine, the second-largest republic in population in the former Soviet Union. Bordered by Poland and Romania, the Ukraine holds a vital place in Soviet lore. With its rich land and vast mineral deposits the republic has long held not only economic but political power as well. The Ukraine was one of the hotbeds of the second Soviet Revolution in the summer of 1990, one of the leaders in the reform movement that led to what is now known as the Commonwealth of Independent States. Waysl and Bertha Dyzcko were independent people as well—he, a rugged Russian-Ukrainian, she, a petite and prideful Polish wife. Waysl wasn't an imposing man but possessed enormous physical strength. "He bucked rivets, drove rivets for the railroad," says his son, looking out at a quiet courtyard. "Jesus Christ was he strong. Oh, mother. I remember one time he picked me up just like that. He said, 'You hear me?' I said, 'Yup.'" Waysl was a welder and burner whose job was chopping up railroad cars for scrap. That is, until trouble started down at Scully's Yard back near Carnegie in the early 1920s, and somebody yelled "strike." Times got tough, and Waysl and three coworkers lost their jobs. He found work instead at A&S Railroad in Aliquippa, driving thirty miles each day, moonlighting as a host at the local Ukrainian club in Carnegie. The hours were long, but as they say, the pay was good. Between the two jobs it was enough for the Dyzckos to buy a nice three-bedroom home with a garden Waysl liked to tend.

Mike Ditka, Sr., was eight years old when he sipped his first beer, down at the Ukrainian club. Watching the old-timers knock back their Boilermakers, he was curious and tried a sip or two himself. "Took a little whiskey out of their glass and a beer and mixed them," he recalls with a grin. "Oh, yeah."

Mike Sr. wasn't much for discipline—"I seemed to fight authority for some reason"—but he and his neighborhood gang couldn't get enough of sports. They played baseball against gangs of kids from other neighborhoods, losers treated to a friendly stoning as they scampered home in shame. Football. Stickball. Mike Sr. loved playing and hated coming home. He skipped meal after meal. When he did show up, there was a fuming Waysl, strap in hand, ready to raise some welts. "Do I think I deserved it?" he says. "Hell, yeah. I earned every bit of it. Not proud of it, but I earned it. My father said, 'I'm only going to tell you once,' and he didn't tell me again. Next time he clobbered me."

Mike Sr.'s favorite sport was football. He spent his teenage years starring, not for the high school team, but in the local youth league, a 158-pound flash who played without a helmet and with unbridled passion. Iron Mike, they called him. Busting up ribs, banging off parked cars, cutting his head on the ragged, rocky field and hustling right back to the huddle. He got as far as his junior year at Carnegie High School before quitting. It was a Thursday, he remembers. On Friday he hired on with A&S, a brash-mouthed kid trading his ball and glove for a pick and shovel, and a lifelong membership in a fraternity of men who built this country with their bare hands. In the beginning he was as raw as the coke and coal he shuttled from one furnace to another. But the seventeen-year-old learned how to lay track and stock coal fast; how to wield that acetylene torch like a magic wand, patching plates and angles for finish work. He learned from immigrant men with strange last names, who grabbed his arm and said, "Not that way, boy, like this." He watched knowing full well if he failed, there were plenty of others, arriving by the busload every day, from Ohio and West Virginia, ready to take his place—and for far less money than the forty cents an hour he was being paid.

"A hard day's work and a little bit more," he says today. "You better goddamn believe it was tough." There wasn't a day, he says, when your arms didn't ache, your body beg for mercy. Not one day your mouth wasn't drier than Sahara sand. A whiskey shot followed by an ice-cold beer was the absolute answer to your prayers.

"A goddamn reward," says Mike Ditka, Sr.

A reward he tossed down daily up and down Franklin Avenue or in the neighborhood bars near home. Mike made the rounds like everyone else. "He was a pretty good hitter," says longtime friend Sildra. "He drank. You had to drink." That meant beers and some poker at the White Sox Athletic Club, a beer or two at Mill City or the Silver Rail, a bourbon and soda at the Cottage Inn or Barney's. Closer to home it was Ted's or the Linwood Tavern. "If you were lucky," says Big Mike, "you made it home for dinner." After dinner and a shower he walked two hundred yards down a hill to Savin's, where he drank and talked until ten or eleven o'clock almost every night.

"There was never any question of their right to drink or do whatever the hell they wanted," says Aliquippa native Mike Rebich, who remains close to the Ditka family. Now an ABC News cameraman, Rebich's father, Swet, worked for years as a yardmaster with A&S. "You know there was one rule in my house, and that was when my father came home from work, he had a clean white shirt to go out. It was never, 'Where are you going?' The answer was out. 'I'm going out.' And I know that was Mike's dad and every other dad in town."

Big Mike became a father for the first time, at the age of twenty-one, on October 18, 1939, not long after he married Charlotte Keller, the pretty, outgoing Irish-German girl down the block, the crackerjack sister of one of his neighborhood gang. They named their first child Michael Keller Ditka. A year later another boy arrived. He was christened Ashton after Charlotte's brother.

The family of four moved to Linmar Plan just three weeks after the Japanese bombed Pearl Harbor, an attack that mobilized the men of Aliquippa and led Mike Ditka, Sr., to volunteer for the Marines. Basic training was two thousand miles away, at Camp Pendleton near San Diego. He came to resent the assignment, the time and distance away from his family. Consequently, he says, he carried a large chip on his shoulder and dared any jarhead to knock it off. Carried it everywhere he went: on duty with the Military Police, during hours of idle drilling in the sand. All he wanted was out. "I had a guy once who wanted me to sign up again and go to Japan or China with him. I said 'you're crazy, I got two kids at home.' He said 'you'll have a woman to do your work. Women wherever you want.' He said 'think of all the extra money you'll receive.' I said 'I'm not looking to get the money. I'm looking to get the hell out of here. I got two kids. I don't know how my wife is getting along, I don't know.' I said I sure as hell wasn't going."

Charlotte wasn't doing much better. Tough as she could be, and that was plenty tough at times, even she was overwhelmed with these two hellions—not that she'd care to admit it. "Michael," she likes to recall, "was a perfect angel." Others disagree. "He was a little tyrant," one longtime neighbor, Patty Sylvester Palladini, told *The Times* of Beaver

County (Pa.) back in 1988. "And was he bad." As the paper noted, the way Ms. Palladini said "bad," "you would add about ten more *A*'s."

Palladini lived near the Ditkas for thirteen years and recalls young Mike and Ashton taking turns tormenting their mother. Naps were a novelty; no sooner did Charlotte tuck the mischievous boys in bed and step downstairs than they would crawl out a back window, scramble down the rain spout, and sprint toward the playground. Charlotte was at a loss until Palladini's mom offered some help. "My mother told her to put the kids to bed naked. Take their clothes so they couldn't run away," she told *The Times*. "It worked for Ashton, but that couldn't stop Mike." Especially on days when the mellifluous smell of Mrs. Sylvester's dreamy chocolate chip cookies drifted through the air. Says Palladini, "One day there's a knock on the door—it's Mike. He climbed naked down the rain spout, smelled the cookies, and wants some. And in he came for cookies. We were sitting at the table when his mother tracked him down that time. I think she gave up on those naps after that day."

With Big Mike away, Charlotte's brother, Ashton, filled a fatherly role; she beamed with pride when Ashton handed Mike his first football uniform at age five. (Charlotte had a yen for uniforms, too. She liked to dress her "perfect angel" like Little Lord Fauntleroy.) But discipline remained a problem. Young Michael proved a bit more malicious and broke a few more windows than the rest of his gang. "Mike was no saint," says Sildra. "He was pretty mean, a real roughneck, a kingpin. Other kids were afraid of him." So it was, until his father returned home shortly after World War II ended. Then the screws tightened around No. 14. "I expected them to abide by whatever decisions my wife and I made," explains Big Mike. Simple immigrant rules passed from one generation to the next. Respect your elders. Work hard. Listen to your teachers. Speak when you're spoken to. Don't talk back. Right and wrong. Make a mistake and it was the business end of an ex-Marine's belt.

It's unclear exactly just how physical the punishments were. You ask and Mike Sr. says, "I'd say I was strict but not tough."

The difference?

"Well, tough you beat them to the extent   you beat them into line. Strict you tell them, and hey, it's done. They toed the line."

A mighty thin line at times. "He was brought up strict," says West Aliquippa native Mike Dzvonar, a close family friend for forty years. "I tell you there was no messing around. In other words, the old man told him to do something, you do it, or I'll beat the shit out of you. And Mike knew it too. That's where I think all the resentment was. The father said do it or you and I are gonna get into it."

In a child's mind sometimes that line of right or wrong is bright and white and painted right down the middle of the street. They understand if you cross it, you pay a price. Such was the case when Michael, then in third grade, swiped a pack of his father's Lucky Strikes and headed for the woods near the house. He lit one, took a puff, and sure enough, the ground began to spin. He tossed the cigarette aside. The woods caught on fire.

"What happened to the woods?" asked Mike Sr. that night during dinner.

"Well," answered Charlotte, "you'll have to ask your son. He burned them down."

"Got a whipping I'll never forget," the son once said.

But other times, for a child, that line can bend and blur, especially if a parent is tired or angry or has been drinking. You also get whippings you never forget. But for very different reasons.

Mike Ditka, Jr., recalled one such case during an interview with ABC News correspondent Judd Rose for "PrimeTime Live" back in 1990. For a moment or two, during this interview, Ditka was back in No. 14, a child again—angry and frustrated about a beating he didn't deserve from a father who wasn't about to listen. "I went to a Catholic grade school," Ditka told Rose, "and if I got a whipping from a nun, there was nothing said about the whipping from the nun. I got another whipping from my dad automatically." In the show he pauses, then attacks with his words. "It wasn't whether the nun was right or wrong. I was wrong. That was assumed. That was guaranteed. I got another whipping."

One day not long after Mike Sr.'s return from the war, a fresh face walked into the railroad shop. He looked around and started giving a spiel about a new union. "You want representation," said the face who worked in the locomotive shop, "you come see me." Big Mike, who was listening, had a better idea. "Why should we come up there?" he asked. "We got seventy-five men down here. Why should the car guys join up with the machinists?"

"Well, that's the way it is," answered the rep. "If you don't like it, do something about it."

Naturally Big Mike did. He and a buddy started talking up the union, organizing, piecing together support. Soon after, Local 1432 of the Railroad Division of the Transport Workers of America was born. A buddy got appointed president of the union; Mike was made an officer. But it wasn't long before the first real election was held and Mike Ditka, Sr., was elected president. He ran again every two years for the next thirty-four years, seventeen elections in all, often over bitterly contested issues, and never lost. "He was like a Marine sergeant," says Shimrak, "but a very, very fair man. No preferences." Over time Ditka came to represent men in the rail shop, car shop, the machine shop, the signalmen, even the blacks and Italians in Maintenance of Ways. Nobody could touch him at the bargaining table—grievances, contracts, he never backed down. "A real bastard," says Sildra. "He didn't take shit from nobody." Often in meetings he would play games with management, bursting into half-hour homilies, stomping and fussing around the conference table, going nose to nose with Brooklyn-born Jerry Creedon, management's man, who, at Mike Sr.'s retirement dinner, called him "the greatest labor leader I ever saw." Ditka's style and success caught the eye of Mike Quill, who founded the International Transport Workers Union in New York in the 1930s and served as president of ITWU until his death in 1966. Quill, the man who shut down the New York City subway system in January 1966, admired Big Mike's brass and balls and campaigned to get him elected to represent the railroad division on the international executive board. It worked. Ditka was one of only five reps for thirty unions. It meant prestige and some trips to New York. It meant more time away from home.

There are only one or two roads out of steel towns such as Aliquippa. Not shortcuts or detours but long, rugged journeys. All the easy streets tip toward the mill or the military. Almost forty years after he chose a path, in his July 30, 1988, induction speech into the Pro Football Hall of Fame, Ditka talked about his road.

"The way people in Aliquippa and Beaver County should remember me is that I'm no different than anybody else. I was the same growing up as everybody else. I wasn't special. I had the same dreams, the same ambitions, the same dislikes. . . .

"I just didn't want to work in the mill. Not that there's anything wrong with working in the mill. Far from it. It's just that I wanted to go a little further. Athletics was my avenue."

It was an avenue that took his life as far away from the tunnel as possible. The tunnel to the young men of Aliquippa was both a blessing and a curse. "The story goes back a long time," says Sildra, sixty-four, a former mill man. "The greatest men ever to come out of Aliquippa were the ones who didn't want to go down that tunnel." To some, it offered an easy choice, and guaranteed money in your pocket. To others the mill meant dirt and filth on your father's face and clothes and burn marks on his arms, forearms, and neck, where the protective clothing missed. But the dirt would wash away, the burns could heal; what lingered was the life—the alcohol and odd hours, the acetylene stench. The uncountable times Ditka's father left the dinner table and walked out the door, down the hill to Savin's Bar, the thousands of nights his mother did the dishes, washed the children's hair, and put them to bed; the nights she helped with the homework, answered the questions, recited the prayers.

One night, in search of the definitive reason behind Mike Ditka's drive, this theory is presented to Sildra. How perhaps, at a very early age, Mike saw what the mill did to men. Men such as his grandfather and his father, such as his peers who would stay behind. And what it would do to him. And how one day he made a silent vow. *I'll never, ever set foot in that tunnel.*

The phone line sits silent for quite some time.

Then Dan Sildra speaks.

"You hit the nail right on the head," he says.

Mike Dzvonar greets a visitor at his West Aliquippa home with a hardy how-do-you-do, his huge walrus mustache bobbing up and down. An unassuming former math teacher, Dzvonar is sixty-eight years old now, but still vain enough to sweep his thinning gray hair back over his head to cover a balding pate. His simple white wooden row house stands with dozens of others along the murky Ohio River. It is a house of a man and his memories, and Dzvonar has many of those, particularly when the subject is Mike Ditka.

Dzvonar first met young Mike back in the midfifties. The mills were booming. The locals within the "planned" communities were lumped together by either social status or ethnic base, oftentimes both. The town aristocrats, the poetic "cake eaters," were descendants of either the English or Scots; they ran the political machine or were bosses at the mill, and they lived in the fancy homes of Plan 6. The Poles, Jews, and Ukrainians dominated other plans, while the coloreds, Italians, Lebanese, Serbs, and Croatians clustered together in Plan 11 and Logstown, where all the spit-in-your-face kids lived. All day, every day, Ditka and dozens of other brush-cut kids scrambled from plan to plan, from parking lot to cow pasture, in T-shirts and jeans, playing every game imaginable. Stickball. Tackle football. Baseball. Kick the can. There were rock-throwing contests, tomato fights, and the occasional raid on a neighbor's garden.

It was athletic Darwinism at its neighborhood best. You got your ass kicked, you kicked somebody else's, maybe your brother's, maybe your best friend's, more than likely the Serbs or Italians next door. "That's what made us tough," says one of the Plan 11 kids. "That's what made Mike Ditka tough."

Dzvonar coached and witnessed that Ditka toughness on American Legion baseball teams he coached, and later at Aliquippa High. "He'd throw a fist at you, a knee, an elbow," says Dzvonar. "Any way to beat you, Michael would beat you." God forbid if you beat him, or worse, if *he* dropped a fly ball or struck out. Gloves got hurled into the dirt. Bats whipped into orbit. In Little League even the most modest failures were met with spectacular, often comical outbursts of emotion.

"Sewickley?" asks Dzvonar. "Do you know where Sewickley is?"

It's a nearby community, he explains, site of just another American Legion baseball game. In his first two times up, Young Mike had looked pitiful at the plate. Suddenly Dzvonar felt a tug at his sleeve. He looked over at his nephew.

"Uncle Mike," said the nephew, "Michael's really mad."

"Don't worry," said Dzvonar without looking. He'd seen it so many times before. "He's just that kind of person."

Perhaps, thought the little boy. But this mad?

"Uncle Mike, look," he argued. "He's on the ground and he's eating grass."

"You're kidding," said Dzvonar.

Sure enough, there was that Ditka boy over by the side of the field. Sure enough he was yanking grass out of the ground and stuffing it in his mouth.

Dzvonar's bare feet crackle against the newspapers and he smiles and says, "Next time up he comes up and hits the goddamn ball, puts it clear over the fence. Must have been a drive about four hundred feet. I never saw a ball hit like that in all my life."

According to a venerable local baseball legend by the name of Tom Diaddigo, who tutored the eldest Ditka boy for years, Young Mike was "a breed apart" when it came to sports. In many games Young Mike would play catcher, pitcher, shortstop, and outfield—sometimes all in the same inning. If he was playing shortstop and a pitcher walked a couple of batters, forget it. He'd be at the mound in a heartbeat, banishing some ten-year-old to the outfield, bringing in somebody else—a winner—to play short. Then Ditka would pitch. Coaches looked on aghast as Ditka played musical chairs. Nobody was immune. In one Pony League—a step up from Little League—contest, Ditka was on the mound pitching against the archrival Celtics, mowing them down, leading 2–1, heading into the final inning. Leading, that is, until his center fielder dropped a routine, game-ending fly ball and two runs scored. The winning runs. That center fielder happened to be

Ashton. Mike threw his mitt down as if it were on fire and chased after his younger brother, who had recognized the severity of the situation and was hopping the center-field fence, heading for home. It's about a mile from Morrell Park to the Ditka home, down a hill, up a hill, and then a final flat sprint. It was somewhere in that straightaway that Michael caught his quarry. They duked it out. It wasn't the first time. "We had some of the worst fights two brothers ever had," Ashton Ditka once told the *Pittsburgh Press*. "Ashy," as he is known, now a senior vice president for marketing for an oil refinery company in Warren, Pennsylvania, was no pushover. He was a standout athlete in his own right, starring in both baseball and football at Bucknell. He and his big brother used to battle it out upstairs, downstairs, right on the street. "He insisted you do it his way," Ashton told the newspaper. "His way was aimed at winning. It upset him when I didn't do things up to his standards."

Young Mike was an obnoxious little athlete, is what he was. If he wasn't blaming everybody but himself for mistakes, challenging parents who dared call him a "crybaby" to a fight, he was throwing equipment or staging sit-ins. Says Diaddigo, "He used to sit on the ground sometimes. And I'd walk by and kick him in the butt and say, 'Don't sit on the ground.' One time I did that and he came at me, swinging his fists and everything. He was nine years old." Of course, if young Mike Ditka disagreed with coaching strategy he hardly held back, moved to muttering, "Dumb move, dumb move," under his breath or challenging the offender straight out. Dzvonar remembers a substitution that backfired in an American Legion game. Two runs scored. A prepubescent Ditka was right in his face in the dugout.

"Just where in the hell," he said, "did you learn how to coach!"

But no one could criticize Ditka.

"That's the one thing I always had against Michael," says Dzvonar in the quiet of his living room. "He couldn't stand criticism. If you criticized him, he really got teed off at you. In other words, it had to be Michael's way or nobody's way at all. He made more mistakes than anyone else. But when he made a mistake, you had to accept it."

Early on, there was only one man who could criticize Mike Ditka and Mike had to take it. Every last word of it. The original Iron Mike was anything but a meddlesome parent, but he liked to watch his boys play. "I can see the old man in the background, in the bleachers following us," Dzvonar recalls. The father never criticized his children in public, but he rarely praised them in either public or private. If somebody hit two home runs, the old man wanted to know why he didn't hit three or four. If they got five A's and a B, he'd ask about the B. Says one family insider, "There was not much positive reinforcement. It's not that you did well. It was always, why didn't you do better?"

"My husband always told Michael what he did wrong, not what he did right," Charlotte Ditka once said.

"I think sometimes he resented that because I didn't tell him the good parts that he did, just the bad parts," added Mike Ditka, Sr.

"Mike [junior] resented that," says Dzvonar. "He couldn't be told what to do. Just like it was back when I was coaching Michael. In other words, who in the hell are you to tell me what to do? In other words, you're not smart enough to tell me what to do. It goes back to the father. There was always resentment there."

As time went on, no coach could cap the volcanic temper. But Little League and midget ball were child's play compared to grabbing a spot on the Aliquippa High School varsity football team. The 130-pound eighth-grader who liked to "bulldoze" his opponents, who was "hell on wheels," was in for a surprise.

The Kingpin was about to meet "The King."

HE ENTERED THEIR LIVES AT THE MOST IMPRESSIONABLE TIME, LEAVING AN indelible mark on virtually every student and athlete he touched. "He was a father figure to all of us," says football coach Marocco, fifty-five, now sitting in his tight, tidy office at Aliquippa High, a man with a face and fortitude not easy to forget. It's not the jet-black hair and olive skin that belie his age; it is the eyes and a laugh that hold you like a three-year-old after a long day's work. It is his attitude, the conviction you hear in his voice and feel in his hands. In many ways, Marocco fits right in between the two pictures that dominate his office walls.

Mike Ditka on one side.

King Carl on the other.

The latter picture is actually a drawing, a charcoal sketch that, in many ways, resembles a young Tom Osborne, the current head football coach at Nebraska. There's the same thin face, same tight lips and wavy hair. The eyes are intense, hooded, penetrating. Next to the drawing is a plaque. It commemorates Carl Aschman's induction, posthumously, into the Pennsylvania Coaches Football Hall of Fame. It is dated July 28, 1989. The plaque notes how King Carl—"as he was known throughout western Pennsylvania"—was voted into several local and regional halls of fame before finishing with his lasting contribution: "Coach Aschman was a great influence on all the men he coached and their success in life is his greatest legacy."

"A monster of a man," says Marocco.

Monster of a man. The phrase hangs in the air for a second, somewhere between the two photos, between student and coach, similarity and influence. "We all patterned ourselves after Aschman," says Marocco. "I do a lot of the things that Aschman did. Mike's mannerisms, his forcefulness, the way he talks, the way he carries himself, are because of Carl Aschman.

"Sometimes," says Marocco, "I look at his picture and I sit here and look at him and I feel like he's watching me. Like he's looking at me right now."

Carl Aschman was born in 1903. He played high school football in Pennsylvania and later was a star center at then-powerful Washington and Jefferson College in Washington, Pennsylvania. In 1928 he was selected to play in the prestigious East-West Shrine college all-star game out west. He quickly returned to Pennsylvania to coach high school football, first at California (PA) High School, then, later in 1934, at Brownsville, a middle-class coal community about twenty-five miles from Pittsburgh near the Monongahela River. There he won a raft of championships before somebody got the smart idea of making Aschman the baseball and basketball coach too, figuring the same thing would happen. I'm a football man, said Aschman. When the town persisted, he up and quit, taking over in Aliquippa in 1941, where he won 184 games, lost 88, and tied 10 over the next twenty-three seasons. He also won Western Pennsylvania Interscholastic Athletic League (WPIAL) titles in 1952, '55, and '64 and lost in two other title games. He never had a losing season.

Back in Aschman's era, Aliquippa High looked like something straight off the set of "Leave It To Beaver" or "Father Knows Best." The high school, built in 1923, was an imposing two-story, red-brick structure. Today it's still impressive, the centerpiece of a sprawling set of factorylike facilities that spread all over a hillside. There's a sports complex built and donated long ago by J&L Steel; a middle school, a transportation department, and the administrative office. Many of the rooms offer commanding views of the Beaver Valley, home of some of the finest high school football teams in the nation. Back in the 1940s and all during Aschman's reign, Aliquippa had few athletic equals. It was a powerhouse school with impressive athletic programs, the proud home to a thousand students, grades nine through twelve, sons and daughters of steelworkers and mill executives.

Today, much like the rest of the city, Aliquippa High is struggling. Enrollment has dropped—to about 450—grades nine through twelve. Sixty percent are black. About eighty percent are underprivileged. But football is still king, and has been for the last fifty years or so. Marocco is the caretaker of the pride and tradition, and he takes it very seriously. He's at the school six days a week, from seven A.M. to six P.M., even in the summer, when he supervises weight workouts.

He grew up with almost a religious reverence for work, one of fifteen children jammed in a two-bedroom house, the son of an Aliquippa monument maker. "I played football, and when I came home from practice at seven o'clock, I would have to go to the shop and put my hours in," he says. "My father's belief was just because I played football that didn't stop me from my job." His job? Grinding headstones. "Some nights I would work until eleven. My brothers would try and sneak over sometimes and try and pick up the slack because they knew I was tired and they felt bad for me. My mother used to make me sandwiches and slide them through the cellar window so I would have something to eat.

"My dad would sit at home and listen to the radio, and he would come over and spot-check me to see I was doing my job. One of my brothers would sneak in and grab the tools off me and cut and chisel, another would be on the lookout for my dad.

"My dad didn't believe, of course, he didn't understand the value of an education. He was a hardworking immigrant from Italy, and he raised a big family, and to him the way to make things was to work hard. Sports, newspapers, television, bicycles, those were luxury items. You didn't need them in your life. What you needed to know is how to work with your hands. You have to learn to work with your hands. He always told me that, your hands will bring you money. And if you got blisters, you were working hard. It was very, very tough."

So was Marocco. He became an All-American guard and linebacker at Aliquippa High in 1954 despite measuring just 5'9" and 180 lbs., and was good enough to be offered a full scholarship to Big Ten power Michigan State. When Marocco visited the campus, he recalls MSU's All-American guard Frank Kush—later a wildman college and pro coach—driving him around in a brand-new Olds, asking, "So what do you want to do? Want a piece of ass? Want to drink tonight?"

"I'm scared to death," says Marocco, laughing. "I'm just a goody-goody from Aliquippa. I'm afraid to death if something were to happen and it got back to Aschman, he would run me out of town."

Such was the complete power Aschman held over his players. You could be eighteen years old, a thousand miles away from Aliquippa, and have the world at your fingertips, yet all you thought of was Aschman. What would he think? What if he found out?

Carl Aschman never asked permission for anything. He walked into a room and instantly took over. Do this. Do that. Students, assistant coaches, faculty, priests. It didn't matter. He never even bothered to introduce himself; you were expected to know King Carl. A ruthless tyrant one minute, he played the benevolent dictator the next. For sixteen- and seventeen-year-old kids he was a combination father figure and supreme being, God as coach. Says Marocco, "He controlled our lives from the time we got up in the morning until the time we went to bed."

Aschman thought nothing of calling his athletes at home, or dropping by, spot-checking his rigid nine P.M. curfew. "He'd stop at your door," says one former player, "and say, you know, 'Is John there? I'd like to see him.' People are watching television, maybe trying to have sex with their wives. Aschman just walked right in. It was like, 'Oh, he's upstairs. Fine, no problem, I'll find my way.' Then he'd go up to your room, turn on the light, and check."

Says Marocco, "It was fear. If he said be home by nine and it was five to nine and it seemed like I was five miles away, I'd panic. Sure enough, he would call. 'How are you, son? Did you study tonight?' You always had that fear he was looking over your shoulder."

Former players also remember Aschman as a sensitive, emotional, and deeply religious man, who walked with a military step and demanded, above all, discipline and commitment from his athletes. His practices were brutal. "This guy believed in hitting," says Dzvonar, a halfback on Aschman's first team back in 1941 and later an assistant coach for several years. "Carl was really basic. Fundamentals. Good tacklers, good blockers." Yet, as Ditka does today, Aschman tailored his team to the talent on hand. One year it was double wing, the next the split T, the next a pro set. He played no favorites. "Sit down and shut your mouth" was a pet phrase. So was "hell's bells" or "hell's fire."

But for every outburst and embarrassment his players endured, there was uncommon love and protection. The King never missed a trick, drawing more inspiration from a silly jig, a scoop of vanilla ice cream, and four quarters than almost any coach in history. You didn't quit on him because, you knew, if necessary, he would back you to the limit.

"Whatever strength you had," says former Aliquippa High guard and fullback John Evasovich, who played for Aschman from 1955 to '57, "he had the uncanny ability to bring it out of you. You tried to prove you were better. If he put his arm around you, and said, 'Good job,' it was worth eating all the dirt, all the work."

Aschman certainly never dressed like royalty. He wore the clothes of a common man, the same sport coat over and over again for twenty-three years, playbooks and papers stuffed into the pockets. Former assistant coaches can still see his pants drooping down in back, jockstrap exposed. His family life was less distinct; married with two children, he never cared about cutting the grass or painting the house. His hobbies were fishing or a hearty hand of pinochle over at the firehouse, but football was his life. "That's all he talked about," says Dzvonar. His two favorite words were Discipline and Commitment, capital *D* and *C*. If you were truly one of Carl Aschman's boys, you never cut a class, never smoked a cigarette, and never, God forbid, got caught in a clinch with a girlfriend. Because if Aschman saw you—or word filtered back from one of his legion of spies—he was on you like rubber on a tire: "We're playing *Ambridge* on Friday and you're *playing around like this!*" he would scream. And no sooner had he reduced the offender to floor wax than he turned on the shell-shocked female, yelling, *"You're ruining my team!"* He kept it up at practice, too, firing off long litanies on the dangers of sex and heavy petting. How you couldn't think, couldn't get down in a three-point stance, couldn't pivot on that right ankle to trap block. And why not? He hardly slept and barely ate during the season. He took every game to heart, every catch, every call, surviving on faith and his love of Aliquippa football.

Under Aschman, game days all began the same way. Over the school loudspeaker the words *All football players report to St. Titus Catholic Church for the rosary and Holy Communion to beat . . .* were heard, and with them, Protestant, Jewish, and Catholics all trekked up a nearby hill. Aschman was always waiting, arms crossed, standing on the front steps of the church. After mass and morning classes, players filed not into the cafeteria for lunch but rather a third-floor room—for film and skull sessions, where frequently Aschman unveiled a motivational trick or two, often in a sweeping gesture, such as yanking the food off the plate of some overweight or underachieving athlete and handing it over to another, less fortunate but more deserving player.

Final period or Study Hall 29, as it was known, was another mandatory pre-game meeting. More film. More "Hell's bells" and "Son, my grandmother can block better than that!" And if verbal abuse wasn't enough to motivate or enlighten, he'd march right over and yank some poor soul right out of his chair. Then they would dance, slowly, mockingly, around the room. Accompanied, as always, by Aschman's fractured serenade of the Australian ditty "Waltzing Matilda."

On the football field he did it all. One minute he was fine-tuning his multi-option motion offense. The next he barked out defense assignments. He taped all the players, left ankle first, superstitious to a fault. "Hey, Mijou," he would yell to Dzvonar, using the assistant coach's nickname. "Go out and take a look at the field." Dzvonar would do as he was told. Ten minutes later Aschman would make the same request. "Carl," Dzvonar would say, "it's still there."

But checking the field was the extent of his assistants' job. "His assistants had no influence on him at all—none. Zero," says Marocco, a member of Aschman's staff from 1960 to '64. "He was the defensive coach, offensive coach, special teams coach. What assistants did was get on one knee, pick up a blade of grass, and listen."

Raccoon Creek State Park lies about twenty miles southwest of Aliquippa in the town of Frankfort Springs. The park is more a wilderness preserve than a recreational area, operated by the state as a natural habitat of birds, flowers, and deer. But for two weeks each summer it was home for forty-five of Aliquippa's finest football players. Raccoon wasn't so much a park back then as a boot camp, a rite of passage. A badge of courage worn as proudly in Aliquippa as any war medal. Fourteen days of living hell and life's lessons courtesy of King Carl.

"It was like the movie *Stalag 17*," says ex-Aliquippa football star Paul Dinello, now the superintendent of the Aliquippa school district.

"Prisoners had it better," says Evasovich.

It was barracks-style living at its worst. No indoor plumbing. No air-conditioning. Cold showers. Snakes. Uniforms with four and five names written and crossed out on the back. Laundry once a week. The players slept in bunks on mattresses thinner than a sophomore's skin. Every morning at five, rain or shine, there was Aschman, air raid siren in hand, screeching the day to a start. After breakfast, players hustled the mile or so to practice where, before the first drill, they formed a line the width of the practice field and slowly walked from one end to the other clearing the ground of rocks and stones.

Dinello laughs now at the memory. He is a mountain of a man. Balding on top, he has a comedic touch and the look of actor/director Rob Reiner as he stands behind his desk, a black pullover shirt accented with gold chains and glasses hanging loose from the cord around his neck. A cigarette jabs the air punctuating his story. "So every morning we have to pick up stones and throw them over a hill off the field. So one morning Aschman sees down below, on the next field, are these juvenile deliquents. It's called the Morganza Summer Camp for juveniles or something. They were taking these guys out of a regular prison and bringing them to Raccoon State Park to clean up brush and stuff."

Another stab of the cigarette. "So Aschman sees these forty guys sitting in a circle getting their daily therapy from a counselor. He decides to go down and find out what the hell is going on. Rather than introduce himself, he just moves right in."

"What the hell is your story?" Aschman shouted at one of the youths. But before anybody answered, Dinello says, the coach was in the face of another youth, firing away. Then came the counselor's turn.

"Why are these kids here?" asked Aschman.

"They've broken the law," said the counselor.

That's all King Carl needed to hear. "Broken the law? What do you mean broken the law?" He stalked around the circle.

"How come you're not playing football?

"How come you're not home helping your mom and dad?

"How come you're not in church?"

Not waiting for any answers, Aschman told the boys to "get up off the goddamn ground," the counselor too, and form a line.

Before you knew it, says Dinello, they were picking up rocks, clearing the field. All except one holdout.

Aschman was in the kid's face in a heartbeat. *"Hell's fire, boy, don't ever look at me that way or I'll knock your head off! You know who I am?"*

For a moment or two, Dinello is seventeen years old again, his laughter heard down the hall. "He never even gave his name. But the kid bent down and started picking up stones. At night Coach Aschman went down and checked them all into bed."

Dinello's laughter fades into his own story. He was an insecure, overweight sophomore who found himself thanks to Aschman, and his practice of allowing graduating seniors to attend football camp before heading off to college. It was another brilliant motivational stroke for the Aliquippa coach. Trading food and occasional lodging and a chance to work out to the graduating players in return for their pleasure in "teaching" a young team a thing or two about toughness. Dinello's "teacher" turned out to be Frank Marocco.

"Now how do you teach a kid today?" asks Dinello, picking up a head of steam. "You'd put your arm around him and say, 'Son, I want to show you something.' Frank busted me across the head. He said, 'I want to tell you something, buddy. You got two weeks. If you don't do like I tell you, I'm gonna kick your ass.' Well, I was petrified. I got down into the three-point stance, and I was wrong. He hit me again."

Dinello made the mistake of asking how many times this was going to happen. Marocco threw him over the hill and down a steep ravine.

"Eventually," says the superintendent, "you say to yourself, 'Hey, how much more am I going to take?'"

So the sophomore came crawling up the hill—tongue caked with dirt, tears lining his face. And there was Marocco at the top of the hill, screaming like a madman: "If you don't kick that guy's ass across from you, I'll kick your ass!"

Dinello crawled up that hill right past Marocco. "Well, they put a senior in front of me and I leveled him," says Dinello. "That's how it started. You had a choice. You think I was going to back down from a twelfth-grader and answer to Frank Marocco? Frank Marocco was an All-American, one of only three in this town. Mike Ditka never made All-American; Frank Marocco did.

"Frank was mean, and when he got done with you, you were mean. It was that simple."

Yes, it was. Just that simple. That's the way it is in Aliquippa. A message that still passes, hand to hand, face to face, eye to eye on the football field at Raccoon Creek State Park and Aliquippa High. A message mouthed all over town—at the Mill City, social clubs, golf tournaments—by a brotherhood of men who, from high school on up, equate quitting with dishonor; who fight life's battles with training from another time and place. Men such as Marocco and Dinello. And Ditka.

And of course, the author of it all was Aschman. His practices were three- or four-hour ordeals, heavy on hitting and peppered with profanity and shouts of "One last play!" that seemed to never end. When it was over, the players staggered back to the barracks for lunch and a nap. Aschman served the meals himself, dishing it out, pulling it back from the plate of those who "failed" him during the day. At night, after another practice and dinner, he'd walk among the worn and weary, ordering one boy after another to stand up and sing the school fight song. Sing it with pride and dignity, son.

And as he walked, he held a five-gallon tub of ice cream in one hand, a scooper in the other. The moment of truth had arrived.

"Kid," said Aschman, "you did a good job today." Boom. A scoop of chocolate or vanilla landed in your bowl.

And if you failed?

"He'd ridicule you," recalls Evasovich. "This guy wants ice cream? Hah! He hasn't made a tackle all day."

"It was like an insult," says Marocco. "Boom. You put your head down."

"All you could think of," Evasovich says, "is, 'I'll show you. I'll make twenty tackles tomorrow.' "

It was only at night, in the deepening darkness, that a gentle man emerged. The insomniac who couldn't stop worrying about his team, padding about the barracks, flashlight in hand, making sure his boys were snug and safe. "It would be like two o'clock in the morning," says Marocco, "and he would be walking around with his flashlight checking every bunk, covering kids up, putting radios off. Putting a pillow back on their bed."

After two weeks at Raccoon Creek State Park, the Fighting Quips were ready to kick ass—not that Aschman was taking any chances. The team often left the practice field during the regular season on the edge of darkness or in it; pregame meals were not the standard meat and potatoes but honey, poached eggs, and a cup of tea. Church was a constant. So were the coach's powerful pregame speeches. Billy Graham or Norman Vincent Peale had little on Carl Aschman, who would call his team together, order them all on their knees, and begin to rub the rosary in his hands. "I prayed all night, Lord," he'd say. "I can't sleep. I can't eat. I walk the floors just visualizing what Ambridge said about us."

Bowed heads barely moved. "God help us on to victory. God give us the power to run the football. Give us the will to run our Forty-six Trap." By now concrete walls couldn't contain his voice: *"God, give us the strength to beat these sons of bitches!"*

And beat them they did. Aschman was as vexing and volatile in games as he was in practice; certainly not above grabbing a face mask and screaming, "I've got to be nuts to make you captain!" or telling some senior, a broken, bloodied nose splattered across his face, "Hell's bells, boy, put some gauze on it and get back in the game!"

At halftime, players went again to their knees—helmets on, sucking the life out of a quarter slice of orange. Aschman would often, if he was unhappy, slap that orange right out of your mouth.

After the game, win, lose, or draw, nobody breathed on the bus.

48

"Whether you won or lost," says Dzvonar, "you kept your mouth shut. That's the kind of discipline we had." And sooner or later Aschman came down the aisle, the penny-pinching Dutchman, a bag of change in his hand. One year it was nickels. Another year, allowing for inflation, it was dimes. Then quarters. Dinello: "He never stopped to feed us. He would give you a buck and a quarter after a game. Five quarters. We would be on the bus and he could come down the aisle and throw them at you. Boom. 'That's all you came along for—to get that dollar and a quarter.' Boom. He always had a comment, make you feel like you didn't deserve the quarters. If you were forty miles away from Aliquippa, you'd sit and ride the bus all the way home with the quarters on your pants or shirt. You wouldn't touch them. That's the way it was.

"And if we lost—I mean, everybody has to lose sometime—he'd go around and your hand might be out, and he'd say, 'What do you want?' You'd have to say, 'No, Coach, I don't want to eat because we lost.' I'll never forget those quarters."

And they will never forget Aschman. Certainly not Dinello. Or Evasovich. Certainly not Marocco, who twice found the course of his life changed by the old man. The first shift was in 1956 shortly after the All-American signed with Michigan State. At football camp one day Aschman introduced him to a couple of coaches from down south. "Coach Smaltz here is an Aliquippa boy," said Aschman of one of the men. "He's from North Carolina State and wants to talk to you."

Smaltz got right to the point. The Wolfpack was looking for a linebacker and Marocco fit the bill. "Coach Aschman recommends you, and we want you to come to North Carolina State," Smaltz said.

"Thank you very much, Coach," answered Marocco, "but I'm going to Michigan State."

Aschman cut him off, ordering the eighteen-year-old to listen up, shut up, and take a recruiting visit to NC State.

Says Marocco, "I went down to there and never came home."

Four years later, the road shifted again, this time shortly after graduation. Marocco was headed north to Canada and a career in the Canadian Football League. Aschman, ears ever pressed to the ground, got wind of the idea and asked Marocco to meet him at school.

"So, son, what are you doing?" said Aschman.

"Going to Canada."

With that, Aschman reached into his desk drawer and pulled out a slip of paper. It was a contract, preapproved by the superintendent of schools, for Marocco to teach gym and coach football. Before Marocco knew it, the paper was signed, Canada was forgotten ("My wife couldn't believe it," he says. "I told her Aschman made me do it"), a new heading set. He stood around listening and learning, munching blades of grass for three solid years. In 1963 he told Aschman he was quitting—tired of warming up athletes and no responsibility.

"So what do you want to do?" said the old coach.

"I want to run the defense," said Marocco.

"Then do it."

So he did, the first official title Aschman ever granted. Later that year, just minutes before the Steubenville game, Aschman went stone white in the locker room. He called Marocco over, whispering how the young assistant should take over his team.

"What about the other coaches? They're more experienced."

"I want you," breathed The King.

It's been almost thirty years since that moment, that 32–0 shutout Marocco engineered, and the pride in his voice rings out as if it were yesterday. "I guess he figured if I had enough balls to stand up to him, if I had been strong enough to do that, I had balls enough to run his football team."

The Steubenville scare turned out to be a heart attack. The 1964 season would be King Carl's last. He died seven years later. By pure coincidence Marocco was at the hospital when the ambulance roared up. It was Marocco who picked up the Hall of Fame plaque in Aschman's honor; the old coach had distanced himself from his family, giving his time and attention to football. His wife was dead. The daughter Aschman loved had died early in life, and that crushed him. His estranged son was nowhere to be found. So Marocco drove down to Hershey, Pennsylvania, and picked up the plaque. He was coaching at Aliquippa's archrival Ambridge at the time, unable, for political reasons, to get the one job he'd always wanted. Finally, in 1989, he did. Now that plaque hangs right where it always should, in Aliquippa High.

"You'll play hell getting it off me," says Marocco, glancing up at his wall. "I bet Mike Ditka would like to have it. Mike Ditka would probably give me ten thousand dollars for it."

Mike Ditka.

A tiger only King Carl could tame.

6

Carl Aschman was the biggest influence on Mike Ditka's life. Aschman was the guy who put Mike on track . . . the greatest thing that ever happened to him.
                    —Dan Sildra, longtime Ditka family friend

THEY LAUGHED AND CALLED HIM CHICKEN LEGS. ASCHMAN TOOK ONE LOOK at the wimpy tenth-grader and kicked the fourteen-year-old kid off the field at Raccoon Creek State Park for his own protection. Clean the latrines, he told him. Once the season started the skinny sophomore was little more than an afterthought. A charter member of the "Ghost Battalion," whose ignoble job it was to hold the blocking dummies in practice. But this sophomore was different. Sure he was skinny, but he had an air about him. An intense, festering fire that crackled every time he missed a block or tackle. "Come on!" the kid would yell. "Hit me again! Do it again!"

In the locker room before games, as Aschman pleaded for pride and dedication, the only other sound was the sophomore, crying in the back. Banging his head against a locker. After losses he was worse, smashing his helmet against a bench, cursing; and he hadn't played a down. "You saw the fight in him," says Marocco. "He worked so hard he would cry. If you beat him to the ground, he would bite you, kick you. He was going to be a ballplayer. He was going to be a ballplayer if it killed him."

It almost did. Aschman knew straightaway this one was special. But he never let on. Not until the football mom asked him why he was picking on her son all the time.

51

"Because he's got all that it takes to be a good one," said Aschman.

Still after his sophomore season the kid was ready to quit. He had taken a terrific pounding in practice. Again the mom approached Aschman. Was her boy "too small" to play? Should he give it up? Go home and drink some milk, he told the boy. Run. Build your body. Have some pride, some dedication. Work.

That's all Mike Ditka needed to hear. Soon he was gulping milk by the gallon, eating for five and rattling the upstairs floor with push-ups. He shook the house, says his dad. By the time the summer of '55 rolled around, the junior-to-be had added thirty-five pounds to his six-foot frame, up to 165 now, ready to make his mark. He started on both sides of the ball—at linebacker and at end—and played spectacularly at times. His finest moments may have come in the championship game at Mt. Lebanon, when the Quips pounded their way to the state AA title. In that game ol' Chicken Legs himself caught a long pass setting up the first touchdown and sparkled on defense. From there he was off and running, basketball, baseball, American Legion, push-ups, cross-country runs, whatever it took. By the summer of '56, Ditka had grown another inch and added thirty more pounds of lean, mean muscle.

"Carl," gasped Dzvonar after catching a glimpse of Ditka that summer. "Have you seen Michael? I can't believe it."

"Yeah," said Aschman. "The kid looks good."

The kid was a kid no more, more like a mad dog straining at his leash. "Usually," says Dinello, "you start off the season at half-speed or three-quarters. Mike started at full speed. Aschman was the only one who could control him. He knew he had a firecracker."

For Ditka that senior year was strictly storybook: captain in football, basketball, and baseball; class president; going steady with the prettiest girl. In football, he shifted from end to fullback on offense to help a team hurt by graduation. On defense he was everywhere. But personal discipline was still a problem. Just as in Little League, he raged at his teammates for not giving 150 percent. He lost his cool completely against Ambridge. In addition to being double- and triple-teamed he got an earful of "dumb hunky" insults. "Coach," Ditka told Aschman, "they're hitting me from all sides, they're killing me." Aschman offered a cold stare and replied, "Well, what do you want me to do? I can't go out there and play for you."

But most of the time it was Ditka who did the intimidating. Some seventy schools offered a scholarship, that one-way ticket out of the tunnel. As a Catholic, Ditka had his heart set early on Notre Dame, so much so that summer he skipped a chance to meet his childhood idol, Stan Musial, the star of the St. Louis Cardinals, to visit Notre Dame. But for some reason, the visit to South Bend fizzled. That left in-state rivals Penn State and Pittsburgh as his primary suitors with Penn State leading, thanks to a certain hard-charging assistant coach by the name of Joe Paterno.

"One of the best high school players I've ever seen, and I haven't changed me mind on that in thirty-five years."

It's that same Paterno on the line, calling back, looking back on his days with Ditka. Joe Paterno is sixty-five years old now, pilot of the Penn State program for the past twenty-six years, one of the four or five faces sure to be chiseled on any Mt. Rushmore of college coaches if and when the NCAA decides to buy itself a mountain. But back in '56 Paterno hadn't climbed any mountains, hadn't won 240 games or two national championships; he was just known as Rip Engle's right-hand man. Paterno had known King Carl way back at Brownsville. "An operator, a conniver, and a great actor," says Paterno today without a hint of malice. Aschman, he says, was well versed in the vagaries of college recruiting. Ever so skilled at convincing young eager assistants of the importance of, say, working the Fighting Quips football camp for free, or speaking at the Beaver County Coaches Association annual dinner—and not showing up empty-handed. "He'd say, 'We're a little short on cash. Can you bring up some beer?' You'd drive over with a couple of cases."

Paterno remembers the moment exactly. It was the summer of 1955, right there in Raccoon Creek State Park. "Ditka stood out like a sore thumb," Paterno says. "He was about six-three and lean. He was just so explosive in everything he did. So intense. Ferocious. A fierce competitor if there ever was one." Paterno was pretty fierce, too. So once or twice a week, whether he liked it or not, he made the drive over to Aliquippa to chat with Charlotte and Mike Sr. (as much as one could), before watching Mike play in one sport or another. Ditka's most impressive performance in 1956, says Paterno, was on the basketball court against Farrell High, which would go on to win the state title. "He must have had twenty rebounds and he dominated both ends of the floor," Paterno says. Aliquippa lost in overtime, but Paterno left with a smile on his face.

That smile widened in the summer of '57, right after Ditka's senior year when Ditka verbally committed to Penn State. In those days there were no formal "letters of intent," the written commitments of today. Your word was your bond—a bond rival recruiters and their boosters

53

thought nothing of trying to break. "I laugh today when people complain about recruiting," Paterno says.

Paterno knew the verbal commitment meant nothing. Not with Pittsburgh and its boosters still snooping around. He never let up. When summer arrived, he phoned up a Penn State alum and made sure Ditka got a classy—and rather cushy—surveying job. And when the kid wanted two weeks off to prepare and play in some big baseball tournament in Altoona, Paterno persuaded the alum to let Ditka have it. "He even got paid," says Paterno. In those days Ditka's baseball talents equaled or bettered his football ability. Scouts liked his outfield arm, his glove and speed. But they raved about his power. In one tryout, at Forbes Field, Ditka had left several Pittsburgh Pirates scouts open-mouthed after blasting a series of shots over the 406 sign in left center field. "He graded out great," recalls Sildra, who coached Ditka on several summer teams. "But the scouts felt he wasn't built for baseball; his upper half was too muscle-bound."

Still, in August, Ditka was selected to play with some Pittsburgh all-stars in a big tournament in Altoona. It was right after that tournament that Paterno got the phone call. "I was on the turnpike," he says, remembering the call as if it were yesterday, not thirty-five years ago, "and I called into my office. They told me to give Ditka a call."

"I got to talk to you, Coach," said the high school graduate when Paterno finally phoned. "I've got a problem."

Paterno's heart sunk six inches. "What problem?"

"I don't know what to do about school."

Wait, said Paterno, I'll be right there. He drove to Aliquippa only to have his worst fears realized. Ditka was going to Pittsburgh.

What had happened?

"I don't know," says Paterno, his voice suddenly soft. "I think you ought to ask him that. Pitt never let up on him. I think their boosters got to him. Something happened at that all-star game I don't know about. Some insurance man in Altoona along with a couple of dentists talked to Mike. Mike was very impressed with that Altoona insurance guy."

Paterno pauses . . . then speaks again. "Losing Mike was one of the toughest losses I've ever had to take. He would have been icing on the cake. I really thought he was going to be a great player."

John Michelosen felt the same way. Which is why when he heard Ditka was playing in a all-star tournament in Altoona, Pitt's head football coach went scrambling for the phone.

* * *

Ken Clapper remembers Michelosen's call as if it were yesterday too. He is sixty-four years old now, gray but trim from long walks and hikes along the Appalachian Trail. "A crazy story," Clapper says one afternoon. "One I've been waiting to tell for years."

Clapper was just twenty-nine at the time, bubbly, smart, with a thousand-watt smile, ready to take on the world. He had a sociology degree—from the University of Pittsburgh, naturally. His charm, college education, and discipline led him to selling insurance for Northwestern Mutual Life to businesses and professional people in the tri-county area around Altoona. Clapper was good at it, damn good. So damn good he earned a seat at the industry's Million-Dollar Round Table just about every year, made plenty of money, and bought himself some freedom. That eventually led to the presidency of the Blair County Pitt Club, a title Clapper held for more than twenty years. Clapper and his cohorts were so good Penn State rarely signed an Altoona boy to a football scholarship, even though Altoona is right between Penn State and Pitt. "Engle used to get on his Penn State alumni all the time," says Clapper, laughing. 'How come we can't get any of those kids!' The reason is we started with them in junior high school. By the time they were seniors they were all set to go to Pitt."

But Michelosen's call wasn't about an Altoona boy.

"Ken," he said, "there's some baseball thing in Altoona next week. We have a Pittsburgh team in it. There's a left fielder on that team by the name of Mike Ditka. He's going to Penn State. I wish you would at least talk to him."

Michelosen was a four-square football man, a block-and-tackle kind of coach, a Carl Aschman, minus the theatrics. Ditka was the poster child for his kind of football.

"Ken," said Michelosen with an unmistakable urgency, "I want this boy."

For Clapper those words were not a wish but a mandate. He had to get him. He had never failed in a recruiting mission, and he wasn't about to start now. He found the aging Colonial, one of the host hotels for the tournament in which about two dozen teams were competing. He rang up the room, surprised when this "monster-sized" kid turned out to be so gentle and polite in person. "Well, Mike," began Clapper, the natural-born salesman, trying to get a foot in the door, "I hear you're going to Penn State."

"Yes, sir, I am."

"Well, that's nice. How'd you like to go to dinner?"

The left fielder said fine, as long as his roommate could tag along. No problem, said Clapper. He took the boys to the snazzy Penn-Alto Hotel for a scrumptious meal. The next day Clapper was in the stands as Pittsburgh split its first two games in the double-elimination tournament. Care to have dinner again tonight, Mike?

This time Clapper began to work the edges of the sell. "So," he asked Ditka at dinner, "what are you studying?"

Ditka told him he was thinking about becoming a dentist.

"You know, Mike," Clapper said, seizing the opportunity, "Pitt has a fine dental school and Penn State doesn't."

Ditka barely flinched, suggesting only that he was contemplating a career as an oral surgeon.

Clapper almost dropped his fork. Did Mike know that a new oral surgery clinic had just opened six miles away . . . right down the road between Altoona and Hollidaysburg? Brand spanking new. Would he like to take a tour?

"Oh, yeah," Ditka said. "That'd be nice."

Soon after, Clapper was on the phone with Ditka's manager—a "Pitt sympathizer"—whom Clapper had been working behind the scenes since the first pitch. Clapper spelled out his plan: as soon as your team loses, how about taking a little detour and letting Ditka tour the clinic. "We could stop," said the coach.

On Thursday afternoon Ditka's team got eliminated. Clapper: "I'll never forget that. It was a day off for the professionals in Altoona. I called Joseph Haller, one of the oral surgeons associated with the clinic. He was on the golf course. I told him, 'Joe, get your ass over to the clinic as soon as possible. We just might be able to steal this kid from Engle!' Sure enough, when the five-car caravan pulled up outside the gleaming one-story clinic, Clapper and Haller were waiting outside. Quickly ushering Ditka inside, they worked to close the deal. Dr. Haller pointed out instruments and talked shop; Clapper mused about the polished furnishings and the cathedral ceiling in the waiting room. The trio finished and walked outside. "I can still see us standing there," Clapper says. "All three of us. Five cars waiting until we dismissed them. He looked at me. He was such a polite, courteous kid, easy to talk with."

"Mr. Clapper," said Mike Ditka, "do you think Mr. Engle would be mad if I changed my mind and decided to go to Pitt?"

The booster club president swallowed his smile concealing the kind of glee he felt when one major corporation canceled its insurance and decided to sign with Northwestern Mutual. "Oh, well, no, Mike," he said. "The only thing Mr. Engle and Mr. Michelosen are interested in is your future and welfare. You can play football anywhere. But I feel certain if you obtain adequate grades as a pre-dent student, you'll get admitted to the dental school."

"Well, all right then," said Ditka, beginning a sentence that would haunt Penn State forever, "I think I'll go to Pitt."

The cars weren't even out of the parking lot and Clapper was on the horn to Michelosen. "John," he said, "get your butt down to Aliquippa right now, and you better be at his parents' [house] when he gets home." Michelosen was sitting in the kitchen when the kid walked in the door. He left with a verbal commitment to Pitt.

Not that Penn State gave up easily. In what Clapper now calls the "sequel" to this story, about ten days before school started, Ditka and two other prized recruits were preregistered for classes, then spirited away to an alum's home on Lake Erie. There, according to Clapper, like gangsters on the lam, they hid the athletes out for two weeks, until three or four days *after* classes had started, a slice of recruiting espionage right out of Bear Bryant's book. It proved prophetic when, Clapper says, Penn State recruiters converged on the Pitt campus demanding to know what happened to Ditka.

Three years ago Clapper says he wrote Ditka a letter in care of the Bears. In it, he related the whole crazy story. He never received a reply. "I'd sure like to shake his hand," says the insurance salesman. "I'd love to tell him if it hadn't been for ol' Ken, you'd never have gone to Pitt. He'd probably have been the same success at Penn State.

"But he did go to Pitt, and it was only for one reason."

Looking back on my college career, Pitt means my whole life to me—what I am now.

—Mike Ditka

LOOKING BACK, FOR MIKE DITKA LIFE AT THE UNIVERSITY OF PITTSBURGH WAS a passage to fame and fortune, the perfect place for a good athlete to grow into a great one. For Mike Ditka it proved a joyous, satisfying journey. A journey that began with the baby steps of freshman innocence and ended in the giant strides of college stardom—a man among boys. "I wasn't as big a name as some of the other guys," Ditka once said. "I think that's where I understood that the harder you work, the more you get out of life. I became a pretty good football player, not because I was faster or could catch the ball better, but I taught myself to do a lot of things that other guys didn't."

A consensus All-American his senior year (known more for his savage play as a stand-up defensive end than a receiver), he was sixth in the Heisman Trophy balloting as the finest football player in the nation in 1960. He captained the football team; he even got a guest shot on the Ed Sullivan television show.

But football was hardly the only sport in Ditka's life. He was an athletic whirlwind, moving from football to basketball to baseball. Twice he lettered as a sixth-man enforcer on the basketball team, and he started in the outfield on the baseball team, where he continued to clear fences and fracture bats. He won several interfraternity wrestling titles, never losing a match. But more than honors or awards, he left a legacy, a reputation that some thirty years later still overshadows other

58

Pitt alums such as Tony Dorsett and Dan Marino, a reputation built, as always, on his fury and fire. "Mike Ditka," says Ernie Hefferle, seventy-seven, who coached the ends at Pitt and later become player personnel director for the New Orleans Saints, "was the toughest, meanest, best football player I ever came across."

"The toughest guy ever at Pitt; the ultimate competitor," says ESPN college football analyst Beano Cook, whose skills and charm as the school's sports information director helped make Ditka a household name.

With that name comes images, personal snapshots in a four-year roll of film. For Cook it was an Army defensive back picking off a pass intended for Ditka and then racing to the end zone. And Ditka, somehow recovering, chasing the speedy back down from behind. "Greatest play I've ever seen," Cook says. For others it's a freshman, pumped up on beer, ripping a stop sign right out of the ground. For a college roommate, hung over after a night of drinking down at the Sigma Chi fraternity, it is Ditka up at the crack of dawn, snapping off push-ups to beat the band. "Amazing," recalls that roommate, David Kraus, now an orthopedic surgeon near Pittsburgh. "I feel like I can't get out of bed and he's doing push-ups. I thought, 'Oh, man, this guy has got a lot more self-discipline than I do.'"

For Ralph Conrad, a star guard and teammate of Ditka's for three years, it is a different kind of photo. "You have to see pictures of him after a game," Conrad says. "They're something that belongs in the Hall of Fame. You don't see it today. The blood, mud, dirt, sweat, and tears . . . he was so much above everyone else in his ability and desire, a man among boys. He was the epitome of sacrifice and commitment."

And the most final and fitting image: the year is 1960. The senior star sits alone on the Fifth Avenue porch of the Student Union, decked out in his dark blue varsity jacket, the one with the block *P* on the breast. Schoolbooks are tucked tightly under his arm. His hair cropped close to his head. Gazing out across the grounds, looking, at that moment, every bit of the Big Man on Campus . . . the most popular guy around.

In the late 1950s, the University of Pittsburgh was never confused with the ivy-covered schools of the East or the sun-drenched universities of the West. It was mainly a commuter college, a drive-in, drive-out place where the local kids and occasional imports from nearby Ohio and West Virginia could go. Most students took the bus, trolley, or drove to school, located in Oakland, an uptown section of the city about fifteen minutes from downtown. There were dormitories for the students who stayed on campus; the athletes, meanwhile, were afforded the finer comforts of the converted Schenley Hotel, built in the shadow of Forbes Field, home of the Pirates and the Steelers.

Ditka arrived on campus in the fall of 1957. In some respects Pitt was an outstanding academic institution. Its medical and dental programs were top drawer, but overall Pitt was as working class as the city itself—an image school president Edward Litchfield sorely wanted to change. His vision was of an Ivy League outpost, an academic tradition that would one day overshadow football legends such as Pop Warner and Jock Sutherland, who had both coached for the Panthers. The current man, Michelosen, hired back in '52, preached the same kind of in-your-face football made famous by Warner. "When you played for John Michelosen," says former New York Jets head coach Joe Walton, who was an All-American end doing just that, "you knew how to block and tackle."

A detail man, Michelosen prized every possession. His teams, it was once written, were "unversed in theatrics and sleight-of-hand magic, known for relentless hard-driving ground attack and sturdy defense." More Landry than Lombardi, Michelosen's standard pregame speech went something like this: "You know what you've got to do, now go out there and do it."

"He was never loud, never shouted," recalls Hefferle, his best friend and key assistant for many years. "If he was unsatisfied, he would talk to the player in a manly way."

It was Hefferle who did most of the talking when Ditka checked in for football. Hefferle liked to set the tone early, even for the first-year players, giving what he calls today "my All-American speech."

"Boys," he would begin, "there is one way to become an All-American, and that's to get voted on your all-opponent team. Make seven or eight of them in a year and you become an All-American. When you rush the quarterback, make sure you take on the [running] back. Those guys don't like to block. Don't disappoint them. Put them on their back. They may not know your name, but they can sure as hell look up and see your number. Do that enough times and you'll make All-American."

It took all of one practice for coaches to notice Ditka's number and learn his name. In late fifties, freshmen weren't eligible for varsity play. So their role, much like sophomores at Aliquippa High, was to act as cannon fodder for the varsity. To run opponent plays. Hold dummies. And get beat up. Not Ditka. He wanted to hit right away.

After the first practice Hefferle bumped into assistant coach Jack Wiley, who had recruited Ditka.

"What do they look like?" asked Wiley.

"That Ditka's something," Hefferle said.

He certainly was. Ralph Conrad, then a freshman, remembers his first exposure to the burly No. 89 just prior to the latter's sophomore season. "My dad and I arrived at Pitt on the first or second day the varsity had come back from fall camp," says Conrad, who would later tangle with Ditka in some memorable interfraternity wrestling matches. "Now I'm just out of Altoona, where I had a pretty sheltered youth. It was August, the hottest, most humid month, and the varsity was having its third and last preseason scrimmage.

"They had an A team and a B team. They'd sold tickets and had a pretty good crowd around the practice field. Well, the A team loses the coin flip and has to kick off to the B team. Ditka is at the left end of the kickoff team. They kick off to the deep back on the right—right in front of Ditka. The kid goes up the middle with the other back as the lead blocker.

"Ditka is the first one down. Like a fanatic. He turns into the center to intersect with the ballcarrier. Just as he does, the other back cuts in front of the runner and blocks Ditka. He crouches down and cuts Ditka across the waist and thighs. Well, Ditka is going so fast he's lifted up in the air. He does a complete somersault, comes down on one knee and one foot, and still makes the tackle."

On the sidelines Conrad turned to his father and said, "Dad, I think I'm in over my head. Let's put my stuff back in the car and go home right now."

Conrad stuck around, but it was that pounding style mixed with an ineffable air of confidence that set Ditka apart. The Pitt practice field was hard as a prison yard, but Ditka didn't care. Not after Aschman. Not after Raccoon Creek State Park. "I'll practice out on the concrete," he told Hefferle.

He hated Hefferle's ritual of easing into contact: checking the three-point stance, exploding into the dummies, driving the legs, the two-man, then seven-man sled work. "Why do we have to do this?" he screamed one day. "These dummies aren't going to be out there Saturday. Let's go live."

Ditka began the season as the third-string end, but by the eighth game had earned himself a starting spot against Notre Dame. He caught two passes, played tough defense, and punted for the Panthers, angling one punt out of bounds at the 1-yard line. The next day Ditka couldn't walk for the bruises.

"Never saw anything like it," publicity director Cook says today.

Neither, evidently, had the Irish. They voted Ditka a member of their all-opponent team.

For the season—Pitt ended 5-4-1—he caught 18 passes, averaging 14 yards per reception, while punting 14 times for a 42.5-yard average. After the season, in keeping with the times where two- and even three-sport athletes were not uncommon, Ditka breezed right into basketball. It was there he earned the nickname The Hammer for his indelicate play under the boards. "He hits the first guy he sees," said basketball coach Bob Timmons. Says Carm Cozza, then an assistant basketball coach at Yale, "All I remember is this guy with a brush cut who pounded the hell out of the boards."

Off the court Ditka had seemingly settled into the life of a typical nineteen-year-old college student. His social calendar revolved around weekend visits from his high-school sweetheart and occasional beer runs into Oakland at such places as The Luna and Pitt Pot, or parties at the Sigma Chi house, where Ditka was a member. "We had our share of wild nights," says former roommate Kraus, the orthopedic surgeon. "Some occasional destruction but nothing vulgar." Kraus, a small-town quarterback from Wheeling, West Virginia, shared a room at the Schenley with Ditka during their sophomore and junior years. He remembers an intense, talkative young man interested in current events. "He was a good thinker. We talked about world things. He was focused on athletics, but he didn't live for them."

Not yet, anyway.

By the beginning of his junior year, Ditka was an unquestioned star. In fall camp he had scattered bodies about like so many tenpins. The *Pitt News* carried reports on how bird dogs from the Baltimore Colts, Cleveland Browns, and several other pro clubs felt "Ditka can't help but make good in the play-for-play ranks after seeing 'The Hammer' take part in recent practices."

If Ditka wasn't a question mark, the Panthers certainly were. Cook, the school's publicity maven, pegged the season at 3-7; sportswriters' predictions ran from 5-5 to 8-2. The wild card was Pitt's murderous schedule, laced, as it was, with five Top 20 opponents. The opener, however, was expected to be easy—Marquette. It was anything but. The Wildcats played inspired ball and Pitt trailed the home club 15-13 in the fourth quarter. Then Ditka took over. First he barreled in to block—and recover—a punt on the Marquette 7-yard line. Two plays later he caught a TD pass, his second of the day. Pitt won 21-15. It was a stunning show—and he paid for it. "Hardest game I ever played," he told the student newspaper after the game. "They had a real good team. I wasn't supposed to rush in on the [blocked] punt. The play was set up for the ends to drop back for the receiver. But on the previous punt I noticed that their fullback was paying no attention to me, so after I took three steps in, I knew he wouldn't be bothering with me, so I just put my head down and went in."

After a 23–0 loss to USC the following week, Pitt reeled off wins over UCLA (Ditka caught a TD pass and twice punted more than 50 yards) and Duke (another TD catch). He was a team leader now who felt comfortable excusing the coaches from the locker room so he could rattle the roof. "He'd get up and start ranting and raving," recalls Conrad, who started at both guard and middle guard as a sophomore. "He was yelling things like, 'Goddamn sons of bitches, lack of pride, you're letting these sons of bitches push you around. By the time he was finished we had a couple of injuries, guys getting out the door. It was a combination of being fired up and nobody wanting to be left in there with Ditka."

Other times, Ditka greeted mistakes or slackened effort with everything from a stinging rebuke—"C'mon, man, get your shit together!"—to a ringing blow to the back of the head. Conrad got the latter shortly after jumping offside on a crucial third-down play. He was halfway back to the huddle when the lights went out. "The next thing I heard was someone screaming, 'Did you get the play! Did you get the play!' He had come up behind me and rapped me on the helmet with his fist. He knocked me senseless."

But after Pitt was upset by archrival West Virginia, a "breather" game that backfired, some students decided to steal a page from Ditka's book. For weeks the student paper had criticized the students' apathy. Not anymore.

Players quickly discovered what form this protest would take—the hanging of Michelosen in effigy in front of the student union. A players meeting was called. A watch would be posted, they decided, with two men on duty every two hours. But when nothing happened by three A.M., the athletes figured the crisis had passed. Wrong. In the ensuing hours the students made their move. The next morning, hanging from a tree like an outlaw, was the ersatz head coach, a "Mike—Take a Hike" sign draped around his neck.

Frustrations built as first Texas Christian University and its All-American tackle, Bob Lilly, won 13–3, then No. 1-ranked Syracuse and its All-American running back, Ernie Davis, blitzed Pitt 35–0. The Syracuse game revealed Ditka's major weakness—his temper. The Orangemen's offense featured a "scissors" play, a deceptive bit of backfield movement, made all the more effective by the blocking of twenty-two-year-old Fred Mautino, a 6'3", 195-pound end Syracuse coach Ben Schwartzwalder called "the best I've coached in eleven years." Mautino was nicknamed The Chief by his teammates for the Indian cast of his face. He reveled in the physical nature of the game and was a fitting foe for Ditka.

"Come on, Freddy," Mautino recalls Ditka snarling as the game had barely begun. "Come on, tough guy."

Freddy buckled up his chin strap and let his blocking do the talking. Between that and the razor-sharp cuts of Davis, Ditka was useless. "There was one scissors play where Ernie Davis got about twelve yards," Mautino later told columnist Milton Gross, "and Ditka made my block on him a little easier. Ditka went with the fake and Ernie cut back and got his yardage. I got up and I could see he was dying for another shot at me.

"He kept calling me out to see who was better. 'Come on, Freddy,' he kept saying. 'Come on, tough guy.' He was trying to get me mad, but he was getting madder all the time and he was losing his composure. It gave me a great deal of satisfaction because I knew he was the best end I'd play against all year and he didn't do too well against me."

According to the student newspaper Ditka had suddenly become a bust on both sides of the ball. After catching 14 passes for 244 yards and 4 touchdowns in the first five games, he had caught just one other pass in the next two. And now Mautino had embarrassed him defensively.

The sports editor of the campus newspaper took notice. "The two biggest disappointments for the Blue and Gold to date have been the play of their two biggest stars, [quarterback] Ivan Toncic and Mike Ditka," wrote Ted Colton. "Ditka, who was slated for All-American honors at the beginning of the year, and Toncic, who played like an All-American against UCLA, have looked like anything but good football players in the last four games."

Now 3-4 and reeling toward Cook's preseason prediction, Pitt recovered to beat Boston College 22–14, scoring its first touchdown in ten quarters. The following week the Panthers knocked off No. 17 Notre Dame, 28–13, before more than 52,000 in the rain. The students, who had been ready to lynch Michelosen, were so stunned (or soaked) they took Monday off, celebrating with rallies and parties all around campus.

Yet most folks figured the fun was over. Pitt would undoubtedly finish the season with a loss to Penn State, ranked twelfth in the nation. The Nittany Lions, led by All-American quarterback Richie Lucas, had lost just once in nine games, that coming a week earlier, 20–18, at the hands of Mautino and Syracuse.

But Pitt had about enough of the frustration and second-guessing. Pounding away on the ground, the Panthers prevailed 22–7 to finish the season 6-4. When the final Associated Press poll came out, they were ranked twentieth in the nation. Caught up in the euphoria, the normally bookish Litchfield canceled classes for an hour Monday morning and sanctioned a postgame rally at the Soldiers and Sailors Memorial.

No sooner had the hubbub died down then Ditka slid back into his reserve role in basketball. By now Timmons had changed his tune a bit, citing Ditka's hustle and how "he commands a lot of respect under the boards." Others had a different opinion. Sportswriters called him "a hatchet man." Somewhere in between was an effort such as the one Ditka unleashed in late February against Penn State, which Pitt edged in overtime 64–63 with No. 54 pulling down five key rebounds.

When he wasn't playing basketball, Ditka was pinning opponents in the interfraternity championships. The bouts took place in the school's wrestling room, a hot, malodorous box packed with rabid frat rats. Ditka wrestled heavyweight. He was so tough the school's wrestling coach, who also handled the U.S. Olympic team, predicted Ditka could have been an NCAA champion. As it was, he pinned every opponent he faced—all except Conrad, an undefeated high school wrestler who now represented the Delta Sigma Phi fraternity. The 6'3", 220 lb. Conrad twice drew Ditka in the fraternity finals. When the two stepped on the mat, Conrad says the room got so raucous "it was like ancient Rome, like throwing someone to the lions."

"He beat the tar out of me," says Conrad, now a salesman for the Scott Paper Co. in St. Louis, "but he couldn't pin me. That was my claim to fame."

In March, Ditka's game changed to baseball. "I want to play," he told baseball coach Bobby Lewis. It didn't matter that the crowds of fifty thousand or more were reduced to what Lewis now laughingly calls "I-F—immediate family." Or that unlike the football team, the baseball team bused or drove vans to games. "There was no 'What do I get because I'm Mike Ditka,'" said Lewis. "It was just 'When's practice?' and 'What do I do?' like everyone else. Here was an All-American who just wanted to play. He asked nothing because his name was Mike Ditka."

But despite good hands and an above-average arm, Ditka's temper was increasingly ill-suited for the hums and rhythms of the college game. When he hit the ball which wasn't very often now, it was gone. But as Lewis notes, "unfortunately, it wasn't enough to be Ralph Kiner," a reference to the former Pirates slugger. Adds Lewis, "Mike played with the same intensity as football, and sometimes, it wasn't good for baseball. It's an inner thing in baseball. You get up [to bat] four times a game. If he didn't get a hit the first time . . . I thought many times he'd take some of our bats and just grind them into sawdust.''

Summer baseball was where Ditka's emotions truly ran free. During one game he took a headlong dive into third base. The field was rain-soaked and muddy.

''Who in the hell do you think you are,'' yelled the mud-splattered infielder. ''Mike Ditka of Pitt?''

Up came a dirt-stained face. ''Yeah,'' said the runner. ''That's exactly what I think.''

But as much as Ditka liked to dish out the dirt, he still couldn't take it. Never could. Never would. Especially now, in the summer, where the taunts were often fueled by alcohol, and Ditka wasn't up to taking grief from anybody. Paul Martha, who followed Ditka to Pitt and later starred at safety for the Panthers and the Pittsburgh Steelers, spent a summer on the same local semipro baseball team. He remembers a game at old Fowler Field on the north side of Pittsburgh near a rash of neighborhood bars. ''There were a lot of drunks at the game,'' says Martha, the former vice president and general counsel for the Pittsburgh Penguins of the National Hockey League. ''They were getting on Mike pretty good about the McKeever boys [Mike and Marlin, stars at USC]. They started to kid and taunt him, and unfortunately, Mike was having another bad night at the plate.'' It was a night, says Martha, compounded by a bonehead play in the outfield.

''There was a fly ball to center field and Mike misjudged it. They got on him again. He just started running in from center field.''

And kept running. And running. Pretty soon the drinkers got the message.

''He cleaned them all out,'' says Martha, laughing. ''Drunks flying all over the place. The fact that he started running at them was all they needed.''

Given his appetite for sports, Ditka was forced to drop his dream, however short-lived, of dentistry. In its place was the less strenuous liberal arts education. Chemistry and biology, he discovered, were incongruous with football and fraternity fun. His favorite subject became history. Still, Ditka never graduated. According to the school's certification office, he fell a ''few credits'' short of a degree. ''I didn't have good study habits,'' he once said. No matter. Despite Litchfield's crackdown on athletic privilege, Ditka retained an edge. ''Mike was sorta exempt," says one former teammate. "It was his senior year and he was important to the program."

Make that *most* important. He had "stolen the show" at the spring game. He was now 6'3" and 218 pounds of sinewy muscle and bad attitude. Says Martha, then just a freshman, "A lot of [guys] considered him bigger than life."

Pitt opened the 1960 season against UCLA, then ran a gauntlet of other great programs, including Michigan State, Oklahoma, TCU, Syracuse, Notre Dame, and Penn State. It was another suicide schedule; one designed to inspire a great team or murder a good one. In Pitt's case, it proved to be the latter.

On the first week they went west and lost 8–7 to the Bruins in Los Angeles as a game-winning touchdown drive was kept alive when a referee ruled a Bruin wide receiver in bounds with just seconds to play. The next week, on national TV, Pitt tied Michigan State 7–7, thanks to what *Pitt News* sports editor Colton called Ditka's "second All-American performance."

Part of that performance come on the field in the form of a TD pass from ex-roommate Dave Kraus. The other was undoubtedly in the locker room.

Near the end of the first half, Chuck Reinhold, Pitt's scholarly senior safety and a Sigma Chi fraternity brother of Ditka's, had allowed MSU running back Herb Adderly to shake off a tackle. Reinhold had also dropped a sure interception. As the Panthers clattered into the locker room, Reinhold made the mistake of yelling, 'Let's get 'em in the second half!" Ditka lost it. "Seven–nothing!" he screamed. "That's bullshit. It doesn't matter what we're down. You had a chance to make a play and you didn't make it!"

He lunged for Reinhold. It took several teammates to pull him away.

After the game, which ended in a free-for-all, Ditka spoke his piece: "We can't continue to play only fifty-nine minutes and fifty-five seconds of football. We have a team that should be winning ball games."

Such was the story of the season. Up and down. Shoulds and coulds. A 1-point loss to Oklahoma. A win over Miami. A shutout of West Virginia. A tie with TCU. In that game Ditka dove and caught a deflected pass just before it touched the ground. Or so he thought. The officials ruled otherwise; even Michelosen told Ditka to shut up, saying the coaches could see from the sidelines. The thing was, the films later showed Ditka had caught the ball; a proper call would have resulted in a game-winning field-goal attempt. Either way the game ended in another near riot; fans poured out of the bleachers, Ditka got blindsided, and Pitt running back Jumbo Jim Cunningham, Ditka's roommate, stood alone at midfield, fist clenched, and challenged the entire TCU team to a fight.

The following week, in his most memorable game since his sophomore start against Notre Dame, Ditka led Pitt to a stunning 10–0 upset of Davis and Syracuse. On defense he helped limit Davis to just 41 yards on the ground. "It was our best team effort of the year," Ditka said. "If we had played that way in every game, no one would have touched us." Syracuse coach Schwartzwalder agreed, saying, "We saw too much of Ditka."

Pitt, now 3-2-2, was now ranked No. 14 in the nation. Notre Dame was next. Ditka had never lost to the Irish.

He never will. Pitt won 20–13. Ditka caught one long pass setting up a touchdown, while his blocking was described as "fearsome." On defense, the papers noted, "he was roaming in the Irish backfield all afternoon."

Covering the game for the Associated Press was a Chicago-based sportswriter by the name of Joe Mooshil, raised a couple blocks away from Wrigley Field. Mooshil had covered the Bears since 1954 and, like most reporters of that day, was close to Bears coach George Halas, who liked to pump the press for information. Says Mooshil, "After college games he'd say, 'Hey, kid, who'd you see, who impressed you?'"

"Well," answered Mooshil after viewing the Notre Dame game, "I saw this good, tough—"

"I know who you're talking about," said Halas, cutting him off. "Mike Ditka."

Ditka's three-year college totals were 45 catches for 730 yards (a 16.2 average) and 7 touchdowns. He punted 44 times for a 39.7-yard average. Yet Ditka scored his most impressive numbers on the Hefferle Index: seven of Pitt's ten rivals would choose all-opponent teams in 1960.

All seven selected Mike Ditka.

And sure enough, the postseason honors rolled in: *The Sporting News*, coaches, NEA, *Look* magazine, and both wire services (AP and UPI) named him All-American, joining the likes of running backs Joe Bellino of Navy and Davis of Syracuse, linebacker E. J. Holub of Texas and tackle Bob Lilly of TCU. He was selected the Pitt MVP by the Curbstone Coaches booster club. He placed sixth in the Heisman balloting, getting more votes than any other end. Pittsburgh Steelers head coach Buddy Parker summed up what so many other pro coaches were saying: "The best football player in college today."

Ditka was enjoying his fame, spending more and more time at places like Frankie Gustine's, a neighborhood haunt near Forbes Field, the Pitt Pot, Luna, or The Sandscratchers, a private club in Oakland frequented by football players. Ditka admits he cut a "wide swath" through the bars that season, but kept his fists and temper to himself.

"He wasn't a wild and crazy guy," says one former teammate, "but he wasn't a shrinking violet either. He was a participant, but he wasn't out of control."

In the winter of 1961 scouts from five National Football League teams made their annual pilgrimage to the Roosevelt Hotel in Pittsburgh for their skull session before the upcoming college-player draft. At this gathering, Hefferle ran across Bears assistant coach George Allen. Allen would go on to a remarkable coaching career with the Washington Redskins ("Over The Hill Gang"), the Los Angeles Rams, and even, at age seventy-two, Long Beach State, where he led the Forty-Niners to a winning record. He died on New Year's Eve, 1990.

The meeting at the Roosevelt was child's play compared to the sophisticated scouting methods employed today; it was part bull session, part mock-draft. As the names of linebackers, quarterbacks, and running backs were listed on a blackboard, the pros and cons of various players were discussed. Most teams, particularly Pittsburgh, Washington, and San Francisco, projected Ditka as a linebacker. The Bears had other plans. But Allen never said a word. Later he cornered his old friend Hefferle.

"Tell me," said Allen in conspiratorial tones, "what do you think of Ditka?"

Hefferle smiled. He knew the cagey Allen had purposely clammed up on Ditka and was not about to tip his hand.

"George," he said, "you can take all those names up on the board and forget them. He's my number one pick. Disregard position. Everything. He's the number one pick of them all."

But it wasn't so easy. There was another suitor—the upstart American Football League. With money to burn and a network-television contract, the AFL was armed and dangerous, a serious threat to a league that treated its players as little more than indentured servants. Halas had sensed danger from the start; he proposed an immediate merger. The other NFL owners balked. So when the Bears went ahead and made Ditka their first selection (fifth overall), they faced a bidding war with the Houston Oilers, who had also picked "The Hammer" No. 1. The Oilers had some of the AFL's deepest pockets; team owner Bud Adams was a true Texas oil baron, and he had wined and dined Ditka during the athlete's visit to New York for the *Look*

All-American team, peeling three $100 bills from a roll as if he were tipping for a shine, pressing the money into the twenty-one-year-old's palm.

"Have a good time in New York," said Adams.

(Ditka did—but he sent the money home to his mother.)

As for the Bears, all Ditka knew was the image: rough, tough, the Monsters of the Midway—lunch-bucket guys like Bill George and redneck hell-raisers like Doug Atkins. The Oilers promised to make Ditka an offer as soon as he returned from college all-star games in San Francisco and Hawaii. But Halas wasn't taking any chances. He contacted Joe Kuharich, Ditka's coach in both games, and arranged it so Ditka had to change planes in Chicago on his way back from the Hula Bowl in Hawaii. Sure enough, when Ditka boarded a flight from Chicago to Pittsburgh, there was Allen sitting right beside him. A charming rogue with an infectious attitude, Allen was destined for coaching greatness. If Ditka got a word in edgewise during the two-hour flight, it was an upset; Allen could sell cookies to Girl Scouts. The next thing Ditka knew the Bears assistant coach was at his house in Aliquippa putting a call in to Halas.

The Old Man offered Ditka $12,000 for his first year, plus a $6,000 bonus.

As described in his autobiography, Ditka turned to his dad. "What do you think?"

Mike Ditka, Sr., thought back to the days of making forty cents an hour—$13, $14, $15 a week, less than $700 a year.

"That's a lot of money," he said. "You work a long time to get that kind of money."

So the son signed, less for the money than the opportunity to test himself against the best. The next day the Oilers came calling in a big way: two years for $50,000. But the deal was done. Ditka was a Bear.

In a January 25, 1961, column for *Chicago Tribune* writer Dave Condon, Ditka put his young life in perspective. He credited his parents and football for opening the right doors and humbly acknowledged the task ahead. "Being unanimous All-American was an honor," he told Condon, "but it doesn't make me feel any better than other guys my age. If I feel good about it, it's because of the glory to my parents. They're thrilled about it.

"The greatest thing I've gotten out of football? Well, being right here at Pittsburgh. My parents didn't have the money to send me to college. I'd never have been able to raise the money. If it wasn't for football, I wouldn't have an education. I'd be just another guy, probably in military service. Football opened lots of opportunities; people I met, and places I went.

"The bonus for signing? . . . Well, I'm going to start saving. I'm not a big spender. I think I'll give some of it to my folks. They've done so much for me.

"The next few months I'm going to work myself into top shape. You can count on me checking into the Bears camp in the best possible shape. I know it won't be easy to make the transition to pro football. It won't be as easy as moving from high school to college ball. The Bears plan to use me as an offensive end, tight. I'll have to learn to shorten my stride going out on pass patterns so I can make sharper breaks and quicker feints. I'll have to learn the league's defensive backs.

"I'll have to learn about blocking. I'm accustomed to just bowling over the other guy, or just knocking him flat. I won't be able to do that against those big pro linebackers. I'll just have to learn to tie up those big guys."

Though he never mentioned it in this article, that $6,000 would come in handy. Three days later, on January 28, 1961, in Aliquippa, Pennsylvania, before family and friends, Mike Ditka married his high school sweetheart, Margie Dougherty. Their first child, Michael P. Ditka, was born on August 21, 1961.

IN THE SUMMER OF 1961, CHICAGO WAS SPINNING IN THE SPELL OF CAMELOT. The previous November, John Fitzgerald Kennedy had been elected president by a razor's edge—just 119,000 of the more than 68 million votes cast—thanks, in part, to the political handiwork of Chicago mayor Richard Joseph Daley, the former Cook County clerk well on his way to turning patronage and power politics into an urban art form. But Daley was not the only artist. In another section of the city, the folk tunes of John Prine and Peter, Paul, and Mary sweetened Old Town cafés. And something new and hip was happening over on Rush Street: "singles" bars replacing nightclubs and smoke-filled taverns. The Chicago sports scene, however, was steady as ever, ruled by Chicago White Sox owner Bill Veeck and the obstinate founder of the Bears. At sixty-six, Papa Bear was in no hurry to retire and collect, God forbid, social security. He still prowled the Bears sidelines spewing one epithet after another—*cocksucker* was a personal favorite—exhorting his players one day, disparaging them the next, particularly come contract time. Halas had a way of arranging the furniture so a player sat squinting into the sun, looking up at an owner who literally seemed to tower over the room (in fact Halas was sitting on a raised chair). Oftentimes Halas dimmed the lights and showed a specially made film clip—of the player's worst moments. And if that didn't put a stop to all the foolish money demands, Halas might reach in his secret files and read reports filed by a network of private detectives and contacts all over town, often detailing the players' X-rated off-field exploits. By now the player was ready either to kill the owner . . . or sign on the dotted line, both of which only added to the legend of what the Bears now rightly call "one of the most enduring personalities in sports history." And why not? How many people can say they shared the stage with Bob Hope in New Guinea? Or played right field for the New York Yankees, only to be replaced by Babe Ruth the following season? Or were friends with the contemptible Ty Cobb? Or returned a fumble ninety-eight yards with the world's greatest athlete, Jim Thorpe, giving chase? Or had signed and coached the likes of Red Grange, Bronco Nagurski, and Sid Luckman? Only one. George Stanley Halas.

He was born on February 2, 1895, on Chicago's west side to Frank J. Halas, an enterprising reporter for a Bohemian-language newspaper, and Barbara Poledna, a proud and perfection-minded Polish woman. The Halas (pronounced Halash) family included two brothers and a sister (four others had died in infancy). George was known as The Kid. He loved to run the streets playing stickball or softball or sneak through the gates at the West Side Grounds to watch the Cubs. When George was still young, his father left the newspaper business and began making ready-made suits. But it was the mother, as so often happens, who taught her sons an early and lasting lesson. It was all about buttonholes. Mother sewed them day after day, and one day, as Halas

72

later recalled, a customer doubled his order for no other reason than "Halas buttonholes are the best."

It was hardly lost on George. "Halas buttonholes became part of the family's everyday speech," he wrote in his 1979 autobiography. "The words always made Father beam with pride and Mother smile with happiness. Halas buttonholes taught me that a person must pay attention to the smallest details and joy comes with any task well done."

The Halas family worked hard—was there any other way?—and invested wisely. Frank Halas bought a three-story brick building, rented out apartments, and opened a grocery and dairy store on the ground floor. Later it became a saloon. Tight-knit and tight-fisted, Frank Halas demanded neatness, punctuality, and discipline. Once, when George was caught shooting dice with friends, he caught the business end of a horse switch. The family dream was a university degree.

Every morning young George was up before dawn delivering fruits and vegetables on foot. He earned fifty cents a week, along with the admonition that the money was meant for college. Chores went unpaid; it was part of family life. "I became frugal," Halas once said. "By being careful with money, I have been able to accomplish things I consider important."

If so, he would have to wait until after high school, where he never missed a day of school other than for trips to athletic events. With his scrawny stature (110 pounds), Halas was a weak but willing athlete, not big enough for varsity football, so he played the "lightweight" version along with indoor baseball and excelled in both. It was in high school that Halas began to jot ideas and thoughts in notebooks, words and phrases, Halas said, "I wanted to make a part of me." After high school his father died, and Halas took work in the payroll department at Western Electric where he learned the importance of precision and detail. In 1914, he left Western Electric and enrolled at the University of Illinois, where he majored in civil engineering and minored, it seemed, in athletics. He gained thirty pounds—to a solid 178—and made a name for himself in sports. Eventually he captained both the basketball squad and several championship baseball teams. Playing end, he was a second-team Walter Camp All-American in football.

After a stint in the Navy (where he was named player of the game in a 1919 win over the Marines), Halas signed with the Yankees and played eleven games in right field, eventually being replaced by some slugger named Ruth.

It was here the course of pro football history began to change in the most unlikely of places—Decatur, Illinois. Halas went there to work as a railroad worker for A. E. Staley, a sharp, self-made millionaire, who had made a fortune selling tobacco and starch, then lost it all in a fire. Unbowed, he amassed another fortune, this time in corn products. Staley cared as much about sports as he did about corn; he sponsored a top semipro baseball team and yearned to try his hand at pro football, which, at the time, consisted of several semipro or industrial-league teams playing against one another. Staley picked Halas as his coach and manager; George accepted without a second thought. Railroading was one thing; pro football quite another.

He loved the challenge, traveling around, recruiting talent from top schools, bringing organization to the here-today, pay-tomorrow world of pro sports. Halas wanted order. Precision. He convinced owners of other industrial teams, including Ralph Hay of the powerful and popular Canton Bulldogs, to band together, and they did on September 17, 1920, in the most famous meeting in pro football history. It was there, sitting on a running board of a Hupmobile in Hay's showroom, that Halas anted up the $100 franchise fee of the team that eventually became his Bears. That first year the Decatur Staleys, as they were known, went 10-1-1, the tie coming before 12,000 fans at Wrigley Field in a championship game against the Akron Indians. Still, Staley was concerned about the cost of underwriting a team. So he signed the club over to Halas and urged him to take it north to the big city of Chicago. But where to play? Terms were a concern. The first year profit of $2,322.77 (Halas had it right down to the penny) had left Halas with little room to dicker. He needed help. He got it from Bill Veeck, Sr., the Cubs' president, who offered his field for 15 percent of the gate receipts and concessions. It was a handshake agreement that would stand between the two men for fifty years.

Over the next thirty years Halas helped build the foundation of pro football and was later responsible for reshaping it. Halas had a hand in establishing the modern T-formation, man-in-motion offense, collegiate draft, and College All-Star game. He also supervised the rewriting and simplying of the NFL rule book. And he won four more world championships.

Halas called everybody "kid" and pleaded with his team to have "the old zipperoo." "He was a great idol to kids in the neighborhood," says AP sportswriter Mooshil.

Halas had a way with the press, plain and simple, reveling in the give-and-take. In the early days of his Bears he had written articles about his team and hand-delivered them to the papers. When that failed to generate interest, he hired his own public relations man—a writer for *The Chicago Evening Post* for $25 a game. He let scribes into the locker room before games. But if his team lost, Halas was rarely in the locker room. Says Mooshil, "He would go to the Pink Poodle [a local bar] and break out a bottle of bourbon and a bottle of scotch, knowing that nobody could write a story without talking to Halas. This was his way of keeping the writers away from the players. If you wanted to get quotes from the coach, you had to go there. By the time you got through, the players were gone."

He'd do absolutely anything to win a game, to get an edge. That ranged from placing the band behind the visiting team's bench to forgetting to stock soap, towels, or programs in the visitors' locker room. A favorite story has a game official dropping his cap to mark a spot where an opponent's punt had tumbled out of bounds only to find Halas had nonchalantly pushed the cap with his foot in favor of the Bears. The distance was immaterial. The thought was not: *Doing anything to win.*

Because of his background, and the fact that he had survived several financial scares (he almost lost the Bears for good in 1932, beating a noon deadline for a $5,000 payment to a local banker by just ten minutes), money meant everything to Halas. On the field, discipline and determination were paramount. That meant mandatory weekly weigh-ins, where Halas weighed the players himself and levied stiff fines for every extra pound. He warned against gambling and outlawed tobacco and smoking in the locker room.

He would have his hands full with the 1961 team, including a rookie All-American from Pitt.

9

Nothing comes too fast. You put yourself in a position in life to get somewhere, and once you get into that position, you go. If you can't handle that, that's your problem.
—Mike Ditka, 1991

BILLY WADE LIVES IN MUSIC CITY NOW, NOT THE WINDY CITY. HE'S AN ex-banker, and after twenty-three years of loans and legalese, he's settled comfortably into the solitude of a seven-acre farm on the outskirts of Nashville, Tennessee. Today Wade devotes his time to his children, his church, and his community. He is a local boy done good, a Vandy dandy, dating back to his playing days at quarterback for the Commodores of Vanderbilt University. Back in 1952, Wade was the No. 1 draft pick in the nation, a "bonus" selection of the Los Angeles Rams. He threw for 8,572 yards and 56 touchdowns in seven seasons on the West Coast before the trade winds blew him east, to the Bears, in 1961. Smart and studious, Wade was a Bible-toting believer long before born-again religion in sports became popular. However, he also preached full-throttle football. "A key phrase for me has always been, 'Formation dictates defense,'" he says today. "You can dictate what the defense does by the way you line up."

Which was why, in the steaming summer of '61, Wade warmed to the sight of the 6'3", 225-pound No. 1 draft choice from Pittsburgh. "A muscular, hard-hitting type person," Wade recalls.

Naturally, Ditka had come to Chicago to dominate. He had no intention of waiting his turn, spending time on the sidelines. Just as he had in Aliquippa, and at Pitt, it was time to step up again, to prove himself once more—to show Halas and the Bears and the rest of the NFL he belonged. So it was that every day for three months, from May through July, Ditka, center Mike Pyle from Yale, and running back Bill Brown of Illinois—the Bears' top three draft choices—conducted informal ninety-minute workouts at Soldier Field. Wade did the throwing, and Halas and assistant coach Sid Luckman did the teaching. Halas watched, hoping his idea would work. He knew Ditka had speed (a 4.7 forty-yard sprint on grass) and blocked like a bull. Halas needed to know if he could run pass routes and catch the football, so day after day, hour after hour, they drilled Ditka, nodding as the rookie quickly mastered patterns and techniques most rookies took four or five years to learn. Wade also knew this brush-cut collegian was special: "I had seen tight ends of this caliber before," he says. "Most teams didn't throw to their tight end. The Rams did. We had a guy named Bob Carey, a four-letterman out of Michigan State. He was six feet four, two hundred forty-five pounds, and a super athlete. But then he got hurt and his career slipped away. Mike wasn't the biggest tight end. John Mackey in Baltimore and Leon Hart in Detroit were bigger. But Mike was like a heavyweight fighter. He had a ferocious spirit about him. His was a dominating nature."

Ditka wasted no time dominating. Scrimmaging against the Bears prior to playing in the College All-Star game against the defending world champion Green Bay Packers, Ditka tore Bear defensive back Pete Manning apart.

Halas was stunned.

"Who the hell hit Manning?" he asked one day.

"That's your first-round draft choice," came the reply.

"That's okay then," Halas said.

After the all-star game Ditka drove down to Rensselaer, Indiana, home of St. Joseph's College, for training camp and continued his assault. "He'd get into two or three fights a day in practice with our defensive guys," Ditka's best friend and longtime Bear teammate, Ed O'Bradovich, once said. "To him, practice was no different than any game. I never saw dedication like that in my life." O'Bradovich was part of a veteran team searching to rebound from a sorry 5-6-1 season in 1960—outscored 119-13 the last three games—after racking up 8-4 records in both 1958 and '59. The '61 team was a rebellious, drink-happy group divided neatly down the line of scrimmage, offense to one side, defense to the other. The divisive split was actually encouraged by Halas, who believed a little animosity, even among teammates, went a long way. Nicknamed Goo Goo by the players (after the nearsighted cartoon character Mr. Magoo), Halas loved pitting offense against defense, player against player, even coach against coach.

The defense was the star attraction, a motley mix of rednecks and blue collars. It was led by three of the greatest competitors the game has ever seen: middle linebacker Bill George and defensive ends Doug Atkins and O'Bradovich. The offense, by comparison, was white bread. Critics dubbed it "eleven sticks of dynamite in search of a fuse." It was talented, to be sure—guard Ted Karras, backs Rick Casares, and Willie Galimore, and wide receivers Johnny Morris and Harlon Hill come to mind—but it was a rather rudderless ship sorely lacking in leadership. Enter Ditka. In the first game of the exhibition season, against Philadelphia in Hershey, Pennsylvania, he caught a short pass, outrunning three defensive backs en route to a 71-yard touchdown. From that moment on he was a seemingly indestructible force who dominated in an anything-goes era when linebackers could chuck you all the way down the field and defensive backs could bust you in the middle of a pattern. Ditka didn't care. He dished it out, bodies banging and bouncing off him like raindrops on a roof, a one-man wrecking crew. "He wasn't afraid of anything," says Wade. "To come into the world of professional football and do what he did was truly remarkable. Very, very seldom do you find players that good that early. Dick Butkus was like that. So was Gale Sayers. Ditka was another."

"If you look up *football player* in the dictionary, you would see a picture of Mike Ditka," says one of the team's defensive tackles, "Fat" Freddie Williams, at 6'4", 255 pounds, an early model of the Refrigerator.

"It became very evident, very quickly," says former center Pyle, "that this was the most intense, motivated football player I had ever seen." Rookies Pyle and Ditka were thrown together as roommates. Pyle was a local boy from nearby Winnetka, the erudite industrial-engineering major from an Ivy League school (Yale) who overcame nerves and naïveté to start his rookie year and never leave the lineup. He and Ditka hit it off from the start, remaining roommates during Ditka's six seasons in Chicago. They are still tight today. (Pyle hosts Ditka's weekly WGN radio show syndicated to fifty-two stations in the Midwest and such Bear outposts as Phoenix, Reno, and Denver. They are also partners in a company called Cheer-Up Marketing, which produces various bibs and baubles sold at Ditka's restaurants and via "fan-direct" marketing on the radio show.)

Pyle has one of the few open windows into Ditka's adult life and, looking back to the early sixties, clearly likes what he sees. "The most inspirational football player I had ever seen in my life," says Pyle. "He was my model, my idol as a football player. I have never known anyone with such total dedication and commitment to task." Pyle's mind flashes back to the time Ditka met some of Pyle's high school buddies at a party, then a year or two later remembered all their names; to Ditka's "quirky" habit of fastidiously folding the corners of his dress shirt, just so, flat and tight across the stomach and back, two folds on each side, precise, meticulous. "He wasn't obsessive or compulsive," says Pyle. "Just very, very neat." Pyle says Ditka's competitive core never varied. They squared off for endless hours at the slide bowling machine over at Pat Haran's bar on Rush Street, drinking forty-cent beers until the lights came on at four A.M. "It was the only game I could beat him on," says Pyle, "and Mike wasn't going to leave until he beat me."

And Pyle recalls an incident years later, during a Colorado ski trip, when a female ski instructor—"a real energetic gal," says Pyle—and Ditka played racquetball, shortly after Ditka had run six miles and skied all day. Susie was short, cute, and athletic. Ditka, says Pyle, "proceeded to beat the shit out of this little girl. I mean he really beat her. Wacked her a couple of times with the ball. Just beat her to death."

"What the hell's the matter with you?" Pyle demanded as Ditka stepped off the court.

Ditka got hot. "Pyle, you know damn well what I'm like. You should never have let me in there with her."

Yet Pyle knows, better than most, that as much as Ditka likes to dish it out, he swallows virtually none of it. "He does not take kidding well," says Pyle. As evidence he mentions the annual birthday party he and his wife threw Ditka during his Chicago playing days. It was all rather routine except one year Ditka showed up late and in a miserable mood. He had lost money playing cards. "So the next year," says Pyle, "my wife got all the gifts. She got all these handmade orange T-shirts that said, 'Same Shit . . . Different Year.'" Pyle's wife personally, and rather dramatically, we might add, handed out all the presents.

"Where's mine?" said Ditka, all excited.

Finally he got his gift box. Inside was the same orange T-shirt. Only the lettering was different. "The Shit," it said.

The reception Ditka received as a rookie was decidedly mixed. Opponents took an immediate dislike to his relentless, right-to-the-whistle (and sometimes beyond) blocking, and the way he barreled down the field looking for people to run over. Wayne Walker, the

Detroit Lions' great outside linebacker, once recalled that he and Ditka wasted no time exchanging unpleasantries. "Hold me again," Walker told Ditka, "and I'll kick your head off."

"If you think you're man enough," snarled Ditka, "go ahead and try it."

Walker's teammate, Hall of Fame safety Yale Larry, hated playing against Ditka. So did former Steelers safety Clendon Thomas, who once told the *Pittsburgh Press,* "He was the meanest, toughest rascal in the league, and I've got the dent in my head to prove it . . . anytime you came near Ditka you had to expect forearms and fists. You came away bruised. He was mean, but he was also as talented as anyone I ever lined up against."

That style endeared Ditka to his teammates. They called him Bucky Beaver for the way he looked: that Wilson single-bar face mask, locked jaw, and chubby cheeks all puffed out. Bill George, the crusty captain, who defined the middle-linebacker post in the 1950s, took a particular shine to Ditka. He showed him how to block linebackers, shake free in the secondary, and how to read a defender's feet and exploit every weakness. Ditka learned it all, and more, his heart and skills quickly adding a terrific new dimension to the team. In effect, Halas and Ditka had redefined the position of tight end. In previous seasons the Bears had never spread the "end, tight," as Halas called it, off the line of scrimmage, making the position little more than a "third tackle." With Ditka, tight end immediately evolved into an attack position; a simple three-yard shift outside the tackle influenced five defenders. "It totally changed the defense," says Wade, who loved this kind of chess match, working the speedy Galimore alone against the free safety, leaving Ditka matched against a strong safety, which in those days, was often no match at all. "I liked to get him the football," says Wade. "I liked to find ways to get him the football."

So he did, 56 times in 1961, to be exact, for 1,076 yards—a stunning 19.2 yards per reception—the best per-catch average of Ditka's career. He also scored 12 touchdowns, another career high. He was named Rookie of the Year over New York Giants quarterback Fran Tarkenton, another future Hall of Famer.

Off the field, Ditka was rushing headlong into the trappings of such fame. He was just twenty-two years old, handsome, already a hero on a team that loved the party life, in a city so in love with their sports stars even sports *columnists* got the treatment in restaurants. And unlike New York or Los Angeles, where the nightlife was sprinkled across vast sections of town, Chicago seemed to be a series of never-ending neighborhood parties. "A group of small towns," is how Fred Williams describes Chicago. People of like-minded interests getting together for fun and frolic. In the early sixties Chicago offered up any kind of frolic you wanted. There were the neighborhood Wrigley Field bars up north, folk music and the beatnik scene in Old Town, and the hip happenings down on Rush. All on the edge of the late sixties and the sexual revolution.

In an effort to at least slow down the off-field activities, Halas took a page from J. Edgar Hoover's book and hired several off-duty security officers from the local Burns Security Agency. They were paid to shadow the players and file detailed reports, including reports on any wild drinking and dalliances that occurred. "I remember one time," says ex–defensive lineman Williams, who now spends his days walking his sheepdog in Conway, Arkansas, "it was me and a tackle, Bob Wetoska from Notre Dame. He and I were out and we happened to run across these two young ladies that wanted to go to another place to a party. I wasn't above going to a party, so we all got in the car and started off to some girl's place."

It was at this point, says Williams, one of the girls turned and said, "I know that guy following us is a detective."

"Bullshit," said Williams.

"No," said the girl, "I know him."

"Shit," Williams said, "it's probably one of those guys that Halas hired." He turned to Wetoska and pointed down a one-way street. "There."

Wetoska made the turn and sure enough the headlights followed. At this point Williams says he jumped out of the car and sprinted back down the street. The dick was trying to roll his driver's window up, but Fat Freddy got there first.

"You a detective?" he said in none-too-friendly tones. The man answered yes. "You following us?"

Another yes.

"Halas hire you?"

Yes again.

"Now, friend," said Freddy in a manner that meant this guy was anything but, "I don't know how you folks act up here about something like this, but if I hear it from Halas that I've been doing this, then someone is going to get hurt seriously."

The most serious injury sustained by detectives was undoubtedly either writer's cramp or flat feet following the various drinking cliques around town. Veterans such as George, Atkins, Fortunato, and Williams, generally drank at old-line places up north close to their homes and Wrigley. Their favorite hangouts were Chicago classics: The Berritz and Buena Chimes (owned by the beloved Bucas brothers), and The Cottage, on Clark near Belmont. Dark and dimly lit, The Cottage was what Pyle called a "shitty ass" bar long on atmosphere and short on comfort. "It was a singles place before singles places," says one ex-regular. The Cottage was home to Chicago Shirley, who, legend has it, slept her way through the National League. The Cottage was a great place to drown your sorrows and party with your 'mates. Monday night the Bears took over, and the drinking often ran long into the night. Sometimes Casares would cruise by and play the drums. Or a liquored-up Atkins might provide his own brand of comic relief.

Doug Atkins was a country hick blessed with a world-class body (6'8", 280) and awesome athletic skill. A high-jump champion and scholarship basketball player at the University of Tennessee, he went on to play in eight pro bowls and was all-NFL from '60 to '62; to many he remains the greatest defensive end in NFL history. Atkins also had the heart of an old hound dog. He was eccentric and lovable, known to show up at a full-pads practice in nothing but a T-shirt, helmet, and shorts. Then he would just jog down to the far end of the field, check around for a four-leaf clover or two, and scoot back into the locker room. "Just breaking in my new helmet," he'd say.

But Lord, don't piss him off. "Then," says former Bears fullback Ronnie Bull, "he was completely unstoppable."

Atkins took much the same approach to alcoholic intake. He was known to gulp martinis straight from a pitcher. It was usually after two or three gulps that he'd spice up the evening by calling Halas on the phone. "Why don't you come to the party, your dirty cocksucker!" Atkins would roar. "Come on down and have some fun with us! You call us names. *Let us call you some!*"

At which point, Atkins routinely thumbed through his four-letter dictionary. Says Pyle, "He'd call Halas everything but human."

The downtown drinkers were a more sophisticated, upscale group, a merry band of men led by Casares, the bruising fullback out of Florida. In ten seasons with Chicago he would run for more than 5,600 yards, second only to Walter Payton, and score a team-record 49 touchdowns. By the time Ditka arrived, Casares was well on his way to scoring even more points with the ladies. "The guy ought to be in the Hall of Fame on his cruising ability alone," says Williams. Casares had Cary Grant's looks, Gable's lines, and Dennis the Menace's flair for fun-making, forever stirring the pot, then slipping away before it boiled over. But when Casares did show up, everyone knew it. He usually had a drink in one hand and a gorgeous lady in the other. "That man forgot there were hours on the clock," Atkins says.

Headquarters for the Casares crowd was Pat Haran's place, 1007 Rush Street. Today Haran owns a bar on State Street that bears his name, a sliver of a spot packed with football posters and Old Style beer drinkers. Standing behind the bar one day, Haran says he didn't know it back in the sixties but Haran's on Rush was probably the first true sports bar in the city. "In those days before Division Street, Rush Street was it, the street of streets, the best street in the country," he says. "People partied all night long, the street was jammed until four in the morning." Haran talks about the good old days when the Singapore restaurant, right next door, had the best ribs in town. The Trade Winds and Mr. Kelly's were across the street, Kelly's the place where Streisand got her start, and where Shelley Berman, the comedy king of 1959, and stand-up comic Dick Gregory did their thing. Haran's fit right in. From an athlete's perspective it had it all: a big bar, a pool table, that slide bowling machine so popular with Pyle and Ditka, and the best burgers around. And oh, yes, women.

"A lot of women," says Haran.

It was the kind of place Johnny Unitas or Frank Gifford would drop in when they were in town, and two or three times a week, Mike Ditka would hold court.

Ex-teammates say Ditka was one of few Bears who crossed party lines and was welcomed by both the sophisticated Casares crowd and the down-home Wrigley Field boys. The Wrigley vets respected him for his steel-town toughness, while the Rush Street rowdies loved his humor and style. And Ditka did his best to accommodate both crowds, eventually falling into a Three Musketeers mentality with Ed O'Bradovich and Joe Marconi. O'Bradovich was a reckless, relentless defensive star with a hair-trigger temper and unquenchable thirst. Marconi, who arrived in a trade from the L.A. Rams in time for the '62 season, liked to wait in the wings, staying sober enough to chauffeur Ditka—who lived right across the street from Marconi—home. Marconi deserves an honorary chauffeur's license, for Ditka brought the same intensity to his drinking and partying as he did everything else. "Ditka?" says Haran. "Busiest man I've ever seen. He was always moving around. Only guy I ever knew who could drink beer, shoot pool, bowl, and talk to a girl all at the same time."

"Ditka and O.B. were the ringleaders," Atkins says. "They were wild."

"Rush Street commandos is what they were," says AP sportswriter Mooshil, who covered the team. "They were young guys having a lot of fun. They were very colorful, on the wild side, especially O.B. He'd have a few beers and he'd be hard to control. You wouldn't want to get in his way."

Halas knew his team needed discipline. He sensed his team had both the physical tools and emotional capacity—"the great desire, mental heat, the old zipperoo," he so aptly put it—to unseat the world champion Green Bay Packers. But they needed structure, purpose. So in training camp in 1962 he handed every Bear a manual. Even thirty years later it reads like a Hammurabi's Code of coaching, a list of football fundamentals guaranteeing success on the field, and (as Ditka would say) in life. Halas, in order, listed:

1. Mental Aspects—Strength and character of personnel determines the strength and character of the team.
2. Pride & Tradition—The team with the greatest desire to win will win. Desire comes from, in part, pride.
3. Aggressiveness—The single most important quality in a football player. Eighty percent of your success comes from the fight and spirit you show on the field.
4. Concentration—It is essential in knowing every play precisely, exactly, immediately.
5. Determination—Setting an objective and achieving it.
6. Leadership—The ability of the captains, coaches, and players to pull together as a team and follow orders.
7. Reliability—The quality every employer seeks.
8. Confidence—Believing in yourself and your teammates.
9. Cooperation—Burying your ego for the good of the team.

It was in '62 that Ditka's great confidence and leadership began to blossom. He had earned the right to talk, and he did. "Goddamn it," he'd growl in practice. "Let's work." Fullback Ronnie Bull, then a rookie, says Ditka "infused" a team with a particular attitude, one that said, "If he had to run over somebody, to destroy somebody, he would." Even Halas wasn't immune. "What the hell we running that play for?" bitched Ditka one day.

"Get out of my face, you dirty cocksucker," Halas said.

"That was a dumb fucking call."

Ditka and Halas had clashed earlier. Ditka wanted a raise, but naturally the cheapskate balked. He offered $14,000.

"Coach," Ditka recalled in his autobiography, "you're making a mistake. I made eighteen thousand dollars last year. You're giving me a four-thousand-dollar cut."

Halas said, "How do you figure you made eighteen thousand dollars?"

Ditka replied, "Twelve and six is eighteen."

"Well," Halas said, "The six is a bonus, remember? The bonus doesn't count."

They dodged and dickered until Ditka finally said, "Look, I won't sign for a penny less than eighteen thousand dollars."

"Okay," said Halas, "sign right here."

It proved another famous Halas bargain. The Bears won five of their last six games to end the season with a 9-5 record. Ditka caught 58 passes for 904 yards and 5 touchdowns. He made All-Pro again. The champagne season of 1963 was next.

PAPA BEAR FELT IT IN HIS BONES. THE 1963 TEAM, HE BELIEVED, HAD "A touch of destiny" to it. To insure a date with destiny Halas made a bold move. He called Pyle and Ditka together and briefly spoke his piece. "Just a changing of the guard," he told them. "Got a pretty good football team this year, and I'm asking if you both want to be offensive captains." Pyle recalls the moment: "Man, I thought I had gone to heaven. To be asked the same time Mike Ditka was asked was perhaps the greatest honor, the greatest unspoken honor, I've ever had."

On defense, Bill George was flanked by two excellent outside linebackers in Larry Morris and Fortunato. Up front, Atkins and O'Bradovich patrolled the ends, while cagey safety Richie Petitbon headlined a hard-nosed secondary. The offense was built around the versatility of Galimore, Marconi, and Bull. Sticky-fingered Johnny Morris and speedy Bo Farrington were stationed at the ends. The offensive line, anchored by Pyle and guard Ted Karras, was strong and steady. And while Wade was no Unitas at quarterback, he was smart and stable and accurate with his passes. Yet the most important and combative Bear in the clan was the twenty-four-year-old tight end now known as The Monster to his teammates. He had injected a sense of purpose and passion into his team, just as he had done in Aliquippa, just as he had done at Pitt. He was a man who raised the level of everyone else's play. Ditka, as usual, deflected any highbrow analysis of his effort. To him it was as simple as black and white. "I just like to play football," said Ditka at the time, "and I only know one way to do it."

Despite high hopes the Bears early schedule afforded no comfort at all—five of the first six games would be away from Wrigley, including the opener against the defending champion Packers in Green Bay. In preparation for that game Wade had spent considerable time with assistant coach Jim Dooley. According to Wade, the assistant coach was a "laboratory genius" in breaking down game film and finding loose ends in an opponent's seam. Only Dooley wasn't working with computers, videotape, or remote-control devices as teams do today. All he had was a film projector and the computer whirring between his ears. Wade says Dooley studied ten years of Packers games, charting, checking, and rechecking before he found that dangling thread. "On passing downs," Wade recalls, "he found they only rushed one guy, [defensive end] Willie Davis, ninety-four percent of the time. [Tackle] Henry Jordan was responsible for breaking up the pocket, and Davis would rush either inside or outside to get to the quarterback. Most people didn't know that." But Dooley did.

Dooley also noticed something else: how head coach Vince Lombardi liked to drop his linebackers into pass coverage. So when Davis rushed and the linebackers dropped, the Pack was vulnerable to short, safe passes to the running back. This pleased Halas to no end. He was tired of all this "eleven sticks of dynamite and no fuse" crap, the public calls for more variety in the offense, deeper passes. Dynamite blew up in your face if you weren't careful, and with his defense, who needed bombs? So Halas shelved all the long throws, the "ten percenters," he called them, and went back to basics. "Short passes, high-percentage plays," says Bull today.

Wade didn't wait. He started throwing swing passes on first and second downs to Galimore, Marconi, and Bull. It worked, thanks to Ditka, who had drawn the assignment, as always, of blocking the Packers' All-Pro, 235-pound middle linebacker, Ray Nitschke. With the score tied 3–3 in the third quarter Ditka found Nitschke standing on his feet completely out of the flow of the play. Ditka and Nitschke had a bit of a battle going at the time, dating back to an exhibition game the previous summer. It seems that at a dinner after the game Nitschke had accused Ditka of dirty play, adding, "I'm going to get you."

"I don't even hold anymore," Ditka replied. "You guys are the only ones who feel that way."

"I'm still going to get you."

"Too bad you feel that way," Ditka said. "But you better get me first because if you don't . . ."

Nitschke didn't. Ditka did. He smashed into Nitschke, knocking him out of the game. Without the bald-headed enforcer to worry about, the Bears' short passing game took hold. A 1-yard plunge by Marconi upset the world champions, 10–3. The ball from that game still rests in a second-floor trophy case at Halas Hall, marked PAPA BEAR IS PROUD! In subsequent weeks the Bears whipped Minnesota, Detroit, Baltimore, and Los Angeles, then dropped a close game to San Francisco before reeling off three more wins. A rematch with the Packers, who were still in pursuit of the first-place Bears, was up next. On Monday night, as usual, Halas and Wade watched films together, jabbering back and forth, the fire still burning in the Old Man's eyes. "He wanted to win so bad," says Wade. When Halas got home, he called Fortunato. The linebacker was still up, watching film, charting Packers' plays according to down and position. "We studied other teams," Fortunato says. "If a guy was leaning on his hand, if his feet were level, one foot behind, we knew exactly what they were going to do." Now Halas was on the phone, wanting to know how the Bears defense was going to do. Fortunato didn't hesitate: "I think we're going to shut them out."

He wasn't far off. Six days later the Bears whipped the Packers 26–7. The winners were now 9-1.

The following Sunday, November 24, found the Bears in Pittsburgh, the first chance since Ditka's days at Pitt that the Aliquippa contingent had to cheer and honor their native son. But on Friday, November 22, a presidential motorcade rolled past a grassy knoll near Dealey Plaza in Dallas. Shots rang out. In an instant Camelot crumbled, a president was dead. Over the next several days a grieving nation stayed home, staring at the television, glued to black-and-white images: caissons rolling, John John at his mother's side . . . the riderless horse . . . a leaderless nation grieving, reeling to . . . where? To Vietnam, Kent State, and Watergate? To greed, apathy, and homelessness? A numbing helplessness gripped our nation in November 1963 as schools closed and scores of sporting events were canceled. Only the NFL wavered, floating the notion that a nation in mourning needed comfort; it needed a distraction from the assassination of JFK. To its credit the league later (much later) admitted it had made a mistake. The nation wanted no such shows of violence; neither, it turns out, did many of the players. "The last thing you wanted to do," Wade says, "was hit someone." Ditka felt the same way but decided it would be worse to go out and play a bad football game. Worse not to win.

So under a smoky western-Pennsylvania sky Ditka dug deep and unleashed what the Bears coaching staff later called "the greatest individual effort on a single play" ever observed on a football field. Today it is known, quite simply, as The Run, what Halas himself called "a superhuman effort." It was a run that seems to summarize and symbolize one man's career.

"Seven guys had Ditka tackled, but he ran through each guy," said Luckman.

"It was the greatest run I've ever seen," added then–Bears defensive coordinator George Allen. "It wasn't the speed that got him down the field. It wasn't his moves. It was just sheer determination."

Says Pyle, "I've never seen a more phenomenal display of determination. He was just completely unwilling to give up."

"Knocked over ten guys," Atkins says.

Actually, as highlights attest, it was a short pass into the left flat—not over the middle. And Ditka buried just five—not six or ten players along the way. But it was still a classic catch-and-run, as much for the timing as the effort. Trailing 17–14 with just over four minutes left in the game, the Bears faced a third and 33 from their own 22-yard line. Wade, understandably, wanted to go deep. But Ditka nixed it. He was dead on his feet; he had already caught 8 or 9 passes. So Wade opted for a 9-yard curl to the sideline. Taking the pass, Ditka twisted past Clendon Thomas at the 31 before slipping past another Steeler. He was on the move now, shoulder down. At the 40 he was greeted by three more Steelers, split them like an old pair of pants, and headed for the end zone. About 45 yards later, nearly out of breath, he stumbled and was caught by Thomas—the first and last person to hit him. Ditka collapsed at the 15-yard line. He lay spread-armed on the ground for minutes, like a snow angel, the play having covered 63 yards. "I felt like I had died," he said later. Four plays after, the Bears kicked the tying field goal.

Today Ditka downgrades the play as "the luckiest run in the world" and remembers how hard the teams played and some brighter personal moments: 13 catches against Washington in '64; 4 TD catches against L.A. earlier in '63; an awesome grab against the 49ers in '65. But over the years The Run seems to have taken on a life of its own. Partly because it happened the weekend of the Kennedy assassination, on a day nobody really wanted to play; and partly because it happened in front of family and friends. But the most important thing about The Run is so many Bears believe they would never have seen postseason play without Ditka's storied effort. "He saved us," O'Bradovich once said. "If he doesn't make that play, we don't wear the rings. We wouldn't have won the championship."

In the locker room after the game, Halas, who had seen just about everything pro football had to offer, pointed to his tight end. This time he delivered the ultimate compliment: "Ditka is going to be one of the greats in this league." Later he told sports columnist Milton Gross of the *New York Post,* "There hasn't been a game this year where he hasn't been great, but this was the key play of the season because it set up our tying field goal and we were able to keep the division lead with the tie. Without it we'd have been in real trouble."

The Bears, after tying Minnesota by the same score the next week and then whipping San Francisco and Detroit, won the Western Division by a half game over Green Bay. The Pack's record was 11-2-1. The Bears were 11-1-2. Ditka led the team in pass receptions (59), yards gained (794), touchdowns (8), scoring (48 points), and bone-crunching blocks. No. 89 was rapidly becoming a human highlight film, one of the NFL's greatest talents in only his third year in the pros.

December 29, 1963, the day of the NFL Championship game, was arctic even by Chicago standards—the temperature hovered around ten degrees and the wind whipped off the lake like a hurricane. Wrigley Field was a sheet of solid ice when players began arriving for taping at nine A.M. Outside, the windchill dipped toward fifteen below. The Bears, even Ditka, were not rah-rah types and found no reason to blow hot air now. That was best left to the stadium grounds crew, who, thinking fast, had borrowed huge blowers from the airport in a desperate attempt to melt the Wrigley rock. Around ten A.M. Wade left the locker room, as usual, and walked a few blocks to a Japanese Christian Church for services. "I sat in the back and thought about things," he says. He returned to Wrigley about eleven-fifteen. The stands were starting to fill with the 45,801 fans and celebrities, including mayors Wagner of New York and Daley of Chicago. Those not fortunate enough to have the honor of freezing their behinds could watch the game on television or closed-circuit television, for this game would mark the beginning of a new era in sports TV. Sixteen years earlier WKBK had paid $900 to televise a Bears game. Now the rights fees had jumped one-thousand-fold, to $900,000. The game was also being carried on closed-circuit TV. Receipts would reach $1.5 million.

The New York Giants and their great bald-headed quarterback,

Yelverton Abraham Tittle, otherwise known as Y.A., were some kind of attraction: 11-3 record, winners of eight of their last nine games, five All-NFL selections, eight Pro Bowl players, and a passing attack that had produced 488 points (still a club record), and an average of 35 points per game. On the other hand, the Bears boasted the league's finest defense, allowing just 144 points (an average of 10.3 per game) while leading the league in rushing defense, pass defense, and total defense—to this day, one of only a handful of NFL teams to accomplish that feat. Something had to give.

"Usually, when it's the best offense against the best defense," says Fortunato, "the best defense wins." But Fortunato couldn't get Tittle off his mind, and with good reason. Old No. 14, had completed 221 of 367 passes for a staggering, in those days, 3,145 yards and 36 touchdowns. He began the game on a tear. But then a blitz by Morris left Tittle with a twisted left knee. He quickly recovered and hit glamour-boy Frank Gifford with a 14-yard touchdown pass. Giants 7, Bears 0. It would have been 14–0 if All-Pro wide receiver Del Shofner, who caught 64 passes for 1,181 yards during the year, hadn't been blinded while running from shade to sun, dropping a certain TD pass in the end zone. The Giants were driving again when some of Fortunato's film work paid dividends. "Watch the screen pass," he told Larry Morris, who was already alert for it. On the next play Morris picked off the screen pass and raced 61 yards to the Giants 5. After Bull bore down to the 2, Wade called his own number. "I wasn't going to let anyone mess with the ball," he says now. "People get so fired up in playoff games they do superhuman things. Pyle and Karras could drive guys out. I felt we had the advantage with the quarterback sneak." So he snuck it in himself. The score was tied 7–7.

A 13-yard field goal by Bob Chandler, who had led the league in scoring, gave the New Yorkers a 3-point lead. But just before halftime Morris blitzed again. This time, in a clean, yet controversial play, he banged into Tittle and wrenched the QB's knee. This time Tittle crumbled and left the game. He returned after intermission, but he wasn't the same threat. In the third quarter, the Giants, nursing a 10–7 advantage, showed a tendency that Fortunato read. "Watch the screen," he warned O'Bradovich in the huddle. Sure enough, Allen's down and distance charts paid off, and O.B. picked off a Tittle screen pass, rumbling ten yards forward. Up in the stands, longtime Halas assistant Luke Johnsos spoke on the phone to the bench: "Now is the time for the Ditka special."

"Remember I said 'formation dictates defense'?" says Wade. "Well, with the Giants, when the running back went left, the linebacker followed." So the Bears lined up Ditka on the right, where he was covered by the strongside linebacker. Behind the linebacker, eight yards deep, was the strong safety. Wade sent a running back in motion to the left, drawing Sam Huff, the Giants' head-hunting middle linebacker. That left Ditka one-on-one with a linebacker and room to run over the middle. Ditka released into the vacated area, and Wade put a pass in his belly. Ditka bullied down to the 1, and Wade, two plays later, leaped over the pile for what proved to be the winning touchdown.

Not that it was easy. With under two minutes left Bull missed a critical first down by a foot. The Bears had to punt and sent the Giants back to their own 20. Still enough time for one last surge. "There was one twenty-three to go," remembers Bull. "That time will be burned in my brain forever." Tittle was back on a bum knee for one last shot. He passed his club out to 42-yard line with 1:03 left. After a series of incomplete passes, he went for it all—to Shofner, his greatest receiver, who hadn't caught a pass all day. He wouldn't get this one either. Instead, Petitbon snared the overthrown ball—the Bears' fifth interception of the day—and he did a pretty backpedal out of the end zone. Wrigley erupted into a symphony of sound heard in only one ballpark and one locker room each year, all of which had to be music to the ears of Halas.

The locker room afterward was a zoo. Beers, tears, and laughter all around. Somebody lit a victory cigar. Halas told him to put it out. Even in triumph the maestro would not break company policy and allow smoking in his clubhouse.

Two days later the championship celebration moved to Mike Ditka's Willowbrook Lanes in the village of Willowbrook, about twenty miles from downtown Chicago. Before the '62 season Ditka joined a group of eight investors in the construction of the bowling alley. He put up no money, but received 12½ percent of the profits in return for use of his name. Business was good. It would have been even better, says Lou Viren, president of the bowling alley for the last 30 years, if Ditka and his teammates hadn't been drinking up the profits. "He was a drinker," says Viren, who more than once complained to Ditka about too many of his football friends drinking for free. "They started coming in right after we opened," Viren says. "Mike was greedy in the sense he expected them all to drink for free. Every Friday and Saturday night, there was a whole crowd of them. They all got drunk and took over the bar."

On New Year's Eve, Ditka and several of his teammates, friends, and their wives headed over to Willowbrook for the biggest bash since the August opening. For $25, couples would receive open bowling, and all the food, beer, and champagne they could drink.

For Mike Ditka, January 1, 1964, proved a day he will never forget.

CHICAGO, Jan. 1 (AP)—Tony Parrilli, who was voted the most valuable football player of the University of Illinois in 1961, was shot to death early today in a scuffle at a New Year's party.

Mr. Parrilli, who played guard, was killed in a washroom at a bowling alley in suburban Willowbrook. The police said he had been accidently shot above the left eye by Chief of Police Robert G.

92

Winthers when the chief tried to break up a fight involving Mr. Parrilli and an unidentified man.

Also injured in the scuffle was Joe Marconi, fullback for the Chicago Bears, one of the stars of that team's world's championship victory over the New York Giants on Sunday. He was treated at the hospital for head wounds.

The third man in the scuffle slipped away unnoticed, the police said.

Mike Ditka of the Bears, the All National Football League tight end, is a part owner of the establishment, the Willowbrook Lanes.

Capt. Herbert Mertes of the Du Page County sheriff's office said that Chief Winthers, who was in the bowling alley when the fight started, had attempted with another officer to break up the scuffle. When he was unable to separate the three men, he struck Marconi on the head with his pistol, which discharged, the captain said.

Mr. Marconi said he had gone to the washroom after the scuffle started.

"I don't know who the other fellow was," Mr. Marconi said. "I tried to calm things down and was starting to wash my hands when I was hit on the head."

A tragic accident. A bathroom fight. An unidentified man fleeing the scene. Sketchy details. A star athlete clubbed on the back of the head while *innocently washing his hands?* How could that be?

It was a tragedy all right. A harrowing night that left Mike Ditka feeling hurt and helpless. One friend was in the hospital, another was dead, stretched across the entrance to a men's room with a bullet between the eyes.

Strangely, the incident seemed to pass quickly in the press. And for that reason it remains one of the most intriguing yet least publicized incidents of Ditka's life. But as it turns out, buried in the memories of several of those involved in the incident, and in the dusty depths of Du Page County Courthouse, are some answers, answers that magnify the senselessness of the shooting. Included is sworn testimony by Marconi and others indicating Marconi's hands were not only out of the sink but far from clean during a night where the wrong things lined up the right way, and a traveling salesman lived up to his last name.

According to sworn testimony in the case, Ditka, Marconi, and a neighbor arrived at the bowling alley around eight forty-five P.M. By nine-thirty their wives were there, too, joined by several other Bear couples. It was just about this hour when three other couples walked in, including Ray Messmaker, a salesman for Osh-Kosh B'gosh Work

Clothing, in Wisconsin. Originally, Messmaker's group had planned to attend a party with nine other couples, but at the last minute the party fell through, so Messmaker and his friends headed over to Willowbrook Lanes. Messmaker wasn't much of a partier. He hardly ever drank. But this was New Year's Eve. "We were drinking champagne," he later told authorities. "We started drinking champagne. I had more than I should have had."

Ditka and his buddies were drinking and bowling, too, right up until midnight when the wives started to complain. "Are we going to celebrate New Year's out here on the alleys or at our tables?" one wanted to know.

Five minutes after horns blew and seventy-five couples exchanged hugs and kisses, Winthers and the two members of his department—the only two—walked into Willowbrook Lanes. Winthers had been hired as police chief on a part-time basis a year earlier; by trade, he was a full-time carpenter. His main partner that night, Sgt. Stanley Yotka, made his living as a plumber. A carpenter and a plumber. Their police presence, such as it was, was mandated by a local ordinance, passed just one week earlier. It stated any special extension of business hours—in this case from the regular closing time of one A.M. until four A.M.—required the presence of at least two police officers for security. So the bowling alley had paid the village $90 ($10 an hour times a total of nine hours) for the police officers to "maintain order" if necessary.

Winthers and his men weren't wearing their uniforms. They wore no visible badges or other obvious means of police identification. Earlier in the week Winthers had discussed how to dress with Charles Purcell, the manager of the bowling alley. "By the way," Winthers asked Purcell that day, "do you want us to be in uniform or do you want us in plain clothes?"

"Bob," Purcell had said, "if you don't have to be in uniform, if it's not required—as far as we're concerned, we don't anticipate any trouble—and you can come in plain clothes, we'd just as soon you have it that way."

But as midnight moved toward one A.M., trouble, big trouble, was about to begin.

The champagne had plainly made a mess of Messmaker. Earlier in the evening he had staggered to the tiny men's room next to the snack shop and vomited. He then cleaned up his mess as best he could. He said he returned to the buffet table to try to ease something into his stomach. It didn't help. Feeling nauseous again, he wobbled back to the bathroom. He was "sitting on the pot," as he later recalled, when Parrilli walked in.

Parrilli, twenty-four, was a physical specimen and then some—at least six feet tall, 225 pounds of packed pecs and rippled muscles. The pug-nosed, curly-haired lineman had been drafted by the San Francisco 49ers in 1962 only to be waived and later signed by the Bears. He never saw regular-season action with Chicago, but was known to run around with Ditka and O'Bradovich and the party crowd at Haran's. In 1963, he had signed with the Washington Redskins, but a preseason shoulder injury cut his career short. He never played in an official NFL game.

"Oh, my God, does it stink in here," Parrilli said as he entered, overwhelmed by Messmaker's earlier vomit.

Messmaker was in no shape to respond. Walking out of the stall, he somehow forgot his previous puking. "I don't know why it stinks in here," he said, "because I didn't even go to the toilet."

What happened next is one of many blurred moments of the night. Certain court testimony suggests the two may have argued about the Bears-Giants title game; Messmaker said they did no such thing. In a postshooting statement all he remembered was "he [Parrilli] started to nail me."

Messmaker was tall but reed thin. Parrilli was a bull. He began to work Messmaker over, pummeling him with shots to the head, eyes, and mouth.

In another part of the bowling alley, Thomas Giles, who owned the alley's restaurant, had just fed 150 partygoers and was sitting down to eat. Almost immediately, he testified, he heard a "thump, thump" sound coming from the lounge area. He quickly realized the source of the sound wasn't the lounge but the men's bathroom. He got up and tried the rest-room door. It wouldn't budge. He tried again. Still nothing. Finally, he squeezed into the six-by-three-foot rectangle. Inside was a single urinal, sink, and toilet on the left side, nothing but a cement wall on the right. There were also two men fighting. "Break it up," he yelled. But the two men continued to battle. Giles ran back to the snack bar, straight to the two men sipping coffee, the ones, he had noticed earlier, with the guns under their coats.

"Officers," he said, taking a wild, and in this case correct, guess, "there's a fight in the washroom. Come on." Winthers bounded up and began sprinting toward the bathroom door. He charged in first, followed by Giles and Yotka. There were now five grown men jammed into a john barely big enough for three.

"Break it up, fellas," commanded Winthers.

Parrilli had Messmaker pinned up against the splash board behind the sink. Winthers saw the blood splattered on the partition separating the sink and toilet.

"All right, fellas, break it up!" Winthers ordered.

According to Giles, Parrilli was the first to speak: "I'll turn him loose if you won't let him hit me."

"They'll be no more hitting," Winthers said.

Parrilli broke his hold and started to back away. "Get over in the corner," Winthers told him. He grabbed Messmaker and dragged him toward the toilet. Yotka pulled Parrilli up near the urinal. Only two feet separated the two men, who, according to Winther's statement, were still yelling and screaming at one another. Just as Winthers was asking who started the fight and taking names, Giles slipped out the door.

As he did, out of the corner of his eye he saw Marconi coming out of the lounge.

Marconi, in his testimony, said he had just finished a second helping from the buffet line when one of the wives mentioned a "disturbance" down the hall, a fight or something in the men's room. Marconi said he had no idea who was involved. According to his testimony, he said he calmly walked into the bathroom and asked Parrilli how he felt. "I'm all right," Parrilli said.

"Well," answered Marconi, "if you're all right, let's get out of here."

"So I tried to get to him," Marconi testified. "The next thing I know I was hit from behind [not standing at the sink washing his hands as he told the newspapers]. The next thing I knew someone . . . had their arms underneath my arms and they had me out in the hall.

"I said, 'I'm all right.'

"They said, 'You've got to get to the doctor. Your head is busted.'

"I said, 'Oh, it's not that bad,' and put my hand up on my head. I brought my hand down and it was filled with blood."

Marconi said he was carried to the lounge where he ran into Ditka, who had been on the other side of the lanes.

"What happened?" Ditka said.

"I don't know," Marconi said. "I think somebody hit me with a bottle."

But during a January 24, 1964, coroner's inquest into the death of Anthony Parrilli, William J. Bauer, the state attorney for Du Page County, had some questions for the Chicago Bears running back. Bauer is now the celebrated chief judge of the U.S. Court of Appeals for the Seventh Circuit. He was at a New Year's Eve party in nearby Lombard, Illinois, when he got the call about the shooting. He hustled over to investigate. Under Bauer's prodding at the inquest, Marconi admitted he had done more than just stand idly at the sink.

Had anyone identified himself as police officer?

"No," Marconi said.

Did you ever see a gun in the room?

"No, I didn't."

Was there a fight going on when you came into the room?

"No, there wasn't."

Did you push, shove, hit, or strike anybody when you first came in, or at any time while you were in the room?

"I don't remember, but when I was going towards Tony in the corner, there was either a fella on my left, or he was on the right side of me . . . and he could have gotten in front of me and I could have pushed him out of the way."

You didn't strike anybody, did you?

"No, I did not."

When you shoved him out of the way or pushed him out of the way, how did you do it? Would you give me a demonstration? Did you push with your hands, or what?

"Yes, I kind of pushed with my hands, and that's when I got hit."

Both Giles and Winthers told investigators it was Marconi who precipitated the incident. Certainly, the policemen's plain clothes, failure to identify or more clearly identify themselves, contributed to the tragedy. So did Winthers's flawed and ultimately fatal decision to draw his gun. But as sworn testimony attests, both Messmaker and Parrilli were separated and cooling off when Marconi burst through the door like a fullback breaking through the line of scrimmage.

"What the hell are you guys doing with my buddy?" Giles heard Marconi shout. Winthers said that with one hand Marconi shoved Yotka, who bounced off the washbasin and into the urinal. With his other hand, Marconi shoved the police chief aside. He grabbed Parrilli and hauled him toward the door.

"About this time," Winthers said in a statement, "you know, the guy behind me [Messmaker]—they're still mad. I mean they're mad and going back at it . . . whirling around and arms are flying, and I reached down and I get the gun by the cylinder, and you can't do anything in there. You're in this washroom. I come up with the gun to hit him [Marconi] over the head to lay him out and an arm comes over behind me—Bill [to Attorney Bauer], there are arms just all over the place.

"I think I hit him, I don't know. I mean, I was trying like hell to hit him. I heard this explosion of this gun go off and I look and this guy is dropping to the floor.

"I felt just like this thing on television when this guy got shot down there in Texas [Lee Harvey Oswald, by Jack Ruby]. I look and this guy's going to the floor. I just drop right on my knees and I go after him."

Bauer breaks in to ask if Winthers's finger was on the trigger when he swung the gun.

"Not to my knowledge. I don't know. The only thing I remember when I pulled that gun is having it around the cylinder so I can use it as a club."

But you thought it was necessary to draw your gun when you did? asked Bauer.

"I couldn't do anything," Winthers said. "I had to subdue him. I mean the only thing I could keep thinking about was this whole bar is going to be out here in this rest room, and what are you going to do?" A moment later Winthers concluded his testimony. "Bill," he said, "that's about it. All I know is there's a guy dead on the floor and I'm half-sick myself."

The gun Winthers pulled from his swingaway holster (he mistakenly left a blackjack in his overcoat) was a Smith & Wesson .38 Special "Masterpiece" target revolver specially mounted on a .45 frame. A large weapon. Too large, certainly, in these close quarters, perhaps anywhere for this carpenter–cum–police chief with little formal training in firearms. The Chicago Police crime-detection lab was asked to do a test on the weapon. "They gave it [the gun] all kinds of tests," a captain in the Du Page County Sheriff's Office testified. "They used a hammer, they dropped it, and everything else." And according to the lab report, "the weapon would fire only with the trigger in the rearward position," in other words, with a finger in the trigger guard and the trigger pulled *all* the way back. In the heat of the moment, Police Chief Winthers had panicked and killed Tony Parrilli.

Bauer, of course, knew none of this as he entered the bowling alley (shortly) after one A.M. and headed straight to the men's room. There, stretched across the entryway to the washroom, half in and half out, was the deceased. Some thirty years later sitting in his U.S. Court of Appeals chambers, Bauer seems a charming adjudicator. A former U.S. Attorney and U.S. District Court judge (he was a finalist in the U.S. Supreme Court nomination process that culuminated in Nixon's offering the nomination to John Paul Stevens), Bauer became the political godfather of Du Page County, the Illinois counterpart of Westchester County in New York or Orange County in California. The counties are Republican enclaves for those who worship at the twin altars of money and power. But Bauer was ascending in 1964, and he wasn't about to play politics. He recalls how by the time he arrived at the scene several Bears had disarmed the Willowbrook cops. "Just walked right up and took their guns away," he says. The county police had also arrived. The place was surrounded. It was too late, however, to stop Messmaker, who, in the shocking tumult, had drifted away unnoticed.

The Bears group was in a separate room when Bauer entered. Nobody knew Parrilli was dead ("before he hit the floor," said the judge). Bauer broke the bad news. O'Bradovich, he remembers, went crazy, jumped up, ready to even the score with the local cops. Says Bauer, "I explained to O'Bradovich that there were *real* cops out there now and they had guns and they knew what to do with them. He calmed down quickly and things remained under control. It was close there for a while."

Ditka was present through the initial investigation. He and Bauer later walked out to the parking lot together. "Wait till the Old Man hears about this," he told the attorney. Bauer knew Ditka was not talking about his father; he was talking about Old Man Halas.

At a subsequent coroner's inquest the jury found that Parrilli died "accidently . . . as a result of a struggle and the apparent accidental discharge of a pistol by Police Chief Robert Winthers." Nevertheless, the jury recommended a Du Page County grand jury investigate the case. Winthers was subsequently indicted on involuntary manslaughter charges. (Ditka gave a deposition and one lawyer remembers him as "one of the most gentlemanly and cooperative individuals I met during my many years in the practice of law.") Bauer, meanwhile, then head of a twelve-man legal staff, decided to prosecute the case personally. "I wanted to make the point you do not just give a man a gun and a squad car and call him a policeman. Policemen should be trained. They should be especially trained in the use of weapons."

After three days of trial Winthers and his lawyer entered a plea of guilty. "There was a holiday in the middle of the trial," Bauer says. Charles Bellows [Winthers's attorney] called to ask me what the judge [future Republican patriarch Bert Rathje] would do if Winthers entered a plea of guilty. I told Bellows that I thought Judge Rathje would put him on probation. Bellows asked how I could be sure. I told him being stupid was not a penitentiary offense, and that Judge Rathje would understand what we all understood—that Winthers was guilty of stupidity. I just wanted Winthers permanently out of police work and permanently barred from carrying a weapon."

Rathje, as predicted, sentenced Winthers to probation. Parrilli's mother and family had been present throughout jury selection and the presentation of evidence. The widow, Nancy Parrilli, was not among them, but plenty of Parrillis were in the courtroom. The moment the judge put Winthers on probation, Parrilli's mother stood up, wailing and screaming. "I knew this case was fixed," she screamed. Rathje's bailiff ran over to take her out of the room. Rathje told the bailiff to bring the woman up before the bench. Rathje explained to her patiently and at great length that Winthers was not a killer. "He is just dumb," Rathje told her, according to Bauer. "We don't put people in jail because they are dumb."

After listening to everything the judge had to say, and perhaps wondering about the political wisdom of putting police chiefs, however dumb, in jail, and the lives of men with lesser intellect spent behind bars, the woman again started wailing and screaming about a "fix." The bailiff told the judge he would escort her to lockup. "Don't you dare," replied the judge, according to Bauer. "If it were my son, I would say the same thing."

But the case wasn't closed, not from Nancy Parrilli's perspective. Later that year she filed a civil lawsuit seeking damages for the loss of her husband. At the time of Parrilli's death, the law limited recovery in wrongful death cases to a maximum of $30,000, and it limited what were called "dram shop" cases (cases against a tavern for damages caused by someone the tavern overserved) to $10,000. On the eve of trial in 1967, the case was settled, according to Parrilli's attorney, for about $14,000—not bad considering her husband could have well started the chain of events that cost him his life. Oliver W. Gregory, the attorney representing the village of Willowbrook and Winthers, recalls vividly that Nancy Parrilli was "adorable" with "amazing doe eyes." A highly successful and respected insurance defense lawyer, Gregory says, "This was one of the most adorable plaintiffs I ever saw. I told the [insurance] company that her presence all by itself made this a good case for her in front of any jury."

Parrilli evidently had a similar effect on another person close to the case. After her husband's death, she married O'Bradovich. In an odd twist, their daughter, Amy, later married Ditka's son Mark.

12

PARRILLI'S DEATH HIT DITKA LIKE A CRACKBACK BLOCK, THE PORTENT OF more grief and heartache to come. For Ditka the 1964 season was one of tattered edges and missing parts. It was a season, in retrospect, when Ditka's professional career truly began to unravel, not wildly but slowly and steadily, dragged down by injury and his continued carousing off the field. He suffered the first major setback—a shoulder injury—in a game against the College All-Stars in August. Meanwhile, players were angry at Halas for reneging on the big rewards he had promised after the championship season. Fortunato recalls a $3,500 bonus figure being mentioned. Husbands and wives has visions of those bonuses— mink coats and color TVs or, at the very least, rings fit for a king. "But nothing happened," O'Bradovich said on a 1988 WBBM-TV special. "It turned a lot of attitudes the wrong way." The mumbles and grumbles, what Wade called the "divisionary forces" arrived in Rensselaer and never left. "Slowly but surely the team was torn apart," says Wade. Perhaps, but what affected morale even more was the sudden, shocking death of two of its most talented and popular players.

Like so many of their teammates, Willie Galimore and Bo Farrington had traveled over to a nearby country club to catch the Summer Olympics on television. It was the logical place to drink a couple of beers and spend a summer night. On the way back to camp, however, their car missed a tricky S-curve and smacked a high shoulder. The car, a convertible, flipped over. Farrington flew out the open roof and died. Galimore was killed when the car rolled over and broke his neck.

Ditka didn't learn about the crash until the following morning. He, along with Casares and George, went down to the morgue and identified the bodies. Ditka was devastated. "It took everybody by shock," says Fortunato. "Everybody was already upset because Halas didn't come through with the raises he promised. That got everybody depressed. When Willie and Bo got killed, that killed us as a team."

Still, in a true testament of his will to win, his threshold for pain, Ditka played in all 14 games (for the fourth straight year) and caught 75 passes, the most ever by a tight end—an NFL record that stood for 16 seasons. Yet those 75 catches gained just 897 yards, a 12-yard average, the lowest to date in his career. And only five of those 75 went for touchdowns. The Bears, meanwhile, fell apart, winning just five football games.

Ditka's threshold for pain was sorely tested during the 1965 season. Physically it was the arch this time, left cracked and twisted when a defensive back fell on his right foot in a scrimmage. Serious foot injuries are anathema to athletes, especially injuries to the arch or instep. Running, cutting, or firing out of a three-point stance is next to impossible with a bad one. The pain is unbearable—"like rubbing sandpaper across a raw nerve," according to fullback Ronnie Bull, who suffered an injury very similar to Ditka's. Most athletes would have rested. Not Iron Mike. He dulled the knifing pain with needles and novocaine, courtesy of the team doctor, and played all fourteen games. Numbed or not, as Bull notes, "there was no improvisation like with a shoulder [injury]. You can use another shoulder. You need both feet to run."

But the arch was only the beginning. Next came constant knee and hamstring trouble, the result of constant shifts in stride to compensate for the injured arch. Ditka caught just 36 passes for 2 touchdowns that season, a frustrating year compounded by disputes with Halas over money. The '65 draft brought two future Hall of Famers—Dick Butkus and Gale Sayers—to the franchise, but their six-figure contracts, at a time when veterans were making $25,000 a year, didn't help morale. The team opened with three games on the road—and lost all three. Despite going 8-2 from then on, '65 remains as painful as that instep to Ditka. "I thought we had better talent than '63, but we just didn't have [what it took to win]," he once said.

Neither, it appears, did Ditka.

At a point in his career—his fifth season—when Ditka should have been peaking, he was slowing down and according to some former teammates, burning out. It wasn't just the arch injury, though it certainly can't be downplayed, or the arrival of Sayers, which limited Ditka's pass-catching opportunities. No, more and more, Ditka's escapades off the field were catching up to him. Four years of hearing last call all over town were starting to take a toll. Billy Wade, the Nashville banker who praised Ditka as far back as '61, is quite blunt about it: "What I saw hurt Mike more than anything was his extracurricular involvement in Chicago. It seemed like it started in 1964 and got a little worse each year. Mike's mind was somewhere other than football. It was like he was tired, getting hurt and stuff. You could see him slowing down; he seemed to be straining, and he was not that old." Wade takes a deep breath and begins anew. His words are slow, measured, and heartfelt. "You could see Mike changing and you knew it wasn't for the best. The marriage . . . all those things. You hope, the guy is your teammate and you care for him. You could see things starting to come apart, almost like you yourself were coming apart."

Actually, husband and wife had slowly been drifting apart for some time. The married glow of two young kids from Aliquippa taking on the world had faded, replaced by the stark realization that they weren't made for one another. Worse, they didn't *know* each other. Says Mike Pyle, with obvious care, "Mike married very young. I think . . . I don't know how to say this. I was going to say *mistake,* but I can't judge that. He was just in the same category as an awful lot of other professional football players, and a lot of other professional athletes at that age. People got married young. Pro athletes do it right out of college—and this is just a personal opinion—so many times they weren't really ready. They just thought they could do it, so they should do it. We all know that a life of a professional athlete did not add up to a growing marriage."

Indeed, the move to Chicago had been a jarring one for both Margery Dougherty and Michael Ditka. Marge was a Pennsylvania original, bright, beautiful, funny, and tougher than tempered steel, a virtual carbon copy of her husband.

In high school she was known as a pretty brown-haired girl who did wonders with a cashmere sweater. She had taken a shine to her handsome 6' 1", 190-pound senior classmate, a football star who loved to roughhouse with his buddies but still served communion in church. He was also shy and just a little bit backward with girls. But as the story goes, it wasn't until after football camp that the all-American boy mustered enough courage to ask the all-American girl for a date. Yes, she said. From that moment on, remembers one good friend, "they were like peanut butter and jelly." High school sweethearts who stuck together, for better and worse, for the next seventeen years.

But Chicago, Marge felt, had changed everything. And everybody. Suddenly her husband was a media star. Rookie of the Year. All-Pro. Running with an older crowd. A twenty-two-year-old dining at a buffet of beautiful opportunity. Marriage? His only point of real reference on

103

the subject was back home in Aliquippa—"I'm going out"—or in the locker room at Wrigley, where monogamy was hardly a household word. Plus, it was the tenor of the times. Marriage in the fifties meant mothers stayed home, cooked, cleaned, and took care of the kids, which is exactly what Marge was doing. (After Michael Jr.'s birth on August 21, 1961, Mark E. Ditka arrived on Dec. 15, 1962. He was followed by Megan Ditka on the first day of November 1964. Marge was now mother to three children, two of them boys, under the age of three and a half before she hit twenty-five years old. A fourth, Matthew, would be born on December 22, 1966, making it four children under the age of six.)

The problem was, Ditka was also following in his father's footsteps. He was hardly ever home. If he wasn't at practice or a game, he was over at the bowling alley, or he was playing poker or gin or golf, or hanging out at The Cottage, Berritz, Buena Chimes, Haran's, Gus's . . . anywhere on Rush. Home in the suburbs was often his final option in a city packed with possibilities.

In a fine WBBM-TV profile timed to his induction into the Pro Football Hall of Fame in 1988, host Johnny Morris deftly asked if "personal sacrifices" to win had been "costly" to Ditka in other areas. "I think I've done some things that haven't been too smart," he answered. "I wish I could have spent more time with my kids when I was younger and they were younger, but I didn't." And in 1991 Ditka told ESPN's Andrea Kremer during a "Sunday Night Conversation" his "priorities" had been out of place. "I was doing what I thought football players had to do," he said.

What has rarely been explored, however, is how his "priorities" affected others. How his maniacal will to win impacted on those closest to him—those who loved him the most. Many a time Marge let him know, fighting from the beginning to make her marriage work. "She went nose to nose with Mike plenty of times," says Pyle. "Oh, there were some great ones, some great ones." More than one such "discussion" took place on Sunday night during the football season, during midnight meals at Riccardo's on Rush Street. Riccardo's was, and still is, a classy Italian restaurant, a hangout for journalists and artists where the Ditkas and several other Bears teammates and their wives drank and dined, relaxed and partied after a Sunday home game. Jeannie and Johnny Morris were often there, so were Richie and Faith Petitbon, Joe and Noonie Fortunato, Joe and Jan Marconi, and many others. The postgame party often started at a bar called The Silhouette then moved over to The Cottage. Most often it ended at Riccardo's for a late dinner. Ric Riccardo kept the kitchen open until the guys felt like eating, which could be anytime, as they continued to drink at the bar. "I feel soooo good," Ditka once crowed, "I could piss right across this bar and down those stairs." Riccardo would probably have ignored it, too; he loved this crowd and pampered it like movie stars.

For the women, it was a special night, a chance to steal a few hours away from the kids and enjoy their husbands' company. After a while, however, they tired of waiting for their men to break away from the bar. "Joe, are you coming over here or what," Noonie Fortunato might yell at her husband. "Let's eat." As dinner was served, the wine and drink began to flow; stories were shared among old friends, their lives and laughter filling an otherwise empty restaurant. Sometimes they'd eat and drink until three or four in the morning. Sometimes frustrations slipped to the surface. Complaint turned to criticism. An attitude into argument.

"The Sunday Night Fights," says Jeannie Morris, laughing. "They were really classic." Morris's laugh is a bubbly one and it fills the front room of her Lincoln Park apartment just north of downtown. "Joe and Noonie Fortunato would just scream at each other, and they were happily married, too. Noonie had this great Southern accent, you know. 'You know my granddaddy would be turning over in his grave if he knew I was married to a son of a bitch like you.' You know, screaming."

When Marge and Mike argued, it was mostly about Mike's not being around enough or being too drunk to walk, let alone drive. Marge never drank much because she had to drive, so occasionally she had some fun. Like the time they all piled a useless Ditka into the car. It was about six below outside, Morris remembers, and by the time they got home, Marge was in no mood to wake and lug her pickled partner inside. So she left him in the car.

Jeannie called the next morning. "So, how did it go getting home?"

Marge never missed a beat. "I don't know. Mike's still out in the car. I guess I better go check on him."

The laugh lights up Morris's face, a familiar one to Chicago TV audiences. Not only did Jeannie Morris raise four children, but she later starred as an Emmy Award–winning correspondent for the local CBS affiliate for fifteen years. Today she is a free-lance writer (she wrote the best-selling autobiography of Brian Piccolo) and TV producer. She admits to a "peculiar relationship" with Mike Ditka—thirty years of friendship and trust tested by the trials of day-to-day journalism. Thirty years. It provides perspective on a man, his moods, and his marriage.

But an even deeper perspective springs from the reporting Morris has done the last few years. During that time she's interviewed about twenty former Bears wives for a book, and after hundreds of hours of interviews she chose to profile four women, all divorced, all recovered from their failed marriages: herself, Linda Sayers, Faith Petitbon, and Marge Ditka.

Morris takes a sip of coffee from a mug cooling in her hands. The book research has been an awakening of sorts. "You can't believe how many of these women are just totally mystified about their lives," she says. "Faith, Marge, Linda and myself *do* understand. The others have no perspective. They've just been beat up, that's all they know. It's really, really sad."

Beat up? "Beat up in the sense of just not understanding why their life got messed up. They don't really understand it. They don't understand the forces . . . Thinking you're going to heaven and finding out it was hell instead. They don't understand these men at all."

The Ditka marriage, Morris believes, like many others of that time, was dysfunctional from the start. "I don't think it was ever any good," Morris says carefully. "Mike and Marge, I mean, you can put it in a nutshell. Mike and Marge never got along."

From the beginning?

"You can read all the tea leaves in Aliquippa. I don't think any of them get along. I don't think Charlotte and Mike [Sr.] get along. I don't think Marge's parents got along. I think if you go over to the Linmar Plan, you'll find two hundred couples in their seventies that don't get along and are still married.

"You know, I think the deal is that when they got married, they got married with the idea of being married forever. I mean, there was nobody else he wanted to marry and he thought he was supposed to get married. Both are very strong-willed and they're very much alike, and Marge tried to go by the rules for a long, long time like we all did."

The rules being what?

"The rules being he's the boss and we do everything his way, and if he doesn't feel like being here for whatever period of time, he doesn't have to be. He doesn't have anything to do with the kids but he wants her pregnant all the time. He wants to have a bunch of kids because he knows he's supposed to."

Morris takes another sip of coffee. "I mean none of us were involved in their lives. They just had separate existences from us, and I've just learned to understand that now, as a reporter. Most women never have the opportunity to understand that."

But at the same time, says Morris, the men wanted love and comfort at home.

"They all needed to be cared for because their mothers cared for them. They very much needed to be cared for and have the kind of orderly home that they grew up in; in Mike's case, a very orderly home. They require that stability, so they can do what they have to do, mainly pay for it and feel like that's what they're supposed to do. You were in Aliquippa. You saw the pattern there. The guy comes home—Marge's father did this too—and he eats dinner and he goes to the tavern. It's a cultural thing. That's why so many of these guys are great football players. They're permitted to concentrate."

Morris takes another sip and shakes her head. "As Marge says, they make great businessmen and football players, but as far as husbands and fathers . . ."

"I asked my mom once," says Megan Ditka, Mike's only daughter, during a long interview one afternoon. "I said, 'Mom, was he the same person when you married him?' She said honest to God, he was a very shy and unassuming person before he got into the Pro Bowl. Then it was women. Fame. This and that. She said the priorities in his head became a little crowded."

Megan Ditka was born during a time those crowds began to form. She is twenty-seven now, with a little girl's giggle and spirited laugh. Chicago is a bit of a blur, but she remembers Dallas. The family moved when she was five, providing Megan an education (University of Texas/Dallas) that led to a sales job with Hilton Hotels. She left the city in the fall of 1991, returning to the Chicago area to work for Hilton. "I have very few recollections of my father," she begins. "My mom basically raised us by herself. I love my mom a lot. She's a real brave woman. I couldn't ask for anybody better. My dad was never really around a lot." And even when he was, she admits, he wasn't. "We were always pretty much afraid of my dad. My dad is just like his dad. You didn't have conversations with him. He's a little intimidating when you're a kid . . . I don't think he knows how to love."

Moreover, the bonds that tie little boys and girls to their daddies—the bear hugs, bedtime stories—were missing much of the time. And when he was home, his moods swung wildly. The wins were celebrated with the boys; the family suffered through the losses. A tense silence filled the house for a day or two before vanishing with a heartfelt apology from Daddy. But the damage was done. A wife and children had been caught in emotional whiplash.

Megan continues, "It was hard for him to connect on an emotional level. I think a lot of that came from his family, his upbringing. My grandfather, the same thing."

Why?

"I don't know. The football tough-guy image. I used to have a real problem with it. Thinking maybe it was me. That I was the problem."

Complications were setting in all around Ditka's life. He had been on a high since his junior year in high school, but now a ten-year winning streak had snapped. First came Parrilli's death. Then the injured shoulder, the aching arch, and business problems. A marriage rolling toward the rocks. For the first time in years black was enveloping white. The losers were winning. Ditka says he never changed during this time, never played a down any easier. Never forgot the team. But others remember it differently. "What's the word I'm looking for?" says Ronnie Bull, now president of a Chicago-area silk-screen company. "Not irritable . . . frustrated. He seemed to strike out, unable to do things he wished to do."

"It was a madness rather than a sharpness," Wade says. "He seemed to be pissed off at the world."

And more and more, during the '65 season, that ire was directed toward one man—Halas. They argued over money and play selection. They argued about who should be playing quarterback (Ditka favored Rudy Bukich over Wade). Ditka ignited a public controversy when he and Morris sided with Bukich at a local banquet. Ray Sons, an ace newspaperman, was at the luncheon and wrote the story. Halas got hot. He called Ditka at home, well after hours, and cursed him out. He ordered him downtown immediately. Ditka refused. See you in the morning, he said. The first thing that morning Halas called Ditka and Morris, demanding they apologize to the team. Morris said he was sorry. Ditka declined, insisting he had done nothing wrong.

But the biggest rift came over, quite naturally, money. In the wake of the Butkus and Sayers signings, Ditka was pushing Halas for a bigger contract, accusing the tightfisted owner of "trying to pay players with the salaries of the 1940s and 1950s." Times were changing, and Halas, who balanced his books to the cent every season, was reluctant to change with them. Halas wanted nothing to do with Ditka's demands; he put his son George S. Halas, Jr., better known as Mugs, in charge of the talks. Mugs finally offered about $200,000 for three years—triple Ditka's pay in '65. Ditka refused, mainly because the upstart American Football League, financed by NBC money, had thrown some mean green in his direction. It was Houston again, and this time the figure was $300,000 for three years, including a $50,000 bonus if Ditka would agree to play out his option after the 1966 season and sign with the Oilers. The AFL had declared open warfare on the established NFL, and now it was raiding as much top talent as it could get. Among those willing to listen were quarterbacks John Brodie of San Francisco and Roman Gabriel of Los Angeles, Packer running back Jim Taylor, and Ditka, who was making just $25,000 at the time.

In fact, in May of '66, Ditka secretly signed an agreement with the Oilers and banked the fifty grand. About three weeks later the Bears discovered Ditka's deception when his contract surfaced during peace talks between the NFL and the AFL. Ditka says his decision "really wasn't that big a deal," adding it was more about "value." The Oilers, he said, were just willing to shell out more money for a player who had never played a down for the franchise. The Bears' idea of "value" was $100,000 less, despite five All-Pro seasons. "That's the only thing I never could understand," Ditka wrote in his book. "It bothered me." He told *The New York Times* if he hadn't taken this opportunity, "my wife would have looked down on me for the rest of my life. I have four kids and this will assure their college education. I'm as loyal as any player to his team, but I have to be loyal to my family first."

If loyalty was what it was, he certainly took a starkly different attitude toward the ten-year-old National Football League Players Association (NFLPA). The NFLPA was fighting for a better pension plan and extra pay for preseason games. Yet Ditka never supported the union—despite his father's legacy, and a roommate who was the NFLPA president at the time.

"He fought for his own money," says Pyle, the Association's president, "but . . . he did not follow the movement." No, what Ditka followed was what he has chased for years, the dollar. He took the money, then lied about it. Then he cashed the check.

For the first and only time there is an edge to Pyle's voice when he says, "The [Dave] Parks, the Brodies, the Ditka's, they put one hundred thousand or two hundred thousand dollars in their pocket that the AFL couldn't get back. It forced the merger, or helped lead to the forcing of the merger, but they didn't do it for the league. They did it for themselves."

In reprisal for Ditka's duplicity, Halas cut his '66 salary 10 percent, a legal but rarely invoked rule allowing teams to reduce salaries of players in option years. Ditka's memories of that season are as bleak and bitter as the Bears' 5-7-2 record. After averaging 57 receptions his first five seasons, he caught just 32 passes, failed to make the Pro Bowl for the first time, and bitched about almost everything. He claimed because of his contract squabble and his "personality conflict" with Halas that he was "not being thrown to as a pass receiver," a curious stance given Halas's zest for winning. Ditka called coaches idiots. He questioned pass routes and meeting times. It was just like Little League. The coach was wrong. Mike is right. Apologize? Forget it. So what if he played hard off the field—damnit, nobody played any harder on it, did they?

Then came the clincher. What is now one of the classic quotes—and cleverest cracks—ever delivered by an employee in any profession. At the height of the contract mess, Ditka said, "Halas is so cheap, he tosses around nickels like manhole covers." Halas was not amused. He was even less pleased when, in February 1967, Ditka publicly disclosed he was "obligated" to play for the Oilers in the fall.

"I've got a valid three-year contract with Houston," he told the press during a business trip to New York. "I won't say for how much, but they gave me a fifty-thousand-dollar bonus to play out my option with the Bears last season. I keep that no matter what. It's in the bank.

"The Houston people have said they will forget about it to keep peace, if the Bears give me the same contract I have with the Oilers. I don't want to hurt anybody. I just want to play for the team that will use me the most."

Despite Halas's advancing age—he was seventy-one now—the old coach wasn't willing to forgive or forget. He didn't like threats, and he didn't like deception. If Ditka wanted to play for a team that "wanted him most," he'd oblige, all right. Ditka's speed was slipping, no doubt. Papa Bear had seen and heard enough. He needed a young, agile quarterback to replace the aging Bukich and Wade. Philadelphia was shopping Jack Concannon, twenty-four, a 6' 3", 205-pound scrambler out of Boston College. So it was on April 26, 1967, four days before Ditka would officially become a free agent, that Halas got the last word. He traded the heart and soul of his team, the tenacious tight end who had never missed a game in six seasons, to the lowly Philadelphia Eagles for Concannon and a draft choice.

Ditka was left in the lurch. He could report to the Eagles. He could ignore the trade and sign with Houston and, if the NFL squawked, take the league to court. Houston released Ditka from his obligation and wrote off the fifty grand as "an investment that didn't pay off." Ditka, shocked by the trade, replied that "after taxes, Uncle Sam has most of [the bonus], anyway."

GARY BALLMAN KNEW HE WAS IN TROUBLE WHEN HE SAW THE PLAYBOOK.

Five years earlier the former Michigan State All-American had played for Joe Kuharich in both the East-West Shrine and Hula Bowl college all-star games. Now it was the summer of '67 and Kuharich handed Ballman, just obtained in a trade with Pittsburgh, the new Eagles playbook. Only it wasn't so new. "This is five years, I mean five years," says Ballman, "and he gave me that playbook and that fucker was identical to the East-West game playbook."

Ballman is a long way from Philly now, Denver, Colorado, to be exact, where he does remodeling and new construction work. He's sitting in the backyard of the current object of his affections: a two-story brick and stucco home, a complete redo, 2,200 square feet of hardwood floors, plush carpeting, Jacuzzi-style tub, island kitchen, and oak cabinets that Ballman and his son have sweated and strained over for months. It's a spec job; Ballman bought the seventy-year-old Congress Park house, in a gentrified section of the city, then ripped off the roof—"popped the top" in construction terms—and started over. In the backyard are the fresh remains of the restoration—a demolition derby of pink toilets, empty paint buckets, and piles of splintered wood. For some reason there is also a battered ski boat and the backseat of some long-lost van. He shakes a balding head covered, as best can be, by a red/white baseball cap emblazoned with the words THERMO-PLY. A mint green T-shirt that has seen better days is tucked under a carpenter's tool pouch resting on a belly fond of beer.

"We had some fucking characters on that team," he says. "We had—what the hell was his name? The kicker. Baker . . . Sam Baker. Man was he funny. Baker always lived alone in the preseason. He'd

111

want to go out after curfew, so he actually had a makeup kit. He would make himself up—usually as an old man. One time he just walked right out the door and around the corner, and here comes Kuharich. And here's Baker in makeup and a fucking cane. He says, you know, 'Good evening,' and walks right by Kuharich.''

Despite his crested belly Ballman has the hearty look of an outdoorsman. His calves, especially, are thick and muscled. They are the same booster rockets that twenty-five years earlier had propelled a sure-handed wide receiver known for his shifty moves to All-Pro honors with the Steelers before he was traded away to Philly in the spring of '67, about the same time as Ditka, or as he calls him now, Mr. Ditka. "I've tried to get ahold of Mr. Ditka a number of times in the past," he says, "but he never had the courtesy of returning my call. I guess he's running with a different crowd now."

But back in '67 and '68 Ballman and Ditka were kindred spirits, soul mates in what turned out to be a witches' brew of shaky ownership, quirky coaching, and injured players, and Ballman shared every hellacious minute of it. They roomed together, partied together, and even got suspended together. Most often, however, they shared the agony of playing for Kuharich. "Jesus," says Ballman, wincing at the name. "Mike got so damn frustrated, and I got frustrated. We'd go to Kuharich and say, you know, your passing game is all screwed up. He'd just say, 'I'm the coach, and I'll take care of it.' He said, 'You guys just play, you're players.'" Ballman yells at two dogs to stop yapping at some squirrels scrambling up and down a nearby tree. "Kuharich was behind the times," he says. "I mean he was *substantially* behind the times. The game passed him by. He totally did not understand the passing game."

Of course, understanding Kuharich wasn't any easier. Chairman Joe, as he was known, was a burly, wavy-haired man with a tough immigrant face, who had gained national attention in 1951 by coaching the University of San Francisco—enrollment 1,276—to an unbeaten, untied season, and sending eight, count 'em, eight players to the pros. At Notre Dame, however, from '59 to '62, Kuharich never had a winning season. He later served as head coach of the Chicago Cardinals and Washington Redskins with little distinction. A martinet on the practice field, he was known as a stickler for conditioning and fundamentals. Off the field, he proved an utterly colorless personality void of idle chatter or repartee. At his best, he seemed to inspire loyalty in his troops; most often he was a baffling mix of malaprops—"That is a horse of a different fire department" was one of his most famous. An ignoble, autocratic man, Kuharich gave the impression that no matter how badly his team got beat, it boiled down to one or two fringe plays. "A missed block here, a missed assignment there, adds up," said Kuharich after one such 56–7 slaughter.

Halas knew this attitude would drive Ditka up a wall, and it did. As it was, Ditka says, his two years with the Eagles were the low point of his life. The absolute pits. "If there's such a thing as purgatory on earth," Ditka wrote in his autobiography, "I was in it there." The Eagles had hired Kuharich in 1964 shortly after business tycoon Jerry Wolman bought the club for more than $5 million. Eagles fans, among the most jaded in sport (they booed Santa Claus one year, pelting him with snowballs), started screaming from the start. To heap further misery on the masses, a year later, with the team at 6-7, Wolman abruptly pinned the title of general manager on Kuharich's chest and gave him a guaranteed fifteen-year, $900,000 contract (an NFL record at the time). You needed earmuffs to handle those howls. But Kuharich didn't care. "Joe Kuharich is different than you or I," Wolman said at the time. "We, both of us, are up and down. [But] nothing happens will affect his thinking."

Kuharich abhorred the star system; he viewed players as interchangeable parts. Early on, in an effort to rebuild the club (or break up cliques), he sold or traded popular stars such as future Hall of Fame quarterback Sonny Jurgensen, wide receiver Tommy McDonald, linebacker Maxie Baughan, and cornerback Irv Cross. Kuharich's reasoning for trading Cross: "Excessive thinking."

Said Cross after his departure, "I had the choice of keeping my mouth shut and being traded or of opening my mouth and being traded."

Fans were not pleased. One fed-up season-ticket holder was actually caught carrying a rifle into Franklin Field. And on one occasion Wolman was forced to duke it out with a fan who had heckled both his head coach and team. "This," said a rookie, watching Wolman during the dust-up, "is a madhouse." If so, in 1966, the Eagles briefly got their house in order. They won their final four games (and seven of their last nine) to finish with a 9-5 record. Not even a loss to Baltimore in the Playoff Bowl dimmed hopes for the '67 season; the writers predicted that Philadelphia would challenge Dallas for the new Capitol Division crown. So it was, in quest of that crown, that Kuharich made more than a dozen trades during the off-season. Trades No. 13 and 14 brought Ballman and Ditka to town. Kuharich had dreamed of getting Ditka ever since the Houston mess surfaced, but gave up once learning Halas was looking to land either John Brodie or George Mira from San Francisco. Then he got tipped that the Ditka market had reopened and he flew to Chicago to discuss a deal. In a blink of an eye the trade was made. "To get an incredible All-Pro like this is incredible," said an incredulous Kuharich afterward. "I feel very lucky because you could never get a boy like Ditka without extenuating circumstances."

The question was, how extenuating? Halas figured it better to get rid of Ditka while the getting was good. With his failing health, Ditka's role now, at twenty-seven, would be simple: carry the emotional torch for a team whose flame had flickered. "We were looking for his leadership," says former Eagles captain and fullback Tom Woodeshick, who is now in the limousine business in Atlantic City. "Not only verbally but on the field. We looked for him to teach us how to win." Ditka flew to Philadelphia alone, separating himself once more from Marge, who wanted no part of the move. "She was trying to keep the kids in school and lead a normal life," Judi Ballman, Gary's wife, says today. So Ditka's new home was the old Sheraton Motor Inn that Wolman had bought and renovated. It suited his needs. It was on the University of Pennsylvania campus, hard by Franklin Field, site of the Eagles practices and games. And for good measure there was a lively bar downstairs.

Any questions about Ditka's potential impact were answered early. In the third exhibition game, the Eagles tangled with the upstart New York Jets of the American Football League. For the Jets, the game was anything but meaningless. It was more like a vendetta against "the other league." Ditka got ejected late in the first quarter, shortly after annihilating Jets cornerback Johnny Sample with a vicious downfield block. Sample, a noted cheap-shot artist, had earlier racked up halfback Timmy Brown out of bounds. Ditka was about to deck Sample when the refs stepped in. Instead he got ejected. But the Eagles won, 34–19.

Ditka took pride protecting his teammates off the field, as well. Brown tells a story of some fan placing a hand on the running back's shoulder during that preseason, an act of consolement actually. Ditka didn't see it that way. Says Brown, "Ditka saw the guy put his hand on my shoulder and he comes right across the room. He says, 'This guy bothering you, man?' He was ready to take him out. He didn't like anybody coming up to players, especially after losses."

So it was in the first few weeks Ditka seemed happy. The Eagles had won three of their first four games. Quarterback Norm Snead was looking sharp, Woodeshick was piling up yards, even the fans seemed sated. Marge was flying in on Friday for home games. That night, more often than not, the Ditkas and Ballmans and several other Eagle couples would head down to the water and grab some crabs. "We'd have these crab parties at our house every Friday night," says Judi

Ballman. "We'd have crab races across the kitchen floor." On Saturday nights before Mike and Gary checked into the team hotel, Judi Ballman served dinner, then watched as Ditka wore a hole in her kitchen floor. "Jesus, Mike, sit down!" Judy told him more than once. "Or you're gonna buy me a new floor." Says Judi, "He would pace, pace, and pace, back and forth, back and forth." That night, when the men had left, Judi and Marge would talk about raising children and the difficulties of being players' wives. "It was tough on a woman because lots of other women in the world want any man that's a football player," Judi says. "It's real hard on most women and most marriages."

In the fifth week of the season the Eagles lost 28–27 to San Francisco. At halftime about fifty eighteen-year-old kids were formally inducted into the U.S. Marines, which, at this point, was basically a one-way ticket to Vietnam. In the Franklin Field press box, Sandy Padwe, a young, crusading columnist for the *Philadelphia Inquirer,* took exception to the ceremony. Padwe, whose diverse writings on such subjects as race relations and sport in society were as powerful as they were prescient, had just completed a six-year stretch in the Army and Army Reserves. That night he wrote a column questioning how the Eagles and the NFL could publicly sanction the induction of teenagers to war while pro teams were slipping able-bodied athletes into reserve units, which had no chance of action. "It was a strong column," says Padwe, now a senior editor for *Sports Illustrated.* "A pointed column."

Too pointed for some people. By coincidence Padwe had arranged a locker-room interview with Ballman for the next day. Ballman's locker happened to be at the very back of the room, right next to Ditka's. The Eagles, still smarting from the 1-point loss and—some at least—stung by Padwe's words, were in a foul mood when he walked in the door.

"You fucker," screamed one player, "you saying I'm a draft dodger?"

Padwe, who looked more like your average high school kicker, replied, "You're the only one who knows whether you are or not."

Whack. A balled-up piece of adhesive tape, a knuckled rock, struck Padwe in the head. Whack. Another. Whack. Whack. Suddenly he was a sitting duck.

"You motherfucker," growled another player. "You saying I'm yellow?"

Padwe kept walking and talking. "Well, if the shoe fits, put it on."

Bam. Another tapeball banged off the back of his head.

From the back of the room Ditka surveyed the scene. He had known Padwe casually for years dating back to college when the newspaperman covered Pitt and Penn State football. Padwe says he had long understood Ditka, primarily, because his "hard-playing style" in college "absolutely personified" the western-Pennsylvania work ethic. Perhaps Ditka also understood where Padwe was coming from, or maybe he didn't like the odds. Either way, he began walking toward the columnist. "I remember he came up to me and backed me toward [Ballman's] locker," says Padwe.

But Ballman wasn't there.

"All right," said Ditka. "Just wait right here."

"He just stood there and protected me," Padwe says. "The players knew better than to mess with Mike Ditka." When things cooled off, Ditka offered the newsman some sound advice. "Sandy, there's a way to get out in the back. Take it."

"At that point," Padwe says, "I knew I had better get out."

It was about that point, five games into the 1967 season, that bad luck, injuries, and a comedy of errors combined to put Philly on the skids. The team lost four of its next six games (it would finish the year 6-7-1, never winning more than twice in a row). Ditka played in just nine games, the first time after six NFL seasons he had missed a game. This time it was an assortment of ankle and knee problems as well as the nagging arch, which had never really healed. It showed. "He was not the same player," admits Woodeshick. "Once in a while, on a slant-in, he'd knock people over like bowling pins . . . but he wasn't physically able to step into it.

"Don't get me wrong. The guy gave us everything he possibly could. But we needed more than that. We needed Mike's leadership by example. To show us, to point the way on the field. To radiate that championship feeling he exudes when he's right. Like he did with the Bears. We didn't get that kind of leadership. I'm not faulting Mike. He just wasn't physically capable of doing it." And every moment off the field, every second in the whirlpool just added another degree to Ditka's disgust. He started sniping at Kuharich, clashing over passing schemes, game calls, double-coverage calls, blitzes, stunts. Worse, here was Kuharich spouting off, as he did in November after a 44–7 loss to the Giants, saying things like, "The Eagles are improved. When I first came to Philadelphia, we were only selling forty thousand season tickets. Now we're selling fifty-three thousand."

Life in Philadelphia had become something out of a W. C. Fields movie. One time when Kuharich implored his troops to "roll and steam and juggernaut" down the field, Ballman turned to Ditka and said, "What the fuck does 'juggernaut' mean?"

"Fuck if I know," replied Ditka, shaking his head, "but let's roll and steam."

The following season they "rolled and steamed" all right, right off the edge of a cliff. It began in training camp when one of Wolman's relatives, who were always traipsing in and out of the locker room, decided to play a practical joke on the players. He dumped some potent itching powder into athletic supporters, the result being a terminal case of teamwide jock itch. Even today Ballman squirms at the memory. "There ain't nothing worse than having a chapped crotch and you gotta go out there in goddamn pads and sweat," he says. "It was the worse goddamn preseason I was ever in." But that's not all. The liniment prescribed to help soothe the scratching stung like a swarm of hornets. "You talk about stinging. Jesus Christ, I couldn't believe it!" says Ballman. Neither could Ditka. Before anyone could warn him about the liniment, he'd lathered it on. In seconds he was a human hot tamale. Says Ballman, "Well, it just so happens we all had these hooks to hang our pants on. So Mike is underneath the son of a bitch and he puts this shit on, and he goes, 'Yow!' and he fucking jumps up and down and that fucking hook *spikes him in the head!*" Ballman bursts out laughing.

Ditka didn't. "Giving us fucking jock itch! Nobody can play football on this fucking team. A bunch of fucking losers . . . plus they can't even give us the right fucking medicine."

"He went through the whole rag," Ballman says, still amused by the memory. "We were all laughing, and he's so pissed off he doesn't even know he's injured yet."

If those signs weren't powerful and clear-cut enough, on the very first play of the first exhibition game, Norm Snead, who had looked sharp in training camp, called a halfback pass by Izzy Lang. Omen one: the pass was intercepted. Omen two: Snead, while turning to try to make the tackle, caught his cleats in the turf and broke his left leg. Kuharich called it a "dastardly event." But, he added, "you have to learn to live with these things." You also learn to live with losses, the backbiting, thin skin, and the misery of a myopic head coach, and owners on the brink of bankruptcy.

Which is just where Wolman, a D.C. developer, was as the season began. There were real estate losses and a $5-million cost overrun on the one-hundred-story John Hancock Building in Chicago. By November of '68 he had thrice tried to reorganize his assets and failed; he was some $70 million in debt and technically no longer in control of his club, already held as collateral by a major New York bank.

Kuharich was out of control, too, well on his way to setting some kind of NFL record for unpopularity. Not that he noticed. Like Captain Queeg, he steadfastly resisted the roar of mutiny around him. Philadelphia fans had long since jumped ship, fed up with Joe's lame excuses and insipid postgame summaries. Franklin Field had become a clearinghouse for "Joe Must Go!" fever. There were pennants, bumper stickers, buttons, newspaper ads, and tables with "Joe Must Go!" petitions. Some of it was funny, like the portable toilet perched on the back of a flatbed truck. JOE'S HOME read the sign.

Some of it was humorless. One stadium sign suggested DO THE FANS A FAVOR AND KICK THE BUCKET, JOE.

"There was a lot of strain," recalls Woodeshick, a stalwart on offense from '63 to '71 and the team's fourth-leading rusher of all time with more than 3,500 yards. "Kuharich's job was on the line. He was the GM and the head coach. The trades didn't materialize. Things got a little tense." Kuharich started pointing that finger again, only this time he was looking for scapegoats.

He found one in the oft-injured Ditka, who by October was coming apart emotionally.

He wasn't playing—spot duty in nine games.

He wasn't contributing—just 13 catches for 111 yards.

He wasn't leading—"Mike was a leader by example," says Timmy Brown. "When you can't contribute, it's hard to tell other guys to go out and break their balls."

He wasn't really married—Marge flying in weekends, Ditka now treating her as if she didn't exist. "He was aloof," says Ballman, adding, "Let's just say he wasn't romantic."

Injuries. Kuharich. The pitiful season. A faltering marriage. All gnawing away at the meat of the problem: Ditka was facing the reality that his All-Pro career was over. He had just turned twenty-eight, but was looking more and more like a washed-up father of four with no real plans for the future. It was an abyss all right, a huge black hole that Ditka crawled in about as deep as you can get, escaping, as so many do, on the icy straits of alcohol. "Double jeopardy" is what Woodeshick calls it now, and he isn't talking game shows. But rather a period when Ditka would order two drinks at a time, drowning his sorrows, reliving his highs with scotch and water, whiskey, beer, wine, whatever was around. "Everything was great until he started drinking Courvoisier," says Ballman of an after-dinner cognac Ditka digested by the bottle in those days. "After that, anything could happen. When he started on the Courvoisier, that's when you left. He would get mean. Mike is not a good drunk. He is a mean drunk."

The sun is still high in the sky, bright and warm in Denver, as Ballman turns to the dark days and nights of his Philadelphia friend. The nights so often began in the hotel bar, where Ditka would drink heavily, before heading out the door, "making the circuit," in Ballman's words, driving off alone to clubs in New Jersey, private hangouts. When Ballman warned Ditka to take a cab, Ditka just turned and told him to "fuck off" and walked out the door.

In his book Ditka is vague yet unusually blunt about this period. "I was about trying to kill myself with the drinking," he writes. "Even though I had good intentions of going out and having dinner, I would start drinking. I would always say I was going out to eat and would be back in the apartment at eight o'clock at night. But I know I woke up in some strange places, not knowing how I got there or why I was there or who I was with or anything like that. I could have been in Alabama as well as Philadelphia. I would go through the day after like I was in a fog, not being able to distinguish between what was real and what wasn't real. I just know things weren't going good and I wasn't playing much and I was in the doghouse. . . . I wanted to escape from it and the escape was to go back to a restaurant or a bar and that was it."

The Eagles hit the skids right along with Ditka. They were 0-10 after a 7–6 loss to the Giants in New York. Ditka and Ballman stayed overnight. Neither had played in the game despite being healthy and available. Both had personal appearances scheduled at banquets on Monday, and even though Ditka's was on one side of town and Ballman's was on the other, they were united in ripping Chairman Joe. Ballman joked about commissioning a special pair of cuff links for Kuharich—an Eagle with 0-14 underneath. He tossed in a dig or two about a "stereotyped" offense. Ditka, according to the papers of the day, was a bit more personal. "I don't want to leave the Eagles," he was quoted as saying at his banquet, "but I don't want to play for Kuharich again next year."

Their comments hit the newsstands before they boarded a late train back to Philadelphia. Ballman picks up the story some twenty-five years later. "We had the papers spread all out in front of us, we're laughing like crazy, having a few pops, saying, oh, shit, we've had it. Because I had made headlines everywhere about Kuharich. We were laughing, wondering what was going to happen." What was going to happen was Kuharich got one whiff of this insurrection and hauled both men into his office. They maintained they had been misquoted. "What appeared in the paper was not what I said," Ditka said at the time. "I was asked if I would come back to play for the Eagles under Kuharich next season. I said, 'No, I wouldn't. I don't think he wants me to play for him. And I don't want to play for a man who doesn't want me.'"

Kuharich wasn't buying it. "You're suspended for conduct detrimental to the National Football League," he told them both.

That's rich, thought Ditka. You can fuck up a franchise, have an owner in hock for $70 million, and *this* is considered conduct detrimental to the league. Ditka just laughed right in Kuharich's face.

The next day a telegram arrived in the office of NFL Commissioner Pete Rozelle. It was signed by several Philadelphia city officials requesting he step in and halt action by the Eagles that "could be detrimental [that word again] to the economic success of the city's new $46-million stadium now under construction." Kuharich and his rebels met again, and this time after what the coach then called "a harmonious conversation," the suspension was lifted. He told Ditka he would play extensively that week against Cleveland. But Kuharich wouldn't forget; neither would Ditka.

"I'm done," he told Ballman that night as they watched a Flyers hockey game.

"What'ya mean?" Ballman asked.

"I'll never play for this guy again."

Ditka meant next year; Kuharich was thinking short term. Despite his pledge for forgiveness, Ditka hardly left the bench in the game against the Browns. Watching from the stands were his parents, who had come to Ohio hoping to see their son play. But now instead of his heroics in Chicago and his run in Pittsburgh, what they saw was not unlike what you see in Aliquippa today: aging relics left to rot on the side of the road. And they sat there waiting. And he sat there wondering, crying, tears of shame, anger, and blame coming to his eyes. But who was to blame? There was no time for soul-searching now, only self-pity. When the season ended, Ditka left town faster than an Emery envelope, driving through a blizzard nonstop . . . going home . . . but to whom and to what?

14

IT WAS A TROUBLED MAN WHO TRAVELED TO THE DALLAS COWBOYS TRAINING camp in Thousand Oaks, California, in the summer of 1969. Much like the country itself—torn apart by antiwar protesters burning flags and draft cards, denouncing the long, deadly war in Vietnam—Mike Ditka was uncertain about his future. His playing days were numbered—or worse, over. His legs were lead. His body puffed and bloated by alcohol. His family life was tense one day, indifferent the next. So as he headed west, Ditka knew, deep down, all he had left was what he started with, his solace in times of trouble. What had created him, sustained him, made him the star he once was: the fury burning in his belly. The belief that nobody, nowhere, no how, was ever going to beat him when it counted.

Tom Landry and Tex Schramm, the Cowboys head coach and general manager, respectively, had rolled the dice on Ditka. Schramm had long been a fevered admirer of the New York Yankees and how that dynasty had obtained championship players late in their careers, guys such as Don Larsen and Johnny Mize, to spark the ball club. How about Ditka? Both Landry and Schramm felt the fading star with the "wild nature" could produce given the right set of circumstances. So it was that Landry called Ditka shortly after the 1968 season ended. "We don't know if you can play anymore," he told Ditka, "but we're going to bring you down and take a look and see if you can play a few years."

So in the same roiling waters that Joe Kuharich had fished two years earlier, Tom Landry, old Stone Face himself, was casting a line. He was looking for a catalyst, a leader for his leaderless club on the cusp of becoming what would soon be known as America's Team. The Cowboys had flirted with greatness for years. They had made the

121

playoffs from 1966 through '68 only to flame out in playoff games against Green Bay. They had earned a reputation as a finesse club that came up short when it meant the most. Looking back on that period, former star fullback Walt Garrison says simply, "Dallas didn't know what it takes to win," especially, he adds, after two of its biggest winners, quarterback Don Meredith and running back Don Perkins, retired after the '68 season.

In July, Ditka reported to training camp at California Lutheran College with the dozens of rookies and free agents the Cowboys annually entertained in hopes of discovering a diamond in the rough. Only one other veteran was in camp, a popular running back rehabbing from recent knee surgery. He and Ditka were casual acquaintances, nothing more. But now in the soothing California sunshine they warmed to one another. They worked out every morning and afternoon, lifting weights, running sprints, playing pitch and catch alone on the practice field. A former college quarterback threw and the tight end caught. It was seven days of friendship fused by competition and, as they discovered, their indomitable wills to win.

In time Dan Reeves and Mike Ditka would become inseparable, "tight as ticks" in the words of former *Dallas Times-Herald* columnist Frank Luksa. "Everything was Mike and Danny," says a former Cowboy official. "They were always together."

But on this September day Dan Reeves is alone. Sitting in his plush corner office in suburban Englewood, Colorado. The vice president and head coach of the Denver Broncos gazes off to his right out the picture window at a panoramic view of his team's practice field. The second-floor space is just above a lobby that seems more a modern art museum than the seat of a football franchise. It is decorated in busts, statues, and a flotilla of multicolored flags. Now forty-eight, Reeves retains the handsome look that sent so many female hearts aflutter during his days in Dallas. Reeves was fond of magic tricks and practical jokes back then. "Oh, he was Mr. Entertainment," says a former Cowboy official. All capped off by that sweet Southern drawl of Americus, Georgia, and the hint of Texas twang.

On this day his graying hair—the only obvious sign of age—matches the steel-framed glasses and designer shirt rolled up at the sleeves. A Bible sits on one corner of his desk. Four pencils, sharpened to perfection, are lined up like tiny toy soldiers before him. Stacked to their right are enough legal pads to please Perry Mason. Not one hair or item is out of place, a testimony to the obsessive organization that marked Reeves's years as a player and now, as a coach, an organization that he has led to three Super Bowls in eleven seasons. As obsessive as Reeves can be, he is equally as competitive—a perfect match for Ditka. "Everything we did was so competitive," says Reeves. "He's like I am. I love to compete, too, love anything you keep score."

There were gin games so fierce that Ditka once fired a chair so hard all four legs stuck in the hotel room wall. There was backgammon in the back of every plane, and golf games that went on *forever,* the loser refusing to concede, yelling, "Emergency nine," pushing the stakes and the competition deep into the dark. "There was one course where we'd play the tenth hole and the eighteenth because they were side by side," Reeves says. "Nobody else would be out on the course, and we'd play ten, and then it was, 'Okay, let's play eighteen.' Back and forth. I got home late more times because of Ditka. My wife would be mad at me. You know, 'Why do you want to play golf at night?'"

But the true blood battles came elsewhere, behind brick walls and closed doors, in the same sweaty box night after night. Pounding away, man against man. Best of three. Always to twenty-one. An hour and a half of nothing but elbows, hips, and hard-core racquetball. "What was bad," Reeves says, "is they were smaller courts, not regulation size. It was great as far as exercise was concerned because you can get more shots, but it was also more physical. He definitely had the advantage because he was so big."

But Reeves had some advantages, too; he was four years younger and a little bit more of what Ditka wasn't: a naturally gifted athlete. A former University of South Carolina quarterback, Reeves had caught the Cowboys' eyes as a free agent back in 1965 before going on to define the phrase *all-purpose running back* during his eight seasons in the pros. Reeves was never the fastest or biggest guy in an NFL backfield—just one of the smartest and toughest. "Neither one of us would ever quit," he says. "You hated it when it was over because whoever lost was mad.

"Mike broke several racquets. Threw several racquets over the building. . . . I think's that why Coach Landry traded for Mike because he felt we needed some toughness on offense. Mike was a guy who would take no prisoners."

For that reason, Reeves says, Ditka fit right into the football team despite the obvious fact he was overweight and out of shape—at least 235 pounds of bloat and blubber. During training camp Ditka showed some fire, starting fights during preseason scrimmages against San Diego and the Los Angeles Rams. Another time during a team meeting he stood up and challenged the entire team. "I'm trying one hundred percent. You're not trying one hundred percent," he charged. "Anybody who is not is going to answer to me." But like a punch-drunk former champion Ditka was only good for a round or two. He kept pulling muscles; Landry figured he had made a mistake. "I really thought his career was over," he once said. "His legs were not under him." Pettis Norman won the starting tight end spot, leaving No. 89 languishing on the bench, used mostly in short-yardage and goal-line situations. It fueled Ditka's frustration—and as before, his drinking.

In Thousand Oaks, Ditka had fallen right into the veteran crowd— Reeves, Walt Garrison, star tackle Ralph Neely, and linebackers Dave Edwards, D.D. Lewis, and Lee Roy Jordan—guys who enjoyed a brew or two after practice. But in those days Ditka didn't stop at one, two, or even sometimes, ten. "He competed just like he did on the football field," says Jordan, the Hall of Fame middle linebacker and one of the finest men ever to play the game. "He had more endurance than anyone else."

Once back in Dallas, Ditka recreated the Philadelphia story. He moved alone into an apartment (Marge and kids remained in Chicago). Almost every night he made a postpractice stop at a bar called The Dirt Dobber, a private club named after owner Mike Stevenson. For some reason Dallas only had about four bars at that time, and The Dirt Dobber was the newest and most popular, at least among the singles crowd. It was located out near what was then the main Dallas airport, Love Field. (A more fitting name you'll never find since the club served as something of a love connection for the sports celebrities and stewardesses who called it home.) Don Meredith, Lance Rentzel, Ditka—they all hung out at the Dobber, sitting in with the band, checking out the Braniffs, Americans, and Uniteds flying in and out of Love. "Mike was equally popular with the stewardesses," says Stevenson, who became a close friend and one of Ditka's business partners. "He was one of the bigger names." According to Stevenson, Ditka was something of a permanent fixture at the club, a wild-tempered, fun-loving, free-spirited Cowboy who loved his wine. What kind of wine? "Anything that had a screw-off top," says owner Stevenson.

"He would come into the restaurant; we had a bumper pool table, it was kinda a gathering place for everybody, and it was one of those winning-players-stay-on-the-table kind of deals. Mike would get back there and get beat and you could just hear the pool cues cracking in half against the tables.

"He'd also get into his wine pretty good, and that fired him on. I never saw him get violent with anybody. He was a typical hard-core

Pittsburgh type, lots of jawing, lots of mouthing, lots of redneck, a rooster.

"A lot of nights he closed the bar. Mike was a young man, just like the rest of us, full of life. He did everything to the extreme. . . .

"We had a hamburger at the club called the Dobber Burger. It was a gigantic hamburger with greasy french fries. Mike would get one to go every night. Our lure to get him out of the club was to let him take a bottle of wine home. And when Mike Ditka wants to take a bottle of wine home, I'm certainly not going to stop him, especially at two o'clock in the morning."

He was drinking to numb the pain, believing his personal miseries could be deadened like an injured arch or dislocated shoulder. But no matter how much medicine he consumed, sometimes those problems just don't heal.

Lee Roy Jordan, one of only seven Cowboys inducted into the club's "Ring of Honor" and now the owner of a Dallas lumber company, makes it clear he still carries enormous respect for Ditka. "Mike and I had a few battles. He was the most aggressive player I ever played against. . . . I was never so delighted to see anyone as when I saw him with the Cowboys. We needed battlers, and Mike was a catalyst." Yet his words soon shift, depicting a different kind of man. "I think Mike was searching for himself. He had been such a superstar in Chicago— all of a sudden injuries reduced his ability to perform. He was trying to punish himself for something. I don't know what, but he had this self-destructive attitude about it. He was really driving himself to drink hard, making drinking a display of Mike Ditka, of his manhood. 'I can outdrink anybody as well as outplay them.'

"He was going off the deep end. I was always concerned Mike would get himself into a situation with drinking that he didn't know what might happen. You always wondered what condition Mike would be in today for practice. He had a wreck or two and battered himself up pretty good."

Stevenson says one night, ten minutes after Ditka left The Dirt Dobber, burger, fries, and bottle of wine in hand, the owner got a call.

"Come and get me," Ditka said.

Says Stevenson, "He had cracked up his new sports car. He had dropped his Dobber Burger on the floor of the car and reached down to get it. By the time he looked up, he had run into an embankment or another car. Just destroyed it. We went out and got him. But before he got out of the car he had to get his Dobber Burger, his fries, and his wine."

Another endless night, just before the final preseason game, a car suddenly darted out of a side road right in Ditka's path. Ditka says he never saw it and only remembers slamming into the side of the car at about fifty miles per hour, getting a face full of steering wheel. Somehow he struggled home and called Reeves, who lived two streets over. It was well after one A.M. when Reeves, rousted from a dead sleep, finally answered the phone.

"Dan," Ditka said, "I've been in a wreck. I damaged some teeth and need to go see a dentist. Can you pick me up in the morning?"

Reeves agreed. But wait, he thought, maybe he's really hurt. Reeves threw on some clothes and raced over to find Ditka's teeth mashed up into his gums. "Mike," Reeves said, "we don't need to wait until the morning. You need to go see somebody tonight."

Reeves called a dentist friend. The dentist called two colleagues—an orthodontist and an oral surgeon—who all went to work on the pulpy mess that was Ditka's mouth. It was now around two o'clock Friday morning. Ditka mumbled to the men come hell or high water he was playing Saturday night against the Baltimore Colts. Right, they said. You can't play with those teeth.

Ditka spit out his response. "Then take them out."

The dentists negotiated a compromise, and the teeth were saved, protected by a plastic mouthpiece. Ditka missed Friday's practice, but sure enough, on Saturday he played the entire game against the Colts. He blocked Bubba Smith, a bitch of a ballplayer, and never gave or asked any quarter. The late-night mission rescue brought Reeves and Ditka closer together and today remains the rock on which their friendship rests. "I can never forget that," Ditka says.

These nightly drinking bouts at the Dobber—where else could he go?—cost Ditka. Not outwardly, for he still displayed inhuman recuperative powers, but inside the locker room where, as Jordan deftly puts it, "his extracurricular activities jeopardized his leadership abilities." Ditka eventually got the message, particularly after the Cowboys finished the season 11-2-1 before losing to Cleveland (38–14) in the playoffs. He saw the promise and opportunity. He realized this was it. His last chance.

So he moved the family down to Richardson, Texas, a Dallas suburb, swapping houses with a guy from Sears who got transferred back to Chicago. The Richardson house was huge—the biggest and best on a pretty block, 4,035 square feet, two stories, with a wide-mouth creek in back. There were six bedrooms and five baths and a living room decorated, Matt recalls, with red, white, and blue patent-leather sofas trimmed in stars and stripes. "An ugly, ugly room," he says. There was also a game room half the size of a high school gym and a pool out back. It was perfect for the kids, who were growing up fast and furious and needed space. The boys, Michael and Mark, were now eight and seven years old, respectively. Megan was five and Matthew three. No more bottles. No more diapers. No more sleepless nights for Marge, who'd come to enjoy Dallas. She and Mike tried to make it work, to spend more time together. They got into riding dirt bikes with the Reeveses and several other Cowboy families in the woods and hills near Lake Grapevine. They took family vacations. But Ditka's focus, as usual, was football. To limit outside distractions he paved his backyard and covered it with AstroTurf. So much for yardwork. He worked out like an Olympic hopeful: lifting weights, running mile after mile on grassy fields without shoes to save his weakened arch. By the time the season started he weighed 210 pounds. "That weight program gave me the body I had eight years ago," he said. He was thirty-one going on twenty-three again and Landry noticed. He caught only 8 passes but played in all fourteen games for the first time since 1966. The Cowboys won the NFC Championship, losing 16–13 to Baltimore on a last-minute field goal in Super Bowl V.

The following season, 1971, began with the grim reality that the Cowboys were working on a five-year streak of playoff failure. "They were always next year's champions," says Luksa, referring to playoff losses to Green Bay in '66 and '67, Cleveland in '68 and '69, and Baltimore in '70. It didn't help that the club stuttered to a 4-3 start, and then, in the midst of a seven-game winning streak, Ralph Neeley broke an ankle during an unauthorized dirt-bike battle out in the hill country around Lake Grapevine. Landry had outlawed the rides because he was concerned about player safety. If he only knew. In those days Reeves, Charlie Waters, Cliff Harris, Neeley, Mike "Dobber" Stevenson and Ditka used to go at it like pros, in knockdown, drag-out races through the woods at death-defying speeds in full riding gear, a precursor of the futuristic movie *Rollerball,* only outdoors. "We kicked each other off bikes, literally trying to run each other off the trail," says Dobber, talking about how they whipped between the trees, up and down the gullies. At night, he says, it was worse. "We'd do crazy things at night," he says.

How crazy? Dobber says as darkness settled in, the tired Cowboys would build themselves a roaring fire. They were eager to quench their thirst so out would come the beer and wine, cases of it. Strawberry Hill wine was the big craze back then, says Dobber. "Inevitably, as the

Strawberry Hill and beer went down, we'd start to crank the bikes up. It was a monkey-see, monkey-do kind of deal. We would ride through the fire. It was crazy. It was a lot of fun and we loved it, but you look back and wonder why we didn't blow ourselves up!"

Somehow they survived. Now, down the stretch in '71, it was Ditka—not Roger Staubach or Chuck Howley or Bob Lilly—who provided a spark. He brought to the team a sense of willpower and want missing from other playoff drives, sublimating his ego for the first time in his career, replacing *me* with *we*. "He *was* our spiritual leader," says Jordan. "He got across the urgency of competing on every play, how every play was critical."

In the first round of the playoffs Dallas whipped Minnesota, 20–12, on the road, a breakthrough win. A week later San Francisco fell 14–3 in the NFC Championship game. Two weeks after that, in Super Bowl VI, MVP Staubach passed for two touchdowns in a 24–3 mauling of the Miami Dolphins. The final touchdown, fittingly enough, came on a crossing pattern down near the goal line to No. 89. It was a meaningless score, really, but not to Ditka. He has long considered the '71 season the most memorable of his career. "I only caught thirty-one passes [actually thirty, his most since 1966], but I contributed to the team," he once said. "I became a team player instead of an individual player. It felt so good to be a part of that team. It was a fun part of my life."

For Dallas the Super Bowl win was cathartic, a coming-out party for a city and its team. "When they won, it was like a huge sigh of relief. A huge anchor had slipped its chain," says Luksa. Suddenly the Cowboys were media darlings, "America's Team," with the unflappable Landry on the sidelines. The Doomsday Defense. Staubach. Lilly. Bullet Bob Hayes streaking down the field. Ditka, as always, was looking for ways to capitalize on this popularity. Many a night after The Dirt Dobber had closed, he and Stevenson and Dave Edwards, a linebacker from Auburn University who happened to live next door to Ditka, had talked about opening a new place. Says Stevenson, "We had this vision, this concept that we all put together, really kind of the first sports bar in the country."

Fast-forward twenty-one years. It is Saturday afternoon in Dallas. Edwards is sitting not in The Dirt Dobber club but in a Mexican restaurant hard by the SMU campus. On this day it's filled with able-bodied sorority sisters whom Edwards takes full pleasure in undressing with his eyes. If they choose to return the look, they'll notice an amazingly fit fifty-two-year-old man fresh from a forty-four-mile bike ride. Edwards sports a day-old stubble and goony metal-framed glasses straight from the fifties. Otherwise, he's decked out in standard Texas fare—black cowboy boots, jeans, flannel shirt, and a jean jacket. Only most jean jackets don't bear an NFL fiftieth-anniversary patch. Edwards pulled it off an old Cowboy jersey and put it on the right breast pocket, a perfect conversation piece—"Oh, did you play for the Cowboys?"—in close quarters, so to speak. He wears a black onyx Super Bowl ring on his right hand.

Edwards retired from the NFL back in 1975. He rode the oil boom for a while, buying crude and selling field equipment before the market went south. He went back home to Alabama and worked a few years before returning to Dallas to manage construction jobs for one of Staubach's companies. It's been tough at times but Edwards isn't bitching. His dark eyes brighten as he talks about Ditka. They were next-door neighbors, business partners, and roommates on the road. All for one, one for all. Buddies till the end.

In fact, Edwards says, just a few weeks earlier he was watching the Bears on "Monday Night Football" and the memories flooded back. He wrote his buddy a long letter. "Stories of the old times," he explains. The *good* old times, it appears, as Edwards recounts in a two-and-a-half-hour expletive-laced interview their partying and playing days in Dallas. Ditka, in his book, downplays the debauchery, saying, "I didn't quite make the level of hell-raiser, but I was probably in tune with the guys who were." Edwards disagrees.

"He and I have been through some shit," Edwards says, pulling on a beer early in the interview. "He was a wild and crazy guy who liked to have a good time. So was I. . . . He was a great guy to party with. We were a couple of party animals. We went through some unbelievable times."

Like the time the infamous Varmint Brothers rang up and invited Ditka and him to a combination campaign rally and dove hunt down on Dolph Briscoe's ranch near the Mexican border, Dolph being a major Texas politico and a candidate for governor at the time.

Edwards: "We had these friends, the Talbert brothers. They invited us down to promote his [Briscoe's] damn campaign. So Ditka and I had to get up at fucking five o'clock in the morning. We were flying to San Antonio to meet these guys, but we weren't really looking forward to it because these guys were so fucking wild we might not make it back. We knew that. Going hunting with these fuckers? Old Diron Talbert and his brother, Don, I gave them the nickname the Varmint Brothers. One of them played with the Washington Redskins, Diron did, and Don played for the Cowboys. Don and I were roommates his rookie year. He went to Vietnam for a while, and when that fucker came back, he was nuts.

"Anyway, we were going hunting with them. So we get down there [to San Antonio] and it's about six in the morning. Ditka said, 'Goddamn, I really don't want to go, do you?' I said, no, not really. He said, 'Why don't you go back and see if we can get a damn flight back to Dallas. I'll wait here, and if they don't show up in a few minutes, we'll go back.' "

Edwards finishes a beer, then finishes the story.

"By the time I walk off, I heard this goddamn car with tires squealing, and goddamn, here they come. Yeeehawwww! They were drunk as hell. They were throwing beer bottles out. We get in the car with them and off we went. It was the damnedest dove hunt you've ever seen. There were about thirty people there. Briscoe was there. He had this damn ranch house that was down by the Mexican border. He's got a foyer that goes all the way around the house with beds lined up. It would sleep a hundred and fifty people.

"So one night, the Talberts and the guys go varmint hunting. Ditka's playing poker with all the damn politicians. He and I were staying in the same room. I decided to go to bed around midnight, and about that time one of the Talberts walks in and he has this little rabbit, and its feet are tied together. He stuck it under Ditka's pillow and turned the lights out.

"About fifteen minutes later I heard that fucker come down the hall. He had lost and he was screaming, 'Those motherfucking cheating politicians!' He came into the room and he didn't turn the lights on. He just started taking his clothes off and jumped in bed. Then he let out one of the most bloodcurdling goddamn screams you ever heard in your life. He says, "Goddamn, there's a fucking rat in my bed!"

Ditka scrambled out of bed, flipped on the light. He saw he had the tiny Bugs tied up in his bed.

"Goddammit," he screamed at Edwards. "You don't have to tell me. I know who did it! Those fucking Varmint Brothers—those sons of bitches!"

Ditka quickly exacted his revenge.

Says Edwards, "He killed a goddamn coyote or something and hung it over their beds. Scared the shit out of them!"

Briscoe lost the election, but Dallas—city and team—kept right on winning, riding the oil boom and the Super Bowl triumph like a runaway train, and Ditka, Edwards, and Stevenson were determined to jump aboard and fulfill their late-night vision. Ditka and Edwards anted up about $125,000 total and opened the SportsPage—the city's first upscale, singles sports bar. Dobber, who had sold his stake in his restaurant, took over as operating partner and general manager, while Ditka and Edwards handled the fine art of promotion (making sure the Cowboys and other sports celebs showed up). The final piece of the management puzzle was a local real estate guy named Ben Pinnell, who owned the strip mall where the SportsPage was located. In exchange for a couple years of free rent Pinnell got 25 percent of the action.

And it was some action. The vision turned out to be a thing of beauty—a multileveled sports bar/restaurant with all the right touches: a projector showing old 16mm NFL films that Ditka and Edwards obtained on loan from the league; ski movies; slide shows featuring shots of Ditka and Dobber riding their trail bikes; training camp and sideline photos; and pictures from other Dallas sporting events, all courtesy of shutterbug Stevenson. The rest of the bar was ersatz barn walls, huge stained-glass windows, and plenty of Foosball and pool tables. And of course a dance floor packed with bodies throbbing to the latest pop tunes.

Ditka reveled in the celebrity, even though, as Stevenson attests, he sometimes overstated his popularity in a town hung up on Staubach, Lilly, and Landry. Ditka got a real good dose of reality one night when Stevenson asked him to participate in one of their many nightly promotions. "Mike didn't like to give out his autograph, but I said, Mike, look, let's have a promotion for the next thirty minutes that anybody that comes up and buys whatever drink it was, you'll give them an autograph. We had stacks of pictures in the back of Mike and Dave."

But Ditka wasn't buying. "I don't want to do that," he told Stevenson. "I'm tired. I've had a hard practice."

"Look, Mike, go along with me," his partner pleaded. "This is going to be great."

"All right."

So Ditka pulled out his pen and stood by the bar as the announcement was made. Stevenson says there must have been six hundred people in the club that night. Fifteen minutes went by and not one drop of ink had been spilled. "We kept announcing it and announcing it, and you could see Mike really getting nervous now because he realized, all of a sudden, nobody was going to take advantage of this deal."

With about four minutes left a young woman walked up to the bar. She ordered the drink. With a flourish Ditka grabbed a picture, autographed it, and passed it to the girl.

"What's this?" she said.

"Well, this is my autographed picture. You get it with the drink."

"Oh, great, I needed something to put my glass on."

Sure enough, says Stevenson, she put the picture right down on the bar. "Then she set her glass on it just like it was a coaster."

For about two years it was that kind of place—wild, crazy, a little off-the-wall. "The place to be," says Edwards. All the old reliables from The Dirt Dobber were there—the Cowboys, the Dallas Blackhawks minor league hockey team, the Texas Rangers, and the stews—just moving the party four blocks down the street. "Man oh man, was it ever something else," says Stevenson. So crowded and so crazy that when E.J. Holub, a former center for the Kansas City Chiefs, shouted, "Can I do anything I want to in here?" Stevenson just blew it off. "E.J.," he said, "you can do anything you want to."

E.J. kept at it. "Are you sure I can do anything I want to?"

"E.J., you can do anything you want to."

"Well, how about if I bring my horse in?"

Stevenson was too busy to bullshit. About horses or anything else.

"Fine, whatever," he recalls answering. "Just bring your horse on in."

"Well, sure enough," says Stevenson, warming to the story, "one night he came. We had a big line waiting outside and E.J. pulled his horse trailer up, unloaded his horse, rode him through the front doors, and backed him up beside the bar. We were giving away cardboard boxes of popcorn at the time. He filled up a big popcorn box with beer, gave it to his horse, and he sat in the saddle and drank his drinks."

Thanks to colorful characters like ol' E.J.—and the swinging singles who flocked to the place—the owners recouped their original investment within six months. Cash was piling up, and increasingly Pinnell, who had gained their trust, was being called upon to invest it. "His one function in life," says Stevenson, "was to make sure we all made a lot of money, made good investments." Early on, that's just what he did, particularly a couple of land deals out near what would become the Dallas–Ft. Worth airport. Says Stevenson, "We really got our confidence in this guy."

At Pinnell's urging, Ditka, Edwards, and Stevenson explored the possibility of a much bigger buy—taking over a run-down, mismanaged ski resort in Wolf Creek, Colorado. Pinnell's wife—"my bride" as he always called her—had grown up in Wolf Creek and tipped her husband to the possibilities. "He went to us and said, 'Hey, guys, I've got this beautiful investment for you, tax shelter and everything.'"

Ditka and Edwards were like most other professional athletes, meaning naive and emotional when it came to business decisions. Stevenson wasn't much better. They listened as Pinnell enthusiastically outlined the deal, which proved a bit unorthodox. Stevenson: "He tells us he has to represent himself as a single entity in this thing because the people of Wolf Creek are so closely knit they don't want outsiders in. His in was his wife. He said go along with me. We'll do the paperwork, but they're gonna think I'm the only one involved."

They trusted him. "We went to the bank and borrowed a sizable amount of money, $250,000, $350,000, somewhere along that line," Stevenson remembers, "Plus we put a lot of our own money in that had accumulated in the bank. So I'm gonna take a guesstimate at around a half million dollars. And we poured it into Wolf Creek. We did all the improvements to take over Wolf Creek. And Ben became a local hero because he saved it.

"Ben's thank-you for saving Wolf Creek was he was going to bring up a couple of Dallas Cowboys for opening day of ski season as his guests. So we chartered an airplane, Mike, Dave, and I. I don't know, there must have been fifty people on the plane. We all flew to Wolf Creek . . . with Ben beating the drums and tooting his horn with his bride, as he called her, as he made his triumphant return to Wolf Creek.

"I'm telling ya," says Stevenson, "they laid the red carpet out for us. He was a local hero. We went to a big dance at the VFW hall. Ben kept saying, 'You got to buy your lift tickets. You can't get anything comped. You got to act like you don't own any part of this.' And we went along with it. As far as the people of Wolf Creek knew, we didn't own any of this thing."

Pinnell was treated like a returning war hero. He got the keys to the city. A crown was placed on his head. Flowers tossed at his feet. As his coronation continued, Ditka, Dobber, and Edwards stood on the sidelines, scratching their heads wondering, as Stevenson recalls, "Just what the hell is going on here?"

By now Ditka's radar was picking up something strange. "Do you think this is right?" he asked Stevenson on several occasions during the day. "I don't know, Mike," Dobber answered truthfully, falling back on the only hope he could: "He hasn't screwed us yet."

For Ditka it was a risky business move at a most perilous time. After eleven years in the NFL, his earning power had evaporated. There would be no more signing bonuses, no more bidding wars for his services. He was on the line for at least $150,000 in Wolf Creek, hardly pocket change back in 1972, which would turn out to be the end of his playing career. He caught just 17 passes but played in all fourteen games as the Cowboys went 10-4 and marched to within a game of the Super Bowl, edging San Francisco 30–28 in the divisional playoffs before dropping a 26–3 decision to Washington. By that time Ditka knew it was over; his weight was dropping like a bad bond market and his back felt as if he had slept in the garage all night. His quickness and strength had diminished. The Cowboys' brain trust had sensed Ditka's skills were slipping and had protected themselves by drafting a tight end on the thirteenth round, Jean Fugett from Amherst, and keeping him on the roster.

Ditka's marriage was in equally sad shape. "It was disintegrating pretty good," says Cowboy running back Walt Garrison. Why not? Between football, off-season golf, gin games, and now the time and temptations at the bar, Ditka was missing in action around the house. "Mom was all alone with four kids," Megan says. "He was no help at all."

And even when he was home, the results were often as humorous as they were disastrous. A former neighbor of Ditka's tells the story of how after the Cowboys won the Super Bowl in 1972, Ditka and several friends decided to take a family vacation, the tight end springing for an expensive camper. "There were nine cars that pulled out that morning," says the neighbor, "each with a trailer behind it. It looked like *The Grapes of Wrath* when the procession left the neighborhood. All of us stood out on our lawns and waved good-bye. Then a few hours later, they all came back. Seems Mike had pulled into a gas station in Weatherford [more than fifty miles away] and sheared the top off his camper when he hit the awning over the pump. Everyone laughed except Mike."

Overall, however, Ditka's demeanor was, as with so many other pro athletes, ill suited for fatherhood. All too often his silences and glowering presence—especially to small children—passed through the front door with him. Matt Ditka was just five years old back then but remembers being "scared" of his father, scared of his hands, how he used them on Mark and Mike. "I was a little intimidated by him, scared of him, and that was my fault, you know," he says one night, just off work as a restaurant manager at Ditka's downtown. Matt Ditka is a spitting image of his dad, the same square build and ambling gait, the comforting face without the rough edges and probing eyes. "I didn't talk to him," he says softly. "I tried to avoid him because I was intimidated." Some twenty years later he still remembers the moment he felt that first wave of fear. Somebody had walked on his mom's car with wet paint on their feet. The prints were little ones, so Matt took a beating—"a pretty good beating"—even though he swears it wasn't him; all he remembers is the beating and how he felt differently around his father. "My dad would be in the room and it would be like I wouldn't talk. You know everybody noticed it and there was no reason for that. But I'm not like that anymore. I hope not. It took me longer than you think to be able to talk openly with him in the room." Megan sees Matt's silence as simply a response to her father's "Don't bug me with it, I don't want to deal with it" attitude. And when he did "deal with it," his actions sometimes confused the kids. Megan vividly recalls getting "rapped" on the head for leaving a piece of bread on the counter; screamed at for dropping french fries on the floor of the car. "He was real meticulous about how the house looked, how the car looked," she says. "He forgot he had four kids. Four kids are going to be messy."

Mike and Marge were getting messy, too, reaching the point of lifeless kisses and cold shoulders in bed. Friends say by this point they had resigned themselves to separate lives. On weekends, for example, when other Cowboys would bring their wives, girlfriends, and families to the dirt-bike parties, Ditka now showed up alone. When he and Marge were together, their hostilities sometimes spilled out into the open. "They used to battle it out verbally quite often," Jordan says. At home, some screaming matches grew so loud frightened neighbors called the police. One of those neighbors, Lareda Pappas, who has lived on the street for twenty-three years, says, "The stories about his temper are legend. One time he threw a football at his house after a fight with Marge and took the front door off its hinges. A policeman friend of mine . . . used to come over and stop the fights all the time. It was like part of his beat." (The policeman, who requested anonymity, confirms the story, though, he says, no public reports were ever filed.)

Diana Trantham had grown up dirt-poor in Little Rock and Pine Bluff, Arkansas, the daughter of an abusive, alcoholic father. "My dad was always beating us up," she told the *Sun-Times* in a lengthy 1986 profile. "In that kind of atmosphere, you don't grow up dreaming."

Trantham quit school after the ninth grade and started working full time by the time she was fourteen. Her perseverance and uncommon common sense led to a series of better jobs. At twenty-six, she tired of small town Arkansas and moved to Dallas to live near her brothers. For the first six months, she said, she was disgusted, heartsick that her dreams of a better life had fizzled. It was then, she recalled, she met Mike Ditka, one Sunday afternoon in his bar called the SportsPage. She didn't care who he was, didn't know he played for the Cowboys.

Actually, it appears, as far back as 1969 and his days at The Dirt Dobber, that Ditka had settled into a steady, somewhat clandestine relationship with Diana—a striking blonde who Stevenson admits was a "real good customer" at The Dirt Dobber and quite particular about the men she talked to. "She was going through what I would call the interviewing process," says Stevenson. "I think she knew what she wanted. I don't think she knew it was Mike. But I do think she had a profile of pretty much who she was going to end up with. She had a real nice head on her shoulders.

"It started at the Dobber and evolved over to the SportsPage when everyone moved over there. It was a relationship that was kept pretty much under wraps until Marge and Mike made their split."

According to Dallas County court records, that split came on May 20, 1973, when the couple officially separated. Mike rented a one-bedroom apartment in a singles complex about four miles away. Almost two months later, on July 19, 1973, according to those same Dallas court records, Marge Ditka filed for divorce contending the "marriage between the parties has become insupportable because of discord or conflict of personalities." On September 21, 1973, twelve years and eight months after their wedding day in Aliquippa, the marriage was dissolved.

Megan's voice is soft and cuddly as a child's as she says, "I love my mom a lot. They were two people much better off not together. I think my mom probably would have killed him. He was dragging her down emotionally. Her self-esteem was so low. They were much better off away from each other."

"Hi, would you like to try some wine?"

The words have a harmony all their own, flowing as smooth as the pouilly-fuissé she is selling. It is a sweet, syrupy voice that blends with the bakery smells around her, a voice that slows and often stops the upscale Saturday-afternoon shopper strolling the fine-wine section of this North Dallas supermarket. "It's from France," she says brightly, carefully pouring wine into a Dixie cup for a browsing middle-aged couple. "A white burgundy, 1990 vintage." They take a sip and after a brief exchange of glances decline to buy. Margery Ditka thanks them kindly. As they move down the aisle, she discards the cups behind the portable tasting counter she has so appropriately decorated: the checkerboard cloth, basket brimming with a fresh loaf of bread and bunches of grapes. "Bought them just before I came in," she says, smiling.

A yuppie couple wanders by. "Would you like to try some wine?" They inquire about the red. "Salice Salentino," she says, pronouncing it "sah-lee-chay," like a pro. "From Italy." Her hair, honey colored, soft and wispy at the ends, is pulled up in back. Her face is void of lines or creases; she looks ten years younger than her age—fifty-two. She wears no jewelry save bronze, triangular earrings and a basic black watch. Her jacket and top are black, too, long, matched with a stylish Indian print skirt that dances around her boots. She has been in the wine business for about a year now, putting in long hours, doing in-store demonstrations by the dozens for a Dallas-based boutique wine distributor, which, it so happens, is owned by her ex-husband's sister Mary Ann, her husband, Bill Stowe, and . . . the ex-husband himself.

Seems the coach bought out Stowe's partner during the summer of 1991. It's a natural connection given Ditka's Chicago restaurant and his affinity for fine wines. "I'm certainly not what you would call a connoisseur," Ditka told *FYI*, an upscale *Forbes* magazine supplement for a 1991 feature story. "I'm just a guy who enjoys wine. Studying it, drinking it, giving it to friends when I find a good one. It's something I'm interested in." Interested enough, apparently, to have his picture taken in a tuxedo with a sommelier's cup dangling from his neck, to subscribe to *The Wine Spectator* and build a hundred-case cellar in his home.

It is Ditka's recent investment in the wine distributorship that forced Marge to abruptly cancel our dinner engagement the night before. "We've been divorced nineteen years and that's the first time he's ever called and asked me not to talk to somebody," she said in explanation. (Megan offers a more reasoned and rational explanation given the circumstances: "Dad owns a big chunk of the company. Mom doesn't want to upset him. That's the bottom line, what can I say? Her hands are tied.") But over the course of a couple hours in the supermarket on Saturday and a few minutes on the phone the night before, Marge loosens the bounds a bit. At this stage of her life those looking for an embittered, vindictive woman will be disappointed. If she were, she could have cashed a big check years ago. "I've been approached lots of times by people to write a kiss-and-tell book about Mike. I could have made a lot of money. I could never betray our relationship. We have a very strong loyalty. We've known each other since tenth grade. He still plays a very important role in my life."

Today, she refuses to psychoanalyze her ex-husband, but nevertheless her comments, when directed toward Ditka, hit home. While discussing trips back to Aliquippa to visit her ailing mother, Marge mentions how Mike remains the town's "pride and joy." But she doesn't stop there. "The town gives [the men] things that makes very successful businessmen," she says, ". . . not necessarily husbands or fathers, but a lot of very successful people." She also says, "During the football season I won't hear much from him." A pause. "You have to have tunnel vision." She runs an index finger across the countertop. "I don't have tunnel vision." A few customers later, she relates an anecdote about champagne: "We just had a tasting on the Fourth of July, and you know, *nobody* buys champagne in Dallas in the summertime. So I thought, why not celebrate our country and the return of the [Gulf War] troops?" Her eyes glitter. "I sold three cases in one day!" Another pause. "I don't have to go to the Super Bowl to make me happy. I just have to sell thirty-six bottles of champagne."

She is a wide-eyed woman these days, free as a bird, thinking for herself. Successful. Proud. Happy to sell a few bottles of bubbly on a hot summer day . . . not obsessed with having it poured over her head on national TV. These are the billboards on the long road to recovery for Marge Ditka. "Marge is so strong a person now you can't believe it," says longtime friend and former Ditka teammate Lance Alworth. "She's a beautiful person. But things have not happened in her life the way she would have liked them to happen." Indeed, Marge doesn't date much anymore. Matt believes his mother now "has a thing towards men in general," the thing being perhaps an aversion to making the same mistake twice. So she finds comfort in a good book and in tending to her shrubs after standing on her feet for four and a half hours in a supermarket. She keeps to herself, shunning the lifestyle of the man she once married. "I have an anonymous life and I like that very much," she says. "I've totally built my own separate life." Is she happy? "Yeah," she begins. "I have four great kids. They all turned out great." She pauses. "I guess," says a wistful Marge Ditka, "no one can ask for more than that. That's the way I look at it anyway."

It was Marge who filed for divorce. By '73 she had had enough of separate lives and losing herself in her husband's large shadow. Both Matt and Megan remember being in the car driving somewhere when their mom broke the news. Says Megan, "I remember my mom telling us they were getting a divorce, then saying, 'Let's go to the pet store and get some fish.' I thought, 'Oh, okay, that sounds like fun.' That's all we thought." But it wasn't fun. Far from it. Marge never stopped loving Mike; she just couldn't deal with the absences, the infidelity, and the subjugation of her self. She sold the house, packed up the kids, and headed to California, living near Lance and Marilyn Alworth, in the San Diego suburb of La Mesa, for about a year. Lance had come to Texas in the twilight of a tremendous career started in 1962 with the high-flying San Diego Chargers of the AFL. He was truly a sight to see, all elegance and grace, beyond smooth. They called him Bambi. In 1971 he was traded to the Cowboys and played just two seasons. It was there, however, that he and Marilyn, especially Marilyn, grew close to the Ditkas. Marge needed their comfort and support. "She was very disoriented," Lance Alworth says. "She didn't know where her life was. I think she was struggling with her own identity as a woman."

After a year in California she was still struggling. So were the kids. They missed their friends. So the family moved back to Richardson, right back to Blue Lake Circle, six doors down from the old place. But even in familiar surroundings Marge seemed lost, detached from life. Matt's earliest memories are of a mother who was his best friend, a "perfect human being." "I just remember we always used to go out," he says. "Out to dinner, to the movies. Just me and my mom." Not anymore. "She went through some tough times," says Matt. "She wasn't as caring like she normally was. I was younger but I saw, you know, she changed." Jobs were hard to find. Discipline slipped. Frustrations rose over stretching the $1,500 a month Marge received in child support and alimony. "I think," says Alworth, "she wanted to have somebody come in and sweep her off her feet, after Mike, to have it happen like Mike happened. I think God has other plans for her, that's all."

Soon Marge moved back to San Diego. The kids moved in with Mike and Diana in Plano. At first Marge lived with Marilyn (who had separated from Lance by then). Then Marge moved in with Lance for a month or so, down near the beach in La Jolla. Over time the two lost souls drew closer. "She sort of opened herself up to me and I sorta opened myself up to her. [But] we never had any other kind of relationship other than a great friendship," Lance says. The relationship they shared most, he says today, was with God and how to "get us out of where we were." Marge told Alworth of the changes in her life, how she was beginning to find peace and harmony in something called "Bible doctrine." She had been drawn to the charismatic teachings of a Houston preacher who stressed simple forgiveness for all sins and that Christ died for those sins. Most important, she says she learned what happens in your life *after* you believe, how Bible doctrine opens up your eyes to a better life. It certainly changed two lives. "I'd been searching for something like that all my life," says Alworth, now remarried and a successful San Diego businessman.

And Marge? "What she has now nobody can replace," he says. "I mean I love Mike . . . but what she has, if she had it before, maybe things would have been different."

THE COWBOYS OF THE 1970S (BRILLIANTLY DEPICTED IN SKIP BAYLESS'S best-selling *God's Coach,* a biography of head coach Tom Landry) were little more than false gods, their oversold public image masking all manner of abuse, from drugs to drinking to vicious front office politics. Given all the hype, what sustained the franchise and its success was Landry's love of simple concepts—organization, discipline, and preparation. The unofficial team motto seemed to be "If I can predict you, I can defeat you," but few would have been able to predict that Landry would bring Ditka on staff as special teams and tight ends coach in 1973. Ditka was just another ex-jock at the end of a broken marriage struggling to stay out of debt, hanging on to his football memories, when Landry called. "Have you ever thought about coaching?" Landry is quoted as asking in Ditka's autobiography. In his book Ditka portrays himself as "ecstatic" at the thought about becoming an assistant coach, especially after weighing life as a bar owner against an NFL coaching job. Others weren't so sure. "The whole nagging thing about him,"

says Luksa, "was how can he control players if he can't control himself?"

But it readily became apparent that Landry had been drawn to hiring Ditka on several different levels. One, he had a soft spot for Ditka, his alter ego, or *altar* ego, as Bayless wrote, referring to Landry's born-again bent. Bayless: "I think he was amused by the temper tantrums that Ditka threw, that Landry *wanted* to throw, but couldn't because of his stone-faced image." Beyond the image came the reality, what Bayless calls "the wacko factor," that drew Landry to this human hurricane. Given the departure of Reeves in '73 to private business, Landry's player connection had been severed; he needed a direct link. Enter Ditka. Or so Landry hoped. "Mike was Landry's hit man," says one former Cowboy. "Landry expressed certain opinions in staff meetings, then Mike would come out and let everybody know how Coach Landry felt." The salary was half of what Ditka made his last year as a Cowboy, just $22,000, but Ditka attacked the job with the same zeal he did football.

"He was an inspiration to me and a lot of other players," says former Cowboys running back Doug Dennison, a Ditka favorite who sparked the special teams from 1974 to '78. "He talked the same way all the time. He was like Muhammad Ali—rapid-fire, constant movement, shaking his fist. He was in a class by himself as a coach."

Ditka's method of communication was often as bold as a punch in the nose. He yelled. He threatened. He intimidated. Sometimes all three at the same time, as when he challenged an entire roster of receivers to a fight. One at a time. All at once. It didn't matter to Ditka.

Back in 1973, Drew Pearson was nothing more than a free agent wide receiver out of the University of Tulsa. When he retired eleven years later, he would do so as the Cowboys all-time career reception leader (489 catches). But in '73 he was just a scared college kid, "living each day on the edge," trying to make the team. Pearson remembers a wide-eyed assistant coach, a little "over his head" in technique ordering his troops to buckle their chin straps—"Okay, boys, strap it on"—before summoning the defensive backs down for drills. And we mean *drills.* Gone were the powder-puff pleasantries of the past, the fancy-dancy shadow blocking, replaced by Ditkaball, a scorched-earth philosophy that was equal parts Carl Aschman, George Halas, and Attila the Hun. Ditka never let up, either, spitting chew, screaming a few lines from Papa Bear's book. *"Cocksucker* was a definite favorite of his," Pearson says. "Such as, 'You sorry cocksucker. Why'n hell you out here wasting my time?' All you could think about was getting through the drill." Early on, Ditka showed zero tolerance for mistakes. After Pearson missed a block and a linebacker flung him to the ground during a short-yardage drill, Ditka dressed him down.

"You cocksucker," he snarled, "I don't know why we've got you on the field."

Pearson, fed up with the constant abuse, snapped. "You sorry cocksucker, why don't you help me out, show me how to block instead of cursing me out." Ditka went crazy. "He thought it was a reflection of his coaching," says Pearson. Teammates had to step in to break them up. But contrary to his combative nature Ditka experienced somewhat of a spiritual awakening under Landry, learning he was a very tiny piece of a large, complex operation. "You know," Ditka told Al Michaels during a "Monday Night Football" halftime interview in 1991, "when I worked with the Cowboys was the happiest I've ever been. I was at great peace with myself and my life, and I knew what I wanted to do and I was happy doing it. . . . I think that the happiest I ever was probably was in Dallas. That was a great learning part of my life." In a 1991 book entitled *The Meaning of Life*, Ditka went a step or two further. "People pump up professional athletes saying, 'You're the greatest,' telling you from day one you are it. Then, all of a sudden, you're not *it* anymore. You're part of it. Once I stopped playing ball and became an assistant coach, I started understanding that I was just a small part in this big machine. And it sunk in."

To be sure, for Ditka the adjustment from player to coach was a lot like scrubbing floors with a toothbrush—painfully slow. On game days, several players say, he'd roam the locker room like a caged cat, pacing, pacing, pacing, psyching up. Several times a year—or a game—Ditka had what Pearson calls football "flashbacks," where clipboards got tossed, face masks grabbed, and players, referees, and especially defensive backs were verbally abused. "We're trying to just get through the game," Pearson says, "and he's instigating all this shit, talking about guys' mothers, brothers, fathers. And once he got their attention, he'd just abuse them. Every other word was a cussword."

"He'd be calling players out, cussing them and everything," adds Dennison. "He'd say things like, 'You still can't play. You couldn't play when I was playing, and you still can't play.'"

Ditka had a particular distaste for a head-hunting safety named Kenny Reaves, who had starred for both Atlanta and St. Louis. "There was bad blood between the two," Pearson says. It was so bad that Ditka began one game with a medley of rank remarks, informing Reaves everyone in his family tree, from mother on down, sucked in one form or another. Reaves took absolutely none of it.

"That's all right," he said, adding an epithet or two. "I thought you were supposed to be in retirement. I put you in retirement."

On the sidelines, receivers like Pearson and Bob Hayes looked askance. "We're thinking, man, 'Mike, *shut up*, we've got to play against this guy,' who's getting more pissed off by the minute," Pearson says. "Every chance he gets he [Reaves] spits or jams his finger in my eyes. The more Mike provoked him the more he wanted to kick our butt."

Ditka began coaching the tight ends, but where he really made his mark was special teams. Rank had no privilege with Ditka. First round, last round, free agent, all he cared about was toughness. He reveled in taking the athletic underclass and shaping it into a kind of kamikaze squad intent on inflicting pain and misery. "If you want to play, prove yourself," he informed them right off the bat. "If not, I'll find someone to replace you."

"He gave pride to the team," says Dennison, a free agent out of tiny Kutztown State in Pennsylvania. He also wasn't above resorting to a favorite Aschman or Halas tactic: motivation by fear. Shank a punt, miss a tackle or a block, and Ditka either set a world record in the clipboard toss or tried to chew off part of your face mask. But the guys who made it, made it big. Under Ditka, Butch Johnson became the NFL's best kick and punt returner and cornerback Benny Barnes was the best cover guy in the league. Linebacker Thomas Henderson, tight end Jay Saldi, backup safety Randy Hughes, all made marks on Ditka's special teams.

Off the field, however, despite his profession of personal bliss, Ditka was struggling financially. The SportsPage had lost its draw, the victim of changing tastes, hipper spots, and a hostile racial atmosphere. Both Stevenson and Edwards say the bar was "targeted" by militant black groups because of its popularity, the result being a steady stream of racial incidents: customer harassment, fights, and threats. "I remember one night," says Edwards, "we got a damn bomb threat. The blacks would come in and harass the whites and they'd be fighting back and forth. One night the 'Black Mafia' called up and said they were going to come over and blow it up. So me and Ditka and Dobber went down to the gun store and bought us some .357 pistols and shoulder holsters and wore them in there one night." The bomb threat abated but race was not the only issue. Some patrons, said Edwards, were killed on their way home following ugly arguments started at the bar. And one night the police captured right inside the place a rapist whose picture had appeared in the local newspaper. "Bad publicity," admits Edwards.

Then one day all the worries about Pinnell and Wolf Creek came true. The realtor called Ditka and Dobber—Edwards had wisely sold his interest—into the back office, beginning with, "Fellas, I've got some bad news for ya."

"Oh, yeah," said Ditka, "what is that?"

"The note is due at the bank."

Fine, they said, let's pay it or renew it. Wolf Creek was proving a success. What's the problem?

"Well," said Pinnell, "the bank won't go along with that. The bank wants all its money."

Ditka and Stevenson did some fast math. In round numbers it was about one hundred grand per man. "I've got my third," Pinnell told them. "You guys are going to have to come up with yours."

Neither man had that kind of cash. When they made that point Pinnell said, "Well, I don't know what [the bank] is going to do then. They're probably gonna foreclose." What about collateral? What about the ski resort? All the improvements? Pinnell said things had changed; the bank no longer accepted out-of-state collateral. "Now," says Stevenson, "we're thinking how are we going to get out of this deal. Ben said, the only way out is, I'll go down to the bank and see what I can work out.

"Well, he went down and talked to them, supposedly, and the only way we can get out is if we signed our collateral over to the bank or they would foreclose right away. Our collateral was Wolf Creek. The SportsPage too. [The corporate owner of their Wolf Creek investments.] Later we found out there was a lot of collusion involved in this deal. We signed our collateral over to the bank, which, in turn, went to Ben. The banker was Ben's personal banker and Ben's good friend.

"Did we ever sue? No, never. At that point I think all of us were so naive as to what was going on that we were glad to get out of it. We thought Ben had done us a favor. It didn't dawn on me until a year or so later what the hell really happened to us. That Ben comes up with one hundred percent ownership, and all he had done with the banker was work a little deal. . . . Mike and I ran into each other and he had figured it out about the same time I did. . . . Mike wanted to kill him. Mike was so pissed that he literally wanted to kill him."

Stevenson's voice cracks a bit as he says, "We lost everything we owned on that Wolf Creek deal. Everything we had worked and saved for. We lost all of the land he had got us into. We put Wolf Creek up as collateral. We put SportsPage up as collateral. We put a lot of our own money up too. And we lost it all. I mean every nickel of it." He forces a little laugh. "Here's the ironic part, if there was any justice, because

Ben lived and died by his bride, quote, unquote. Anything he could do for *his bride*. Never his wife, always his bride. Well, he came home one day and his bride had run off with the piano tuner." Stevenson pauses to control his laughter. "So I guess if there is any poetic justice . . . I guess Ben kept coming home and about once a week the piano tuner was there. He couldn't figure out why his piano was so out of tune." [Efforts to reach Pinnell for comment were unsuccessful.]

Soon after, Stevenson left to open up a SportsPage franchise in Shreveport, while Ditka, who was now divorced, continued to carouse around town. He particularly enjoyed hanging out at the hottest spots with the coolest people, places like Wellington's, a North Dallas bar that packed about as many tight bodies and nasty thoughts as humanely possible into one place. At Wellington's, the finest women in Dallas paraded around, autograph pen in one hand, phone number in the other, waiting, watching, hoping to rope themselves a Cowboy. "If you wanted a woman, it was just a matter of showing up. You could get anything you want, you just had to be there," says one team star. "The girls would sit around and wait their turn to approach you for an autograph, so to speak. Then they'd smile and give you their phone number.

"You just had to be there. Mike and [another Cowboy star] used to sit back in VIP section, like kings on a throne, watching. Watching guys like Ditka operate, how they handled women, I had good training. Mike just sat back and waited for them to come to him."

These late-night antics caught up with Ditka, usually around ten every morning during film sessions. As Landry and Reeves, who had rejoined the team in 1974, worked the projector from the middle of the room, Ditka nestled up next to a side wall and waited. As soon as lights went out, so did he. "We used to make fun of him in the meeting," says Pearson. "He'd be taking some serious z's, sleeping so hard his head would be bouncing all the way forward then snap back." In the back of the room receivers Drew Pearson, Bob Hayes, Golden Richards, and Jean Fugett, along with running back Calvin Hill, would giggle like schoolgirls, betting how long it would take Ditka to doze off. Ditka's lack of discipline seemed to have little effect on Ditka's stature with Landry, but then again, he was low man on the totem pole and had nowhere to go but up.

Landry's staff was envied around the league. There was Gene Stallings, the current head coach at the University of Alabama, and behind him Landry's four Rocks of Gibraltar—Jim Myers, Jerry Tubbs, Ernie Stautner, and Ermal Allen—who, between them, would leave the organization with some ninety years of NFL coaching experience. Ditka, Stallings, and Reeves were about the only assistants to challenge Landry—not that he listened much. "Tom never let anyone stray too far off the path," says Ed Hughes, another assistant on Landry's staff. But to hold his attention, coaches were forced to defend every square inch of their game plan.

Sometimes, in the heat of battle, Ditka would bypass Landry and call for a punt block or kickoff reverse. Invariably, it failed. At that point Landry would turn and stalk his way down the sideline, taking a bead on his special teams coach. Ditka would retreat to the outer limits of the coaching box before Landry finally hemmed him in. Staring out at the field of play, barely moving his lips, Landry seethed and said, "If you ever do that again without telling me, you'll be looking for another job."

Before the '74 season, in an effort to gain a stronger voice and greater respect from Landry, Ditka took another long, hard look at himself. He started cutting down on his drinking. He swore off scotch for beer and wine, and he began listening more and more to Diana, who was proving to be just what Ditka needed in his life: smart and sassy, stable and tough-minded, and a steady influence on a man in desperate need of some direction. Sherman Millender, the principal at Plano High School, where Diana eventually worked as a switchboard receptionist from 1978 to '82, paints a picture of a woman much like her future husband. "She was perfect for the job she had with us," says Millender. "As our switchboard receptionist she was the first person anyone who called or came to the school talked to. You had to be a special person in that role. She had to be tough. She had to be blunt. She had to be smart. She had to know how to handle abuse from parents who were upset because she heard from a lot of parents. She learned how to tell people, 'You calm down or I'll hang up on you.' And she did do it."

"A terrific companion," says Jordan. Indeed, it was obvious to Ditka's closest friends that Diana's love and latitude could not have come at a more opportune moment. "When Mike needed somebody, Diana was there," says Reeves. "She loved him so much, she could overlook any shortcoming he might have had. I mean she just absolutely loved him. You know, that's probably what attracted him to her. Whereas probably in the past . . . he had been told how many times, you're a lousy father, you're a lousy daddy, you're, you know, a lousy husband. Here's someone telling him, you're great, you're wonderful. It came at a time when he really needed it."

It showed. The '74 season was postponed by a players strike, but when the team finally assembled, it found a slimmer, more mature Ditka waiting for them. Pouring energy into a new training regimen, he knocked off marathonlike training runs almost every day, arthritic hip and all. It all came in handy when Landry, angered by the strike, ran four weeks of three-a-day sessions lowlighted by a fifteen-minute, before-breakfast trek through sheep shit up a nearby mountain. Talk about fun. Every day Ditka led the charge and won every time. "No matter how in shape we were, nobody ever caught Mike," Pearson says. "He'd always win by a big margin. He'd half-showered by the time everyone else was done."

Yet Diana was not a miracle worker. Ditka may have slowed down some but he was still running well ahead of the party pack. On Saturday nights during football season he could be found in the middle of a poker game with the major domos of the Dallas media, such as Luksa, Blackie Sherrod of the *Dallas Morning News*, games that normally didn't start until eleven P.M. or midnight and ran well into the wee hours of the morn. It was a bachelor party of sorts—cigars, all forms of alcohol, plenty of food, and raucous good humor. In those days, Ditka was the designated pigeon. "A terrible poker player," says former Cowboys public relations director Doug Todd, a regular at the games. "We all won money off him. Mike was the kind of guy who after he's had some wine gets a pair of deuces and somehow strangles them until they become a full house. He wouldn't quit. We got some good pots because of him. He was always in there."

On other nights, particularly during training camp, Ditka would revert to form and party till dawn, often with Reeves, the two of them cruising in at five or six in the morning, slipping on coaching shorts just in time for the run and morning meetings. One incident— allegedly involving a one-punch knockout of a bartender in a place near training camp—forced Ditka, once again, to reassess his life. He recalls having all the material things in life: a nice home, car, celebrity, yet feeling spiritually adrift, hearing the echoes of his Roman Catholic upbringing. An altar boy from grade school through college, Ditka realized he had performed church rituals hundreds of times but rarely felt their full meaning. Landry, on the other hand, seemed to epitomize religious tranquillity. The head coach had never pushed his born-again beliefs on anyone. Sure, he regularly made Fellowship of Christian Athletes speeches, but he kept his feelings private. Yet he was such a powerful figure, so impressive a man, that his assistant coaches couldn't help but make the connection. Former Cowboys coaches say Landry had a calming effect on both Ditka and Reeves. Reeves says it was next to impossible not to be affected by Landry's approach to life. "I think the thing you admired about Coach Landry is that he was never overbearing with his Christianity," he says. "You saw it in him. You couldn't understand why he had this calmness about him in crucial situations. You know this is something that was special about Coach Landry, his faith in the Lord really did make a difference.

"You know," Reeves continues, "Mike had a drinking problem and the reason he was able to turn that drinking problem around was the fact the Lord came forth to him."

Consequently, said Schramm, "Mike started to see the other side of life. He became a great coaching influence." Dennison saw that difference, too, describing how Ditka was "tenderized and nutured" by Landry. "His mannerisms had changed," says the former running back. "He idolized Landry."

Jordan says much the same thing: "Certainly you saw changes in lifestyle. He was still competitive, but he got to be more moderate in his drinking, the women, his verbal attacks on people."

Pearson, however, finds the whole religious-conversion business quite humorous: "If he was a born-again Christian, so was I. I didn't see any adjustment made that made me believe he was born-again. He certainly didn't exemplify it in our meetings or certainly not off the field."

On the field in 1977 Dallas jumped to an 8-0 start, setting the stage for a Super Bowl showdown with the Denver Broncos. On January 15, 1978, Dallas defeated Denver, 27–10, the Cowboys' second world title in six years. Over the next four seasons—1978 through '81—Dallas would play in the NFC Championship game three times, and born-again or not, Ditka occasionally lost touch with coaching reality. Case in point: a nationally televised game against Houston on Thanksgiving Day in '79. A substitute special teams player got confused between the field goal and punt return teams and ran out onto the field at the wrong time. The extra-man penalty kept a critical Oilers drive alive. The Cowboys lost, 30–24, and Ditka quickly broke his previous world record in the clipboard throw, firing the thing so far that Landry warned him, if he did it again, he would be checking the want ads. Another case in point: Ditka was known to put a bounty on opposing players, especially Doug Plank and Gary Fencik, the head-hunting Chicago Bears safeties. "He used to tell us if we took out Plank or Fencik, we got a free dinner at his restaurant," says Pearson.

Yes, *his* restaurant. Ditka was nothing if not persistent when it came to owning eateries. After the SportsPage folded and the ski resort flopped, he somehow bounced back and opened up the Hungry Hunter, a sophisticated dining experience known for its wild game, with items such as buffalo steaks and pheasant on the menu. Problem was Ditka brought along a former SportsPage manager to help run it. "I told him not to take the guy," says Stevenson. "I don't know, the guy had a hold on Mike, but it was from the past. This guy was bad business and Mike, I don't know what he is now, but he was a terrible businessman. So he took the guy as his general operating manager and I think the guy fleeced him pretty good." Good enough to force yet another restaurant failure.

After the '80 season Reeves found the out he was looking for, leaving Dallas to take the head job in Denver. He had been chafing under Landry's iron-fisted control of the team for years, complaining privately about his frustrations. Ditka kept his mouth closed, exhibiting a stronger sense of loyalty. Yet by now he harbored no illusions about the so-called Cowboy mystique. Bayless remembers walking into the media headquarters one day out in Thousand Oaks, stunned to see Ditka watching "All My Children" on television. Turning to Bayless he made reference to the continuing Cowboy soap opera, starring the dueling egos of Landry, Schramm, and vice president of player personnel Gil Brandt, saying, "You don't buy into all the company policy around here, do you?"

"I try not to," said Bayless.

"I like that, I really like that," said Ditka.

In Reeves's place came another boy wonder, John Mackovic, now the head football coach at the University of Texas, and former head coach with the Kansas City Chiefs and the University of Illinois. Ditka got additional duties involving the Cowboy passing game, but Landry held the reins. Serious doubts remained as to whether Ditka had what it takes to be a head coach. The temper was a question mark, certainly. Though Reeves was competitive, he at least, as one club official noted, had "a veneer of civilization." Ditka's sideline outbursts and foul mouth made him out to be something of a loon. He had never coached at any level other than NFL; he had no experience organizing a staff; he had never constructed a game plan; he had never handled the media or evaluated scouting reports. Worse yet, his caveman approach to football was the antithesis of the subtlety and sophistication common in NFL head coaches. "Quite frankly," says one longtime member of the front office staff, "he never looked like a guy who was going to be head-coaching material."

Still, one day Ditka asked Schramm for a favor. He had a dream and wanted a blessing. "I thought it was a long shot," says Schramm, who nonetheless consented to let Ditka apply for a job. So, long shot or not, Ditka sat down and carefully crafted a letter. If opportunity knocks, he thought, I want the Old Man to know I'm ready to answer.

GEORGE HALAS PICKED UP THE PHONE AND PUNCHED IN AN EXTENSION, telling his trusted young aide to hustle on over to his office. It was early December 1981. George Halas, eighty-six years young, the patriarch of the Chicago Bears, was in a cantankerous mood. His team was faltering, missing the heart and what Halas had called the "old zipperoo" of the '63 championship team. Head coach Neill Armstrong was a sweetheart of a man, a "wonderful gentleman" in the words of Gary Fencik, who says Armstrong was a coach cut from the cloth of Bud Grant, who believed ballplayers should be treated as men and motivate themselves. Still, Armstrong liked getting close to his players, coaching the kind of touchy-feely football that, in the NFL, works about as often as the Cubs win the World Series. The '81 team abused him right and left, showing up late for practice ("Had a flat tire, Coach") and missing meetings ("Alarm didn't go off, Coach"). Most players were more concerned about their radio shows and love life than their won-lost record. The last straw, says Fencik, was when one player, a high draft choice who was riding the pine, walked off the field in the second quarter of a game to make a phone call in the locker room. "We figured this guy was gone," recalls Fencik, who would play for the Bears for twelve seasons, several as a star. "The next day Neill said, 'You know, we've had a tough season, we're having a lot of problems, but we have to stay together.' That's when we knew this guy was not getting canned. That's when I think every rat on the ship jumped. If you can't mete out discipline evenly, then you just don't have the respect, and it was at that moment that everyone lost respect for Neill. I'll speak personally. I lost respect for him."

So had Halas. The '81 team would be the twelfth Bears ball club to finish under .500 in the last eighteen years, and after a particularly miserable showing, the Old Man roared at his offense, *"This is a football. Hold on to the *%$%##@ thing!"* It was time for a change.

As young Jerry Vainisi walked through the door, Halas held up two folders. Both were about four fingers thick. "Go through these and organize them for me, will you?" asked Halas, handing them over. Vainisi noted the name on the files. *Ditka,* it said.

The team comptroller and in-house counsel repaired to his office and went to work. Inside the folders were hundreds of handwritten notes on fines, curfew violations, contract negotiations. There were articles, memorandums, investigative and private detective reports on everything from the shooting at Ditka's bowling alley back in 1964 to his active social life. "The kind of files that you could have said we were building a case to either blackmail or sue him," says Vainisi a decade later.

Vainisi was almost to the bottom of the pile when he saw the letter. "One page out of five hundred pieces of paper," Vainisi says. "The other four hundred ninety-nine would have buried Ditka." But not this. My God, thought Vainisi, as he read it. Halas must be considering Ditka as a head-coaching candidate. The counselor mentally flipped through the Rolodex of reasons why it would never work—the meager coaching experience, the hair-trigger temper. Then he read the piece of paper again. Vainisi remembers that "it was a heartfelt, handwritten letter saying he was not applying for Neill Armstrong's job, but that there had been a lot of speculation as to what the Bears were going to do and that he had a dream, much like Halas, of bringing the Bears back to their days of glory, and he would like to be a part of it if at some point it would work out. It was not meant to be taken as anything to undermine Neill. Independently, if the Old Man was going to make a change, Mike wanted to be considered as the guy to replace him."

Halas died of pancreatic cancer on Halloween night, October 31, 1983. He passed away believing he had left his club in the hands of the two men most capable of protecting his legacy. Vainisi was one of them.

Vainisi is now vice president/football management for the World League of American Football. He was hired in May 1990 to scout, evaluate, and eventually, stock the league with talent. His NFL days with the Bears ended abruptly in January 1987 when he was fired by current Bears president and chief executive officer Michael B. McCaskey for the age-old "philosophical differences," of which Vainisi freely admits there were many, most having to do with McCaskey's insufferable ego, penny-pinching mentality, and maddening habit (despite authoring a business book called *The Executive Challenge: Managing Change and Ambiguity*) of prolonging problems rather than solving them. Vainisi, an attorney, filed a grievance over his firing. He took McCaskey and the Bears to NFL arbitration because he had two years left on a contract, a contract signed by Halas, not his interloping grandson. Vainisi says he won every legal issue. By then he was working in Detroit, first as legal counsel (1988) then as vice president of player personnel the next two seasons.

In the summer of 1991, the forty-nine-year-old Vainisi brings to mind the actor Ed Harris, slimmed down and tanned in a pink Ralph Lauren polo shirt trimmed with white stripes. Vainisi's office is hardly Architectural Digest material. It's a little antiseptic actually, the back half decorated with helmets and football memorabilia, the front half, where Vainisi sits, stark yet scenic given the man-made canal just outside his window. The canal gives this Irving, Texas, business park, home of the World League, a soothing sense of calm. Today Vainisi needs the view. Between cups of decaf coffee and handfuls of microwaved popcorn, he has put out one brush fire after another: skittish owners continually call to check on the fragile future of the league. In October of 1991, NFL owners would decide whether to cut $15-million first-year losses or fund the league for another season. Time and time again Vainisi outlines the four options to these nervous Nellies. Fold. Fold for a year and come back. Reduce the number of U.S. teams and bolster Europe. Stay the course and continue funding all ten teams. "I think it will be option number four," he tells the owners confidently. He knows the NFL and particularly Commissioner Paul Tagliabue want to continue the league, hoping an infant international TV market will catch its U.S. counterpart, and team licensing divisions will someday become the multibillion-dollar enterprise that NFL Properties has become. If that's not enough to worry about, the Orlando Thunder head coach called, agonizing over a three-year, $530,000 offer from the Canadian Football League to jump ship and coach in the CFL. That sets off a flurry of phone calls to some NFL types, WLAF commissioner Joe Bailey and the Thunder owner, vacationing in the Bahamas. Vainisi handles it all with aplomb. Why not? There is a lot of football in his blood.

* * *

Jerry Vainisi, Mike Ditka's dearest friend—so close, they became known as "Vainitka"—grew up on Chicago's North Side, one of Tony and Marie Vainisi's three boys (they had a daughter, too). Tony, the tenacious, hard-drinking Italian immigrant, and Marie, his dutiful wife, headed an Italian family bound together by work, willpower, and love. Tony never got much past grade school and, in the beginning, peddled fruits and vegetables to survive. In time he had a grocery/delicatessen, then another, and another, all along Wilson Avenue near the old Sheraton Plaza Hotel, where a lot of Bears lived during the season. Players such as Gene Ronzani, George Musso, and Danny Fortmann would wander in and out all the time, getting sandwiches and sodas, morning coffee, while hollering hello to Jack, Sam, and Jerry. The Vainisis became family—and vice versa. Sometimes the players would even show up at St. George High, a perennial Catholic football power and watch Jack Vainisi, an All-American tackle, tear up the opposition. Jack went on to play at Notre Dame but left college near the end of World War II to help the Allied forces clean up Hitler's mess in Europe. Then Jack got rheumatic fever. It left him with an enlarged heart, ending his athletic career for good. By the time he graduated from Notre Dame in 1950, one of his dad's old customers, the ex-Bear quarterback Ronzani had become head coach of the Green Bay Packers. He hired Jack as a scout.

Every time Jack came home to Chicago he'd take his young brother Jerry up to Evanston to St. George High for an audience with legendary coach Max Bernell. Bernell's eyes widened at the sight of the husky grade schooler. "You coming to St. George, Jer?" he'd say, throwing his arm around the kid. The young boy would nod and say, "Oh, yeah, Coach, all set." But it wasn't. Much as Jerry dreamed of following in his big brother's footsteps, his dad had other plans. The grocery business was booming now, so his father could afford to send his young son away to school just as the doctors and lawyers did. It meant a lot to an immigrant grocer. So off Jerry went to Campion Jesuit High School in Prairie du Chien, Wisconsin, a prayers-in-the-morning, prayers-at-night place whose slogan was "Give Campion a boy and get back a man." Strict? With five-hundred boys? Are you kidding? They had rules for rules. Jerry was in and out of hot water. Throwing butter. Missing curfew. He hated it. He had his sights set on Notre Dame. But every time he came home, his parents and uncles would call him Jack—he looked just like his brother. "No," he'd say, "it's Jerry." He started thinking maybe Notre Dame's not such a good idea, especially since they shut the power off at eleven P.M. every night. He had been in the dark long enough at Campion.

But what really clinched it was when he was seventeen and a ball boy at the Packers' training camp up at St. Norbert College in Wisconsin. It was 1958. Jack was officially the team's business manager, but he was putting in twenty-hour days running the player personnel department, signing players, doing all the scouting and Lord knows what else. He had one dorm room for sleeping, another next door that doubled as his office. One night he slumped in from his office, lamenting how a second string center from his alma mater, of all places, was being offered $20,000 from the Boston team in the new American Football League. "If we gotta start paying back-up centers twenty thousand dollars, the Green Bay Packers will go under."

"I remember that conversation like it was yesterday," says Jerry Vainisi. "We were just sitting there and he was lamenting the amount of money he had to pay. A light went on that night and I said to myself, 'Well, I want to be in professional sports management,' and to me that meant football."

It's a Saturday morning now. He's on his back patio dripping sweat down the front of his World League T-shirt, fresh from a long trip on the treadmill. The house is in a ritzy section of Dallas, a roomy ranch with a pool and rock garden. Vainisi figured contracts were the wave—more like a tidal wave—of the future and that negotiating said contracts would be his entré into Jack's world. So, he thought, who knows contracts? Lawyers. Okay, I'll go to law school. But what about college? Okay, I'll select a college that has a good law school. "That," says Vainisi, "is when I started thinking about going to Georgetown."

He was in his second year at the Washington, D.C., university, studying accounting, just before the big Thanksgiving weekend, when Jack's heart gave out. He was thirty-three years old. At the time, the Packers were 5-4, including a recent Thanksgiving Day defeat in Detroit. Jack, says his brother now, "absolutely lived and died" with the team. Lombardi was the coach by then, in just his second season, and half his starting lineup—guys like Bart Starr, Paul Hornung, Jimmy Taylor, Jerry Kramer, Willie Wood—had been scouted and signed by Jack. They loved him and dedicated the rest of the year to his memory. They ended the regular season 8-4, and before flying off to Philadelphia for the playoff game, Lombardi praised Jack to the fifteen thousand fans who had gathered at the airport to see them off. "A great deal of this team," he said, "is due to Jack Vainisi who is no longer with us."

Jerry never forgot him either. "Everything I did," he says, "I focused around sports management."

He got his degree in accounting, then after a brief foray into

Mike Ditka, Sr., the original Iron Mike. (Beaver County Times files)

Charlotte Ditka, the doting mom who once called her son "a perfect angel." (Beaver County Times/Bill Gilmore)

Family photo of Mike and his first wife, Marge, and their son Mike, Jr., after Ditka's spectacular rookie year. (Beaver County Times files)

The tunnel: The one walk Mike Ditka never wanted to take. (Beaver County Times/Clif Page)

A forlorn Franklin Avenue, the symbol of a boom town gone bust. (Beaver County Times/Dan E. Stauffer)

The King—Carl Aschman, the man who made Mike Ditka. (Beaver County Times/Pete Sabella)

Fiery Frank Marocco, who brought the spirit of Carl Aschman back to Aliquippa High School football. (Beaver County Times/ Pete Sabella)

Downtown Chicago parties hard, celebrating the Bears' Super Bowl victory. (Bill Smith Photography)

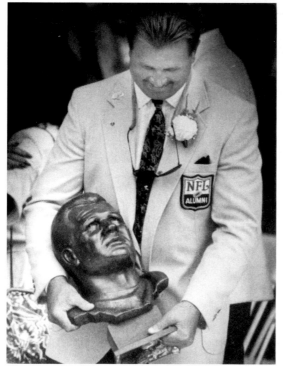

One shining moment— Mike Ditka's induction into the Pro Football Hall of Fame in the summer of 1988. (Deaver County Times/ Brian Plonka)

**The captivating, intimidating coach deals with the media on his
own terms.** (Bill Smith Photography)

**Former Bears
GM Jerry
Vainisi and
Ditka shared
the dream of a
Super Bowl
season.** (Bill
Smith
Photography)

". . . and another thing . . ."—"Da Coach" on the set of "The Mike Ditka Show" during a 1991 taping. (Bill Smith Photography)

Jim McMahon, the punky QB who drove Ditka crazy but was brilliant at picking apart defenses. (Bill Smith Photography)

William "Refrigerator" Perry weighed in at a cool 380 pounds during the 1991 season. (Bill Smith Photography)

Kicker Kevin Butler's roller-coaster year mirrored the Bears' 1991 season. (Bill Smith Photography)

Mike Singletary, the heart and soul of the Chicago Bears. (Bill Smith Photography)

The heroes of '91—quarterback Jim Harbaugh and wide receiver Tom Waddle. (Bill Smith Photography)

Farewell, Mellow Mike. Ditka promises ''no more Mr. Nice Guy'' in 1992. (Bill Smith Photography)

basketball play-by-play, he went to law school, first at Georgetown and then closer to home at Loyola of Chicago. He found it tedious and pretentious and soon turned back to radio where, at the urging of Ray Scott, the voice of the Packers, he enrolled in a thirteen-week broadcasting course. That led to a sports director's job of a local radio station in Monmouth, Illinois, covering high school games. His new bride, Doris, was right at his side, acting as his spotter, pounding the table, cheering the local boys on. Then Doris got pregnant, and despite an offer of a bigger job (and $110 a week) for a station in Galesburg, Illinois, Vainisi realized the gypsy life of a radio reporter wouldn't work for a family man. So he quit and returned to Chicago. He took a job in the tax department of the accounting firm of Arthur Anderson and went to law school at night.

In the summer of 1968, just before his senior year in law school, he flew up to Green Bay and talked to Lombardi about the growing need for in-house counsel given the complexity of contracts and what Vainisi perceived as the future of the NFL. Lombardi liked what he heard, but he said, "If the Green Bay Packers ever have that role, I know another young attorney who would be in line—Vince, junior." As in Vince Lombardi, Jr. "But send me your résumé anyway," the coach insisted, "and I'll pass it around the league." Over the next two years as the NFL merged with the AFL and the league split into conferences, the NFL Management Council was formed to handle player relations. Vainisi barely missed jobs as an assistant to the president of the NFC conference and labor lawyer for the Management Council. He finished second both times but impressed the league with his drive and dedication. Unbeknownst to Vainisi, his name and résumé got passed around among the owners with the preface . . . "If you're ever looking for someone . . ."

One day the phone rang.

"Hello, Jerry?"

"Yes?"

"This is George Halas, Jr. We understand you have an interest in working in football."

"Yes."

"Would you be interested in working or interviewing for a position with the Bears?"

"Yes."

"When would it be convenient for you to come over for an interview?"

"Anytime."

"What about today? Would it be convenient for you today?"

"Sure."

"What time?"

"How about ten minutes."

Vainisi laughs now at the exchange, but he literally dropped his pencil and walked right over to the Bears downtown office. There he met Halas's forty-eight-year-old son, already in his twenty-second year of working in the Bears front office. The Old Man had been stunned when his first child was born in January of 1923. He just naturally assumed it would be a boy. An heir. He left the name blank on the birth certificate. Eventually it was filled in—in pencil. Virginia Marion Halas.

Two years later a boy was born. "Hiya, Mugs," said Halas. The chance remark was picked up. Mugs it was. And Mugs it stayed from his first days as a ball boy right until his ultimely death in 1979. By 1953, at the age of twenty-seven, Mugs was the team treasurer; ten years later he was promoted to team president, just in time to see the Bears win a world title.

"I really want to be a general manager of a football team," Vainisi told Halas Jr. during their interview, one in which the elder Halas popped in and out, sizing up the accountant. "If this job isn't going to prepare me to be a general manager, then let's save us both a lot of wasted time and aggravation."

Halas Jr. answered with a smile, "It will be a good job."

Vainisi was hired on October 1, 1972, and immediately started to update the Bears' prehistoric payroll system, while, every chance he could, sitting in on coaches sessions, listening, learning, observing. The head coach at the time, Abe Gibron, wondered what the hell this *accountant* was doing at all the meetings. "Slow down," suggested Mugs. So Vainisi focused on financial matters, wading, in 1973, into the world of contract negotiations as Mugs started yielding some day-to-day control of the ball club. Mugs was getting worn down by the Bears' futile record since 1963, a miserable marriage, and the tiresome burden of living up to a legendary name. "He was very, very unhappy with what he saw in the mirror," Vainisi says, "and I was taking more and more of a role on a daily basis." It was the role he had always wanted, the role he had dreamed about as a teenager.

Prior to the 1974 season Mugs decided to make some changes. In an emotional outburst he poured out his frustration to his father. "I'm tired of this shit," he said, referring to the team's sad-sack history. "I want to bring in someone to change it." That someone was Jim Finks.

Finks was the executive vice president of the Minnesota Vikings at the time, and he had spent ten years in their front office, the architect of the Vikings' rags-to-riches rise to NFL power—two Super Bowl appearances, five straight NFC Central crowns—and was known around the league as a proud and thorough administrator. "A very efficient operator of a football team," says former Viking public relations director Bill McGrane, who would follow Finks to Chicago as an assistant to the general manager. "I remember him talking about the structure of things. How the system works if you're patient. How the draft works, but you have to give it time."

On September 12, 1974, Finks signed on as executive vice president and general manager of the Bears. Halas Sr. wasn't crazy about the idea, but Mugs argued that while Finks ran the day-to-day duties, Mugs would have the final say. In truth, Finks assumed control of personnel decisions—he and Mugs agreed Finks would take over as president of the club within a year—and went about upgrading coaches, talent, and attitude. At the time, McGrane recalls, "the Bears were looking for ways to lose." Finks waited until the end of the season then fired Gibron—11-30-1 in three years—and replaced him with Jack Pardee. Three years later Chicago was in the playoffs for the first time in fourteen years, but Pardee resigned to chase the Washington Redskins head job, which he got. Finks reached back to Minnesota for a replacement—Vikings defensive coordinator Neill Armstrong. Mugs didn't quarrel with the choice. His life was changing. The Bears were important but not all-important anymore. Now divorced, he had found pleasure and romance in a relationship with a former grade-school classmate, and Vainisi had reworked some club finances so Mugs could finally reap the rewards of his father's team. Better yet, the Bears were in the playoffs again. The Friday before the last regular-season game, he and Vainisi kidded each other about postseason play.

On Sunday, December 16, 1979, a day the Bears won their tenth game of the season, Mugs Halas had a heart attack and died. He was fifty-four years old.

The Old Man's reaction was an overpowering mixture of bitterness and grief. How could Mugs do this to him? To Halas the Bears were something like a Greek coffee shop; only the owner or a member of the immediate family works the cash register. The family controls the money. The family controls the club. He had already told the other side of the family, the McCaskeys, whose son Ed had married Halas's daughter, Virginia, politely but firmly to forget about "working the register" because Grandpa ran the Bears, and when Grandpa was finished, Uncle Mugs would take over. Now Mugs was dead. Halas grieved for six months, a time in which club operations almost ceased to exist. By training camp the following July Halas started to roll out of the fog. He decided he would once again take over the register; he would run the club. With Mugs gone he leaned more and more on Vainisi—much to the dismay of Finks and his backers. "It caused a problem," says Vainisi. "Halas would go to me directly for things that he should have gone to Finks for, and when I would tell him, he'd say, 'If I wanted to ask Jim for it, I would have asked him for it.' Well, it started to cause a deterioration of my relationship with Jim because he knew. Halas ran the club. It was his football team. It was his baby since 1920. To this day I respect Jim and think but for the circumstances we would have worked very, very well. Ultimately I aligned with the Old Man and McCaskey aligned with Finks."

That would be Ed McCaskey, the Bears current Chairman of the Board. "Big Ed," husband of Virginia. As Vainisi explains it, McCaskey had reluctantly been brought into the Bears organization in 1967 and given the gaudy but empty title of vice president and treasurer. His main responsibility at the time, to quote the team's media guide, was "spearheading the club's civic activities and representing the team at the annual owners' meetings." Community involvement turned out to be his football claim to fame. He served on several boards, including a position as chairman of the Brian Piccolo Fund, which generated more than $2 million for cancer research from 1970 to 1987. As for the treasurer's job, it was little more than a mention in the media guide. "He never saw a financial statement," says Vainisi. "When I came in in 1972, I was told to do financial statements. I was to give them directly to Mugs and the Old Man. Or through Mugs to the Old Man. But not to give them to Ed. Not to even let him see them. And he never asked to see them."

McCaskey had three strikes against him from the start. To Halas he was "a ne'er-do-well dance-band singer" who had caught Halas's daughter in a weak moment (they had eloped) and spent too much time at the racetrack. Vainisi says Halas brought McCaskey into the front office "just to watch him and try and control his gambling" and showed no respect whatsoever for his son-in-law. "He hated him," says Vainisi.

"We would have meetings—this was after Mugs died—and McCaskey would sit in on them. We'd get to a part of the meetings and the Old Man would excuse Ed, saying, 'That's okay now, Ed, you can go.' He'd leave and he'd wait at the door. The Old Man . . . would be waiting for him to go. The door would close and it was like a chime. 'There goes the stupidest son of a bitch I've ever met in my life.' Like it was a recording. Every time."

At one point, however, the McCaskeys made what Vainisi now calls "a run at Halas." They wanted to bring in one of Virginia and Ed's eleven children, Michael, as an assistant general manager or some appropriate position to train under Finks in hopes, the family felt, of establishing a new line of succession. An heir to the throne. From a distance Michael appeared an inspired choice. He was a walking, talking Renaissance man. He had studied the classics at Yale. He had spent two years in the Peace Corps in Ethiopia and taught at both UCLA and Harvard Business School, earned a Ph.D. in business, and authored a book on management. He and his wife, Nancy, had created their own management-consulting company. He had grown up around the team, worked as a ball boy at training camp, but according to a January 1992 cover story in the *Chicago Tribune Magazine* "hardly seemed like a kid anxious to take over his grandfather's empire."

Instead, the story goes, he carried textbooks during rides to and from Wrigley Field. He considered the priesthood and spent three years at a preparatory seminary. "It would be a way to help people," McCaskey told writer Michael G. Glab. "Religion has always been a serious aspect of our family's life." Nonetheless he left the seminary and played high school football (backup quarterback and starting defensive back) before lettering two years in the early sixties as a wide receiver at Yale. (According to the Yale Sports Information Office, McCaskey caught 3 passes for 34 yards his junior year. The next season he was listed as a flanker but never caught a pass and does not show up on the team statistics from that season.)

At Yale he studied philosophy and psychology. "Philosophy addresses the very fundamental questions of life," he told Glab. "Psychology is learning about how people behave. That's exciting to me."

George Stanley Halas, Sr., fancied himself something of a modern-day football philosopher and psychologist. So when Virginia and Ed made noises about bringing Michael into the organization, Halas balked. He knew football talent. Lord knows he had scouted, signed, coached, and managed enough of it in his life. Uh-uh, he said. Not this kid. As much as Halas loved his grandchild, the word was he didn't respect him, not when it came to football. "He said he had no street smarts," says Vainisi.

It was December 1981, a week before Christmas, when Vainisi finally finished organizing the Ditka folders, putting all the letters and reports and memorandums in reverse chronological order. The most recent, Ditka's letter to Halas, was on top.

Shortly after Christmas Halas made his move. He called a press conference. Speculation ran wild. Was he going to fire Armstrong?

Despite a 6-10 record the Bears had won their last three games. Would he hire defensive coordinator Buddy Ryan? Ryan, a weather-beaten, pipe-smoking, foulmouthed Okie who looked more like a farmer than a football coach, had built almost a cult following on the defensive side of the football. The veterans loved his irascible charm and his undying loyalty. Finks was pushing to retain Armstrong, or at least not dangle the noose too long. Finks felt it was his choice. But Halas, now eighty-six and caught in cancer's web, had one more trick up his sleeve. He had asked one of his assistant coaches, Jim Dooley, to "observe and evaluate" the coaching staff ("to be his spy," says Vainisi), and Dooley's report clearly indicated that Ryan, as the players implored, was an asset worth keeping. Ryan had, in fact, been campaigning for the head coaching job. So when Halas called the press conference at the Bears offices downtown, early speculation had the Okie taking over. Halas announced Ryan was being retained for three more years as defensive coordinator. Reporters ignored the bulletin and peppered Halas and Ryan with questions about the head coaching post. Had Buddy wanted it? What about Neill? Are you disappointed, Buddy? How do you feel? Ryan kept his cool. About a week later Armstrong was fired.

What now? When the name of a forty-two-year-old Dallas assistant coach surfaced the reaction was as swift as it was savage. The local press took both Halas and Ditka apart. Below a headline that blared "Hiring Ditka Would Be Madness," the *Sun-Times* influential sports columnist John Schulian gave Ditka both barrels. He opened with an anecdote of Ditka cussing out an official and went downhill from there. He blasted Halas for the "inhumane" firing of Armstrong and said that "all Mike Ditka has shown he can do . . . is throw a clipboard and tantrums." He dubbed Ditka's hiring by Landry "a charity case."

"Again and again," Schulian wrote, "you are confronted with visions of him throwing clipboards and cursing officials when he should be sending in the next play on offense or calling the next defense. He is, after all, a creature of brute force, the quintessential Midway Monster, and such is not the stuff head coaches are made of."

On January 20, 1982, another downtown press conference was called. This time the Dallas assistant was seated next to Halas, so quiet and intense, he was a coiled spring set to explode. It didn't matter he would inherit a defensive staff he didn't know led by a coordinator backed by a major show of support by the team owner; or that players cared more about stock plans than game plans. None of it mattered. Halas wanted a coach with "mental heat," someone to put the fear of God back into his players, to revive the memory of his dying Bears, and that's exactly what he got. Critics suggested the reason the new head coach was hired was because he came so cheap. None of which mattered to Mike Ditka, the prodigal son. He was home, back in Chicago, back with the Bears, now coaching the only team—in the only town—he ever wanted to coach.

MIKE DITKA MOTIONED FOR ONE OF HIS ASSISTANT COACHES TO CALL ROLL. *Roll.*

"Well, fellas," he began when the troops were all present and accounted for, "we can only keep forty-nine and we're going to get out there and we're going to see who's best. We're going to separate the men from the boys around here. See who wants to work and who doesn't. If you don't want to win, if you don't want to sacrifice, then you don't want to be here."

They began to find out in the spring of 1982 in Scottsdale, Arizona, the thermometer pushing ninety, Ditka pushing to whip his ball club into shape. Fencik says he'll never forget the first Ditka speech, not an hour earlier, a "good news, bad news" number that wiped the carefree Armstrong era away forever. "The good news," Ditka told them, "is our goal to win the division and then get to the championship game and then win the most important game of our life, and that's the Super Bowl.

"But the bad news is that as I look at you, half of you won't be there when we get there."

He ran them to death and back, patiently and methodically mixing dashes with distance, watching who had heart and who didn't, silently separating the winners from the losers, looking inside their souls.

It was a coaching style rooted in Aschman, Halas, Landry, and Lombardi, who Ditka admired. It might as well have been Raccoon

Creek State Park as Scottsdale. "Too many guys," he warned, "have too many things going on outside football." It was a surprising sentiment from a former player who owned bowling alleys, bars, restaurants, and played more cards than Amarillo Slim and as much golf as Arnold Palmer. But nobody knew enough about Ditka then to notice the contradiction, or even care. He was digging a new foundation for this franchise or, better yet, excavating an old one. The golden rule, he told them, was you played by his. When Rickey Watts, a wide receiver who averaged 17.4 yards per catch his first four seasons with the Bears, missed the first day of minicamp, Ditka cut him quicker than a price tag on new pair of pants. He preached pride, pride in yourself, in your teammates, pride, most of all, in being a Chicago Bear. Turn around, he told them, and tell the guy behind you that you love him. We're going to the Super Bowl, he predicted, maybe not this year or next, but we're going. You make the choice. Either get with the program and get on the train or hop off now before I push you.

"You don't win games just with defense," he told them. "It takes offense, special teams. We're not going to win until *everyone* does his job, because winning and losing depends on all three." Invariably, however, it depends on chemistry, and Ditka was having trouble passing that test when it came to his coaching staff. He was so hell-bent to take the Bears job he would have accepted Benny and the Jets as his assistants, and in Ditka's mind it didn't matter all that much anyway. Much like Aschman, from the beginning he has set himself apart from his coaches, partly because of ego, partly because of personality. "He's never been much with other coaches," says Hughes. That first season Ditka was reluctant to make changes in his offensive staff without a proper evaluation; his only move of note was replacing Ted Marchibroda, who quit as offensive coordinator, replaced by the gifted Hughes from Dallas. Ditka tried to slip a Dallas scout by the name of Steve Kazor into the organization as his administrative assistant. Landry and then Reeves always had assistants, gofers, if you will, to handle day-to-day duties. Ditka wanted one too. Halas balked. "He couldn't sell it to the Old Man without giving him [Kazor] some responsibility," says Vainisi, "so Ditka made Kazor the special teams coach and told the Old Man he [Ditka] would run the special teams. Kazor's a horseshit special teams coach, but he was a guy who works the phones, get information, and he had a pipeline to the coach."

The pipeline clogged continually between Ryan and Ditka, who had stormed into Chicago with the bright idea of shifting the Bears defense to a Dallas 3-4 "Flex" defense. Ryan told Ditka he could flex himself for all he cared, but he wasn't about to mimic anybody else. If that's what Ditka wanted, well, just send me my checks in the mail, said Ryan. Defense was hardly the only issue. Ditka lived and breathed the total team concept, everyone working together for a common cause. He hated the fact defensive backs and linebackers on his own team were cheap-shotting receivers in practice. Ryan stressed the Buddy System, an "offense versus defense" philosophy predicated on his "46" defense.

The 46 defense had been named after Ryan's head-hunting safety Doug Plank's uniform number. The defense was a madcap mixture of about a dozen formations and eighty different coverages Ryan had dreamed up back in 1978. The 46 wasn't actually the 4 or 6 of anything but more like an 8-2-1 lineup that specialized in creating matchups—one-on-one or overloads—that opened up blitz possibilities. The key was controlling the opposing offensive tackles with three defensive linemen. If that happened, the defense had a rocket trip to the quarterback. Yet for all its perceived complexity, the beauty of the 46 was its simplicity, flexibility, and adaptability. Coverages could change with every offensive shift, every audible.

"Now I like Buddy," Vainisi adds, "and I consider Buddy a friend, but I have a real problem when you're trying to run an organization, a football organization. . . . Buddy coaches a system that undermines the overall organization because of the fact that he has certain players that fit the system, and he'll pass up better players because they don't fit his system. Ryan would go with the veteran player who could grasp his system and learn and execute it at the expense of having better athletes on the field.

"There was tension from day one," says Vainisi, "and Ryan did nothing but fuel it."

Finks had a philosophy, too, and wasted no time putting Ditka in his place. In Finks's book, scouts scout, coaches coach, and management manages. He made it clear from day one he held final say on all player personnel decisions—hardly a cause for concern given his track record in Minnesota. The year before, 1981, Finks had drafted USC tackle Keith Van Horne, Singletary, and Ohio State safety Todd Bell, three future stars, in the first four rounds.

For the '82 draft, Finks, Vainisi, and Ditka all agreed the number one need was at quarterback. They also agreed that quarterback was to be Jim McMahon of Brigham Young University.

McMahon had everything you want in a great quarterback—and if the local press had a vote, little in what you'd want as a human being.

163

"He's an asshole," seemed to summarize their sentiment. He was outspoken and obnoxious, a head-butting, headband-wearing original who gladly traveled to his own set of tunes. He partied hard and said things like, "If you've got forty-five beer-drinking fools who love each other, you've got a good chance of having a good football team." He would rather kiss a cockroach than somebody's behind. His career statistics at BYU were staggering: seventy-one NCAA Division I passing and total offense records; an all-time best career-passing efficiency record of 156.9 and a 62 percent pass-completion percentage for 9,536 yards and 84 touchdowns. As a junior, in 1980, he had thrown 47 touchdown passes in just twelve games. But his most striking statistic was this: he averaged 14.6 yards for every completion, amazing because in four years at BYU, McMahon had completed 653 passes of 1,060 attempts (his 9 yards per attempt is also a NCAA record). In essence, that meant not only did McMahon complete nearly 62 percent of his passes, but he wasn't dumping the ball off to his backs or tight ends all day. This guy had both the touch and the gonads to go deep.

What separated McMahon from other quarterbacks was never so much the physical skills, which were hardly reminiscent of an Everett or Elway, but his uncanny, almost psychic ability to read coverages and adjust. "To me Jim's biggest assets were always his brains, the audible play," says Hughes, the team's offensive coordinator for seven years. McMahon's other undeniable asset was the Pied Piper effect he had on his teammates, the way his quirky, idiosyncratic style and death-do-us-part attitude raised the level of other people's play. Before his welcome wore thin in the late 1980s, to McMahon's teammates and admirers he was an antihero straight out of Marvel comics who ran his fingers across the chalkboard of life and got away with it. No. 9 sent out global messages ("POW-MIA") via headband; he was the punky QB perfect for the cover of *Rolling Stone*. McMahon's teammates believed in him, and for many years, so did Ditka, who tolerated McMahon's rock-star status because Ditka knew that when No. 9 was healthy, nobody beat his Bears.

Vainisi has a theory about that, what might be called the ABCs of Bear football: "I really believe the team played to three different levels. We played to a C level if we thought McMahon was on the bench but could possibly come in and play. That no matter how poorly we played, he would come in and salvage the day. We played to a B level if he wasn't available and was completely out, so the players had to pull themselves up by their bootstraps and make up for the difference. Then we played to an A level when he was in there in command of the offense and running the team." In fact, from 1984 through 1988, the Bears were 35-3 with McMahon starting behind center, and during one stretch from October 21, 1984, until November 16, 1987, he was a perfect 25-0.

But at the start of training camp in 1982, McMahon was just another rookie weathering a freak summer storm named Ditka. "He was wacko," says Vainisi. The neophyte coach saw sloth and ego at every turn, blatant violation of team rules, players whining about playing time, complaining about injuries. "Ah, Christ," bristled Ditka after a player broke his jaw, "all you have to do is wire that son of a bitch up and he'll play Sunday." Ditka had no time for nonbelievers, for pantywaists. Hadn't he played with dislocated shoulders? Bad knees? A mangled foot? Says Vainisi, "He felt that everybody should take the game the same way, and play with the same kind of intensity he did." A rebellion simmered but Ditka beat it down by sheer force of will, just as he had a thousand opponents in his life. *One-on-one. You and me. Let's see who's best.* Ditka went with the only real offensive system he knew—the multiple sets favored by Landry in Dallas. Ditka copied the same terminology and numbering system for plays. But it was a miserable move if for no other reason than the Bears had neither the brains nor talent to pull it off, especially since neither Bear quarterback, Vince Evans or Bob Avellini, reminded anyone of Roger Staubach. "Vince had the arm and no brains, and Bob had the brains but no arm," says Hughes with a smile.

With Avellini starting at quarterback the Bears lost the first two games of Ditka's coaching career, 17–10 at Detroit followed by a 10–0 shutout at home to New Orleans. Talk about ugly. The Bears looked as if they were auditioning for "NFL Bloopers." On offense, players were lining up wrong and receivers looked as if they needed Seeing Eye dogs. Pop Warner teams displayed more heart and discipline. The New Orleans loss was pitiful, "a horrible, terrible mess" in the memory of Hughes, who says, "It looked like our team quit before it got on the field." Ditka screamed and cussed and labeled them all cowards. The players rolled their eyes, wondering how long this maniac would be around. Then they walked out the door and didn't come back for eight weeks. No, it was nothing personal, although given Ditka's state it could well have been. It was actually a contract dispute, a labor walkout that lasted two months. In retrospect, says Vainisi, it proved the best thing that ever happened to Ditka because it allowed him to reassess, step back from the mess he was making and fix it. "In my opinion," says Vainisi, "it gave him a very short first season, but it gave him a first season. Then he had an off-season to reflect on it. One thing about Mike. You can tell him he's full of shit. You can tell Mike he's wrong. I mean he may not agree with you and argue with you and get all frustrated over it. But he'll carry it with him and he will think about it at some point, and he'll be the first one to tell you, 'I thought about it, and you know, you're right.''

Which is exactly what Ditka did. He was obviously ill prepared for strategic planning and game plans, so he fell back on his personality to pull him through. The result was overkill—on the sidelines, in the locker room, on the practice field. To his credit, Ditka realized his mistake and softened his approach. He listened more and sought to establish better communication. But his most important decision had to do with McMahon. "If the future is with McMahon," he told Vainisi, "there's no use developing these other guys. Let's develop him and go with what we've got.''

McMahon started the next seven games and, as expected, rode a roller coaster, but ended with far more peaks than valleys. He completed 58 percent of his passes, earning the highest rookie quarterback rating in the league (80.1) and the ninth best overall in the league. UPI voted him NFC Rookie of the Year. The Bears, meanwhile, rallied to win three of their last five games and just missed the playoffs. "Forget the playoffs," says Vainisi today, "nobody cared about that. The point is we were much improved the second half of the season because of his change in approach and going with McMahon.''

In April 1983, Ditka, Finks, and then–Pro Scouting Director Bill Tobin congregated in the second-floor conference room at Halas Hall for a meeting of the minds. Finks was a firm believer in the draft, a patient man who eschewed trades because, as McGrane explains, "Jim felt nobody gave you a player with the express purpose of making you better; something was generally wrong." In the room were all three Bear regional scouts, the second-smallest contingent in the league behind cheapskate Cincinnati, which employed one, count 'em, one full-time college scout. And while the Bears made frequent use of the BLESTO scouting combine, funded by a consortium of NFL clubs, up until 1984, Tobin, Jim Parmer, and Don King were responsible for scouting the entire country, more than eight hundred NCAA football programs. Today the Bears employ four regional scouts, half of what most NFL clubs average, and a far cry from the likes of Denver or the Buffalo Bills, who put as many as twenty scouts on the road at one time. Which is why in 1991, for example, Buffalo boasted several starters from such schools as Kutztown State, Chadron State, Wabash, and Benedictine, collegiate outposts Bears scouts rarely, if ever, visit. The Bears 1991 roster, in contrast, featured thirty-eight players from the top six conferences (ACC, Southwestern, Southeast, Big 10, Big Eight, and Pac-10) and Notre Dame. The Bears also shy away from the high-tech gadgetry creeping into pro sports, the "black boxes" for intelligence and dexterity testing, the psychological profiles. "We're pretty much horse and buggy compared to teams like the Giants," says King, who retired in May of 1991 after seven years with the team and eighteen as a pro scout. "We stagger around with three guys, but the high-tech stuff . . . that doesn't always work. It boils down to guys who can block and tackle."

In the Bears war room come draft time there is generally a huge board with seven hundred names. The players are listed by position and ranking by the Bears scouting department. Chances are the higher-ranked players had three "looks" or personal evaluations and a complete analysis of their junior and senior seasons. The 1983 draft was crucial because the Bears had six choices in the first four rounds, including two No. 1 picks. So as the coaches and staff gathered around the conference table, King says, the mandate was clear—don't waste a single pick. In years past the team had always operated under the familiar "best player available" theory, drafting great athletes regardless of position. But in the '83 powwow Ditka wanted more than just pure ability. "We were looking for emotional players," says King. "Competitors, hard-hitters, guys with a look in their eye."

Ditka, says King, never attempted to impose his will on the scouting staff, which wouldn't have worked much anyway. Finks and Tobin both frowned on coaches suddenly becoming draft experts at the eleventh hour, especially Tobin, who made it a point to see the top one hundred players himself. As in Dallas, Ditka was willing to accept whatever player the scouts deemed best. He listened as King or Toby, as Tobin is called, talked about how there might be ten guys in the entire country who could start for the Bears as rookies; maybe forty after two years, and seventy-five after three. "Tell me about the ten guys," said Ditka. Nine times out of ten he boiled it all down to one question:

"Is this guy a Bear?"

"He was always looking for that kind of mentality," recalls King, who now spends his days fishing for salmon and red snapper in the Pacific Northwest. "You've got to be some kind of nut to play in Soldier Field in January."

So it was the Bears made these selections in the 1983 draft:

1a. Covert, Jim, T, Pittsburgh
1b. Gault, Willie, WR, Tennessee
2. Richardson, Mike, DB, Arizona State
3. Duerson, Dave, DB, Notre Dame
4a. Thayer, Tom, C, Notre Dame
4b. Dunsmore, Pat, TE, Drake
5. (Choice to New England)
6. (Choice to Cleveland)
7. (Choice to Cleveland)
8a. Dent, Richard, DE, Tennessee State
8b. Bortz, Mark, DT, Iowa
9a. Fada, Rob, G, Pittsburgh
9b. Zavagnin, Mark, LB, Notre Dame
10. Hutchison, Anthony, RB, Texas Tech
11. Worthy, Gary, RB, Wilmington
12a. Williams, Oliver, WR, Illinois
12b. (Choice to San Diego)

It was a work of art, really, something to hang on the wall and admire for years to come. Overall the top nine draft choices from Covert to Fada made the club. Seven of the choices—Covert, Gault, Richardson, Duerson, Thayer, Dent, and Bortz—eventually started on the Super Bowl team of '85. "That '83 draft is really the draft that made the Bears," says Vainisi. Covert was big enough (6'4", 280) to blot out the sun, yet he was blessed with tap dancer's feet. This offensive tackle from the University of Pittsburgh, who listed Twain, Melville, and Hemingway as his favorite authors, was a two-time All-American and never seemed out of control or off balance, one reason he allowed just three quarterbacks sacks in his final three college seasons and none his senior year. He was, absolutely, a cornerstone for Ditka's new foundation. Covert would eventually start 108 of 110 games and be voted to the NFL's Team of the '80s by the Pro Football Hall of Fame Board of Selectors. In one quick pick the Bears had found a rock-solid way to control a pass rush and protect the backside of their quarterback.

The second pick, Gault, plugged another gaping hole, a deep threat to take the pressure off the running game, principally, Payton, the game's all-time leading rusher, while giving McMahon a viable passing option. The next two picks, Richardson and Duerson, eventually formed half the Bears starting defensive backfield. By 1985, Thayer, a four-year letterman at Notre Dame, and Bortz, an all–Big 10 defensive tackle, joined Covert and Van Horne and Hilgenberg to form the heart and soul of the football team.

Dent was, perhaps, the biggest risk. At Tennessee State, a school known for its pass rushers, he had set a career mark with 39 sacks, despite carrying just 230 pounds on his six-five frame. His practice habits left much to be desired and so did his body—more legs and butt than anything else, but Tobin liked his awesome first step and power rush. And besides, concedes King, "when it's your eighth-rounder, you can gamble a little bit."

Dent and Gault and Bortz and Thayer wouldn't really pay off for two more years, but the 1983 season showed signs the Bears were finally headed in the right direction. It wasn't easy. The front office was hardly a cohesive unit, with Finks increasingly concerned that Halas was cutting him off in favor of Vainisi. In fact, in the spring of '83 shortly before the draft, Halas had asked the young comptroller to assume contract negotiations, a challenge Finks successfully beat back, at the expense of increased paranoia and turf wars around the office. Still, by August, when all the draft choices were signed, Finks had had enough. He called McGrane into his office on the twenty-fourth of August. "Bill, you're a good writer," he said. "I need you to write something for me."

"What?" said McGrane.

"I quit."

McGrane went back to his office and knocked off a one-paragraph statement, "boiler-plate stuff," he says today, something about how Finks was resigning in the best interest of all parties concerned. Actually, says McGrane, who left the team in 1989, Finks could have predicted his future from the day Ditka was hired. Finks, remember, is a proud man (he is now the president of the New Orleans Saints and nearly became NFL Commissioner before Paul Tagliabue). "Jim felt you either do the duties spelled out in the contract or you don't," says McGrane. "Finks had hired both Pardee and Armstrong. But when Halas hired Ditka, Finks felt Halas no longer had confidence in his ability to operate the team. Jim is a guy who has strong beliefs in his own talents."

That night Vainisi was ready to leave the downtown office when the phone rang. It was Halas.

"Where are you going?" he asked.

Vainisi said, "Up to training camp."

"Would you mind stopping by my apartment before you go."

Papa Bear was propped up in his hospital-style bed in pajamas and robe when Vainisi arrived. Halas made some small talk then got to the point: "Are you aware that Jim Finks is resigning?"

Vainisi hadn't heard a thing.

169

"What do you think I should do," asked the eighty-seven-year-old owner.

"I think you should accept his resignation. I mean, he's telling you he doesn't want to be here. Don't force him to stay here."

"Get him on the phone for me."

Now when Finks answered the phone, the Old Man wanted to know why Finks hadn't told him personally. The call was quick and cool, Halas telling Vainisi to prepare a short press release announcing Finks's decision. Just as McGrane had done earlier in the day, Vainisi knocked one off and handed it to Halas. "Now," said Halas after he'd approved it, "in the next paragraph announce that I'm naming you the general manager to succeed Finks."

Vainisi was stunned.

Have you told Virginia? he asked. Halas said no. So they got her on the line next and father told daughter his wishes.

"Very well," said Virginia.

The next call went up to Halas Hall, to public relations director Patrick McCaskey, another of Ed and Virginia's boys.

"I have a statement for you from Mr. Halas to read after Jim's announcement," Vainisi told him. "Write what I'm telling you down word for word. I'll be available to meet with the media afterward."

So, as the media gathered in the basement classroom at Halas Hall, Finks stood behind a podium and announced his decision. He spoke for five minutes, no more, adding little to his prepared statement. Then he walked away.

Now it was Big Ed's turn to meet the press that was hungry for some answers. Soon after Pat McCaskey walked in the room and handed his father a single typed sheet of paper. "I just got handed a note from George Halas," Ed said, speaking before reading. When he was finished reading about Vainisi, McGrane says, "Ed about fell off the podium."

Before the night was through, Vainisi, armed with a new five-year contract offer, not only met with the media but briefly with Ditka, McGrane, and most importantly, the McCaskeys in a preemptive attempt to quiet any dissention. He spoke of unity and efforts to avoid all the infighting. The next morning he told Ditka he wanted to talk to the team—five minutes, no more. "The switch from Finks will have no bearing on you," he told the players, who were nearing the end of training camp. "But from now on everything will be totally open around here. What Mike knows, I will know, and what I know, he will know. No more ends against the middle. We're all here for one purpose, and one purpose only." He paused before delivering the last

170

line. "As long as we're moving in that direction, you will have my complete support."

Vainisi was no sooner out the door than Singletary was at his side. Singletary, the ultimate team player, was fired up.

"I want to negotiate an extension on my contract," he said.

Vainisi had one more person he wanted to see. For two years now he'd been observing the man, watching him "fight a thousand different demons" in the ever-changing form of the press, his players, his temper, his drinking, and even members of his own organization. Vainisi made it clear, the infighting would stop. No more Halas faction, Finks faction, Ditka faction. "I said from this day forward we are united in one purpose only, and that's to bring the Bears to the Super Bowl," Vainisi said. "I said I'd do anything possible to help you win. That was the only concern I had in life." But Vainisi also warned Ditka he was going to have to change his approach and drop the madman act. This creating a controversy every single day, at every single practice, for the sole purpose of motivating your football team had to stop. One day it was a holdout, the next day lack of effort, the next the sorry facilities. You are diverting attention from the task at hand.

"Your technique is you coach by crisis," Vainisi told Ditka. "You always have to have some crisis to overcome. It diverts attention from the game itself. The players don't understand it. They think you're crazy."

Ditka didn't care. Who was this guy anyway? What did he know? How badly did he really want to win? Seven games into the '83 season, five of them losses, Ditka found out. It was Saturday night before a game against the Eagles in Philadelphia and the pressure was building again. Ditka wasn't irrational, exactly, but he was bouncing from one bizarre incident to the next, showing a lack of control in himself that ultimately affected his football team. It began, in earnest, in late September. That's when he broke his hand smashing a locker after a 22–19 overtime loss to the Colts in Baltimore, the second OT defeat in two weeks. In a fit of pique he had yanked Covert, playing only his fourth game, off the field and screamed at wide receiver Ken Margerum for dropping a pass. During a 23–14 loss to Minnesota he berated officials and raged again at his players. He benched McMahon. Evans came in and fumbled and got blasted. The players had had enough. Margerum, the Stanford grad and possessor of some of the best hands in pro football—and possibly, the slowest feet—said these tantrums were counterproductive; they were eroding the players' confidence. Closed-door meetings followed and—voilà!—yet another new Ditka emerged. "I'll be the most relaxed guy you've ever seen," he was quoted that week. "If I fall asleep on the sideline, I don't want anybody to say anything."

It was a nice act for a while, but Ditka, as usual, couldn't sustain it. Winning remained his sole energy source, a point that became abundantly clear when "the most relaxed guy you've ever seen" ordered rookie Duerson to "go get" Detroit Lions kicker Eddie Murray, after Ditka mistakenly assumed Murray and Lion quarterback Eric Hipple had faked a field goal late in an eventual 31–17 win over the Bears and Hipple scrambled for an 8-yard score. Ditka felt his team was being shown up; he retaliated in a move that saw him chastised for cheap tactics from one coast to the other. Ditka would eventually receive a written reprimand from NFL Commissioner Pete Rozelle for his action.

So it was on that Saturday night before the Philadelphia game, with the Bears 2-5, that Vainisi sat down with Ditka at dinner. In the years to come, Saturday nights on the road would be their night together. A favorite restaurant. A fine bottle of wine. Relaxing conversation between two men who could have been brothers. But not this night. Today Vainisi says this dinner "may have been the one time we had a very direct conversation where I laid it on him and told him and he knew." Translation: Vainisi had seen enough. If Ditka didn't change, changes would be made.

"You know," Vainisi told Ditka that night, "I have worked all my life to become a general manager of a football team. I never believed it would be the Chicago Bears, which, in my opinion, makes the accomplishment even better, and I'm not going to let you do anything to screw that up." Catching Ditka by surprise, Vainisi kept on talking. "Now, I'll help you, work with you, do anything I can to help you win football games, but you have to work with me. You have to control yourself. You can't just go off on a tangent and carry on like you're doing. Work with me and you'll get the world."

Ditka stared across the dinner table.

The GM glared right back. "Do you understand me?"

"Yeah, I do."

Years later, referring to that night, Vainisi says, "I wasn't calling his bluff. I was just trying to tell him that this was as much my dream as it was his."

If so, it was still in the formative stage as the Bears continued to display an almost supernatural ability to drop passes, miss tackles, and false-start. The natives were getting restless. One customer, getting in the spirit of the season, sat in the first row of the north end zone for a

Halloween game against the Lions with a pumpkin that had the words GO BEARS carved into it. Right below was a banner that read DITKA'S HAUNTED HOUSE. That it was. The Lions won 38–17 to drop the Bears to 3-6, the same record as the strike season in '82. Ditka was escorted off the field by three beefy security guards. Fans were throwing beer, cussing him out. But Vainisi's words held meaning. Ditka kept his temper in check. Most of the game he had stood on the sideline, staring at the artificial turf. Now in the media tent he held his anger inside. "They've got a lot of pride," he said of his players. "Unfortunately that's hard to explain to people when something like today happens."

"I think he's responding very well, considering," Evans told the press, referring to Ditka. "The one thing he said after we came off the field was, 'Hey, we've got to stick together.' I can't agree with him more. It's so easy to give up. He's a guy who doesn't give up. I just hope that kind of personality is conveyed throughout the team."

A week later Old Man Halas died. Ditka had kept a vigil at his bedside right up until the end. Just before Halas passed away, he surprised Ditka with a bottle of Dom Pérignon champagne. Attached was a note that said, "Mike, don't open until you win the Super Bowl."

It was up to Ditka and Vainisi now to carry on the Old Man's vision. Two men, destined to become allies, business partners, and best of friends. "There was a love relationship between the two of us in the proper sense and everything," Vainisi says. "There was just a real understanding, a close bond between us. We could greet each other and we both understood, without having to say it most of the time, what it was we wanted. I'm not talking about what the Bears needed. I'm not talking about other things in life. But we both knew we would be there, we would support each other and do the things necessary to accomplish the goal. Which was to do anything to make the Bears winners."

It would prove to be anything but easy.

18

THE BUSES INCHED UP LASALLE DRIVING TOWARD THE DALEY CENTER AND THE biggest victory party Chicago had ever seen. More than a million fans swarmed the sidewalks and streets, oblivious, it seemed, to the minus-thirty-degree windchill and arctic gusts. Hell, in a way, it was a perfect day! *Bears weather!* Confetti and ticker tape swirled in crazy patterns. Air horns honked. Balloons blew wildly in the breeze. Strangers smiled and hugged like long-lost friends.

Inside the lead bus Mike McCaskey and several of his players waved and smiled right back. It was crazy. One lady, catching a quick glimpse of kicker Kevin Butler's college ring in the window, started screaming, "The ring! The ring!" carrying on, believing the players were already wearing their Super Bowl rings. Butler, his fiancée, Cathy, at his side, laughed and kept on waving. Unbelievable, he thought, just like watching those ticker-tape parades for the moon-walking astronauts when I was a kid back home in Georgia.

By all rights, Cathy, his college sweetheart and a former cheerleader at the University of Georgia, and Kevin should have been on the moon. A honeymoon, that is. Eight months earlier, right after minicamp, Kevin had called Cathy and told her to change the date of the wedding. Kevin was just a rookie—a two-time All-American out of Georgia, a fourth-round pick who was in a dogfight with veteran Bob Thomas for a job.

"What do you mean?" asked Cathy, whose mother owned a bridal store. Future husbands, she knew, especially this future husband, don't change wedding dates. They just don't. They may cancel weddings, but change them, never.

"We're going to the Super Bowl," Kevin said.

174

"I was so hurt," says Cathy today. "I thought he was trying to find an excuse." Here was her future husband, who hadn't even made the team, and he was talking about going to the Super Bowl.

"We fought about it for a while," Kevin said later, "but I was a firm believer this team was going to the Super Bowl. I just knew it because Ditka came in . . . he didn't talk about anything else except our goal is to win the Super Bowl this year."

Win it they did, capping a season that must have felt like a hundred honeymoons to Butler. He set an NFL record for most points scored by a rookie—144—breaking Gayle Sayers's mark of 132 set back in 1965. He made 31 of 38 field goals, including 28 of 29 inside the 40-yard line, and all 51 extra points. A monster year. He had even kicked 3 field goals in New Orleans the day before. Now he was somewhere between hung over and cloud nine, having partied all night in New Orleans, first upstairs on a private floor with all his teammates, then downstairs in a big ol' ballroom with three thousand of his new best friends. Bill Murray showed up. So did actors Jim Belushi and John Candy, Chicago guys to the bone. It was wild stuff for a clutch kicker affectionately known to his buddies as Butt Head.

Now Butler was feeling a little claustrophobic, so he eyed an escape hatch in the bus's ceiling and called out to the driver, "Can I go up? Can I go out?"

"Yeah, yeah," the guy said, "just pop it up."

Butt Head stuck his head out. "Incredible" is the word he used six years later to describe the sight and sounds. People were hanging on the lampposts, sitting on crosswalk signs, screaming their names, spontaneously breaking into cheers about the Bears.

"Guys," Butler said, "you gotta get up here."

So they all went up. Butler. McMichael. Punter Maury Buford. Tight end Jim Thornton. Defensive back Jeff Fisher. Up the hatch and on top of the bus, and on top of the world. People dressed in every form of Bears attire were tossing up coats, watches, unopened bottles of liquor. "Somebody even tossed up a bottle of Dom Pérignon," said Butler, smiling. "Unopened."

Ditka had celebrated with his own special bottle of Dom Pérignon, the one the Old Man had given him on his deathbed, Ditka saying a silent thanks to Halas, Landry, Aschman, and even his father, men who had inspired and instilled the desire and discipline. Ditka had opened minicamp with an impassioned speech about sacrifice and unfinished business and the need to take that final step. "I don't know about you guys," Ditka had said, "but second best isn't good enough for me."

175

"My God, that first meeting he really had us, he had us," says Fencik, then entering his tenth season with the team. Now it was November '91 and the former dreamboat defensive back with all the right moves was eating some low-cholesterol eggs at Le Tour, a hot downtown Chicago power-breakfast place that suits Fencik's Yalie/yuppie image to a T. "I was talking last night to Steve McMichael and we talked about the Super Bowl being as magical as it was because of that first meeting. To get that many guys committed for an entire season, to put a lot of high-priority things behind you—family, girlfriends, wives, everything, they were all disappointed—it was hard, yet it was so easy to do because we all converged at that one moment in time to want to do it. I think that was a combination of Mike raising our self-expectations and us focusing on one dot every week, no matter what we did."

It was an impassioned plea for solidarity that, despite some inevitable distractions (Todd Bell and Al Harris held out the entire season), took the team on a magic carpet ride that connected twelve straight dots from September through November: 12-0. The '85 Bears, in the words of Otis Wilson, were "a gift" to the game, a picture of pop-star personalities. A team so fresh and appealing in the otherwise mundane NFL that media from all over the world flocked to moneyed Lake Forest, the Gap clothing capital of North America, to report on them. And why not? Some teams offer one or two intriguing angles or personalities. The Bears list looked limitless, offering endless possibilities . . . the endearing Papa Bear–Baby Bear angle . . . the simmering feud between Ryan and Ditka . . . a mouthy punk-rock quarterback . . . Samuari Singletary . . . the Buddy System . . . the heartwarming Payton profile . . . a phenom called The Fridge. And when the players weren't being interviewed or signing autographs ($1,500 for one hour), they were lighting up the local airwaves (eight starters had TV or radio shows of some sort), or making commercials. Only a loss to Miami on "Monday Night Football" the first week in December prevented a perfect season. As it was, the Bears finished the regular season 15-1, allowing an average of 12 points a game. During one three-game stretch in November they outscored opponents 104-3. "You knew when we got on the field the other team wasn't going to score," says Singletary, sitting in a suburban Chicago restaurant two months before training camp 1991 was to begin. His almond eyes give tiny hints of Cherokee Indian, German, Mexican, and African American heritage and not his hardscrabble Houston youth, where, as a child, he slept six to a room. He is the son of a Houston contractor who doubled as a fire-and-brimstone preacher, a man who willingly spread the gospel on street corners and in a small white-framed cottage church next door to the family home. Mike was a sickly child, in and out of the hospital with pneumonia and high blood pressure. Sometimes he got so sick his mom just looked at him and started crying. Michael cried, too, thinking about how his father was "living a lie," too busy preaching to others to spend much time with his kids. "None of my brothers or sisters really ever talked to my dad," he wrote in his 1986 autobiography. "He was too busy attending to others, comforting the sick, the wicked, to see what was happening in our home. Somebody always needed him more than he thought we did. Mom believed in being there for the kids. But not Dad."

Now in his eleventh season, he remained the unquestioned leader of the team. A proud and principled man, he had been captain of the defense since 1983. The eight-time Pro Bowl-er had been named the 1990 NFL Man of the Year for contributions on and off the field. Singletary's voice is sad and a bit distant as he talks about the '85 Bears defense. "You knew the other team wasn't going to score, that was a given. How were they going to score? They couldn't throw it on us. We had really good defensive backs. [Cornerback] Leslie [Frazier] was one of the underrated players of all time. Leslie is the guy who kept Mike Richardson pumped up. Leslie's the guy who kept telling him, 'You can do it.' When Mike would slack off, Leslie would tell him, 'Hey, Mike, it's you and me. We're in this thing together. I'm going to shut out my side. You shut out your side.' Fencik and Duerson are in the middle saying, 'Don't worry, man, we're going to shut it off.' Those four guys, hey, you're not going to beat them. Up front you've got Steve [McMichael] and Dan [Hampton] saying, 'Nothing's coming up the middle.' And we all had our territory. Otis [Wilson] on one side, Wilber on the other. Hey, I'm gonna be there for you. And Dent saying, 'Don't forget about me, I'm coming.'"

Singletary has forgotten about lunch. The salad and soup and turkey sandwich sit ignored on the table. For several moments he's transported back in time, six years, to the playoffs when the Bears shut out the Los Angeles Rams and New York Giants on consecutive weekends, when the 46 defense was unstoppable. "The thing we had with Wilber and Otis and Fencik and Dent, we had guys who were killers, had killer instincts," Singletary says. Dent? "I'll tell you," says Singletary, "he's one of the most vicious guys. He just hates. After a while, he just hates people. . . . We had guys who had killer instincts and guys who said, 'Hey, I'm not going to cross that line.' We had a great mixture and a coach who could handle it, who knew what buttons to push. Who to give responsibility. Who not to give responsibility."

It was Singletary whom Ryan chose to carry much of the mental burden. The way the '85 Bears played the 46 called for split-second adjustments and constant, precise communication. During defensive meetings, as Ryan's Captain Black pipe tobacco filled the air, Hampton might sprawl and snooze on the floor, waking only when Buddy yelled, "Big Rook, you got that (defensive) front?" Hampton would answer with a hazy, "Yeah, Buddy, I got it." Meanwhile, the flamboyant 6' 4", 235-pound Wilson, feet propped on a desk, just jabbered away. "I'll stop talking," he liked to say, "when they lay me in a box and throw the dirt down." Ryan allowed—no, encouraged—the freedom and laughter, knowing, in the end, the 46 hinged on Singletary—who watched more film than Siskel or Ebert—and the linebacker's ability to read formations faster than a supermarket scanner.

Ryan had come to love and rely on his middle linebacker like a son. Singletary was to the defense what McMahon was to the offense, a repository of opponent information with the ability to make split-second decisions. Whereas McMahon's memory was near photographic, Singletary spent hours and hours watching film, early in the morning with Ryan, deep into the night at home. No athlete in any sport, past or present, brings any greater dedication or sense of purpose to his profession than Singletary, and for that very reason, from 1983 on, he rarely disappointed Ryan, Ditka, or any of his teammates. Most of the times in defensive huddles Singletary would just bark, "AFC," meaning "automatic front coverages," a reminder to listen at the line of scrimmage for the defensive call. So when the opposing offense broke its huddle, the game within a game began. The quarterback on one side. Singletary on the other. Matching motion and shifts in strength and personnel with one Ryan coverage after another. Singletary yelling out a call. Fencik, another bright boy, relaying it to the cornerbacks. Up front, Hampton and McMichael played some games of their own, slipping predetermined fakes and spins (known as stunts) into coverages. Marshall and Wilson, classic bookend linebackers, begged for a blitz. Often they lined up together on the left side, the "46 Blitz," hell-bent for the quarterback. Or they would fake a blitz and peel around to drag down a play from behind. On the sidelines Ryan received feedback from his troops. "What are they doing?" he would ask after the first series. "How did they react to the blitzing scheme?"

"Well," Singletary or Wilson or Fencik would offer, "they're closing everything up the middle. We can't blitz anymore."

"Okay, blitz one more time," Ryan would say. "If they still have that there, we hit them from the outside."

Next series, boom! Wilber and Otis would come strafing in from the backside, or Dent would go on a tear, McMichael on a stunt. "Teams didn't know what to do," says Singletary. "We're coming from the end. We're coming up the middle. After that, it was over. The quarterback was scared to death. The running backs were scared to death. They didn't want to block. You could see it in their eyes. I felt bad for the other team's quarterback. We were in the huddle—'Get him, knock him out!'

"I would ask the guys, 'Don't you have any heart?' 'Nooooo! Kill him!' That's the way it was. Quarterbacks didn't want to come into the game. Minnesota Vikings. A game there. Wade Wilson, and they had some other quarterbacks . . . knocked him out. We knocked five, six quarterbacks totally out of the game that year."

In fact, the Bears defense was playing to do just that—to knock out the quarterback. As described by Fencik and another starter on the '85 team, the Bears had, for at least part of the season, a $500 bounty on quarterbacks or top running backs such as Tony Dorsett of Dallas. "Buddy never really instituted that," says Fencik. "We kind of imposed it. You know, if you can get Dorsett out of the game, but you had to get him out, he couldn't come back in. There were no ifs, you know, he couldn't be out for a play. He had to be out of the game."

On the other side of the ball, McMahon was getting state-of-the-art protection from what were now known as The Black 'N Blues Brothers (everybody had an act). Across the front, or from left to right, were Covert, Bortz, Hilgenberg, Thayer, and Van Horne. Covert, aka Jimbo, the Pittsburgh guy, on his way to consensus All-Pro in his third year, was the fussbudget of the group, always adjusting mirrors, seat belts, picking up things and putting them away. Like defensive ends.

Bortz, aka Bortzy, 6'6", 270, was a converted all–Big Ten defensive tackle from Iowa, as well as an avid outdoorsman and war buff who soaked up military books like blitzing backers.

Hilgenberg, aka Hilgy, 6'2", 270, was an undrafted free agent signed out of Iowa in 1981—at the time, the latest in a long line of Hawkeyes including his father (Jerry), an All-American center at Iowa in the fifties, brother (Jim), who preceded him as the Iowa center, and brother (Joel), who followed. He loved to ride Harley-Davidsons for fun.

Thayer, 6'4", 270, no aka, just Thayer, was a four-year letterman at Notre Dame who played in an inhumane forty-six games in '85 (twenty-three with the USFL Chicago Blitz, twenty-three with Bears including the playoffs and Super Bowl). Mr. Muscle Beach, the team's most dedicated weight lifter, had an eye on a career in radio and TV.

Van Horne, 6'7", 280, aka Horn, a denizen of the dark, loved to hang with McMahon, married vice president Mondale's daughter, and was an aspiring radio disc jockey.

Thanks to The Black 'N Blues Brothers, McMahon threw 9 TDs in the first four games. In the postseason he was 39-66-636 and 3 TDs, the perfect complement to Payton, Sweetness himself, the human highlight film. Gault, McKinnon, sure-handed Dennis Gentry, and Ken Margerum gave the Bears everything they needed at wide receiver. Butler was on automatic pilot, hardly ever missing. It was an awesome team. "The greatest team, definitely, ever put together, definitely," says Singletary. "The reason is we played well even in the turmoil, the envy."

He is then asked the question many other Bears have been asked. If this team was so good, so powerful, what happened? Where are the two or three other Super Bowl rings? Singletary takes another bite of his turkey sandwich, raising his eyes to look at his questioner. He thinks before he speaks. "You look at the 49ers, the Pittsburgh Steelers, what did they have? Consistency. You think about it, the thing we never had in the last five years is consistency. The 49ers or Steelers weren't in a situation . . . they weren't in a city like Chicago that can tear you apart." Singletary takes a moment to explain. He loves Chicago and feels "blessed" to play there compared to other cities, especially when it comes to the fans and, quite honestly, the endorsement opportunities. He talks about other Pro Bowl players paid $250 or $500 for appearances in their cities, and how he can make ten or fifteen grand in one night if he wanted to. "But it has its disadvantages," he says. "If you have a great team, you've got to have a strong coach, a coach who can keep a lid on things, who believes in what he says and says what he believes. We didn't have that."

When did it change?

"It started," says Singletary, "right after the Super Bowl."

19

TINK . . . TINK . . . TINK . . . TINK! TINK! . . . TINK . . . TINK . . .

The plinks of a piano tuner veer from sharp to flat on this placid summer morning at 59 West, one of Chicago's hottest new nightclubs. The previous night, a Wednesday, when most places around town are dead, 59 West (named after its downtown locale—59 West Grand Avenue) had been hopping. The club crowd came dressed in snazzy suits and sleek black minis. The look seemed to fit right in with the retro restaurant decor, the black Formica tables, black Casbah drapes, and sensual impressionistic art. Most patrons had been drawn by a freebie buffet and Bulls party planned around game two of the NBA Finals. By midnight the scene in the adjoining dance club—a neo-Roman flashback—was hotter than Michael Jordan. The crowd was all hard bodies and dazzling smiles. When the night finally ended, sometime around three A.M., Jimmy Rittenberg and George Shlaes had created yet another slam-dunk success.

Now, a little less than eight hours later, Rittenberg is relaxing in the deserted nightclub. He is a handsome roly-poly kind of guy with a boyish face, shaggy brown hair, and matching eyes that can't sit still. His polo shirt, with its Steinlager Cup Rugby logo, looks as if it spent the night on his bedroom floor. He is a Chicago guy, born and raised, a Rush Street sixties original who has parlayed his special talents and street smarts into a local legend as a restaurant manager and promoter.

All, ever so simply, based on the answer yes.

"My saying is, 'The answer is yes, what's the question?'" he says. "I'm a giant concierge network, all based on the answer yes."

Paul Anka wants to watch the replay of a championship fight at midnight? He calls J.R.

Cosby's around and wants to party? He calls J.R.

CBS Records needs twenty Bulls tickets at the last minute for the rock group Warrant? J.R. to the rescue.

He knows everybody. Everybody knows him. He is a Director of both the Chicago Convention & Tourism Bureau and the Greater North Michigan Avenue Association, a man-about-town who knows every local TV executive and literary agent in town. He talks and talks, dropping names and ideas, always shmoozing—at which, one of Rittenberg's close friends says, "Jimmy is the best, bar none." That he is, a born promoter and marketeer, skilled at popping his name—and that of his latest restaurant—into local columns. "You've got to live the business to do the business," he says as Sinatra's "Strangers in the Night" streams out of the house stereo. "I give to charities. I go to meetings at seven in the morning. There are thousands of little tricks of the trade. It's an easy game to play, a hard game to play well. It's like backgammon. To know the odds. To calculate. To think ahead."

He is always thinking, calculating, weighing the risk of saying yes versus the expected return. "Why do I sit here and talk to you? What's to be gained? Something must be gained. I'm not sitting here so you can make money. I'm not sitting here to get my name in the front of the book. I'm sitting here to maybe tell the story . . ."

It's a story that began almost fifty years ago when Rittenberg "came wailing" out of the city's west side, a former track and baseball athlete who worked his way through De Paul University as a switchman on the Rock Island Railroad. He became a teacher of inner-city kids, speech and English mostly, with a little coaching on the side. To make ends meet he tended bar at trade shows and at spots in Old Town and on Rush. Even back then he had the answer. He'd tell the trade-show suits, hey, guys, stop in, have a drink, I'll get you in anywhere without having to pay a cover. "Monday night I'd have twenty guys at the bar tipping me two, three dollars. Then I would call around, no cover, no cover. Then they'd come back for a nightcap. I'd make one hundred fifty, two hundred dollars on a Monday night." But Rittenberg kept to a personal code. "I had a reputation. I never bought a drink for a customer. I didn't believe in it. I would give them anything else. Introduce them to this guy. Order a pizza for them. Call and make sure they didn't have to pay a cover. I'd do anything for the customer except give away the bar. That's the one reputation I had as a bartender."

In 1970 a schoolteacher friend by the name of Jay Emerich hatched an idea for a nightclub. Rittenberg had eight grand in the bank. He invested it all and quit his job. The club was called Faces. He learned early on that investors knew or cared little about running a restaurant. All they knew was the steak tasted good, the johns needed toilet paper, and what about my party for six on Thursday night? When Emerich made a bold move and took the club private, selling memberships for $50, the partners jumped ship. Not Jimmy. "I became the glue," says Rittenberg. Emerich got sick with lupus. "I took over everything," Rittenberg says. "Sales went up a hundred percent. I got us into private parties. The nightclub didn't start until ten-thirty P.M. I had trouble with the six-to-ten spot. I tried a cocktail hour, giving away food. Didn't work. Then I started working with the convention bureau, donating time to charities, and we started having convention events, trade show events, charity events. Bang! All of a sudden our biggest business was trade shows and conventions. We'd have three or four hundred people in the club. Come nine o'clock the club opens, the place is jammed." People drew people.

Faces, at 940 Rush Street, became internationally known, one of the country's hottest spots. Studio 54 in New York? Tramps in D.C.? Mr. Pips in L.A.? Forget it. Faces was hotter. At its peak, Emerich and Rittenberg had sold eighteen thousand memberships, despite raising the fee to $500. It all fed on what Rittenberg defines simply as the "boy meets girl" mating game everyone else was selling, only at Faces you had celebrity, beauty, politics, and power all in one room. Anka came by all the time. So did Cos, Rich Little, even Mick Jagger and Bob Dylan. The OC guys hung there too, and even, one evening, a certain Scandinavian king with a particular want in women.

As the story goes, one of the king's men approached J.R. and mentioned the king's wish. *The answer is yes, what's the question?* How do you say no to a king? A call was made to a certain strip club around the corner. A few moments later some models arrived. The king, suddenly ill, slipped out a back door to his limo. After an appropriate interlude one of the pretty black models was escorted out the same door. The rest, as they say, was international relations. Another notch on J.R.'s promotional belt, a belt that Emerich eventually felt was getting too big. Rittenberg and Emerich split in 1978. With savings from his $1,000-a-week salary and 30-percent-of-the-profits deal, J.R. bought a condo in Acapulco and some peace and quiet in Hawaii. "Then one day," he says, "I got a call from George Shlaes, who I didn't know."

An hour earlier Shlaes had spun his story in the same empty nightclub. He is something of a Mitch Miller look-alike with the white-beard and regal bearing of a linguistics professor, a far cry from

183

his Depression-era upbringing. The son of a local butcher, Shlaes says he never played much sports, never saw a high school football game. He was the only Jew in a North Side neighborhood filled with Italians, Irish, and Germans. Every day after school George worked in the grocery store, stocking shelves, learning how to cut meat. Now, behind the bar in the other room, there are reminders of how far this man has come. Pictures of Shlaes with Tommy Lasorda. Former boxing champ Sugar Ray Leonard. "I've always been star struck," says Shlaes.

But Shlaes has shined, too. Not like Lasorda or Leonard or even his business partner, J.R. But down at the Chicago Board of Options Exchange, buying and selling stock options, making more in a day than his father made in a lifetime. He quickly realized, however, his strength wasn't in trades—particularly after a silly mistake cost him 2 million bucks one day—but in hiring and managing young talent. At one time Shlaes says he had eight traders working for him and owned eight seats at the Options Exchange. Most years, he says, he made between three and four hundred thousand dollars, but like a lot of traders, he was always looking for another deal, another avenue for his money. One night Shlaes found himself in Faces. He had lived near the bar for years but had only bought a membership a few weeks earlier. "Gee, this is fabulous," Shlaes mentioned to a couple of friends.

"How'd you like to buy it?" asked the bartender.

Shlaes doesn't remember now if it was the excitement or the alcohol, probably a bit of both, but the words "Hey, this is a helluva go" left his mouth. On Monday the phone rang. It was one of his drinking buddies calling about their appointment that evening with Emerich, who by now, drained by lupus and stress, wanted out. A week later Shlaes and two partners paid $800,000 for Faces, the highest price in city history for a bar. "The problem now," Shlaes explains, "is who was going to run it? The guy who used to run it, Jimmy Rittenberg, was in Hawaii. Is he willing to come back?" The answer from the "Yes Man" was yes. But he wasn't cheap: $1,500 a week plus a big percentage off the top; it was always off the top now with Jimmy. "It was astronomical," admits Shlaes, "but we figured we were going to be in this business, we needed somebody with his expertise. The place was basically built around Jimmy Rittenberg."

Shlaes and Rittenberg have been partners ever since, almost fifteen years now, in at least a half dozen different "concepts," from fifties bars to high-class nightclubs. Not partners in the literal sense because only once—and it would prove a critical financial mistake—has J.R. stepped outside management and made himself liable for loans and leases. "I call him my partner and everything else," Shlaes says, "but he has never had ownership in any of the places. Jimmy has a gift to create. . . . In this business it's fairly easy to be a hit for a short period of time. Our thing has always been longevity. How can we make it last? It's no good—a year and you're out.

"We've always catered to people who are closer to our age. The thirty-five to sixties with the young broads. We've always had the ability to have the girls come in, you can get the girls to come in, you can have ten guys to one girl. That's one of the secrets. The other secret in this business is to do the party business. Nobody has ever done the party business. We do parties. We do the convention business. We do bar mitzvahs. The average day-to-day business is not enough to support one of these places. You pay rent twenty-four hours and you only use them six or eight hours a day. The object is to use them as much as you possibly can. Jimmy has always been a great innovator, a great creator of parties. We make parties out of thin air. Last night's a classic. The Bulls are playing the Los Angeles Lakers. Very, very difficult to get people to come out. So we throw a party around that. We basically give away a buffet, and we have these tickets, we actually have a ticket to a ball game. We put a twenty-dollar price on it. Initial it and say, be our guest. Then we have a big buffet and give away chicken, ribs, pizza. People stay for the game. They drink. We pick a Wednesday that is normally a bad night and make it a very, very good night [$8,500]. Well, those are Jimmy's ideas. We did this for years and years before anybody was doing it. We had bar mitzvahs every Saturday and Sunday, year in and year out. The catering business is one where you can control everything. You control the cost before you sell it. . . . We work conventions. We send pretty girls into every convention we can get into. We buy them badges. We have them go in dressed up and they pass out passes. We have a restaurant with a nightclub. That's Jimmy's creation."

Building on the success of Faces, Rittenberg came up with a concept for something he called "Juke Box Saturday Night." The first concept he tried was a country-western bar called Rodeo in 1980, shortly after he returned from Hawaii. Rittenberg had gotten wind of this new Travolta movie Paramount was pushing called *Urban Cowboy*. He remembered what Travolta had done with the disco craze, so six months before the movie came out, he hustled down to Houston and convinced the only bar owner in the country with a mechanical bull on the premises to give him a ninety-day exclusive in the Chicago area; not another bull could be sold in the city for three months after the movie opened. Rittenberg called his good friend Harry Caray, a name synonymous with Chicago and the Cubs, to see if Harry wanted to get in on the action.

"This is a good sidebar," says Rittenberg, who can play the press much like Sandberg does second base. "I was going to do Falstaff beer so I called Harry and said, 'Harry, I got a joint that's going to do a shitload of draft beer. I'll go with Falstaff'—he was with them at the time."

"Hold it," Caray told him. "I might be going with Budweiser. Then you can put Budweiser in and make me look good."

Sure enough, Bud went in, and as J.R. points out with pride, "we sold the shit out of it." Sixty half-barrels a week. Rodeo grossed more than $1 million in ten months. But then, Rittenberg says, after his exclusive ran out, "the amateurs took over." Urban cowboys got tossed off the bull at other bars; patrons got hurt. By then Rittenberg's mind was a mile away, searching for something new, another concept. He noticed how while nobody could really two-step worth a damn, late at night, when the fifties tunes were on—Elvis, Chuck Berry—people danced and drank and danced some more. Time to change, thought Rittenberg. He had seen a store with a catchy name—Juke Box Saturday Night—filled with memorabilia from the fifties and sixties. He convinced the owner to furnish the Lincoln Avenue club on consignment ("I knew nobody would buy anything"), then told him, "Give my bar the name Juke Box Saturday Night and I'll make it famous for you."

He did. Four in Chicago, then in Minneapolis and Des Moines. More investors arrived courtesy of Shlaes's contacts downtown. The Yes Man and the Money Man . . . were on track to a gold mine called Ditka's.

Rittenberg is leaning against the bar now, halfway through a diet soda. Sinatra is long gone, replaced by a soothing sax. For the next several minutes it is 1985 again and another new concept is forming in Rittenberg's head, a combination sports bar/nightclub. He talked to Lasorda about it, inquiring about Toots Shor's, the famed New York saloon. "Oh, it was a great place," Lasorda replied. Could you watch a game? Well, no, he admitted, but it was a great place to hang out. "That's not what I wanted," Rittenberg says. "I didn't want the sports figures so much. I wanted the sports *fan*. Sports figures, you're going to buy them a drink, pick up a meal. Fuck that."

So Rittenberg started shopping for sites. A real estate guy showed him an old trucking garage on West Ontario, corner of Wells and Franklin. It was the absolutely wrong address—too damn close to the freeways, the el tracks and parking lots, right next to an old air-conditioning and refrigeration company. There were only two other restaurants around, Ed Debevic's and Carson's Ribs. But Rittenberg pulled the traffic study from the city. Hmmm. Sixty-six thousand cars a day, going home on a one-way street that fed two major expressways. Something to promote, thought Rittenberg. Feelers were put out to both Harry Caray and Dick Butkus, but neither was available (Harry wanted to keep his name available for future use and a Butkus meeting never came off). Then one of Rittenberg's restaurant managers mentioned how he had gone to school with Jerry Vainisi and the word was, you know, that Vainisi and Ditka were looking to start a restaurant. "Well, shit, let's call 'em," said Rittenberg.

Vainisi and Ditka were, in fact, exploring the possibility of opening a sports bar and restaurant. Vainisi was casually checking land in the northern suburbs of Deerfield and Northbrook, but definitely nothing downtown. He was looking for a three-way split with a manager. Ditka, however, was leaning against lending his name. "We were thinking of 'Champions,' or 'Winners,' something like that," says Vainisi.

A meeting was set at a little Italian restaurant two blocks from the site. Introductions were in order since neither side knew the other. Rittenberg then explained the concept—a man's place, heavy on meats and TV monitors, the kind of place where you could take your wife on Saturday night and still catch a game over her shoulder. He wanted a nightclub, too, and was already plotting to take the Faces "boy meets girl" and convention crowd with him. Vainisi and Ditka were looking for something less touristy and more upscale, a Toots Shor retreat for athletes. But they listened, swayed, at least in part, by Rittenberg's reputation and the kind of numbers he and Shlaes were projecting. Shlaes remembers Ditka being flattered by the attention but leary, given his personal track record in the restaurant business. "He was very, very cautious as to who he was going to get into bed with."

Vainisi remembers it differently. He says an attorney was never hired to "properly evaluate things," that "we're both ethnic and we both deal with gut feel a lot. So sometimes you win and sometimes you get burned. Our gut feel on that was those guys seemed to be very successful on what they did with their Juke Box Saturday Night ventures." Still, Vainisi gave NFL security both names for a background check. The league came back with nothing specific, just a general concern that the restaurant and nightclub business can lead to associations with gamblers or people who bring discredit to the league. But, Vainisi says, "there was nothing that specifically fingered Rittenberg or Shlaes."

Rittenberg was hardly in awe of Ditka. "To me he was a market," Rittenberg says, a way to fill not only the restaurant but most important—as Rittenberg had learned long ago—the nightclub, where the real money could be made. "When you sit in a nightclub and I give you a table, there is nothing on that table. Then I give you a glass and say four dollars. Inside that glass is a twenty-eight-cent shot of vodka. Now you sit in the restaurant and order a four-dollar order of calamari. There you get a tablecloth and a waitress, a cook, plate, a fork, sauce, lemon in a little skirt, salt, pepper, and sugar. It's the same four dollars as the drink. You're done with your four-dollar calamari, we make maybe two or three cents. When you're done with your four-dollar drink, we're walking away with three dollars and fifty cents. To me the restaurant was a loss leader."

A syndication deal was set: $40,000 per unit. Returns on investment were based on annual sales of $1 million to $5 million for the first five years. Shlaes solicited the investors from contacts at both the Board of Trade and Options Exchange. In the end, twenty-eight "outside" investors purchased about 40 percent of the partnership. A direct-mail executive named Gene Pontillo, who had put money into the original Juke Box Saturday Night, invested $400,000, while Ditka and Vainisi, under their D&V Ventures corporation, bought two units for $80,000. Ditka was given another 5 percent of the partnership (worth an additional $80,000) for the use of his name. Shlaes took 20 percent as his fee for syndicating the deal. So the percentages broke down roughly like this: Pontillo, 30 percent; Ditka and Vainisi, 10 percent; Shlaes, 20 percent, with outside investors making up the rest. Rittenberg put up no money. Instead, his J.R. Management, Inc. was contracted to oversee construction and manage the restaurant. For that, Rittenberg would receive a flat 5 percent of the gross. At the time, Rittenberg was still struggling what he called the "signature item," something to sell, to promote on the menu. Steak was out. Too much competition from Chicago landmarks such as Morton's or Gene & Georgetti's. Carson's had ribs, Shlaes suggested chicken. It's inexpensive, he said, and you can sell a lot of it.

"No," said Rittenberg, "I'm thinking of something else."

"What?"

"Pork chops."

Shlaes nearly swallowed his tongue. "What the fuck? Are you crazy? Who's going to pay to eat pork chops? Pork chops are something you eat at home with applesauce. Let's do ribs or something."

"Pork chops," said the answer man.

One of the new chefs suggested a marinade of pineapple and orange juice. Rittenberg and Shlaes, the butcher's boy, then went to Chicago's famed stockyards and shopped for prime cuts of meat, asking packers to create something special. But none of the big names got it right. Finally, a small packer, Allen Brothers, came up with an eight-ounce boneless chop perfect for broiling over coals. With that problem solved, Rittenberg went about building a staff, drafting several of his longtime employees from Faces, promising a percentage of the party profits. "He said, I know we can't afford to pay you what you're worth," remembers Barry Peterson, who set up the City Lights sound system and spun the records at night. "There were about six or seven of us. He said he would make a pool and give bonuses." The nightclub actually opened the first week in August 1985, just in time for the Bears exhibition game in London against the Cowboys, a month or so ahead of the restaurant, which was still under construction. Rittenberg's original nightclub concept in the vast, high-ceiled room was something akin to the Rainbow Room in New York, a white-tablecloth, Big Band atmosphere geared to the Rolex crowd. It bombed early on, because the drawing card, Ditka's restaurant, wasn't ready to open, and those who did show up found the atmosphere *too* New York, the kiss of death in Chicago. "It just wasn't hip," says John May, the club's entertainment director, a friend and employee of Rittenberg's for some twenty years.

But by October, when Ditka's had opened, the planets had aligned and Ditka's/City Lights was suddenly the hottest spot in the city. What happened? Well, two things actually, independent of one another yet intertwined: the Bears beat Washington and San Francisco in a span of three weeks to push their season record to 6-0; City Lights made a dramatic shift to an eclectic mix of everything from Glenn Miller to music videos, the flashy bright-lights, big-city style a perfect anthem for the undefeated team. One entity fed the other, just as Rittenberg had planned, all his "tools" as he liked to call them, in their proper place. The biggest tool of all, of course, was Ditka. On the marquee out front was a larger-then-life caricature, Popeye arms folded across a burly chest with GO FOR IT scrawled in white neon. It brought in the tourists and conventioneers, folks from Missoula, Montana or Muskegon, Michigan, in town for the electronics show. But there were other draws as well. Rittenberg had hired Eddie Minasian, a former catering director in both Beverly Hills and Chicago, as a manager/greeter. Minasian, a gregarious, handsome, cigar-smoking throwback, seemed to know every coach, manager, and player in sports. He spread the word around the leagues, and within days the likes of Lasorda or Texas

Rangers manager Bobby Valentine stopped by. The restaurant itself was no bigger than a couple of pro locker rooms with hardwood floors, standard card-table chairs with some quiet booths in an elevated dining area. A horseshoe bar anchored the middle of the dining room, surrounded by the obligatory Chicago sports photos and memorabilia, two wide-screen TVs, and dozens of smaller monitors. The main fare, The Mike Ditka Special, was three eight-ounce pork chops—twenty-four ounces of meat before broiling—served with scalloped apples. Other signature items included Diana Ditka's chicken, Lasorda linguine, Jerry Vainisi veal, Ryne Sandberg swordfish, Irv Kupcinet's BBQ-broiled salmon.

By the time the Bears trounced Dallas 44–0 to run their record to 11-0, Ditka's was literally in hog heaven. The restaurant was serving four-hundred, five-hundred, even six-hundred dinners a night. Pork chops were a cultural phenomenon, much like McMahon or The Fridge. "It became unbelievable," says Shlaes. "We started talking tonnage. At one point we were near four to five thousand pounds a week. People came by just to eat the pork chops." Ditka so dominated the pork chop market that over at Harry Caray's new restaurant they put it right on the menu: *If you want the best pork chops, go to Ditka's.* And as crazy as it was in the restaurant, City Lights was worse. On weekends you needed a crowbar to get into the place: the lines stretched through the lobby, out the front door, and down the block. The nightclub drew the most diverse crowd in the city, everyone from young, bodacious babes to star-struck conventioneers to slick businessmen, to what Peterson called the "Fred and Ginger types." Five or six hundred people every night of the week, dancing, waiting for dinner, buying those $4 drinks. "It was ridiculous," May says.

But that wasn't all. Rittenberg's promotional skills and network of contacts were beginning to pay off. Soon the club was busy with luncheons and private parties from noon until five P.M., setting up the dinner and drinking crowd. "On Friday and Saturday night we would have eight-hundred people still in the club at five to four in the morning, drinking like racehorses," marvels May. "You couldn't serve them fast enough." And before the day was done, it seemed as if half the people who walked into the place walked out with some souvenir bought in the lobby gift shop where Ditka pins, caps, buttons, T-shirts, baby bibs, were being sold. At its peak, the stand grossed a reported $900,000 a year.

Ditka was certainly doing his promotional part. In the first year he dropped by Ontario Street at least twice a week, usually on Wednesday night after taping his Sunday-morning TV show, and right after home games on Sunday. "He was fantastic," says Shlaes. "He would go around shake hands, sign autographs." Peterson, the deejay, even worked out a system where Ditka could offer personalized greetings to convention groups, which Peterson taped up at Halas Hall. When the tapes were played, Peterson says, "people's tongues would hang out; they thought it was a live satellite hookup."

"How good was it?" asks May. "We couldn't have made any more money if we were printing it."

20

IT IS A SUN-KISSED MORNING IN JUNE 1991 AND JIM HARBAUGH IS PUTTING on a show on the practice field behind Halas Hall. Twenty-yard outs. Forty-yard fades. Posts. Flys. Harbaugh hits them all, one seamless spiral after another. The touch, the strength he hopes to show in September and beyond, is all there. Sweat glistens on his bare shoulders and back. There are no local reporters on the scene, no TV cameras around. The cycle of professional sport in the city is spinning rapidly around other teams now. Bulls fever is peaking thanks to last night's upset win over the Lakers in L.A., tying the NBA Championship series at one game apiece. At Dick's Last Resort, a beachy sandals-and-shorts joint downtown, gorgeous, sophisticated, sports-minded women had howled and cheered until the final horn had sounded.

"There are only two living cities left in America," novelist Norman Mailer once wrote, "Chicago and New Orleans." Chicago lives on today, blue-collar values and the raw sound of bare-wire blues colliding with the magnificence of Michigan Avenue. It is a city where the drugs and despair of the city's South Side increase every day, while yuppie couples stroll down Division Street at midnight, without worry, ready to party at Scoozi's.

Harbaugh had some worries when he arrived in Chicago in the spring of 1987. He knew Ditka had pushed hard for a defensive player in the first round of the NFL draft—speedy linebacker Alex Gordon out of Cincinnati was his favorite—but Bill Tobin and Mike McCaskey fought for the all–Big Ten quarterback from the University of Michigan. Ed King, the veteran scout, liked Harbaugh, too, although he felt Michigan's pass offense was so unsophisticated that Harbaugh— despite throwing for 2,557 yards and completing 66 percent of his passes and rewriting Michigan's passing records—was more like a sophomore or junior at BYU. But nobody—including Ditka— discounted Harbaugh's leadership abilities or will to win. King told Tobin and the others that the Bears had "staggered" around in '86 without a QB. "If you want one," King argued during a draft meeting, "take one now so he can be ready in five years."

Ditka played his typical mind games when Harbaugh walked into his office shortly after draft day. "Welcome to Chicago," he said, handing Harbaugh a team sweater. "You know, we've got four other quarterbacks here already."

"You know," says Harbaugh after the '91 passing workout, an ice pack strapped to his throwing shoulder, sweat still dripping down his face, "I really didn't get the feeling he wanted me here. From everything I had heard, it seemed like he wanted a different player." What Ditka got was an athlete who turned out to be as tough as he was handsome, which is to say plenty of both. At 6'3", 205 pounds, Harbaugh is a mixture of Midwest and California hunkiness (born in Toledo, high school in Palo Alto). His deep brown eyes and wavy brown hair along with the lantern jaw and a quick smile are straight out of some American Dental Association video. The son of a former Bo Schembechler assistant who's now the head football coach at Western Kentucky, Harbaugh was hardly out of diapers when his competitive streak surfaced.

In grade school he played in every youth league around: basketball, hockey, football, wrestling, and baseball. On Saturdays he was up wrestling at six A.M., changing his clothes in the family car in time for a basketball game by ten. By the time he was eight, he kept statistics on his batting average in baseball, scoring average in basketball, and touchdowns in football. During the more restrictive winter months, Harbaugh and his brother, John, who was fifteen months older, devised another test of will using only a deck of cards. The rules were simple. If you turned up, say, a seven, it meant seven push-ups. A face card was ten push-ups, aces were fifteen and the joker twenty. Depending on the luck of the draw, it meant as many as 400 push ups in an hour.

"Without a doubt one of the most competitive people you'll ever meet," says Bears tight end and good friend Cap Boso. "Whatever he does, Jim wants to be the best." Boso said he and Harbaugh ceased guarding each other in five-on-five basketball games because the contact got so rough. No matter what the game—cards, golf, hopscotch—Harbaugh hates to lose. "I'll be totally honest," says Harbaugh, who finds it difficult to be anything but. "I see Coach Ditka just exactly as I am. He'd be a guy I'd hang out with if he was playing now, or if I was playing back then."

It was Ditka who informed Harbaugh he had won the starting job in 1990, right after the last preseason game when he called Harbaugh and Mike Tomczak up to his office. The martial arts classes, visualization exercises, all that walking on a balance beam at home and working on his footwork, had paid off for Harbaugh. "He called Mike and I up to his office and it was kind of dramatic in that we just sat down in the two chairs in front of his desk," Harbaugh says.

Tomczak and Harbaugh, never the best of friends, not friends at all, really, never talked on the way upstairs. "You both did well," said Ditka, "but I feel Jim had a better training camp and I'm going with him."

Harbaugh had control now. This was his team. His year. His time, as they say in sports, to "step up" and make a name for himself. Harbaugh takes the leadership role seriously. Simply, he wants to lead "by example" by "just doing it," by inspiring others in critical moments, theatrics be damned. "People say, you know, you're a leader, you have to show you can stand up to Ditka on the sidelines and take the reins of the Super Bowl team like McMahon used to." Harbaugh brushes some hair off his forehead and puts some pop in his voice. "I honestly don't think it's any of that. I'm not getting into an argument with Ditka in front of the whole team to show everybody I'm the leader. Being a leader is going out between the white lines and making the plays at the right time. When it counts. When it's big. Like Larry Bird hitting the three-pointer when the buzzer goes. Like Magic Johnson. Then when you say things like, let's do this or that, you get people's attention."

The 1991 season's opening game is still some ten weeks away. Harbaugh likes what he sees on this team. "It has changed for the better," he says. "We've got a lot less selfish people who just want to win and aren't concerned with how many endorsements they do, with how many commercials they do, if they're doing more than the next guy.

"For me, I'm not going to have done it until I've won a Super Bowl. I'm not going to take a backseat to anybody. I like our chances to win it this year. I don't see myself as just a guy taking snaps, not making mistakes, handing the ball off to somebody. I think my role this year is going to be very significant. It's going to be one of the major reasons we get to the Super Bowl."

Harbaugh was nowhere to be found as the roar rose from the crowd at exactly 9:04 A.M., Wednesday, July 17, 1991, twenty-six minutes before summer training camp was set to begin in Platteville, Wisconsin. Ditka, naturally, was the subject of the cheering. Just as at minicamp back in May, he arrived on the scene at the University of Wisconsin–Platteville athletic complex in his personalized golf cart, cutting across a road from the stadium to the fields, running a gauntlet of Bears fans who were straining against student security guards for a look or perhaps a handshake as Ditka sailed by, down a hill heading toward two lush green practice fields: fields of dreams to the rookies and free agents shooting for one of the forty-seven spots on the regular roster, but "Hell Valley" to the vets, who had endured this misery before.

Hundreds of fans, family, and folks from Illinois, Wisconsin, and nearby Iowa sat peacefully behind yellow ropes, many on multicolored lawn chairs or Bears blankets. Some held binoculars (they were some two-hundred yards from the action). Others carried Bear cups bought from a nearby souvenir stand. Still others just brought their memories. "I never thought I'd live long enough to see them win it," said one elderly gent who had a huge Bears helmet painted on his garage door back home in Juda, Wisconsin ("sixty-two miles away!"). "Live at a four-way stop. People are always coming by to look at it." His family, he says, went a little crazy when the Bears won it all back in '86. "We have ten kids, five boys. We all danced around the table that day."

Today that champagne season is just a distant memory. The 1991 season had already been summed up, in the words of one reporter, as "one real big question mark." Would Harbaugh finally emerge as the real leader? Would Ditka scrap the ball-control-or-bust philosophy and finally, finally, open it up? Was the offensive line too old? The defensive line too thin? Ditka's hair, cut unusually short and shellacked down to his head, seemed to underscore the seriousness of the task ahead. Players knew it too. They clattered grim-faced across a street to the fields ignoring dozens of little hands wiggling pieces of paper, hoping a hero would stop.

"Can I have your autograph—pleeeease," shouted one child after another.

"Tim, *please,* Tim."

"Trace! Trace!"

"Tom! Mark! Can I have *please* have your autograph, *please!*"

And one by one John Roper, Tim Ryan, Trace Armstrong, Tom Thayer, and Mark Bortz passed by without stopping. "The first day and it only gets worse," sighed John Pratt of Sterling, Illinois, who left his house at five A.M. with his wife and two boys to see the Bears.

Linebacker coach Dave McGinnis can't stand the wait. By ten after nine he has cornered a couple of free agents—"Richard, Charlie, let's go"—and begins running them through drills.

"Pro Squeeze Cover One," yells McGinnis. "Give me all your calls."

But that's not even enough. He recruits a ball boy to impersonate a tailback. "Play Payton," he says.

It was, of course, back in the glory days of Walter Payton that the Bears first made the trip to the southwest corner of this state, and the relative obscurity of the University of Wisconsin–Platteville. Back in the late 1700s Platteville was home to the Winnebago Indians and a few fur trappers. Then one of the trappers, Emmanuel Metcalf, discovered traces of mineral lead in an animal den, and the rush was on. Lead miners poured in and so did the homesteaders. Today the downtown area retains a gritty, frontier charm, particularly if one admires aging brick buildings and bars with such monikers as the Hoist House and Inferno. As in most college towns, the bars and local businesses cater to the young—the 5,200 students from nearby UW-Platteville, but the city, to its credit, has broadened its base, selling itself as one of the can-do summer communities bursting with arts and music festivals.

Encouraged by the summer marriage of Platteville and the Bears, in 1991 two other Wisconsin communities enticed the Kansas City Chiefs (River Falls) and New Orleans Saints (La Crosse) north for adoption by the state. Platteville took this adoption business a bit more seriously than the others, however. For the seventh straight year the local Chamber of Commerce had sponsored an "Adopt-a-Bear" promotion that enabled local merchants to draw the name of a player by chance, then go about dressing up store windows with pictures of the player and other personal paraphernalia. There was a certain delicious irony that the local Domino's Pizza outlet pulled the name of William Perry this year. When The Fridge showed up late for the first practice, it appeared he had adopted every Domino's franchise in the nation.

Perry's blubbery mass was a shock to even veteran weight watchers. At the end of the morning practice he ran six forties with all the grace and gusto of a wounded water buffalo. Then pulled up lame. "Cramping up, man," he gasped to head trainer Fred Caito.

Ditka had spent much of the morning gazing out of his golf cart a hundred yards away from the action. Unlike some NFL coaches he shies away from direct player contact during practice, partly because his crumbled hip joint can no longer handle the pressure of standing for more than a minute or two. At times, his golf cart takes on the look of a talk show couch as one by one friends, business associates, or front office personnel stop by to chat. In the past, some vets have grumbled about the coach's concentration and commitment at practice. Normally, however, Ditka is focused on the field. "I'm thinking all the time," he says. "Looking, observing, looking for the good in people, evaluating."

On this day, the head coach had clearly seen enough. After the morning practice he drove his cart into a horseshoe pocket of reporters and cameras. The press corps numbered at least forty. Eight Minicams, a dozen radio and TV microphones, and assorted tape recorders were all pressed inches from Ditka's face. One hand attached to a local TV mike actually shook while reporters wondered, will he bring up Perry's weight? As happens more and more these days, as Dan Pompei and Fred Mitchell and other beat reporters have learned how to handle Ditka's moods, their initial approach is cool and calm. They ease into the Perry issue, gauging Ditka's tone as he offers a variety of first-day impressions. The result is a wealth of material, more meaty quotes on one subject than most NFL coaches offer in a year. Moreover, not only does Ditka speak passionately but within a larger "in life" context (he drops three references into the full press conference) as well. What could have been a dull and ordinary day is suddenly filled with words and wisdom that resonate around the league.

First-day impressions, Coach?

"It wasn't great," Ditka says. "It wasn't bad. Looked like a lot of guys stumbling around out there. A lot of guys who aren't in shape, lot of guys who are in shape. It's idealistic for me to sit up there and say I want them to be a lot better on the first day. They're not going to be a lot better. . . . They are not a lot of bodies who are in shape right now, I mean football shape."

Mike, what explanation did William Perry have for being late? It's Mitchell from the *Trib*.

"He's said he's sorry. All he said and I accepted it. I'm not into investigative reporting like some people I know. It doesn't matter. Watergate died."

What did you fine him? It's Pompei.

The question is ignored.

How does Perry's condition look to you?

"What do you think?"

He looks a little heavy.

"Yeah. You're right. Those things are obvious. That's an obvious statement that requires no question or answer."

I'd like a little elaboration if I could.

"Elaboration? He's real heavy." (Laughter.) "He's too heavy and he knows it, and he'll try to get it down. I can't worry about that right now. We've got a lot of other football players trying to be football players. I just can't. I just can't. We had our time to do that. That time has passed. That mountain has been climbed. No more."

How about his attitude, Mike, are you concerned?

"His attitude is good. I mean he'll try. But, ah, you know, you can only do so much physically when your limitations are hindered. You can never get to your maximum potential. You can never reach where you should be in life. No matter how good he gets, he'll never, ever, get to where he should be unless his weight is right. And unless he understands that, it will be a fruitless career for him because he'll never really experience what it is to be on top of the mountain, where you are what you are."

Did you fine him? Pompei again, probing.

"Yeah, I fined him."

A thousand dollars? Still Pompei. He was ignored again but still digging. *What does it say that a twenty-eight-year-old man can't be to work on time after six months of vacation?*

"You have to ask him. Why are you asking me that?"

Well, you're the coach.

Ditka sensed blame and criticism coming in his direction, though that's hardly the tack the *Sun-Times* writer was taking. No matter. Ditka suddenly unloaded on Perry.

"Well, I know the rules too. You know the rules. See, you're trying to create controversy. The issue is he's wrong. Dead wrong. I mean you can write it W-R-O-N-G. Wrong. He's wrong. You can elaborate on it and psychoanalyze why he wasn't here, but that doesn't make him any more right or wrong. He's wrong. He's wrong. He apologized. I accepted the apology. He'll accept the fine. That's all I can say. All I know is that if I was twenty-four or twenty-five years old and somebody said, 'Hey, here's what, I'm gonna give you a chance for a couple of years to make yourself a couple of million,' you watch me bust my butt.'' (Heating up.) "That's all I'm gonna say. That's all. Some people think different than I do.''

The writers, sensing momentum now, begin to push. *Don't you get tired of it?*

"Well, you know, I'm not in a position where I can afford to be tired of it. If I'm tired of it, than I shouldn't be doing this. William's a first-draft pick; he's a fine football player. Again, will he ever be as good as he can be? I doubt it, until he understands about his weight. The weight has to come down, no question about it. He's gonna hurt himself out there physically.''

Is he that much above last year?

"He's three seventy. You can print that any way you want. But it goes three, seven, oh.''

What was he doing this morning?

"Taking a stress test. He had to take a stress test before he came on the field.''

Because you were concerned?

"I guess so.''

How did he do?

"He did well on the stress test. He didn't die anyway." (Heavy laughter.)

Mike, do you think it might have come too quick for him?

"That's a lot of crap.''

Well . . .

"Do you think it came too quick for Mark Carrier?'' (The reference is to the Bears' No. 1 draft pick in 1990, who led the NFL in interceptions with 10, made All-Pro, and was named the NFL Defensive Rookie of the Year.)

Well, Mark Carrier didn't have what this guy had.

"Well, I'm asking you a question. Do you think it came too fast for Bo Jackson? For Michael Jackson . . . I mean, Michael Jordan?''

All I'm asking is if you can reflect on it.

"No, I don't think it came too fast. I think he handled it poorly. Nothing comes too fast. You put yourself in a position in life to get somewhere, and once you get in a position to get there, you go. If you can't handle that, that's your problem. . . .

"His weight was down. He was really close to it in the spring, and he threw it all away. It's very disappointing to me because of all the times, all the guys that have gone to bat for him, if he can't trust me, then he can't trust anybody. That's the only thing that hurts me. Never a phone call. Never an excuse. Never a reason. Never, 'Hey, Coach, help me out.' If I'm not his friend, than I don't think he's got a friend. It's a fact. I'm not going to belabor this issue anymore." (He keeps talking, despite already having given writers enough for a half-hour show and two Sunday supplements.) "I happen to love this guy and I happen to care a lot more about him than [just as] a Chicago Bear football player. I don't know how I can get it across any more than I've tried. We tried everything and I tried everything. The rest is up to him."

Five years earlier in July 1986, on the first day in Platteville, Perry could have weighed four-hundred pounds and still not led the sports news. The story of that day was another heavyweight—the suddenly bloated form of Jim McMahon, who had put on twenty pounds over a rather satisfying winter of golf, beer drinking, and autobiography writing. McMahon arrived in camp as the hottest athlete in the country, well on his way to making millions off his hell-bent-for-leather performance during Super Bowl week, a compelling mix of shock theater combined with a boffo on-stage performance. First there was the case of the Japanese acupuncturist whom McMahon needed and McCaskey refused to let on the team plane. Then McMahon mooned a helicopter to show, in effect, that the treatments were working. Blindsided by an erroneous news report in which he report-edly called New Orleans women "sluts" and all the men "idiots," McMahon was found to be innocent of any misbehavior, victimized instead by an irresponsible reporter. In the Super Bowl, McMahon's headband messages became as much a part of the game as the Bears themselves, and a lot more interesting. In a span of four quarters he pleaded the plight of those military men still missing in action ("POW-MIA"), sent a message to a sick friend ("PLUTO"), and raised a tremendous amount of money for juvenile diabetes ("JDF-CURE"). It was sports theater at its best, coupled with a right-on on-field perfor-mance (12 of 20 passes, 256 yards, and 2 rushing TDs) that sent McMahon's popularity into the stratosphere. In no time he was making millions in commercials from such companies as Taco Bell and Adidas. He was on the cover of such disparate magazines as *Rolling Stone* and *BusinessWeek*. McMahon had always scoffed at authority. Now on the heels of his Super Bowl triumph he pushed himself and his rebel image to the max. "If possible," says Pompei, "his head got even bigger."

But when McMahon pulled a hip flexor muscle during the second practice of training camp in 1986, Ditka decided it was time to deflate his star's ego. From that point on they bickered and traded barbs about everything from McMahon's injuries to his lack of leadership. Their family feud was viewed as little more than preseason entertainment as the Bears prepared for their first exhibition game of the season, a transoceanic trip to London, for the so-called American Bowl—the NFL's attempt to mass-market football to the European market. The Bears were one drawing card. The Dallas Cowboys were the other. Immediately after returning home, however, Bears players were greeted with some stunning and potentially career-threatening news: a random drug test. Ditka and Vainisi had talked about the testing prior to training camp. The league had wanted to test before the London trip, but with all the preparations, Vainisi says it just wasn't possible. He suggested the test be scheduled soon after the club returned from England. "Both Mike and I decided not to tell the players about it," says Vainisi. "I mean, we wanted to know. We felt it was management's right to know." When the club finally gave the players forty-eight hours notice of the test, it got ugly.

"They revolted," says Vainisi.

The players gathered for a team meeting in one of the classrooms at UW-Platteville. It was a stormy session. Several players angrily demanded player rep Singletary seek more time before the test (normally it takes at least seventy-two hours for cocaine to pass through the system; marijuana, if smoked in minimal amounts, passes through in about a week). Singletary was not happy about it. Says Fencik, "Mike (Singletary) always felt that we were protecting some people, and we probably were." Singletary and player alternate rep Duerson negotiated a compromise—backed by Ditka—of a few extra days. "Yeah, he backed us," says Fencik of Ditka's decision. "Let's face it, Mike's been there. In a different era, but he knows you've got to stick together, and we just felt the procedure was handled very poorly."

A few days later the Bears got tested. Says Vainisi, "If anybody was on cocaine, then they had enough time to get it through their system, and to my knowledge none tested positive for cocaine. There was one marijuana. In any event, we got through that."

It was just in time for another flap to start. This time it was McMahon's autobiography, a soon-to-be best-seller (four hundred thousand copies, twenty-one weeks on *The New York Times* list). Thanks to the deft touch of *Tribune* columnist Bob Verdi, his collaborator, it was a dead-on dust-up of the NFL and a scathing personal attack on McCaskey. As the team bus pulled out of Three Rivers Stadium in

Pittsburgh after a 33–13 win over the Steelers in the second exhibition game, McMahon walked up to Butler. "I got the book," he told the kicker. "Read Chapter Nine. It's on management."

Butler's mouth dropped a little lower with each paragraph: "Michael McCaskey doesn't have any qualifications to operate the Bears, except his name. . . .

"Michael McCaskey might think we won because of him; he'd be offended to learn that most of us felt we won in spite of him. . . .

"I'd like to play pro football forever, or at least until I'm forty, because I enjoy it so much. But I can't see doing it for the Bears unless Michael McCaskey sells the team. He takes a lot of fun out of the game."

When he had finished the chapter, Butler couldn't see McMahon playing for the Bears a minute longer. "It's been fun playing with you," the kicker said. "You're out of here."

As it turns out, McMahon was hardly the only unhappy camper. In addition to his feud with Ditka and McCaskey, and the surprise drug test, the Bears were experiencing the same kind of emotional meltdown common with any world championship team, i.e., locker room jealousy and resentment over who gets the most credit and publicity, and ultimately, the greatest monetary rewards. Only in Chicago, the fame = money equation was more dangerous because it potentially produced staggering numbers. For example, McMahon would make more than a million dollars on his autobiography alone; Ditka's would sell 140,000 copies and make $300,000 or more; Singletary's book sold 35,000 copies and turned a profit. Car dealers, poster makers, shopping centers, business groups, were all clamoring for a Bear, any Bear to show up at their function. Monday and Tuesday became as known as money days around the locker room. A one-hour, in-store autograph session was worth a quick $500 or more. A speech on Tuesday might bring another $2,000. The rookies and second-line players were happy with whatever came through the public relations department.

But the star players were getting edgy with each other; when Pompei inquired as to how the team might play with Singletary about to miss a game, Marshall piped in with, "What do you mean Singletary? Nobody ever asked about me when I was injured." Marshall and others also started comparing requests for interviews, to the point of actually counting the number of times reporters came up to teammates' lockers. Squabbling broke out over commercials, too. Hampton and McMichael, close friends, got in a messy argument when McMichael won a role over Hampton in a tire commercial starring Perry. "To put it in a nutshell," says Singletary, "we lost our focus. We came back looking for who was going to get more interviews, who was getting the publicity, who was going to get the next commercial endorsement."

Some not only did not get commercials, they weren't even asked. Dent, the Super Bowl MVP, was miffed at what happened. "I think, at the time, Mike stuck William [Perry] back there [in the backfield in some games, where he became a cult hero] and William turned into the all-American guy. He makes all the money. Then you got McMahon coming in right behind him. Then you got Payton behind them. I was the MVP and I didn't get hardly nothing as a major endorsement." His voice cranks up a notch. "Why? The team has got to get behind the athlete, the marketing people have got to be in the same boat. If you're McMahon, the team is in the same boat. Fridge, the team is in the same boat. And Ditka, the team is in the same boat. Fact is, it doesn't leave too much room."

The jealousies and animosity brewing in the locker room soon spilled over at home. Several of the wives proved as star struck as their husbands, principally Willie Gault's and Otis Wilson's. Kim Singletary and Cathy Butler, as soothing and solid as their husbands, saw the nouveau riche attitude first creep into the most unlikely of places— baby showers. Bears wives had always held such showers for first-time mothers-to-be. Back in 1983 and even '84 with the team on the rise, baby bibs, receiving blankets, and single outfits were the most common gifts. Sometimes, says Kim, four or five wives would chip in and buy a stroller. That changed in late '85 and '86. "The showers were unbelievable," she says. "Now one wife would buy a two-hundred-dollar stroller."

"One shower was so unbelievable it was like a wedding reception," says Cathy Butler. "It got to be such a joke. It was like 'Wheel of Fortune,' 'Big money, big money.' "

Soon the overblown displays spread from shower gifts to cars, jewelry, furs, and even homes. "There was such materialistic competition," Cathy Butler says. "Nothing overtly verbal, but it was just there. Guys were getting dealer cars. You'd hear things like, 'I'm sure I'm going to drive a [Chevy] Celebrity.' Who has the bigger house. Who's got the newer Mercedes. It was like a monster, it just kept growing. Everything to the max.

"I didn't want to believe it was happening. It was hard to believe material things could make such an impact."

In years past, Mike Singletary insists, the dueling-egos problem would have been solved by Ryan, at least on the defensive side. But

Ryan was gone, hired as head coach of the Philadelphia Eagles. Buddy had said his good-byes in his final meeting the night before the Super Bowl. "I was sitting next to Singletary and Buddy was giving a speech and he said, 'You know, no matter what happens tomorrow you guys will always be my heroes,'" Fencik says. Ryan left the room with tears in his eyes. Fencik did too. Gone was the 46. Gone were all Buddy's crazy names for defenses, like Mumbo, a blitz, named after some former player's nickname. Gone was what Fencik now calls the "wonderful little history" of Ryan. The one-page "World According to Buddy" memo Ryan would pass out on Friday mornings, filled with folksy, profane reminders. "Now, Richard," he would write to Dent, "make sure your ass is on the outside." "Buddy," says Fencik in a soft, wistful voice, "Buddy would break you down like a sergeant in boot camp. Then he would build you up in his mold. He had an incredible bond. He'd back you. Ditka would come in and tell Mike Richardson, 'You're an asshole,' and Buddy would close the door and say, 'You're an asshole but you're my asshole and I love you.'"

And when Ryan left, the burden fell back on Ditka to soothe the egos and keep the peace. He failed. "We had a great football team," says Singletary, "but it was tough to keep it all under one hat. I think the only reason we were able to keep it under one hat was because you had Buddy Ryan on one side and Ditka on the other. You had two head coaches, that's really what we had—a coach for the offense and a coach for the defense. When Buddy left, you know, it's like a kid hanging on when his parents get a divorce. The kids hang on the mom." But Ditka didn't have the time or the personality to play crisis counselor. Ryan was gone. Good riddance. And so, said Ditka, was the 46. Give it a chance, said the players. We'll work with you. "We could do anything he wanted us to do with it," says Singletary. "We had built up to this eruption, and he came over and put ice on it. We're ready to explode with [the 46]. I mean it's at its peak. In '85 it was great, but I felt in '86, we could just come back and blow everybody away. We needed the guy that was there to say, 'All right, you sorry, no good so-and-sos, kill them.'" They needed fire and spirit and showmanship on the sideline.

What they got was Vince Tobin.

A straightlaced, no-nonsense former USFL and Canadian league defensive coordinator, Tobin is the brother of Bears personnel director Bill Tobin. His credentials in the CFL and for the Philadelphia/Baltimore Stars of the USFL were impressive, particularly for the Stars, where his defense led the league all three years in fewest points allowed. In the first meeting under Tobin, Wilson, coming off a Pro Bowl season, propped his feet on a chair. "Put 'em down," ordered Tobin. In fact, eight of the Bears starting '85 defense had, or would be, in the Pro Bowl: Hampton, McMichael, Dent, Singletary, Wilson, Marshall, Duerson, Fencik. They had made it because of Ryan and the 46, not Tobin, and they let him know it, not overtly, but with blank stares and snide comments, as when Tobin implored the unit to "swim to the ball like sharks," and one defensive star turned to another and whispered, "Oh, boy, that's an inspiring thought."

Singletary is asked to assess Ryan's departure and Tobin's impact on the team. He chews on the question for several moments before answering. "Let me put it this way," he begins. "Our defense now is totally different. When Vince came in he did a great job with the defense, but he had to deal with"—Singletary crosses both arms on his chest and brings a bored look to his face. "I mean Buddy was our *dad,* and we felt like we could pretty much do this ourselves. We didn't need anybody." How bad did it get? "It got pretty bad because Vince does not have a strong character. He's a corporate guy," Singletary says. "I want this, this, this, and he expects you to do it. Bottom line. He'll explain it, but in coaching there's a whole other side to it. Here's a kid who's got a problem at home or needs someone he can go to, or he's got a problem with Coach Ditka. With Buddy it was, 'We'll make it right, we'll make it happen.' But you were afraid to go to Vince because Vince might tell him [Ditka]. So instead of conveying it, you internalize it."

But Tobin had a system, too, a defensive philosophy geared to what Ditka wanted—a standard 4-3 alignment with less blitzing and more zone pass coverage designed to cut down on big plays. It made sense, if for no other reason than cornerback Leslie Frazier had suffered a career-ending knee injury in the opening moments of the Super Bowl. With Frazier out, both corners were vulnerable. But like it or not the defense was nothing short of sensational. Only three teams scored more than 14 points against the Bears during the regular season, and the defense set a record for fewest points allowed (187) in NFL history for a 16-game season. The Bears won six straight games to open the '86 season, running their two-year mark to 24-1. One of those wins came over Philadelphia in the second week of the season, a blood battle with Ryan that Ditka wanted badly. McMahon was hurt, nursing a bad right shoulder, and he and the club were still sniping back and forth. Team doctors and trainers said McMahon's injury was a mild separation of the acromioclavicular joint. McMahon believed something else was wrong. Before the Philly game a number of Bears came by to shake Ryan's hand. Ditka turned his back, staring a hole in the stands. Against Philadelphia, Tomczak, in just his second year, took the reins and, with Ditka playing it close to the vest, squeaked out a 13–10 overtime win. Afterward Ryan cried, Singletary cried. Six hours later Ditka blasted Ryan on his radio show. "He talked about [going to] the Super Bowl in three years," Ditka said angrily. "He'll be lucky to have a job in three years."

For much of the next month McMahon popped in and out of the lineup—the shape of things to come for the next three seasons. He took shots, anti-inflammatory drugs, and tons of Ditka's grief over his health and "pouting." Ditka was taking shots, too. "Get your mouth shut . . . jerk," he bellowed at a drunk who had interrupted a press conference after a game with Cincinnati. Making a circle with his thumb and forefinger, Ditka added, "See that? That's your IQ, buddy— zero."

Yet the Bears kept winning, despite the fact neither Tomczak nor Fuller had inspired widespread confidence within the organization. "Fuller was injured and having an awful year," says Vainisi, "and Tomczak wasn't ready."

So Ditka and Vainisi began shopping for another quarterback. "You know, it's late in the season," says Vainisi. "There's a quarterback out there that's a competitive guy. You've got a helluva football team. Quarterbacks are overrated anyhow. If you can bring the guy along and teach him enough of the system, maybe, you know, maybe, he can get you through."

Ditka and to a lesser extent Vainisi pushed to sign Doug Flutie, the 5'9" Heisman Trophy winner from Boston College who had signed a $8-million contract with Donald Trump's New Jersey Generals of the USFL. When the league folded in August '86, Flutie was content to collect $3.95 million in guaranteed money and remain property of the Los Angeles Rams, who held his NFL rights. Talent scouts had two distinct opinions on Flutie. To some, Flutie was a miracle worker whose scrambling ability and improvisional skills sparked ball clubs and produced points. To others, he was a peanut-sized passer, perfect for outposts such as the USFL or CFL but physically incapable of competing in the NFL (too small to see over linemen). Ditka believed the former; Bill Tobin and McCaskey were adamant about the latter. "For whatever reason," says Flutie's agent, Bob Woolf, "McCaskey couldn't cope with it. He didn't want him there from the beginning."

Ditka pressed the issue and won. On October 14, 1986, one minute before the trading deadline, the Bears acquired his rights from the Rams for two 1987 draft choices. "It may work out we'll have him this year," Ditka said. "That's my original thought—to bring him in now. The trade was my decision and I'll live with it. I had to talk long and hard with a lot of people in this organization before the trade was made."

In retrospect it was arguably the Bears' single biggest personnel mistake in the last six years. Some might argue trading away the deep speed of Gault in 1988 was worse, but as a pure recipe for disaster—for dissension, backbiting, and sending the absolute wrong message about loyalty and unity—the signing of Flutie won the gold medal. All the bitching and moaning about McCaskey, the drug tests, the carping about playing time and endorsement deals, that was Dick and Jane compared to this. "Any questions?" Ditka had asked his players when the signing of Flutie seemed imminent. Before he knew it, Van Horne had stood up, all 6'7", with a question:

"What's this fucking Flutie shit?"

"What do we need *him* for?" demanded Wilson.

"It was definitely heated," says Butler. "We just didn't understand."

To complicate matters, soon after Flutie signed, the Bears waived free-spirited wide receiver Ken Margerum off injured reserve. Many players, particularly those camping in McMahon's backyard, felt it was McCaskey's way of getting even at what McMahon had said in his book. Margerum and the quarterback were best of friends. But it also hurt Ditka. Margerum was perhaps the hardest worker on the team, an exemplary practice player who, says Butler, "we all rallied around in practice . . . a guy who may not contribute on the field but meant so much to the team in other ways."

The battle lines had now been drawn. McMahon immediately mocked the trade, wearing a red "22"—Flutie's number at BC—in practice. When Flutie finally showed up a week later, after signing a two-and-a-half-year contract, he found his locker next to the toilet. Hampton was heard growling, "Just because you have the uniform doesn't mean you're a Bear." The team ordered pizzas—Flutie got a personal pan.

"What's he worth to me?" asked linebacker Wilson. "How much change have I got in my pocket?"

McMahon was taking this a bit more personally than anyone else. Quite personally, in fact. He was injured but still wielded tremendous influence over the team—particularly his offensive line. He publicly questioned why Fuller and Tomczak were being abandoned. Hadn't they suffered through training camp? Wasn't Tomczak undefeated as a starter? It was a noble gesture—one, however, several teammates suspected, mixed with an ulterior motive.

"I think there was a lot of insecurity on his part," says Butler. Because of that insecurity, behind the scenes, players say, McMahon did everything possible to sabotage Flutie.

"McMahon was the guy who destroyed it," says Vainisi, and adds that Ditka saw McMahon's moves as "a complete challenge" to his authority. "It became a battle of wills. Either Mike Ditka or Jim McMahon. Basically it was a matter of who's running this football team?"

So Ditka waged a campaign of his own. He took Flutie to dinner. He praised him in public. He was the first quarterback ever to look at extra film, Ditka said. He called Flutie "Bambi," telling reporters, "You look at those brown eyes and yelling at him would be like yelling at Bambi."

A Chicago Bear? *Bambi?*

"Bambi," said Ditka.

He invited Flutie and his fiancée over for Thanksgiving dinner. Some players saw it for what it was—a friendly gesture to a new player. Others bitched about the "teacher's pet," wondering why they had never been invited to dine. There was even a rumor that Flutie stayed the night at Ditka's home. "A lot of guys were going, 'Wait a minute, what's going on here?'" says Fencik. "'I didn't get invited over to bring my toothbrush and stay at Mike's house.'"

On and on it went. The strain showed after a painstaking 13–7 win over Detroit. "Maybe this is the way it has to be," said Ditka in obvious distress. "I don't know." The Bears, wrote *Sun-Times* sportswriter Brian Hewitt, who had covered the team for years, are the unhappiest 7-1 team in recent NFL history. It got worse. Ditka was openly questioning McMahon's shoulder injury and his inability to practice. Hampton had done the same thing earlier in the year, standing up at a team meeting, yelling, "Hey, McMahon. You plan to practice anymore this year?" McMahon practiced and played in a 12–10 defeat of Green Bay, but his shoulder was shot. He argued with Ditka, then flew to Los Angeles to consult with noted orthopedic surgeon Dr. Frank Jobe, who immediately found a partial tear in McMahon's rotator cuff and some other instability in the shoulder. The gonzo QB was headed for the operating table, out for the year.

Flutie was seeing spot action by now, and while he was turning out to be a good guy with a rocket arm, he was ineffective at quarterback. "He had problems," says Hughes. "He had to get out of the pocket to see things, and we were not that good of an offensive line to get him out of the pocket or keep him in the pocket. You could stand behind

Doug in practice and see the blind spots. If there was a lineman in front of him, he just couldn't see the receiver going through the gaps. For a small guy he had pretty good anticipation; he could lead a receiver, but he might not be able to see how many defensive people were sitting over there."

Fencik, for example, recalls intercepting Flutie time after time in practice, the defensive backs remarking, "My God, he didn't even see us."

"He'd throw it right at you," says Fencik.

Ditka had desperately hoped McMahon would somehow recover and march his ball club back to the Super Bowl. The defense was on fire (five times in the final seven games it held the opposition to 10 points or less). If McMahon would play . . . but it wasn't to be. In response Ditka turned to the former miracle worker from BC, hoping for another miracle. He piled four months of learning into just eight weeks. "We just gave Flutie too much," says Vainisi. "We tried to force-feed too much too soon."

It all came to a head in the worst possible way, at the worst possible time: in the NFC playoffs against Washington. Chicago had entered the game as a prohibitive favorite despite the problem behind the center, despite the fact that seven of the team's fourteen wins had come in the pathetic NFC Central against Detroit, Tampa Bay, and Green Bay, who had *combined* for eleven wins, despite the fact only two teams the Bears played in '86 finished with winning records, Minnesota and Los Angeles, and both had beaten Chicago. Wasn't Washington coming off a brutal wild-card win over the Rams six days earlier? Weren't the Redskins beat-up, injured, and playing on the road? "We have no plans for a loss," McCaskey said before the game. "If we lose it will be like a toboggan that's racing down a hill and hits a log, sending everybody flying."

Ditka chose Flutie to steer the sled against the 'Skins. "A lot of guys were upset," recalls Dent. "We had Fuller and Tomczak on the sideline, who know the whole offense, and we're bringin' a guy in after six weeks and put him in the game. . . . Why break a record that was going good? We've got something going, why tear it up?"

Hughes was against it too: "I would have played Tomczak. Mike brought Doug in. It was his sole idea of bringing him in. Come the Washington game, he was going to play."

It was not a memorable moment. Bob Woolf, Flutie's agent, still has the tape bracelet Flutie wore around his wrist that day, the one with thirty-one different plays written on it. Plays that read, "R R/L

W.O.—49/28 W.G.U. P.O.W." Overwhelmed, Flutie, in the words of Vainisi, "short-circuited" and started calling Boston College or New Jersey Generals formations. "It just got confusing," says the former GM. Very confusing. Flutie was just 11 for 31 for 134 yards, just 5 of 15 in the second half for a grand total of 37 yards. In the third quarter he threw one of those blind, ill-conceived practice-type passes that was picked off by cornerback Darrell Green, setting up a TD that put Washington ahead to stay, 14–13. The final score was 27–13. It was a miserable way to end a miserable season.

Two days later, Vainisi was fired.

Backing Ditka on the Flutie deal had put Vainisi's job in jeopardy, despite the fact, he says, under his stewardship the team had its four most profitable years in history, but McCaskey was tired of internal debates. He and Tobin had squared off enough against the GM and head coach over players and policy. Vainisi, certainly, was no fan of McCaskey's, dating back to his days with Halas. The GM loathed the club president's inability to make a decision, his constant harping for "more revenue, more revenue, more revenue," and the way he wore his high-minded Harvard ways on the sleeve of his preppy blue blazers. There were "endless" staff meetings, and continual evaluations and reevaluations of problems. Says Vainisi, "He would look at it seventeen ways and prevent you from making a decision and keep on continually delaying."

McCaskey's aristocratic attitude and use of the English language as an intimidating weapon, spouting four- and five-syllable words to make others feel inferior, was also wearing thin. In one of his first meetings with other NFL owners, McCaskey lectured the group on economic realities. It went over about as well as the idea of unrestricted free agency. Also unappreciated were his attempts to break the team's Soldier Field lease with the Chicago Park District in favor of a move to the suburbs, and his demands that a piece of lakefront property be donated for a new stadium site.

According to Vainisi, in an effort to get rid of his general manager, McCaskey began "trying to fabricate a scenario to show breach of contract." McCaskey, who declined to be interviewed for this book, eventually charged that Vainisi had lied and deceived him in a deal involving a pilot "Bears fan club" program with NFL Properties, the powerful marketing arm of the league. As Vainisi explains it, Properties made some unauthorized assumptions on the Bears commitment to the fan club. During the playoff rush in '86, the league was about to announce the Bears were starting a fan club when McCaskey, who had liked the idea but wanted to negotiate a better deal, found out about the league's intentions. In early December he summoned the entire front office to a meeting. "Did you authorize this?" he said, going from person to person.

Everybody said no.

He turned to Vainisi. "Did you authorize this?"

"No."

Vainisi says, "He claimed I lied to him. He had his father sitting right there. He had told the staff that you could never lie to him because if he couldn't trust you, he couldn't work with you. Therefore he said I can't trust you and you're fired."

But McCaskey had some conditions. If Vainisi didn't say anything negative about him or the Bears, he could keep his job for a reasonable period of time. The next day Vainisi met with his attorney and prepared to file a grievance.

But of course, there was still the matter of Ditka. Vainisi had been fired around two P.M. Two hours later a drawn and sad-faced Ditka entered his office; he had been told. Vainisi explained he would be staying on for a while, something Ditka didn't understand. "If they don't want you, goddamn it, get out," said Ditka. "Get the hell out of here."

Vainisi patiently explained he had some $75,000 in deferred salary coming due on January 15. The firing would have to be kept quiet for the next ten days or so, until the money was deposited into his account. Ditka left like a man in mourning. Not only had a 14-2 season ended in despair, now this: now his last link to Halas had been severed, his best friend and business partner had been axed right underneath his nose. That night at home Ditka cried with Diana, and he hardly closed his eyes. He was too busy thinking.

"The next morning," says Vainisi, "I went into the office real early and Mike was in the whirlpool. He looked really bad, terrible. I went specifically to tell him not to saying anything, to make sure that the story didn't get out before the fifteenth because I wanted to make sure I got the money."

"Don't worry, I've got a plan," Ditka told him. "I'll talk to you later about it."

That morning Ditka met with McCaskey and others and laid out his plan. Keep Vainisi for one more year, the 1987 season, and I'll walk with him at the end of the year. I've got one year to go on my contract; at the end of the season, we'll both leave. A package deal.

No, said McCaskey. It's a done deal. The board has approved it.

"Fuck the board," said Ditka. *"You're* the board."

No, it's over, said McCaskey.

At this point Ditka stormed out of the meeting and down to Vainisi's office. He paced the carpet just as if he were back in Judi Ballman's kitchen in Philadelphia. "Fuck 'em!" he roared. "They don't give a shit about you. Why should you care about them!"

"Because I've got that money tied up," Vainisi reminded him.

Ditka left the room and said little about the entire incident until January 13, when he asked Vainisi about the check. "He asked me if the wire transfer had gone through," the GM recalls. "So I checked and it had."

The next day it was reported that Vainisi had been fired. Five years later Vainisi was asked a simple question. Was the hiring of McCaskey a watershed moment in the fall of the Bears?

"I can't say it because it comes out sour grapes." But then he says it anyway: "That really was the turning point. He doesn't have the ability to rise above personal feelings and make an objective business decision. All the feelings you would think a guy [teaching] at Harvard Business School would be taught. He may be the greatest theoretician, but in practice he ain't worth a shit."

IN 1987, MCMAHON DID NOT WANT TO PLAY BALL ANYMORE, AT LEAST NOT IN Chicago. Not after the Bears had drafted Harbaugh on the first round. Far more insecure about his playing talents than he let on, McMahon viewed Harbaugh, wrongly as it turned out, as an immediate threat. So he called his agent, Steve Zucker, and demanded a trade. Zucker relayed the message to Ditka and McCaskey. Before things got out of hand Ditka called McMahon and calmed him down. Don't worry, he said, you're still my quarterback.

It was a strange about-face given their fractious relationship at the end of '86. By this time Zucker says Ditka and McMahon were uncommunicative, existing at the subhuman level of grunts and groans. A flamboyant former defense attorney, Zucker had moved into the agent business back in '84 when McMahon asked for his help. Soon Zucker represented nine other Bears starters. "I'd tell Jim, 'Go in there and talk to him, man to man, he really likes you.' Jim was afraid Ditka would yell at him. He'd tell me, 'He's just going to yell at me.' "

So Zucker did most of the talking, which he is quite capable of, acting as a conduit from player to coach and back again. That is just what he did early in '87. He convinced Ditka to sit on the dais for a Juvenile Diabetes charity roast of McMahon, where the QB would receive the "McMan of the Year" award for his consciousness-raising —and fund-raising—efforts on behalf of JDF. The event was held in the Grand Ballroom at the downtown Hilton Towers. It ended up being one of those magical nights, the high-water mark of McMahon and Ditka's seven years together. Says Zucker, "It was like a father and son that fight and finally love each other."

The father spoke first, holding every one of the 1,800 patrons in his seat with a spellbinding speech. "I love Jim McMahon," he said in closing.

Then the son stood behind the podium. The night was already a spectacular success—more than $2 million raised. One couple alone pledged $1.5 million. McMahon was the evening's exclamation point. Speaking straight from the heart, he praised Ditka in words few had heard before. In closing he said, "If it wasn't for Mike Ditka, we never would have won the Super Bowl." They embraced as the Grand Ballroom echoed with cheers and applause.

But the '87 season would reopen old wounds and further spread the divide between quarterback and coach. McMahon was still the star, the dominant national personality, but Ditka was drawing near. The Super Bowl championship followed by the 14-2 record followed by the Flutie gambit had added to Ditka's aura. So did having his name up in lights on Ontario Street. The restaurant was producing some staggering numbers: in 1986, its first full year of operation, Ditka's/City Lights had grossed an eye-popping $7.5 million, $2.5 million more than what the prospectus had outlined for the *fifth* year of operation; in 1987, it was on the way to a remarkable $8.5 million in sales, the twenty-fourth best in the nation. Says Shlaes, "It got so on Saturday night, the [one-hundred-thirty-seat] restaurant would serve six-hundred meals. Nobody ever turned a restaurant four and five times. We would have lines out into the vestibule. Two-hour waits. Ditka was fantastic. I guess we were so star struck, so starved for a winner here in Chicago, he became an absolute God. Old women. Young women. He would walk by and people would want to touch him."

The success of the restaurant and the strokes he received every time he walked in the door fed Ditka's ego. So did the cash rolling his way. Restaurant investors had received a full return on their money plus a healthy profit in about eighteen months—unheard of in this kind of deal. Pontillo earned $600,000 for his original 400 grand. Ditka turned about a $140,000 profit given his split with Vainisi and the 5 percent for use of his name. But Ditka was not happy. He wanted more. Especially after he discovered that Rittenberg, per the terms of his contract, had been paid $375,000 in 1986 based on his 5-percent-of-the-gross contract.

"No one thought we would do those figures," says Shlaes. "That's when some of the problems started."

Problem number one was Ditka.

"What the fuck is this?" he asked Shlaes after realizing what Rittenberg had earned. "You know that's my name up there." Shlaes knew that. He also knew that he and Rittenberg were spending eighty hours a week in the place, working the convention crowd, handling the banquets, the bar mitzvahs, promoting the nightclub. Rittenberg, said Shlaes, was the glue—not Ditka. "Jimmy certainly deserved it. He created it. Mike didn't understand that. He came to us and said, 'How can he be getting this much money and I'm only getting my [7.5%]."

Rittenberg offers no apologies for what he made: "I created everything. Who knew that? Waitresses don't know that. Bartenders don't know that. The partners don't really think about it. All they know is they got their investment back in eighteen months. Well, a contract is a contract. They all signed a contract which said if you make money, we make money. Well, that's what happened! Only I made more." His voice jumps up an octave or two, cutting through the quiet at 59 West. *That was my job! That wasn't their job!* I mean, Ernie Banks and Walter Payton made more money than their coaches. That's the way it is. I was the player. I was the guy who was there, and I made a lot of money. They said, well, we didn't know you were going to make that much."

Ditka had a different view, as expressed by partner Vainisi: "The restaurant would have been successful with the popularity of the Bears and Mike Ditka if you or I had run it. It wouldn't have made any difference who ran it. Now did he get convention business and get the conventioneers over? Yes. Would the conventioneers have come anyhow if the place was going? Yes. He ran the disco. I mean, I would have no use, no use or desire to run any of that kind of stuff. But he did. I mean he deserves a certain amount of credit, but if you put the Ditka name up on the marquee, especially at that time . . . Christ we had just won the Super Bowl! The Ayatollah could have run the goddamn thing!"

Ditka wanted more money. According to Shlaes, Ditka was in the restaurant with two friends drinking "very, very heavily" before Shlaes and Rittenberg, their attorney, and the head coach walked to an upstairs office. Shlaes's relationship with Ditka had been strained from the start. Although technically a partner and a man who had made millions at the Options Exchange, he says Ditka always "treated me like I was a manager of some kind." Shlaes was turned off by Ditka's "demanding" atttitude and "smarter than anyone else" demeanor. "One of the problems," says Shlaes, "is that he got to believe the publicity. Mike Ditka never ran this restaurant. He never had the ability to run it. He's a good football coach. He's a terrible managerial person. Some of the decisions he tried to make, some of the decisions he tried to force us to do, were terrible."

For instance: tablecloths and the wine list. To Shlaes and Rittenberg they stand as symbols of Ditka's meddlesome and misguided ways. From the beginning Shlaes and Rittenberg fought Ditka's attempts to recreate that Toots Shor atmosphere, especially at a time when the restaurant was turning tables like lightening. "He wanted a gourmet restaurant," says Shlaes. "We're not a gourmet restaurant. He wanted a white-tablecloth restaurant. This was never going to be a white-tablecloth restaurant. That's not what we envisioned. That's not what we were looking for. We told him you're chasing away the people who are your fans. He wanted to do the wine list. We said, 'Fine, do the wine list.' He took a wine list for a gourmet restaurant and wanted to make it the wine list for the sports bar. He never, really, to this day, understands the concept of what he's got."

Ditka was naturally making his displeasure known. "We're nothing but a tourist trap; this is not what I wanted," he'd argue at meetings with his partners and Rittenberg. One time Shlaes said Ditka told him, "I never wanted this fucking kind of restaurant. My friends don't enjoy coming into this restaurant because it's too noisy, too loud, and they can't get a table." One night Ditka took his displeasure public. He walked in unannounced with six friends and demanded to be seated. Shlaes pleaded for a moment or two of patience; the place was mobbed. *"Fuck this mother-fucking place!"* Ditka screamed in the entryway, an outburst that made the local papers. *"I can't get a seat in my own goddamn restaurant!"*

Now as the meeting in the upstairs office began, Shlaes was edgy. He had seen Ditka in a drunken state before and found him "obnoxious" and "overbearing," just another football player "who thinks he knows more than the world does." Nevertheless, Shlaes stood his ground this time. The partnership agreement was explicit. There was no provision to put Ditka on the payroll, no provision for any additional royalties for his name.

"Mike," said Rittenberg, "I didn't know I was going to make that much."

"Well," Ditka answered, "we're making money because of my name and your abilities."

"I agree with that," said Rittenberg.

Ditka said, "You're making all the money and I'm not."

"I agree with that too," Rittenberg said. "Of course, you had not won a Super Bowl when we made this agreement. You weren't Mike Ditka, Super Bowl coach. You were Mike Ditka, coach."

Ditka didn't buy it. Rittenberg says now he was thinking the only thing that destroys partnerships is jealousy. So he offered Ditka a deal, one, he says, he would offer again.

"Why don't you take two thousand a week out of mine [pay], take a hundred thousand, plus a twenty-five-thousand-dollar lump, because I think you're right."

Both Shlaes and the attorney broke in. "Jimmy," argued Shlaes, "don't do it. Let's see if we can sit down and work something out. Let's not get hasty. Let's not get crazy. If you want to give him something, let's talk about something less."

Today Rittenberg says he was thinking long term, thinking "we want to be here forever." Weighing his expertise against Ditka's Super Bowl victory, he stood by his offer. He wrote Ditka a $25,000 check on the spot. In Shlaes's words, that "soothed the savage beast." A week later, the first $2,000 payout rolled in. Shlaes's disgust over the entire episode pours out as he says, "I lost completely all respect for him [Ditka] at that point. All my respect was completely lost. There was no Ditka's without Jimmy. There was just no Ditka's. And for him to do this, there was just no respect left. No one knew it except the people in the room because he never told anybody. And we just never told anybody. But every week Jimmy was sending him a check for two thousand dollars."

The Bears looked like a million bucks in the '87 season opener, rocking the defending Super Bowl champion New York Giants, 34–19, at Soldier Field. Signs of Super Bowl fever swept the city once more—and Ditka's popularity hit new heights. "The phone just doesn't stop ringing," said his longtime personal assistant Mary Albright. "Sometimes I feel like pulling my hair out. He could be busy morning, noon, and night if he wanted to."

His leap into the local commercial market had actually started back in 1983 when he endorsed a rustproofing product called The Protector, as little more than a favor for Kushner, who owns an automotive supply company. In the summer of '85, David Hynes of Passport Communications was working on pitching a promotional poster idea to Budget to help move their Lincoln Town Cars. He came up with the theme of "Go With a Pro" and considered Ditka. "I thought, let's take this crazy man out of his element, put him in front of his brand-new restaurant, leaning against a Lincoln." So Hynes took a shot and called Halas Hall. Albright happened to be out that day. When Ditka answered the phone, Hynes said he nearly had heart failure.

"What'ya got?" asked Ditka.

"Mr. Ditka," stumbled Hynes, an otherwise hyperkinetic ad guy, "we're doing this project for the people at Budget . . ."

"Me? An endorsement?" cracked Ditka when Hynes had finished. "What are you talking about?"

Hynes kept talking. "Well," said Ditka, "come on up here."

Ditka eventually told Hynes he would "give it a shot," and once the posters went up, they came down just as quickly—stolen by fans enamored with Ditka's act and the fact his Bears were Super Bowl–shuffling their way to New Orleans. Soon the local marketing crowd was crowing about how Ditka was the perfect pitchman—recognizability, strength of character, and of course, credibility. Entire media campaigns—TV and radio spots, posters, point-of-purchase material—were now being built around Ditka. National advertisers took notice. He signed his first network television spot—for Hanes underwear. He was sensational, the "famous tough guy" who proved a real softie at heart, rubbing those nice fresh undies against his beard. Next came Campbell's Chunky Soups. Sales soared. American Express followed with its classic "Do You Know Me?" campaign. Directors raved about Ditka's preparation and natural on-camera persona, what a quick study he was. "Two-Take Mike" they called him. They also quickly learned he tolerated nothing less than perfection on the set and was not above getting, in the words of a Tallman Bank executive, "fidgety" if a director wanted more takes than Ditka felt necessary to give. "Sometimes, he thinks he knows better than the director when it's a good take," says Tallman vice president Jim Sherman.

Ditka took advantage of his appeal and quickly boosted his price per commercial into the $75,000-to-$100,000 range. Momentum flowed into other areas as well, particularly motivational speeches, where Ditka now commanded $20,000 per talk, leaping into the same league with Notre Dame football coach Lou Holtz and Pat Riley, then coach of the NBA champion Los Angeles Lakers. Some players began grumbling. On one hand Ditka had cautioned his players to cut down on endorsements and devote more time to returning to the Super Bowl. On the other hand, he was selling a piece of himself every chance he could. "Some of the players were saying that Coach Ditka was doing too much," says former Bears cornerback Lorenzo Lynch, sitting in the quiet of a New Jersey Meadowlands hotel room the night before Phoenix was to play a 1991 game against the Giants. "A lot of people talked under their breath. Players were complaining all the time, in the locker room, on the bus. Their comments started to rub off on people. He'd be talking and [the players would be saying], 'Oh, he's just gonna do it for himself.'"

22

IN LIFE, AS DITKA MIGHT SAY, EVENTS OFTEN CONSPIRE TO TEACH ONE A lesson. In week two of the '87 season, the Bears rolled to another win, 20–3, over Tampa Bay. By this time, NFL players were preparing to strike, stressing the same issue—free agency—that helped trigger the 1982 walkout. NFLPA Executive Director Gene Upshaw viewed the Bears as the linchpin of any labor unrest, knowing full well if McMahon, Singletary, Payton, et al. supported a strike, the rest of the league would follow. Dave Duerson was actually the player rep at the time, but when the strike talk surfaced, Singletary stepped up and returned as rep. Instincts told him it was going to get sticky, and as he says, "I'd rather take the heat." He says he placed his faith in the Lord and told his teammates, whatever we do, we do it together, holding several player meetings. On the Friday before the Saturday game against Tampa Bay, he discussed various strike options with Ditka, who was none too pleased. "Don't do it, Mike," said the son of a union president. "It's dumb, it's stupid."

Singletary says he was also getting heavy pressure from Upshaw. Singletary told the union president the Bears were sharply divided, that some players supported free agency and the fight for greater benefits, while others were just as eager to keep the status quo. Fights broke out between teammates. Best friends stopped talking. Veterans worried about mortgage payments while rookies made vacation plans. Some players supported Singletary, calling him "a rock." Others either found him "too militaristic," or a "company man." Singletary says he was simply representing a majority viewpoint, no matter how thin the percentage. He warned Upshaw straight up he wasn't going to take his guys out, set them up for something that might not happen.

"Well, Mike," said Upshaw, "what they're doing is not right."

"I know it's not right," answered the middle linebacker, "but at the same time two wrongs don't make a right. So I'm going to tell my guys to walk? For what? For free agency? What if we don't get it? These guys have got families."

"I know, I know," Upshaw responded. "If you do it, if you walk with me this time, we'll make it."

Singletary was at home at the time, talking into the phone. Duerson was at his side. "Gene," said Singletary, "the only way that we will walk is if you give me your word that we're going to stay out until we get what we're fighting for."

"You got my word," Upshaw told him.

On Monday, by a slim margin, the Bears voted to strike. That night on "Monday Night Football," Singletary went on at halftime to explain both the team's and union's position. Two days later, games scheduled for the following weekend were canceled. Scab, or "replacement," players were brought in. Some coaches, such as Buddy Ryan, openly backed the striking vets and treated the scab players like lepers. Ditka took a different approach. Naturally, he played to win, and his replacement players pounded Ryan and the Eagles 35–3 on the first weekend in October.

The following Sunday, before a game against Minnesota, several Bear veterans set up strike tables in the west parking lot at Soldier Field. Tensions were running high among players. Some were ready for a long fight. Others were already drained by Singletary's constant "keep your nuts hot, keep your nuts hot" speeches, worried the union seemed to have no fallback position on any of its issues. "What were we keeping our nuts hot *for?*" asks Harbaugh four years later. "Hey, let's get a strategy here. Why are we doing this?" Still, much of the team showed up at Soldier Field seeking fan support and a boycott of the game. They found themselves shaken as, one by one, fans stopped to chat, asked for an autograph, then walked right in the stadium. "It was really disheartening," says Fencik. "It made an indelible mark on a lot of people." Around halftime the players adjourned to a private room at Fencik's Hunt Club restaurant where they watched the impostors beat the Vikings, 27–7.

Sitting in the Hunt Club was a team that had learned from the previous year's mistakes. The backbiting, envy and destructive personal jealousies were subsiding. Forty-seven men were now primed for another shot at the Super Bowl. They had believed Ditka to be *their* coach. They had trusted him. But now that trust had been shattered by

Ditka's defiant anti-union stance. After the Philadelphia win he had labeled NFL strikers "goons on the picket line, goon squads," a heartless slap across his father's face if there ever was one. Ditka also praised his replacement defense, boasting how it "looked the same to me. If you take the names off the jerseys and change around the numbers, you'd never recognize the difference." This callous comment followed another Ditka outburst of a week earlier when he lashed out at striking players, charging his team was loaded with "egomaniacs" and "prima donnas" and that the only way to control them was through discipline.

During the week of the Minnesota game Ditka went a step further, threatening fans who wanted ticket refunds. "If I owned a club," he said, "and they turned their tickets in, I wouldn't give them a ticket next year. Seriously, I don't care if people like it or not."

Finally, as if that wasn't enough, the day before the Vikings game Ditka appealed to what he called "real" Bears fans to ignore the striking players out in the parking lot and come inside Soldier Field and support his team. "We need all of the support of real Bears fans we can get for the players on the field playing," he said.

Plainly, Ditka didn't care about the men who had made him famous. All the restaurant backslapping, his name in lights, plastered all over television, heard daily, almost hourly on the radio, clouded his vision at the wrong time. As Singletary says today, "He thought he didn't need us anymore. He thought he could win with any eleven guys he put on the field."

Black or white. Win or lose. He made the choice.

And even though after the victory over the Vikings Ditka tried to backtrack on his statements and talked about how much he respected his original Bears for "fighting for what they think is right," he never came out and said he missed them or supported them. The damage was done.

The back room of the Hunt Club was stone-cold silent as Ditka made his post-game remarks. Somebody swore, the mood darkened by the news the talks between the union and management had broken off again. The next sound was chairs scraping against the floor, guys getting up and just walking out, a lost look on their faces. "That," says Butler, "is when the reality of the strike set in." Fencik, in a TV interview, vented his spleen about the scene at the stadium, how the team would never forget it, nor Ditka's insensitive remarks. The hurt still shows on Fencik's face as he says, "Mike had emphasized the team so much, his team really felt betrayed, and it was *his* team. I mean, he's the one who insisted on two things being on the Super Bowl ring—

220

team and attitude. And boy, I can tell you it was very rough to come back and feel that we were his team. His team was whoever happened to be in a Bear uniform.''

The players also had Gene Upshaw and the NFLPA Board of Player Reps on their side—or so they thought. But on Thursday, October 15, just twenty-four days after the Bears walked out, more than one hundred veteran players broke ranks and crossed the picket lines. The board, following Upshaw's lead, decided players should return without a contract believing management was intractable on the free agent issue. There would be no free agency, no extra benefits, nothing from management.

On the following Monday, after the replacement players had lost to New Orleans, 19–17, the real Bears returned. Sort of. Several players now say something had happened to the soul of the team. Those who hadn't lost respect for the front office and its call for ''loyalty'' over the years felt betrayed by their union leaders. At the time, Ditka blamed his players' lifeless attitude on their public humiliation in the strike, saying, ''the strike took a lot from the Chicago Bears and I'm not sure it's ever going to come back . . . it's almost like when I talk to them, they don't want to hear from me.'' It wasn't *almost* anything. To a man, the players couldn't stand to look Ditka in the eye anymore, or listen to his motivational spiels. Not after what he had said. In meetings, players sat slumped in chairs, sunglasses on, blindly staring into space. Oh, so that's how it is, their look seemed to say.

In an effort to win a couple of ''replacement'' games, Ditka had driven a stake into the heart of his football team. He had lost his entire team.

A strong argument could be made today that if Vainisi had still been in power, this kind of cataclysmic change would never have happened. Before backing the scab players Ditka would have either sought Vainisi's counsel or the GM would surely have offered strong advice. But now Vainisi was gone and with him, Ditka's safe harbor, his sounding board. ''What he missed was someone to go to,'' says Vainisi. ''It was him against the world, it really was. It was him against every aspect of the organization. The players were just one more factor.

''Mike really had nowhere to go. He didn't mean anything by saying 'That's my team' other than to show the 'scab players' that 'You're my team.' You know, 'The Bears are my team. You're wearing Bear uniforms and I'll coach this team.' He didn't know when he said it whether he was going to be playing one week or whether he was going to be playing with these guys the rest of the season, and that's all he meant by it.

221

"We have talked very briefly about it and he said if he had the strike situation to do over again, he would find a way not to take on the veteran players. He would have handled it differently."

Unfortunately, Ditka came to his senses a couple years too late. That critical moment—the backing of the replacement players over the veterans—is what Singletary now terms the "turning point" in the rise and fall of the Chicago Bears football team the last six years. Speaking with the passion of a preacher, his voice rich in resonance and reason, Singletary says, "When he turned his back on us, we felt abandoned. We felt like orphans. Well, who are we playing for? The fans were with him. Then we realized a very cruel reality: we're just a bunch of guys out there, playing for ourselves. We're not playing for the fans; we're not playing for the coaches; we're playing for ourselves. And that's all we've got. Each other."

Adds Singletary, "Backing the replacement players was the single biggest mistake of his coaching career—it was like civil war, a fatal mistake. He tore our heart out. We didn't want to play for him anymore. That's when he lost the team . . . it took us a long, long time to trust him again."

In an early effort to rebuild that trust, to salvage a season, Singletary marched upstairs to Ditka's office and closed the door.

"Coach," he said, "you want your team back? You better go apologize."

"I'm not going to do it," Ditka said.

Back and forth they went. "I'm just telling you," Singletary finally said, "if you want your team back, you better go apologize."

Ditka finally offered up an apology, but it came across as trite and indifferent: "You know, we all make mistakes . . . and I've made mine . . ." It went nowhere.

At the time, the one saving grace was that McMahon's bum shoulder had healed enough to play. In the next three weeks he sparked dramatic wins over Tampa Bay, Kansas City, and Green Bay, all by a total of 6 points. Against Tampa he turned a 23–14 halftime deficit into a 27–26 win, completing 17 of 24 passes for 195 yards and a touchdown. But there was a flip side to this success: games against the Bucs, Chiefs (31–28), and Packers (26–24) had rarely been this close. For the first time since Ditka had taken over, the defense had allowed 20 or more points in three straight games. It added the fourth the following week, a heartbreaking 31–29 defeat in Denver, McMahon's first loss in twenty-six games as a starter. Emotionally, the team was running on empty. Again, instead of admitting his mistake and issuing a call for unity, Ditka resorted once again, in the words of one vet, to act like some Third World dictator, browbeating and threatening his subjects into line.

Like him or not, and many did not, the Bears played on. That is what professionals do. By the end of the year the team was 11-4. McMahon was healthy and ready for the playoff rematch against Washington, once again at home. But Ditka's reaction to the strike had sent a chilling message to his team. A message that to them meant they were just so many interchangeable parts, items on an assembly line. Combine the loss of Buddy Ryan, the surprise drug test, the Flutie fiasco with all the bickering over commercials and endorsements, and the undeniable truth was that this team had changed. The spell that had bound Ditka and his forty-seven men together had been broken— forever. Vainisi calls it an "intangible thing," a reference to how, when games are tight and times get tough, players cough up some courage. "When it's fourth and one and you're down by four points and you really need that yard, you would like to think," says Vainisi, "that they'll do anything short of giving up their lives for the club."

Not anymore. Chicago jumped out to a 14–0 lead against Washington before the Redskins rallied to tie the game at halftime. In the third quarter Cap Boso was just about to tackle Redskin cornerback Darrel Green during a third-quarter punt return when somehow, some way, Green, the NFL's fastest player, leaped right over the sprawling Boso and sped 52 yards for a touchdown. Now the Bears were behind by 7. They got 3 back on a Butler field goal, but with their lives on the line, failed to score in the fourth quarter. Overall, McMahon threw 3 interceptions and was sacked 5 times. The Bears lost 21–17. Four points. The Bears had tried to dig inside, to find that courage, but management and Ditka had torn the heart out of the Super Bowl team. Four points. It might as well have been 40.

23

THE PHONE RANG JUST AS DAN POMPEI WAS CLOSING HIS DOOR AT FOSTER B. Porter Hall at UW-Platteville. For the last eight years Porter has been the media's home away from home during the three-week drudgery of training camp. A regular on the Bears beat since '86, Pompei rated a corner "suite" in the campus dormitory, if two hundred square feet of tile floors, twin beds, and communal showers qualified as a suite under the Holiday Inn index. Just back from pumping some iron at the school's athletic complex, Pompei was headed downtown for a beer or two with friends when the phone rang. It was Harbaugh, worried about the public reaction to his $1.4-million-per-year contract demands. He wanted Pompei—he would also contact Mitchell—to understand how much he wanted to be in camp. He was just minutes up the road, shoes and shorts in the backseat of his car, itching to come in. Five days later Harbaugh signed a new deal: two years, $1.2 million, good news for a team that sorely needed some.

The first blast of bad news in 1991 had come the opening day of training camp when Jimbo Covert injured his back, and it now appeared he was done for the year. That left a gaping hole at the critical left-tackle spot (protecting the blind side of the quarterback, working against the opposition's best pass rusher) in the untested hands of rookie Stan Thomas, the No. 1 pick from Texas. Thomas had made a splash in minicamp with his size (6'5", 305 lbs.), appetite (he loved stuffed pizza), and contract (five years, $650,000-a-year), which Thomas quickly discovered meant absolutely nothing to Ditka. He called Thomas up to his office and, slipping off his reading glasses, motioned for the rookie to take a seat. "I was shaking," says Thomas. Ditka laid it on the line: "You've got the greatest opportunity in the world, don't let it slip by. We drafted you number one because we thought you were a great player. We want you to be a main man, to step up and do the job. If somebody goes down, you're there." With Covert out, Thomas stepped up. Walking off the field that first morning, swimming in sweat, Thomas looked like a man who had gone twelve rounds with Evander Holyfield. "One day of practice here is like a whole week at Texas," he huffed. "The tempo is so much faster."

The Bears team tempo was further disrupted by more bad news, the absence of several key veterans who were holding out: tight end Jim Thornton, kicker Kevin Butler, wide receiver Ron Morris, and tackle Keith Van Horne. Van Horne's dispute highlighted the tendency of Bears management to speak with a forked tongue come contract time. On the eve of training camp, personnel boss Bill Tobin was quoted as saying, "I believe in loyalty," going on to praise the likes of Payton and Hampton as athletes who worked within the system. "Greed," said Tobin, "never entered into Walter's vocabulary or mind-set. He wanted to be a Bear. He was a Bear. He was compensated fairly. It was the American dream." There it was. All the buzzwords. Loyalty. Greed. *A Bear*. The American dream. Tobin's logic suggested if you were loyal, humble, and a team player, all your dreams came true. Sure they did, if you happened to be the leading NFL rusher in history and a franchise athlete showered with investment and endorsement opportunities. What about such loyal soldiers as Butler and Van Horne, who averaged eight years in the league, more than double the NFL average. Van Horne knew full well Thomas's $650,000 deal—$220,000 more than the ten-year tackle was making—was a product of the times, but he wondered why the word *loyalty* had suddenly vanished from finance director Ted Phillips's vocabulary. "I'm just asking for the current market value from someone with my experience at my position," Van Horne told WLUP radio. "Last year I played with some pain in my shoulders. They knew that. They asked me to play with them. But then they turn around and use that against you. They talk about loyalty. It just gets frustrating. You play ten years for them and they still do that to you." They were doing it to Butler, too, currently under fire for his shallow kickoffs. Management, said Butler, was offering a salary commensurate with the eighth- or ninth-best kicker in the league; Butler felt he was in the top three. His statistics surely made for compelling argument . . . NFL holder for most consecutive field goals (24), set in 1989 . . . fourteen club records . . . second in Bear history in points (633) behind Payton (750) . . . converted on 11 of 14 attempts with less than a minute remaining in regulation or overtime . . .

second in the NFC in points (114) in 1990. "No matter what your occupation is," said Butler one day, "when you're trying to claim your worth and someone is telling you, 'You're not worth it,' it gets stressful. We could play stats war our whole life. The bottom line is there hasn't been a better pressure kicker in the league the last six years."

It was back in '88 that McCaskey and his management team made their message clear. Behind the scenes McCaskey had been wringing the revenue towel dry, squeezing every last dollar he could out of scouting operations and contract negotiations. Long-term, multi-million-dollar deals were now the exception rather than the rule as the players discovered back in '88 when management refused to match Washington's five-year, $6-million Plan B offer for Wilber Marshall, allowing the All-Pro linebacker to become the first free agent since 1979 to switch teams. Certainly it was not an easy call. Marshall was coming off consecutive Pro Bowl seasons; his big-play ability and blinding bursts to the ball had keyed the 46 defense. But given Tobin's regimented defensive scheme, the club apparently felt Marshall's price too steep, one destined to set off a money rush from other players. Dent agreed, but added a slight racial twist. "The Bears didn't want to match it because then you got a Singletary that wants more money, then Otis Wilson . . . then Payton," he says today. "You got these guys, and a lot of them blacks. I mean, you got to face it. That's what you're going to deal with."

Dent didn't like the loss of Marshall and neither did several other Bears. Despite receiving two first-round draft picks as compensation— wide receiver Wendell Davis in 1988 and defensive end Trace Armstrong a year later—Marshall's speed would be sorely missed. To Dent it meant nothing less than "the whole team breaking down."

Indeed, after the 1987 season the face of the Super Bowl champions shifted. Some of it was evolutionary—the retirement of Payton and Fencik, for example. Some of it, such as the Marshall move, and another major loss, the trading of wide receiver Gault four months later, was portrayed as purely monetary. Perhaps, but either way, it stripped the Bears of two of their most flamboyant black athletes and biggest playmakers. Gault had demanded superstar money, commensurate with his nickname, Hollywood. Management balked, and in July, Gault was shipped west to the Los Angeles Raiders for a No. 1 pick in '89 and a third-rounder in '90 (which produced starting cornerback Donnell Woolford and QB Peter Tom Willis). In retrospect, the Gault decision proved more damaging than the loss of Payton or Marshall. Sure, Gault could be a self-promoting prima donna who treated football as a way station to movie stardom. Sure, he blathered about ballet and acting lessons as much as he did football. Yes, he had a pushy wife, Redi-Mix hands, and ran meandering routes. But he also had something the Bears and every other NFL team desperately needs: speed. World-class speed. There weren't many Olympic-caliber high hurdlers or NCAA sprint champions running around the NFL. And despite his personal shortcomings Gault had led the Bears in receiving yards and yards per catch every one of his first five seasons. More important, his threat to go deep extended the defense, giving Anderson and Muster room to run, and other receivers room to move.

It was on July 30, 1988, shortly after the Gault trade, that Mike Ditka made a long-awaited, and much-deserved, trip. It was to Canton, Ohio, where on a sun-bathed Saturday, before family, friends, and teammates, he was enshrined in Pro Football's Hall of Fame, the first tight end ever honored. He shared the stage with three other NFL originals: Jack Ham, the Pittsburgh Steelers' brilliant outside linebacker; Fred Biletnikoff, the Raiders' wide receiver who had the hands of a heart surgeon; and attorney Alan Page, the Vikings' stellar defensive tackle. Out in the crowd were hundreds of Aliquippa people who had arrived in Canton despite a serious bus accident the day before. One of the buses carrying the fans to Canton had been forced to stop quickly, and another bus had smashed into it. The windshield of the second bus was shattered, the driver pinned behind the steering wheel. Several fans were banged up—the driver received only minor injuries. But in the tradition of their local hero, all continued to Canton. "Nobody," said one local, "wanted to miss Mike get into the Hall of Fame."

So there he was, standing at the podium in his canary yellow coat, seconds after embracing best buddy Ed O'Bradovich, who made an emotional introduction. Ditka stared out into the crowd, at the IRON MIKE—PRIDE OF ALIQUIPPA, PA. signs. He was a humbled man, a man who had been eligible for the Hall ten years earlier but only now, after a Super Bowl win and national acclaim, was getting his due. Here was a wild child who had triumphed over the tunnel, it appeared, and almost every other obstacle in life. "I didn't know how hard this would be," he said with a quivery voice. "I'm very humbled by it all because I'm not sure I understand it." What he did understand was that all the hard work, the sacrifice no matter the cost, had paid off. "If I'm not the American dream," he told the crowd, "then there is no such thing." He said his thank-yous then closed with this thought: "In life, many men have talent. But talent itself is no accomplishment. Excellence in football and excellence in life is bred when men recognize their opportunities and pursue them with a passion."

A few moments later the final ovation built to a thunderous, Bearlike roar. Mike Ditka stared down at the bronzed bust in his arms, fighting to regain his composure. Photographers focused, waiting for him to raise his head and pose proudly with the bust. Instead Ditka shuffled quickly to the side of the stage, tasting his tears, knowing full well that whatever happened from this day on, all the abuse and the anger, all the push-ups and the needles and the pain, had been worth it. He held the bust tighter, closer to his chest. He was a Hall of Famer. Nobody would ever take it away.

The Hall of Fame selection only enhanced the cultural debate surrounding Ditka. The name struck a nerve all over Chicago. In bars and bedrooms the argument raged: Master motivator? Insufferable fool? Media whore? American hero? Love him, hate him, he was impossible to ignore, especially now, the endorsements and commercials rolling in like whitecaps off the lake. He was tooling around town in his vintage '36 Auburn. He was selling himself right and left, presented as this manly yet sensitive soul capable of selling everything from soup (Campbell's) to suits (Gallagher's of Chicago). Yes, sir, ladies and gentlemen, there he was—washing down Old Chicago Seltzer while taking flight on Midway Airlines, putting Peak antifreeze in his Barrington Motor Werks BMW 750iL, riding in his Iron Mike limo or Budget rental car while reading a copy of *U.S. News & World Report.* The latter's print campaign ("You tackle the issues") had become such a hit that all the Ditka posters for *U.S. News & World Report* on Chicago commuter trains were being replaced twice a month.

Plus, there was the requisite rock music video—the "Grabowski Shuffle," a tacky, champagne-fueled ode to Chicago's working class that succeeded only in making Ditka look foolish. Still, Ditkaphiles snapped it up anyway.

As Ditka's popularity and bank account soared, so did his ego and—contrary to his Grabowski references—his taste for the finer things in life. He was eating like a king, puffing away on imported cigars the size of yule logs, sampling fine wines and his favorite champagnes. He got what friends call "showy" with his drinking and his wealth. Such as the time in Sweden just prior to a 1988 exhibition game against the Vikings. Players and wives and assorted Bears staff, fans, and business travelers were lounging around the SAS Park Avenue Hotel when Ditka started buying rounds, at a place where mixed drinks ran $10 a pop. "He bounced all around the tables buying everybody in the bar drinks, all night long," says a member of the travel party. Ditka half-drowned himself in his favorite champagne. The next morning he showed up at a press conference in sunglasses. Why the shades, Mike?

"If I take them off," he said, "I think I'll bleed to death." After Wednesday, November 2, 1988, those kinds of comments ceased being funny.

As usual Ditka had risen in the predawn darkness, arriving at Halas Hall around five A.M. for his usual ninety-minute workout. It was shaping up as another stressful week. A week earlier his 7-1 Bears, hot off a win over San Francisco, seemed to have regained some of the focus and fire missing from the '87 season, thanks to inspired play from McMahon. But now McMahon's season was over. On Sunday against New England he had damaged a knee during an abysmal 30–7 defeat, putting the club leadership back in the hands of third-year-pro Tomczak, whose considerable physical skills were often overshadowed by his insecurities and his infuriating habit of forcing passes into places they did not belong. In relief of McMahon a year earlier, Tomczak won all seven starts and had thrown for more than 200 yards on three occasions, but he had completed just 49 percent of his passes and tossed five times as many interceptions (10) as touchdowns (2). Those were the kind of numbers that sent Ditka's blood boiling. His sideline blasts at Tomczak were frequent and often profane. Says Hughes, "It was embarrassing how Mike chewed on him on the sidelines. Four-letter words, nasty remarks."

Now, while working out, Ditka dissected the anguished weeks to come. Suddenly the odd burning in his throat returned. It was the same inflamed sensation he had experienced a time or two before. Indigestion, thought Ditka. Or maybe I'm out of shape. His answer had been to push harder. His workouts, as always, were straight out of boot camp: 250 sit-ups, wind sprints up and down the deserted hall, heavy weight lifting in a rubber suit, a treadmill run followed by a steaming-hot shower and sauna. Now, as he sat in the sauna, he noticed how the burning had dropped deeper into his chest, clamping his sides.

A nauseous, clammy sweat swept over Ditka. He ignored it. He was introducing Vice President and Republican presidential candidate George Bush at a local campaign rally that morning. The head coach struggled with his coat and tie.

An hour later at Southern Illinois University, Matt Ditka was just waking up. He was alone in his four-bedroom apartment, the result of a tragic set of circumstances. All three of his roommates were away attending the funeral of two college classmates killed in a car crash while driving to the Carbondale campus just a few days earlier. "I think my phone was unplugged for some reason," he says. Mindlessly he flipped on the television. In the background a WGN newscaster was talking about the Bears. Says Matt, "I remember something about how

229

'McCaskey says he's in good spirits and he thinks everything is going to be all right.' I had a feeling they were talking about my dad."

He thought of the phone. Nobody had called. Maybe it wasn't his dad. He checked the connection. Unplugged. Now he was worried. He hooked it up and speed-dialed home. No answer. Then the phone rang. It was one of his roommates, fumbling for the right words, dancing around the news of the day. "He didn't want to jump right out and say it," says Matt.

Finally, Matt popped the question. "Have you heard anything about my dad?"

Yes, his roommate said, he was working out, got chest pains, and they took him to the hospital.

Assistant coaches Steve Kazor and Johnny Roland had actually made the potentially lifesaving decision. As soon as they saw Ditka that morning, they argued for the hospital. "No," answered Ditka, "I have to meet the vice president." Instead, Kazor and Roland prevailed and Ditka met the emergency doctors at Lake Forest Hospital, the vise tightening around his chest. He was admitted to the cardiac unit. Doctors found blockage caused by a clot in the lower back area of his heart. Later, in medical terms, it was described as "a fairly small inferior-wall heart attack," one of the "best" heart attacks you can have, if there is such a thing.

Local TV stations went live with the news. Halas Hall and the hospital were flooded with calls. (Some 12,000 cards, letters, and phone calls would eventually pour in to the hospital and the Bears offices, leaving Ditka humbled and grateful.) The city of Chicago held its breath, waiting, wondering. Players whispered in the halls. *Did you hear Coach had a heart attack?* Could it be?

In Dallas, Megan heard the news and scrambled to call the hospital. She couldn't get through. She dialed her dad's personal assistant, Mary Albright, and leveled a blast worthy of her father. "I was pissed," Megan says. "I told her, 'You better get me on the [hospital] phone.'"

Instead Diana called back. Ever since the divorce Megan and Diana had been at odds, if for no other reason than Megan refused to let The Other Woman administer any relief for her family pain. "I never thought or expected Diana to take my mother's place," says Megan coolly. At the time Diana was the conduit to her dad, the relay switch for requests for time or money. Nothing more, nothing less.

Your father is fine, said Diana. And guess what? President Reagan called!

"Oh, that's nice," Megan shot back. "I know I'm not as important as President Reagan, but I'd like to talk to my dad."

"It kinda pissed me off," Megan says today. Two days later, she says, she finally got through to her father's room.

Matt was equally upset when he finally arrived at his father's side, but for a different reason. The robust, celebrated Monster of the Midway looked wan and pale, even weak. "You know," said Matt, "he never looks like that."

He did now.

The cardiac episode had a far greater impact emotionally than physically. In Ditka's case it went well beyond the average lifestyle change and right to the heart of his Superman image. "I wouldn't want to say I thought of myself as invincible, but 'bulletproof' probably applies," Ditka told sportswriter Pete Axthelm shortly after the heart scare. "I always figured that heart trouble was something that happened to the guy down the block." But now it was Ditka flat on his back in intensive care with the tubes in his nose, the monitor on his heart.

Close friends and family members say Ditka was more than just scared. He was "embarrassed" by the incident, worried that somehow he had let his team, his fans, his family, down. Says Matt, "It was kind of like maybe he thought we felt less of him because it happened." So it was that just eleven days later, Ditka was back on the sidelines watching as the Bears interim head coach, Vince Tobin, collected his second straight victory, an impressive 34–14 win at Washington. As TV cameras pressed ever closer, viewers held their breath, as if watching a bomb squad approach a ticking package. Friends in and out of the business had urged him to quit lest something more serious occur. What's to prove? His overall coaching winning percentage was the best in team history. He had won a Super Bowl. He was in the Hall of Fame.

Yet there was Diana Ditka telling friends that her husband was coming back to coach against Tampa, less than three weeks after the episode. Why, in heaven's name? they asked.

"He's afraid of losing his job," she said.

The following Sunday, when Ditka did return to coaching, he was a changed man, a man whose relationship to life, his family, his team, and the public had shifted faster than an alderman's vote. To the general public, especially locally, Ditka had suddenly lost his hot-headed, money-hungry image. He was real, again, one of us.

He went public with his heart-smart campaign, telling everyone from *People* magazine to Minnesota sportswriters about the new Mike Ditka. No more high-cholesterol food, red meat, alcohol, and cigars. Even pork, the pride of his restaurant, was out. "I can eat pork, but I haven't even done that," said Ditka. "I've got to keep going back, catch myself, and say it's only a game. I used to think that the whole thing is

231

happening on Sunday afternoon or Monday night. And I can't do that anymore. I refuse to do it. I'm gonna work as hard as I can; I'm gonna try and do the right things. But I'm just not rantin' and ravin', that's all there is to it."

His team responded. Despite the absence of McMahon, Otis Wilson, Perry, and Dent for extended periods, the Bears wrapped up the regular season at 12-4. In the playoffs, the big question was once again the health of McMahon. By now McMahon had worn out his Second City welcome — at least with the local press. It abhorred his pompous attitude and the way he delighted in making the media grovel for the merest morsel of news. In the locker room, feelings were divided. Dent was, and still is, one of the true believers: "He didn't have the best talent, but he had the balls to get it done. You can find talent all day, but you can't find people who will sacrifice. I've seen the guy get shot up three, four times in the arm, shoulder, and you had the press saying, 'Oh, he's broke up.' If you're a quarterback, you're gonna get broke up. You're playing football. You're going to get a doctor bill."

Fencik, meanwhile, found McMahon's never-ending battle with injury wearing thin. "I won't say he milked it, but it was like he was kind of picking and choosing which games to him were important rather than all of them being important." That sentiment surfaced among some players and coaches during the second to last regular-season game of 1988, against the Detroit Lions, over the condition of McMahon's strained right knee. "Steve, they want me to play," McMahon told Zucker prior to the Lions game.

"How do you feel?" Zucker said.

"I don't feel right."

"Go to Dr. Schafer."

McMahon went to see Dr. Michael Schafer, an orthopedic surgeon at Northwestern Hospital who had treated McMahon before but was not a team doctor. After running McMahon's knee through a series of simple mobility exercises, Schafer deemed it unstable. "I couldn't live with myself if I allowed him to play," the doctor told Zucker. "Give it another week, ten days."

"You'd better tell Ditka right now," Zucker advised his client, who did just that. According to Zucker, the head coach "hit the ceiling," despite the fact Schafer backed McMahon. Two weeks later, in the first-round playoff game, McMahon was ready, yet it was Tomczak who started the now infamous "Fog Bowl" against Philadelphia, the pea-soup party the Bears ended up winning 20–12, although if you were farther away than the sidelines, you missed it. Tomzcak (176 yards, 1 TD, 3 Int.) reinjured his left shoulder late in the game and McMahon (2-3, 13 yards) finished it.

The next week the Bears faced their old nemesis, Joe Montana and the 49ers, for the right to represent the NFC in Super Bowl XXIII. Ditka withheld naming his starting QB until shortly before the game. McMahon finally got the nod, followed by this coaching caveat: "I don't want any complaining, any beefing," Ditka said. "You do one wrong thing, I'm pulling you."

McMahon proceeded to have perhaps his worst game in a Bear uniform. It would also be his last.

After the game—a 28–3 Montana-led blowout—McMahon called Zucker. They met at McMahon's restaurant downtown. "Get me out of here," the quarterback told his agent. "I can't play for the man anymore." Zucker listened, probing a bit about the game. "How many audibles did you call?" he asked. McMahon said one, maybe two. McMahon said he was afraid to change plays for fear of getting pulled.

"When a quarterback loses his confidence, especially a guy like Jim," says Zucker, "it's not the same. Jim would call a lot of audibles, most of them a success. That always bothered Ditka."

McMahon and Ditka had feuded over the quarterback's improvising for years. Whether it was ego or something else, Ditka had long kept a tight grip on the game plan. McMahon simply took what the defense gave him, and according to Ed Hughes, an NFL assistant for almost thirty years and one of the league's most respected offensive minds, no modern quarterback was any better at it than McMahon. Two years after he retired, Hughes still marvels at McMahon's almost psychic ability to decipher defensive coverages. "I don't think it was publicized too much, but I coached him for seven years, and to me, Jim's greatest asset was his brains. Looking at films, I don't think there was hardly one time in seven years he'd say, 'Stop the film, run that back, let's see what they did.' I would run it back and he'd say, 'Ed, they're in a two coverage.' It was almost like he had a photographic mind."

Hughes proceeded to tell a story of how before a Washington game the coaches had noticed that when a Redskins safety got into a certain spot on the field, he was going to blitz. Says Hughes, "We conveyed that to Jim and the safety got into that place, he blitzed, Jim audibled and burned him for a touchdown." It happened again, and McMahon completed another pass. The third time, the safety finally caught on. He moved to another spot, still thinking blitz. "Sure enough," says Hughes, "Jim audibles anyway and throws a touchdown. When he came off the field, I said to him, 'Hey, that safety wasn't in that spot.'

He told me, 'I could see he was trying to bluff me. I could see it in his eyes.' "

Hughes traces McMahon's pitiful performance in that 1988 playoff game back two years, to the end of the '86 season. It was a time, says Hughes, for reasons that remain a mystery to him, when Ditka became "infatuated" with running a new motion offense—wide receivers dashing along the line of scrimmage, tight ends shifting from side to side. "I don't want the defense to set on me," Hughes says Ditka told him at the time. "I want to be moving. I'm gonna make them make the mistakes. I'm not going to sit there and let them run any defense they want."

"Somehow this moving thing got ahold of him and he wouldn't let it go," says Hughes, who fought the shifting from the start. He felt it forced the quarterback to concentrate on the movement of his players and not the defense. "To me it was terrible," Hughes says. "I would move only if I knew what the other team was doing or if it would improve a blocking scheme. Sometimes our tackles didn't know if the tight end was on the left or right, if they were double-teamed or single-blocking . . . it hurt us. He'd just sit there and dream up some movement whether it made any sense or not."

The player it hurt the most was McMahon. "Now he couldn't audible," says Hughes. "People were moving. . . . Now he was more like a robot quarterback. He couldn't do the things he was best at, except in the two-minute drill when they couldn't call the plays."

Most often that left play-calling in the hands of the head coach, who, according to Hughes, had neither the brains, mental dexterity, or focus necessary to construct and execute a game plan. To Hughes, Ditka was your basic brown bagger when it came to Xs and Os. "Not an innovative person, not at all," says Hughes. As for play-calling? "He's too busy yelling at players, yelling at officials, to generate the next move," says Hughes. "He doesn't have that play ready to jump to, to know exactly when the ball comes down what he wants. Or, 'I'm running this, but I'm setting this up three plays later.' Or, 'When we've got a second or third first down on a march, I'm gonna hit them with the big one.' He never had the forethought to keep track of that."

Other factors may have contributed to Ditka's losing confidence in McMahon. Certainly the injuries did not help. Neither did the constant carping of assistant coaches, who, Hughes recalls, rated McMahon no higher than the sixteenth-best offensive player on the team in their postseason evaluations. Hughes thought they were nuts and said so. He repeatedly rated the QB first. "We couldn't operate without McMahon," he says, an argument he made many times at meetings with Ditka and other staff members. Instead Hughes pointed a finger at other areas of the offense, including the vaunted offensive line. "I don't know how many times I got in trouble for saying the offensive line was not as good as they [the media] blew them up to be." Hughes traced McMahon's poor health to the battering he was taking in the pocket and the poor play of, ironically, McMahon's good buddy, Van Horne. "I never liked Van Horne," says Hughes. "One year I rated Van Horne twenty-first. They said, 'Why did you rate him so low?' I said, 'I think he's a detriment to the team.' I wouldn't have him around. He's the one who's getting guys hurt all the time. He was a two-step guy and that was it. He had no balance. He had no quickness. A big, tall, heavy guy, almost three hundred pounds, two steps, hit somebody, and Van Horne would be on the ground. Even on a run block, boom!—hit somebody and go down. No mobility.

"I thought Thayer was not that good. I would have played Wojo [free agent guard John Wojciechowski]. I was fighting the offensive-line coach. I'd sit next to him on the airplane. We'd take rides on the airplane and he wouldn't say a word to me he was so mad. But I was the offensive coordinator. I had to say what I felt."

OMENS.

If summer signposts held true, 1991 would be a memorable season all right—for all the wrong reasons. Ditka had seen the signs as far back as spring. Staring out from his cart, he silently measured his team—weighing its advancing age along the line of scrimmage, the inexperience at wide receiver, its lack of breakaway speed—against other teams around the league. "I think *resigned* is the best word for how he feels," says Vainisi one day. "He knows he doesn't have the talent. He sees other teams getting better, and they're slipping." During the exhibition season the slippage was as obvious as Chicago's rocketing homicide rate—a record 609 killings in the first eight months of the year—which Mayor Daley likened to the streets of drug-torn Colombia. The Bears lost three of five pre-season games— wrapping wins against Miami in the first game and Buffalo in the fifth around losses to the 49ers, Cardinals, and Raiders. The offense looked duller than a six-month-old razor blade. It squandered more scoring chances than Ditka had commercials. Mentions of the Bears' dead-last ranking in NFL passing yardage in 1990 popped back in the papers. So did questions about depth as one by one key players were lost to injury. The first to go was Covert, with that severe back injury the first day of training camp. Then 6'7", 275-pound Eric Kumerow, acquired in a trade in January and counted on for depth along the defensive line, suffered a season-ending Achilles tendon injury in the game against Miami. Starting strong safety Shaun Gayle, one of the league's best, went down with a stress fracture of his lower left leg. Brad Muster and Lemuel Stinson had hamstring problems. Stan Thomas had dislocated a shoulder. Omens.

But the offense and injuries took a backseat to what one of the players' wives called "the black cloud" that hovered over the Bears family. One numbing ten-day stretch in August summed it up: a miscarriage for Kim Singletary, a drunk-driving arrest for Kevin Butler, and a murder case involving Neal Anderson's father in Florida. The black cloud swirled and gathered strength beginning the second week in August. The Bears were in Berlin for yet another American Bowl adventure courtesy of the merchandise-minded NFL. Upon arrival Ditka looked about as pleasant as a former East German border guard. "Call off your posse," he warned a WBBM producer whose cameras crept a tad too close as Ditka surveyed the historic Berlin Olympic Stadium for the first time. Without warning, Ditka snapped. He screamed at the producer and reporter. They were doing "horseshit jobs." The producer was "a jagoff," Ditkaspeak for a jerk. Typically the coach apologized for his outburst the next day, but he was clearly unsettled. One minute he was fidgeting as his words were translated to the German press or sarcastically dubbing a WBBM producer "Ted Koppel" after a probing question. The next minute, when a boat filled with San Francisco 49ers drew near the Bears' boat during a sightseeing tour, Ditka donned a spiked World War I German helmet and puffed a long cigar in comic relief, just to show the snooty 49ers who was in charge.

On the field, however, it was the other way around—49ers 21, Bears

7. The offense hit a succession of sour notes: poor timing, bad blocking, four passes batted down at the line of scrimmage.

Back in Platteville on Monday, Ditka leveled a measured blast at Butler, Thornton, and Morris, who were still squabbling with management over money. "In life," he said, "if you want to be somewhere, you go there. I don't care about contracts or anything else. I went through that as a player, and I understand. But if it's time to be somewhere, you get there. That's all there is to it. Get it done. Find a way to get it done. If they aren't here before this week is up, I'd say we're quickly getting to the point of no return."

Butler felt the same way. The black clouds had been hovering over his head for weeks, or so it seemed. On Monday afternoon he picked up his attorney Ed Slowik at O'Hare Airport and dropped him off at Halas Hall. Butler hoped it would be the final contract talk. He was itching to join his teammates in camp. But not even thirty minutes after he left Slowik in front of Halas Hall, the phone rang in a Lake Forest coffee shop. "Come pick me up," said Slowik. "This is ridiculous; a waste of time." Slowik said Ted Phillips, the team's director of finance, was playing hardball, hanging the club's third-round draft choice, All-American punter and placekicker Chris Gardocki of Clemson, over their heads even though Gardocki hadn't hit the side of a barn so far. Phillips was also backing off on incentives and insurance coverage, waging the stats war Butler loathed to play. Slowik and Phillips continued to bicker over Butler's car phone as the kicker ferried his agent back to O'Hare. The seven-year pro stared out his windshield, his mind a mess, wondering if all the field goals, the community service, if all the stomach-turning nights at home with Cathy agonizing over the team, had really mattered. Deep down Butler knew it did. He cared. He loved the Bears. God, remember the buses during the Super Bowl parade! That champagne celebration on LaSalle! That was so much ancient history now. He was just another commodity, bought and sold like the futures contracts downtown. "I think 1985, '86, were easy years, very easy years," he said over that same car phone one day. "All of a sudden you start losing a couple of playoff games and you get evaluated a lot harder." For Butler, the new and persistent knock was his dying-duck kickoffs that seemed, more and more, to settle around the 10-yard line. The kickoffs had become something of a cause célèbre in Chicago, something new to bounce around in the columns and the clubs. To Butler his troubles were quite simple: a bum hip that finally improved and special teams coverage that never did. "They were honest-to-God blaming [special teams coverage] all on me. I don't think that was fair. I *know* that wasn't fair. You've got second- and third-round linebackers that I'm making more tackles than, and they're going to blame me. I don't give a shit if you kick to the forty-yard line, one of those guys should make a tackle. They're getting knocked on their ass, guys are running around them, and they're [the coaching staff and local press] going it's because he kicked it only to the eight- or five-yard line. I don't buy that." At the time, Butler wondered whether the entire kickoff issue wasn't just a back-door move by management to replace his high-priced right leg with Gardocki's left. "I think I was just being set up because my stats prove I should be paid [in the same category as] the top three or four kickers."

What was not so obvious was, on what side of the contract fence was Ditka standing? As much as Butler admired and respected Ditka—which was plenty—they had endured a rocky relationship. The first stone was cast back in '86 during the Ryan-Ditka grudge match at Soldier Field. Butler had missed four from the field that day. Headed to the locker room at halftime, Ditka unloaded with an earful on Butler: motherfucker this, motherfucker that. "Yeah, I missed four that day," said Butler, not mentioning he won it in overtime with a field goal. For much of '90, mainly related to the kickoff issue, Ditka made Butler his whipping boy in team meetings. One of the early blasts came in late September, the Monday after Butler banged in all four field goal tries, two over 50 yards—including a game-winning 51-yard shot on the last play of the game—in a 19–16 win over Minnesota. There was no thank-you, no praise, just poisonous darts about the short kicks. Later in the season Butler and Ditka had it out during a game.

"You motherfucker," Ditka had screamed after one short kickoff. "God damn it, I'm getting rid of you."

Butler wheeled around. "Fuck you," he shot back, "get rid of my fucking ass."

That Monday, says Butler, there was a new kicker at practice. Before the next practice Butler tried one kick before Ditka told him to "get your ass outta there" and put the new recruit in.

"What's the fucking deal?" one of the linemen asked Butler.

"I don't know. I said the wrong thing."

A year later Butler talked about learning a lesson. "I won't say that again," he admitted. "That's one thing I learned. I'll never go say get another kicker because that's exactly what he did. In the heat of the moment he's never really minded that before because that's how he motivates players, he challenges you." Just don't challenge back.

Driving to the airport, Butler thought about Gardocki, the kid out of Redan High in Stone Mountain, Georgia, Butler's old high school. The kid was having a horrible exhibition season, all knotted up from nerves. But there was no denying the leg, it was big league all the way. In Butler's case, pressure was his partner; it fortified him on the field. He lived for those last-second daggers into another club's heart. But now his heart was sinking. Says Butler, "The Bears had done what they wanted to do. They had broken me down."

Turning to Slowik, he said, "Whatever it takes, finish it tonight. In the morning I'm on my way to camp."

Around nine o'clock that night Butler pulled his BMW into the parking lot of his restaurant, Overtimes, in suburban Northbrook. He was edgy, stressed from more O'Hare strategy talks with Slowik. Inside the bar were several local hockey and baseball players Butler knew. The talk soon turned to management, the games people play, one story leading to another, one beer to another. "It was more or less a release," Butler said. "It wasn't a conscious thing, chugging beers, but over two or three hours, talking." At eleven-thirty Cathy called the bar. "Why don't you come home now?" she said. Kevin, who hadn't eaten since lunch, told her he would be home in "a little bit," that he was just sitting in the bar talking.

"Famous last words," says Butler, who had no idea how famous.

Butler's "little bit" extended to around 2:30 A.M. By then he was "pretty buzzed" by the beer, "hyped up" and "preoccupied" over the contract talks. Driving north on Milwaukee Avenue, he missed the speed sign in the village of Lincolnshire, the one warning drivers to slow from fifty-five to forty-five. At 2:43 A.M. a cop clocked him at fifty-eight miles per hour and pulled him over.

"Have you been drinking?" the officer asked.

"Yes, sir," said Butler. "I've had a few beers."

Although field sobriety tests proved inconclusive, the Breathalyzer did not. It registered a blood alcohol count of 0.2—twice the legal limit in the state. Butler was arrested and jailed for driving under the influence and speeding. The officer never mentioned anything about the Bears and Butler never volunteered it. Cathy, however, had something to say to her husband at the station house and later at home, as husband and wife talked toward dawn, dealing with the personal and public consequences of the incident. "I just thank God nobody else was involved in it," Butler says. "This was Kevin Butler's problem brought on by my mistake." It was a mistake, Butler was informed, that would become public record the following Monday as part of the village's weekly press release of police activity.

That afternoon Butler signed a new three-year, $1.25-million contract. He told neither his agent nor Phillips about the drunk-driving arrest less than twelve hours earlier. In Butler's mind there was no correlation between the two; he believed he should not be penalized for one night, one mistake. "In no way did I let it affect the negotiations," Butler said. "In no way did it concern the Chicago Bears. This was Kevin Butler's problem. It wasn't the Chicago Bears' problem. I hired Ed [agent Slowik] to do my contract. To get what Kevin Butler should make from the Chicago Bears. If one night, one mistake, affects all that, I think that's wrong."

And after his bitter contract talks, Butler had no doubts of how the news would have been used. "Believe me," he said, "it would have been used against me by Phillips. If he says it wouldn't, he's lying. It was like an ace in the hole for him." Butler estimated beyond the principle of the matter such an admission would have cost him $100,000 easily, probably more. "It was like a trump card for [Phillips]. I mean, how many murderers testify against themselves? I'm not naive.

"If I had some problem with drugs or alcohol in the previous six years, yeah, I would have had some guilt. But I think my track record, my beliefs in myself, the things I did to rectify the DUI, speak for themselves. But people don't want to accept that. People want to see you suffer."

Whatever suffering Mike and Kim Singletary did the week of August 3 and beyond was done in private, with prayer. She had come back from Berlin on Monday on an emotional high from all members of the Bears extended family patting her pregnant tummy, asking when she was due. This is just like 1984, thought Kim, relying on her baby shower barometer. The showers, she said, were no longer exercises in game show excess. The wives were more down-to-earth, committed to the team. "It's almost like we've come full circle," she said. "Now at the baby showers people give bibs, washcloths, and receiving blankets. That's the way a baby shower should be." On Wednesday, with her husband away in Platteville, Kim went for a regular ultrasound checkup, only it wasn't so regular this time. There was a complication. Her baby, a boy, had died. "The umbilical cord had wrapped around the baby's ankle; it was a lack of oxygen," Kim said one afternoon, her voice sad but not bitter, speaking with the strength befitting her strong religious faith. "The doctor said it was so rare, the ankle is so thin." Her husband flew home immediately thanks to an assist from Ditka, who arranged for the plane. "Everybody uses the term *miscarriage*," she said quietly. "You think, we lost a child . . . that's when it hurts."

The hurt at the Butler household, while nothing compared to the sorrow of the Singletarys, took hold the following day. Worried about a press leak, Butler had called Ditka before he reached camp and explained the DUI arrest.

"You all right?" said Ditka.

"Yes, sir."

"Kevin, you're human. You're allowed to make mistakes. I hope you learn from it. But they build you up to tear you down, and they're gonna start tearing you down. I'll be in your corner if there's anything you need."

The news leaked on Friday, earlier than expected, and with such force that it knocked the macabre Jeffrey Dahmer murders right off the top of the ten-o'clock news. Reporters camped out on Butler's lawn. The phone rang without relief, friends, relatives, and most of all, reporters, seeking some answers to what had happened. One of the local TV stations, the CBS affiliate, naturally wanted an interview. Butler told them he was withholding comment until a court date was set. He had decided to go through classes and counseling before speaking out. He says a reporter at the station turned that comment around and suggested Butler was trying to squelch the story. In a fiercely competitive media market feeding a city's ravenous appetite for sports, Butler became the supermarket special of the week. "It was just exactly like Coach Ditka said," says Butler. "I had reporters trying to look in my house with cameras, like they were going to see me sprawled out on the floor with fucking liquor bottles all over the place. That's when it started to turn for me. The previous years had been too good. It got to-the-bottom ugly. They wanted sudden impact, shock TV, that's when they started to turn on me."

That Sunday as Butler walked onto the grass at Soldier Field, a gang of cameramen and reporters were yelling, "What about the DUI? How are you gonna plead, Kevin?"

"They did everything they could to get a reaction from me," Butler says. He held his tongue, and in the end, he gave them a story. Working with a new holder, punter Maury Buford, he missed four field goals, of 44, 39, 54, and 38 yards—as the Bears lost to lowly Phoenix, 12–10, on national TV.

About a week later, just as things were beginning to quiet down, Butler said he got blindsided again. On August 20, 1991, he awoke to find himself hammered by Ted Phillips in the *Sun-Times* for not coming clean on the DUI arrest during the contract negotiations. Phillips had been sitting in his office when Brian Hewitt, an outstanding Bears beat writer and columnist, walked in. Hewitt was bothered by the timing of Butler's signing and the DUI, but given the reporter's heavy workload, it took him a week or so to get around to seeking Phillip's opinion.

"I've been waiting for someone to ask me," the treasurer replied. "It bothered me quite a bit."

Hewitt quoted Phillips as saying he was "disappointed" by Butler's "lack of honesty" and that the Bears' second-leading scorer in history had "an obligation" to tell the club what had happened. Phillips admitted he might have structured Butler's contract differently, mainly relating to a roster bonus and games played, had he known about the drunk-driving incident. Hewitt said he tried to contact both Butler and his agent to no avail, also quoted Phillips as saying he had not talked to Butler since the arrest. "I may, at some point, talk to him," Phillips said. "I'd like to know why he didn't tell us. I'd like to know."

Phillips didn't have to wait long. No sooner had Butler read the story then he grabbed the phone and dialed the Bears public relations office, demanding to know what the hell was going on. "Is the whole organization turning on me?" he yelled at Bryan Harlan, the Bears public relations director. Harlan was as bewildered as Butler; nothing had come through his office.

As soon as Butler hit Halas Hall, he raced straight up to the second floor and right into Phillips's face. "What the fuck are you trying to do? Crucify me again?"

Phillips tried to catch his breath but Butler wouldn't let up. "No matter how much this might hurt you to hear this, Ted, I don't answer to you. I answer to Ditka and McCaskey."

Phillips had his bearings now. "You were very unprofessional in what you did."

"Ted, I made a mistake. I recognize mistakes. *You* were fucking unprofessional."

With that, Butler wheeled and walked out the door.

In September, a local judge fined Butler $1,000, suspended his license for three months, ordered two hundred hours of community service and one year's court supervision—a stiff sentence for a first-time offender. Now Butler had to worry about the NFL. In July the league had instituted a new alcohol-abuse policy, and he could be suspended for four games without pay. Butler and the Bears management were worried the NFL would use Butler's case as a public relations tool, a powerful message that alcohol abuse of any kind would not be tolerated by a league dominated by beer advertising. As September moved into October, it appeared NFL Commissioner Tagliabue was preparing to come down hard on Butler. Butler remembers sitting in one meeting with Mike McCaskey where Tagliabue made mention of the near-daily calls he was getting from Don Pierson, who covers the

NFL for the *Tribune*. Pierson, also a past president of the NFL writers' association, was pressing for a decision. McCaskey, who reprimanded Phillips for speaking out, told Tagliabue to hold on a minute. "Let's not crucify the kid," he said. "He's done everything you asked of him and you're throwing him in the same category as [repeat drug offender Dexter] Manley."

"That was a side of McCaskey I never experienced or even believed was there," Butler says. "He went to bat for me."

It worked. Instead of a suspension, which Butler said he would have sued the league over, Tagliabue fined the kicker half a game's check and let him off with a stern warning that any repeat violation "of this type will lead to a suspension from NFL play."

"It was fair compared to what they wanted to do," said Butler. "I walked out of there [Tagliabue's office] with great relief that the right things were going to happen."

THE BEARS OPENED THE 1991 SEASON IN THE NATIONAL SPOTLIGHT, ON A spectacular first day of September. Sultry weather earlier in the week had broken a bit, and by the time the game rolled around it was seventy degrees, with just a wisp of wind floating in off the lake, and the famed Chicago skyline seemed more magnificent than ever. All around Soldier Field the smell of charbroiled chicken and steak scented the air. It would prove to be a classic black-and-blue division matchup, Bears versus Vikings, on this brilliant blue-skied afternoon.

Already, in week one, it was a must win for the Bears. Based on its cream-puff schedule, Minnesota was the preseason pick of many to snap the Bears' stranglehold on the NFC Central Division (six championships in seven years). After the Vikes, the schedule called for the Bears to play the Giants, Bills, and Redskins in the next five weeks, with expected rest stops against Tampa Bay and the New York Jets along the way. Parking-lot and pregame sports radio chatter centered on the Bears' need for a strong start, particularly from an anemic offense that totaled one touchdown pass during the exhibition season. And that had come off the arm of backup quarterback P. T. Willis a week earlier, in a deceptive 30–13 thrashing of Buffalo, which was resting most of its star players. Across from the main entrance from storied Soldier Field, with its massive Doric columns and classical Beaux-Arts architecture, in a parking lot bursting with RVs and MTV music, fans debated the fate of Thomas. Not Supreme Court nominee Clarence, set to begin confirmation hearings, but rookie left tackle Stan, who, bum shoulder and all, would face one of the league's best speed rushers in dangerous Chris Doleman.

And when it was all said and done, you had to be six feet under not to appreciate what turned out to be Ditkaball at its ever-loving best—a dictionary definition, played at playoff pitch. "A classic Bear victory," praised former Bear fullback Ronnie Bull. It was a game won not so much on the field as in the heart, and it stamped the Bears as a team to contend with. Minnesota had more yards and more talent but lost 10–6 because the Bears proved hungrier. "I don't care how much talent you have in life, that's wonderful," Ditka gushed in the press tent outside the locker room after the game. "I think heart is the most important thing—attitude, desire, guts, what you want to call it. I'm tremendously proud of these guys."

Guys like Thomas, Stan the Man on this, his first real NFL afternoon. The rookie had played like Covert reincarnate, a wall along the left side. He repeatedly sealed off Doleman's inside rush and sent the four-time All-Pro home without a tackle. Nary a hand touched another guy, the big brown-eyed question mark before the day began, despite his 10-4 record as starter and a club record 173 straight passes in 1990 without an interception—the quarterback who earlier in the summer had said, "I'm not going to take a backseat to anybody," and, "I know my role this year is going to be very significant." It was against the Vikes that Jim Harbaugh stepped right up and did it: 17 of 24 passes for 186 yards and a touchdown. Faced with an eight-man front that flat out dared him to make a play, Harbaugh made all the right moves. He stayed in the pocket, throwing the ins and outs, the corners and fades, just as he had in June. He earned the praise of center Hilgenberg, who admitted, "If it wasn't for him, we're in trouble today."

If one play set the tone of the day—the season—it wasn't the arm of Harbaugh but the hands of Tom Waddle. His second-quarter touchdown catch was the kind of overachieving effort that sparkled just a little brighter than the rest. By all rights Waddle should have been back in Cincinnati or the Boston College area, coaching high school football or something. He was the original boy on the bubble, forever afraid of losing his job—judged too slow, too small, too average, to play high school, college, and certainly, NFL football. On Monday, Waddle's bubble had burst for the third time in three years when he failed to make the official forty-seven man roster and was placed on waivers. It was basically a procedural move by the Bears because, Lord knows, nobody was going to sign Waddle. After clearing waivers, Waddle, who played wide receiver, was resigned by the team (for the third time in his career). Now here he was on Sunday making the play of the day—for the first time in his career.

Waddle's previous pro experience, if you could call seven games in two seasons such a thing, had been a long series of moves between the waiver wire, inactive roster, and developmental squad. He had caught Ditka's eye with his extraordinary reflexes and shortstop hands, the way he shook free from blue-chip defensive backs. "We love you as a receiver," Ditka told the 6'0", 180-pound Waddle in the summer of 1989. "You may never be a starter in this league, but you can be a receiver." The question, said Ditka, was whether Waddle would survive long enough to help: "We don't know if you're big enough to take the pounding week in and week out. You're just going to get hurt." Waddle took it as a challenge and was now the team's third-down-possession receiver. Trailing 3–0 in the second quarter on the Vikes 37-yard line, Harbaugh went deep. Overthrown. But Waddle worked around cornerback Todd Scott and laid himself out flatter than a crisp five-dollar bill. Out went the fingertips. In came the ball. It stuck. Waddle hit on the 1, bounced, and rolled into the end zone. Touchdown. CBS Sports analyst John Madden had found a new hero. After the game in a joyous locker room Waddle, his punky blond hair askew, looked a bit lost among the media horde. Time and time again he was asked to describe the play, his moment in the sun.

"I've been making that catch all my life," he said.

As a child, life for Tom Waddle was a narrow strip of grass about fifty yards long. He didn't have to go far to find it. It was on the side of his house, the corner lot on Bridlepath Lane in the Cincinnati subdivision that was home for a budding Johnny Bench or Pete Rose, a future

Kenny Anderson. Almost every day a dozen neighborhood boys would square off in Wiffle ball, baseball, or football. Twenty of those kids went on to play, if not as a Cincinnati Red, at least some major college football or baseball. A couple, however, did make the pros. One, Billy Long, pitched for the Cubs. The other, Tom Waddle, caught for the Bears.

"I think people can relate to me because they look at me and see themselves," says Waddle. "Maybe they see a little bit of the hard work in themselves."

What you see on this day, as Waddle speaks in the fall of 1991, is a gray T-shirt still soaked long after a Bears practice has officially ended. You see a fresh red crease from his helmet cutting across the top of his forehead, a fluorescent-orange cap with BOGIE'S DINER scripted across the front, sitting back on his spiky beach-blond hair, his eyes the color of dark coffee. In person Waddle is much more of a specimen than he appears to be on television. He had come into the 1991 training camp weighing a muscular 191 pounds, the result of fierce five-day-a-week weight workouts. He assured a reporter he doesn't plan on slowing down. Not now. Not ever. "I think every practice and game, for the rest of however long my career lasts will be a test," he said. "I don't think I'll ever get off that bubble. Maybe in someone else's eyes I will, but in my eyes I never will."

Words that make Bob Waddle, Tom's father, very proud.

"People have always said Tom was too small, too slow, too something, but he's always found a way."

Just like Mike Ditka, Tom Waddle's search for excellence started close to home. His father, who was raised rough in the foothills in Kentucky, married at nineteen. He then set off to make a better life for himself and his teenage bride, Ruth, who was just sixteen when they walked down the aisle.

"It was nothing that he ever really said," says Tom. "It was just the example of what he was doing."

Bob Waddle sighs and says the fifteen-hour days were the easy ones back then. He had started out with General Electric but soon moved into a smaller business that supplied parts for airplanes. "Some nights I slept on my desk," he says. "You had to when you're building a company. But I never, ever, missed any of their ball games. I might have made a lot of phone calls or gone back to work, but I never missed a game. The kids were most important."

Besides his brother, Mike, Tom's best friend was a neighbor named Mark Kamphaus. Kamphaus was Kenny Anderson, the artistic Cincinnati Bengal quarterback. Tom was Fred Biletnikoff, the glue-fingered Raiders wide receiver. From elementary school on up, Kamphaus threw and Waddle caught. They lived out their fantasies, first in that side yard, then at Cincinnati Moeller, arguably the nation's finest high school football team. At Moeller, Kamphaus became an All-American, one of the top ten recruits in the country. Waddle, with his deceptive speed and jaw-dropping grabs, was selected all-state. Every college in the country wanted Kamphaus. Hardly anybody wanted Waddle. Notre Dame coach Gerry Faust told him, flat to his face, he would never play major-college football. Penn State showed absolutely no interest despite Tom's twice attending Joe Paterno's football camps. Michigan State invited him to visit, but never talked scholarship. "I don't even think I met with the head coach," says Waddle. Ohio State? "They wanted me just so they could get Mark." But they decided to stay together, backyard buddies till the end. They chose Boston College, in part because of Doug Flutie and Gerard Phelan, and their Hail Mary pass that beat Miami in 1984. Kamphaus eventually saw his career cut short by injury but stuck around, however, to earn a master's degree in finance.

Waddle caught the eye of an assistant coach named Barry Gallup, a detail guy who always sweated the small stuff. You didn't play for Gallup unless you did it all. It was Gallup who taught Waddle how to turn a defensive back around during a route. Gallup who showed him how to keep a cornerback on the inside or outside depending on the flight of the ball, and how to pivot and come back for a pass. Gallup's cardinal rule was if you can touch it, you can catch it. Says Waddle, "He would keep statistics on dropped balls, and basically anything that hit your hands he wanted you to catch." Waddle caught them. At BC he grabbed passes in twenty-six straight games and left the school as its all-time career reception leader with 139. During his senior year in 1988 he set another school record with 70 pass receptions, including 13 in one game against TCU, another mark. He made all–East Coast and honorable mention All-American. It was good enough for an invite to Indianapolis and the NFL Combine, four days of intense physical and mental testing, where Waddle proceeded to fall flat on his boyish face. He came at a sickly 173 pounds, ran a sluggish 4.8 forty-yard dash, and showed little of his BC flash. "It's intimidating; you kinda freeze," he says. The Bears, he recalls, were the only team to show interest, and he was the last person they signed. Theoretically, that would have made Waddle the worst player in the NFL in 1989. "The lowest of the low," he says.

Minicamp was Indianapolis revisited. Waddle wanted to quit. His dad and his girlfriend, the daughter of ex–Boston Patriot receiving and kicking star Gino Cappelletti, said no. So Waddle went back to BC, where he worked out with Gallup—lifted weights, honed his moves, and caught thousands of balls. At Platteville that summer Ditka noticed the change. He nutured the young receiver between the development squad and the waiver wire, keeping him around. That patience had paid off in the game against the Vikings.

Tuesday, September 24, 1991

IN CHICAGO ON THE MORNING AFTER THE MIRACLE ON MONDAY NIGHT, THE football gods, so active the night before, rested, leaving darker forces at play. A dull, drizzly rain swept the city. The expressways crawled. Teachers in three school districts stayed out on strike. But even the miserable mist could not dampen the downpour of emotion over the game. The city was buzzing about the surreal ending between the Bears and the New York Jets in the early-morning hours at Soldier Field, how under the spell of a harvest moon, strange, poetic things had happened. "Divine intervention," Ditka called it, and nobody was moved to argue. Backs who never fumble had fumbled. Kickers who never miss had missed. In the end the Bears dug about as deep as you can go, Harbaugh came of age, and Chicago came up with one for the ages, a 19–13 overtime thriller sent straight from the heavens.

It was the kind of game that sets a tone for a season, defines the character of a club. The newspapers, columnists, sportscasters, radio stations, had a field day. They sung Harbaugh's praises. They laughed about Boso's face full of grass. They marveled at the play of an aging McMichael, the eight clutch catches from Waddle, and how, once more, Ditka's Bears had shown a "Monday Night Football" audience what heart and courage are all about. After the game, deep into the midnight hour, a coach who looked as if he had worked all night on a rescue squad had just enough strength left to lean into a cluster of mikes and sound more in touch with a team than ever. "The game of football has been my life, my love," he said. "But these guys are my life and love now."

These guys. Four wins in a row now, undefeated, by the grand total of 14 points. After snuffing Minnesota the Bears had traveled to Tampa Bay and eked out a 21–20 win over the Bucs, an ugly but uplifting effort because Chicago had played poorly and still survived. "By far the most screwups ever in a game," reported Hilgenberg, reflecting on a day in which Chicago gained more yards in penalties (131) than they did on the ground (100) and was victimized by a small army of mental errors, mistakes, and miscommunication along the line of scrimmage. Harbaugh had yet another resourceful, productive afternoon: passing for 153 yards and 2 touchdowns, one to Anderson, making a somber return to his home state, where his father had been arrested for murder.

In training camp Anderson and his teammates were shocked when the news broke: Tommy Anderson, sixty-three, Neal's father, had been charged with killing his fiancée, Laura Mae Tyson, thirty-seven, in Graceville, Florida, a poor Panhandle city of about three thousand people not far from Tallahassee. Neal Anderson was born in Graceville and much of his family still lives there, the Anderson name holding considerable sway in town. "When you come from a small city like Graceville, it's like you're coming from an extended family," Anderson told the *Chicago Tribune.* "Everybody looks to you and says, 'Yeah, that's our guy.' I'm everybody's son, it seems like, in Graceville." Shortly after signing a $1.6 million a year contract in 1989, Anderson bought his father a new car as a Christmas present. "Neal is very close to his family, his sisters, and father," says tight end Boso. (As of May 1992, Tommy Anderson was still awaiting trial.)

A three-time Pro Bowl-er, Neal Anderson was, without question, one of the most graceful and gifted runners in the league, the rock on which the Bears' entire offensive scheme rested. A classic cutback runner, his slashing style had made him the all-time leading rusher at the University of Florida and produced consecutive 1,000-yard seasons (1988–90) in the pros. Something of a mystery, Anderson was anything but a self-promoter. Instead he sailed in and out of Halas Hall as smoothly and quietly as a summer breeze. Boso, one of his closest friends, found Anderson to be easygoing and devoted to golf, charity work, and a pet rottweiler named Axel. "He loves that dog," said Boso. "I mean he *loves* that dog." But those who confuse Anderson's laid-back attitude with a lack of toughness are sadly mistaken for, as Boso was quick to attest, Anderson "takes things head-on." For example, said Boso, Anderson was such a competitor that one time while playing Ditka in golf, he recalculated the scorecard after Ditka was done with it and found a $5 error—and called Ditka on it. And one day in Platteville he ordered a free-agent tailback out of a full-bore, all-rookie scrimmage and jumped into the action. "Neal just couldn't stand watching it," said Boso. "He likes the game."

It was with the same kind of fortitude that Anderson faced his father's plight. Returning to the team after a trip back home, he pronounced himself mentally ready to play. "Time to go to work," he told running backs coach Johnny Roland. Boso wasn't so sure: "Neal would never, ever, use that as a crutch. He seemed the same, but I think it had an effect."

In the Tampa game Anderson's mind seemed to be elsewhere at times. Playing before family and friends, he scored twice, on a 12-yard dash up the middle and a 7-yard catch, but uncharacteristically he also fumbled twice and gained just 35 yards on 17 tries, although the Pop Warner blocking up front certainly was no help. "Just another football game," said Anderson. Perhaps, but after two games Anderson's season totals now read 93 yards on 40 carries.

Ditka didn't know what to think about the win. Certainly topping Tampa Bay in this wacky way was not something to shout about off the top of the Sears Tower. But it sure beat being 1-1. "Right now," said Ditka, "we're not on page one yet. We're way back in the comics section. It's going to be a struggle for us. We have a chance to be a very good football team, but after two weeks, school is out. I don't know, I really don't know."

He knew a little more after week three of the NFL season. The New York Giants had enjoyed a huge statistical edge only to end up, like Minnesota and Tampa Bay, on the short end of the score. The hero this time was William Perry, heretofore invisible, despite his girth—no tackles against the Vikes—who batted down Matt Bahr's 35-yard field goal attempt with fifteen seconds left to preserve a 20–17 victory. In sweltering ninety-degree heat Harbaugh had a huge day, 221 yards passing, including a 75-yard TD bomb to wide receiver Wendell Davis. But the play of the day belonged to Anderson. His 42-yard burst down the left sideline and swan dive into the end zone midway through the fourth quarter won the game. Simple as that. Without it, the Bears were 2-1 and in danger of losing their seat in the NFL's first-class cabin. Early in the week, as players fanned out around town for the weekly luncheon speeches, the first big Tuesday payday, Ditka had talked not about revenging the 31–3 playoff loss against the Giants in 1990 but a single word: *resolve*. He had narrowed the focus of the game to a simple theme, acting much like the man in the "Operation Ditka Storm" posters popping up around all over town—a quickie Ditka endorsement deal based on Desert Storm commander Gen. Norman Schwarzkopf. "You identify yourself in life with victories and defeats," Ditka said. If so, General Ditka and his troops had proudly earned the mantle of a winner for at least another week.

Right from the opening, ABC Sports left little doubt who would be the star of their Monday-night matchup between the Bears and the Jets. Chicago's absence from "Monday Night Football" had hurt the network's ratings because love 'em or hate 'em, Ditka attracted a big audience. So in the opening montage ABC made it clear that the Big Bad Bear was back, their video pyrotechnics crashing from one shot of Ditka to another as Al Michaels's dramatic voice traced the story line. Ditka . . . who embodies the Bears. Ditka . . . seeking his one hundredth career win. Ditka . . . and his undefeated Chicago Bears. Finally, cutting live to majestic Soldier Field and the roar of the crowd, cutting down to the sidelines to the man himself, resplendent in blue turtleneck and a white sweater with a big blue *B* over his heart.

The ABC director keep cutting back to Ditka early in the game, drawn to the beaded eyes, the grinding of the gum. Out on the field Stan Thomas, suddenly a long way from opening day and the domination of Chris Doleman, was being manhandled by Jets defensive end Jeff Lageman. Soon Thomas was out and backup Ron Mattes was in, but that did not solve the defensive problems. The Jets tall wide-receiving tandem of Al Toon and Rob Moore, two of the AFC's best, were working over John Mangum and Lemuel Stinson at the corners; the tide had turned along the line of scrimmage. On the sidelines Hilgenberg saw the gaping holes and wide-open receivers and shook his head. He looked around for Harbaugh. The kid had played like a real pro so far. In minicamp Hilgenberg had praised Harbaugh's "dramatic" progress while hoping he would learn to sit in the pocket a little longer, to gain the confidence, like McMahon and Montana, to throw the ball in traffic. "If he can make that next step up," said the six-time All-Pro center, "then I really think he can be a top quarterback." Watching the action now, Hilgenberg decided it was time to help Harbaugh take that step. The Bears running game, minus Muster, still out with a hamstring pull, was stuck in neutral, going nowhere fast.

"You're going to have to win this game for us," Hilgenberg told Harbaugh.

Harbaugh barely blinked. "We'll win it. Don't worry."

Well, maybe a little. Certainly when the fourth quarter opened and the Bears were trailing by 10, fans worried. With four minutes to go Chicago was down by 7 after having been stopped on first down inside the 5 when four running plays, the last a quarterback draw by Harbaugh, came up two feet short. The Bears were history. Two minutes left. No time-outs. All the Jets had to do was make one first down and the game was over. A Soldier Field crowd of 65,255, eighth best in club history, suddenly sounded like 6,255.

In the still of the night Jets quarterback Ken O'Brien turned and handed off the ball to Blair Thomas. Thomas had not lost a fumble in 208 career rushes and receptions. But McMichael fought off a block and stripped the ball loose. Then he fell on it. A deafening roar reached out toward the ramps, the parking lot, calling the faithless back inside the stadium. The Bears had the ball! In seconds the stands, half-empty just five minutes earlier, were jammed. Harbaugh, in the midst of a career night, went to work from the Jets 36. The official clock said 1:54 to go. A sack. An incomplete pass. It was now third down and 19 yards to go at the Jets 45-yard line. Harbaugh, calling his own plays now, went to Waddle up the right sideline. It was a poorly thrown pass, badly underthrown, a intercep—but no, somehow the Cincinnati Kid came back to the ball just as his BC coach Gallup had taught him. Waddle yanked it away from cornerback James Hasty for a 16-yard gain. It was fourth and 3. Harbaugh went to Anderson, his meal ticket, and the All-Pro battered down to the 21. A quick shot of Ditka, spitting on the sideline. A third-down pass to Anderson was complete at the 7. A minute left. No time-outs. Second and goal from the 4. Harbaugh was sacked. Third-and-goal from the 9. Harbaugh scrambled to the 6. The clock ticked down . . . ten . . . nine . . . eight . . . seven . . . six . . . fans were screaming out the seconds . . . three . . . two . . . The snap, another mad scramble, a frantic shot to Anderson in the left corner of the end zone. It looked short. Anderson, falling backward, scrapes his fingertips on the turf and pulls it in . . . Touchdown!

A strange, warm, wonderful feeling came over Harbaugh. It was all a dream, he thought, a made-for-real-life replay of one of his favorite movies. "It was unbelievable," he says. "I looked up and the whole place was going crazy."

It was time for overtime. In short order a personal-foul penalty on Singletary—"Number fifty, blow to the face"—set the Jets up with first down on the Bears 11. There was 3:50 left. It didn't matter. It was over. Pat Leahy, at forty, the oldest player in the league, had made 79 straight kicks inside the 30, excluding blocks. This one was from 28 yards away. But somehow, someway, at the last instant, his kick hooked left. Inches left of the upright. Bears ball.

It was the Harbaugh-Waddle show now. Coming of age, both of them, right there on "Monday Night Football," the three years of sweat and strain, all the practice passes, turned into a telepathic performance. Down the field Chicago went, fifty yards, to the Jets 30. All during the drive Ditka had used four wide receivers. Now he shifted his thinking and went with a double tight-end package, Thornton and Boso. The call was a fake-toss bootleg pass. Thornton was the "under" receiver, Boso the "over" twenty yards downfield. For Boso it was a pivotal moment. Signed as a free agent five years earlier, he knew his body was breaking down. He honestly didn't know how much longer he would play. He could feel the grinding and clicking in his arthritic left knee; he had had a bad ankle and pinched nerves in both shoulders. But now he was running free down near the goal line. Harbaugh fired him the ball. "The ball was rifled, but it seemed like it was in slow motion," Boso later recalled. "I knew I was wide open; I thought I got into the end zone."

So did everybody else. Boso popped up, a divot the size of a dinner plate wedged into the right side of his face mask, like some crazy Halloween costume or some Second City skit. But this was far more heroic than comic. Da Bears had done it again. Boso danced wildly around the field. Harbaugh ripped off his helmet and leaped like a Little Leaguer into the arms of two teammates. *You've got to win this for us.* Harbaugh's right index finger shot like a fighter jet toward the heavens.

"Did you ever see the movie *Everybody's All-American?*" he said less than twenty-four hours later in a silent corner of Halas Hall. "That's exactly how I felt. I just looked up . . . and it's like, my God, is this really here? Is this really happening?"

Only this movie wasn't over. Not yet.

Boso was whooping and hollering in the locker room when Offensive Coordinator Greg Landry rushed in. "They're reviewing it," he said, sticking a pin in the party balloon. Out on the field, the referee clicked on his field mike: "After further review, the ball is down at the one. First down. Return to the field."

Boso didn't want to go. His shoulder pads were lying near his feet. "I didn't want to put my jersey back on," he said. "I just wanted to stay in there."

But sure enough, the camera crews, reporters, and fans were cleared from the field. Ditka trundled back toward the sideline. There were eighteen seconds left in overtime when Harbaugh lunged over Hilgenberg and Thayer toward the end zone. Was it a touchdown? The replay official wanted a second look. The players waited and wondered. Finally, three hours and thirty-seven minutes after it had begun, it was over. Harbaugh had completed 28 of 42 for 303 yards, all career highs, for 2 touchdowns and no interceptions. Cornerback Donnell Woolford had 13 tackles. Waddle, suddenly a star, caught 8 balls for 102 yards, 4 for first downs.

Those kinds of numbers had to be deeply satisfying to Ditka because he knew, deep down, respect equals effort, and the effort he had seen against the Jets was a testament to the bond he had built with his players. Minnesota. Tampa Bay. New York, New York. Sure, each win had showcased athletic skill and, without question, the strengths of the coaching staff, its dedication and preparation. But these games had been won from the inside out, not the other way around.

Overachievers, Ditka liked to call his players, a sporting term so often twisted into a negative, as if going beyond yourself, pushing the limit, meant, somehow, you were limited to begin with. Not so at all. And even though this team was thin and aging and inexperienced in spots, it had heart and soul and yes, at this moment, it had Ditka written all over it. The Bears were unbeaten because they simply refused to lose; somebody had to want it more, and to date, nobody had. "I don't know if it's luck or divine intervention or what, but you'd better have respect for this team," Ditka said after the game. "They didn't quit. My God, what an effort."

Some ten hours later he was in front of the press again, this time at Halas Hall for his customary day-after-the-game briefing. Fresh from a morning workout, his face was flushed, hair plastered into place. He wore yet another different outfit from a never-ending wardrobe—a blue sweatshirt, the words IRON MIKE printed in orange across the front. Again his ego was on hold, the texture of his tone soft, faintly religious. "I think you win a game like you did last night, it makes you believe in the hereafter and beyond. It makes you believe. I know that.

"We do love these guys and they play well for us. I think they take a little of the hokey things I say to heart. Waddle made some plays last night I don't think any other player in the league would have made. He took an interception away from them, made the completion, and gave us a chance to win. That's big-time stuff. That's thinking through the whole play. I can't tell you how big that is.

"I think we've got a lot of pride. I want people to know the Bears are a good organization that plays with pride." Somebody asked a question about Stinson's tentative play at corner. "I talked a little bit about that to Lemuel," Ditka said softly. "He'll be back out there. He's made his living that way, being a little bit cocky. You can't suddenly get timid. But I'm not going to jump on anybody anymore for getting beat, believe me."

Four or five years earlier, given the Flutie fracas and the divisive players strike, such phrases as "We do love these guys" and "I'm not going to jump on anybody" would have sounded like something out of a Fellini film. Constant intimidation and personal attack had frayed the connection between players and coach. Now, as Ditka went on praising McMichael and Anderson, Harbaugh and Waddle, the clock turned back to another 4-0 start, two years earlier, when the cable connecting Ditka to his team and to life had been severed.

Only to be repaired by a surprise visit from an unlikely gentleman caller.

WALLY HILGENBERG QUICKENED HIS STEP AGAINST THE WINTER WIND CUT-ting across the Metrodome Hilton parking lot. He knew game-day schedules often ran like a military mission, and he didn't want to be late for his talk. Michael McCaskey had wanted the uncle of Bears center Jay Hilgenberg to speak at the nondenominational chapel service before the Bears' Sunday-night game against the Vikings on December 3, 1989. About fifteen players and coaches showed up for the service held in one of the Hilton Hotel's meeting rooms. Ditka was there, and in a brief introduction he touched on his stiff battles with the elder Hilgenberg, once a card-carrying member of the Purple People Eaters defense.

In Hilgenberg's own mind, he was fading back to his first meeting with Ditka, summer of '64, Hilgenberg nothing but a cocky fourth-round draft choice of the Detroit Lions with some mayhem on his mind. "It's kind of a funny story," says Hilgenberg, now a successful insurance executive. "I played at Iowa. My brother was a coach at Iowa. I remember Thursday night, in preparation for the game, I called home to make sure everybody was lined up for tickets. I talked to my brother. He said first play of the game, whoever you line up against, give 'em a good shot, let 'em know you mean business." Great idea, thought Wally, who found himself at left linebacker lined up across from the league's premier tight end. Says Hilgenberg, "I'm there in my linebacker stance, and just before the ball is snapped, I cock my arm back a little bit, and as soon as the ball is snapped, I throw a forearm right at his chops. Hit him real good. Popped his head back. He leaned back, then reached out and grabbed me and pulled me right up face-to-face. He looked me straight in the eye and said, 'So you want to play rough, huh, rookie?'

"I thought, 'Oh, my God, here I go.' He beat me up in that game."

Hilgenberg's NFL career eventually spanned sixteen seasons, including twelve with the Vikings (1968–79) where he played in, and lost, four Super Bowls. To Hilgenberg the NFL was a warrior's world, full of scotch, groupies, and the taste of your own blood. He reveled in it. "I was the wildest, craziest, rowdiest, gambling, you-name-it-I've-done-it kind of person," he says.

Looking out at his audience, Hilgenberg forgot about the violence and vice and focused on the void. "The story I would like to share with you today," he began, "is the fact that sixteen years of pro ball, after playing in four Super Bowls, it got to the point in my life where I was looking around and saying, 'Is that all there is?' I had money. A wife and four kids. Position on a great football team. But I was still searching in my life . . ."

So was Mike Ditka.

Just a few months past his fiftieth birthday, it appeared Ditka was feeling more helpless and empty than ever inside. There were problems, it seemed, at every turn. The rumors around the locker room at the time were that he and Diana were having trouble at home, brought on, perhaps, by her husband's frequent absences for football, golf, cards, and business deals. "You know, everyone thinks you have such a wonderful, glorious life," said a football wife and a close friend of Diana's. "It's not so wonderful and glorious when you're there alone all the time." Diana had proved to be a very special woman indeed, a saint to some for her ability to handle her husband's many moods while sparkling so brightly in public. She made it clear she was utterly devoted to her husband, telling the *Sun-Times* a few years earlier, "The only thing that matters is being with him, the *only* thing." That kind of blind devotion worried several of her closer friends. "I've heard her say she just couldn't live without Mike," says one of those friends. "I personally don't like to hear a woman say that."

To complicate matters, the team was well on its way to losing six straight games. And the media was starting to carve up Ditka like a Christmas ham, repaying all the verbal swipes, the put-downs endured during Ditka's post–Super Bowl ego trip.

The week before the Minnesota game had been the worst. The Bears had been pummelled in a 38–14 loss in Washington, their sixth defeat in eight games. Ditka had berated Greg Landry on the field, ripped apart Woolford and Lynch in the locker room, then buried his entire team—and season—in the press. "This is the worst I have ever seen," he said after the game. "We stink. We are absolutely an atrocious football team at this point. I doubt—we have to play the rest of them—but there's no question in my mind that we will be fortunate, fortunate, to win one more game."

Naturally it all made headlines. *Ditka Says Season's Over. Won't Win Another Game.* Ditka offered his traditional mea culpa, apologizing to Woolford and the team on Monday. But it meant nothing. The players knew that. By now they were inured to the apologies. "He wasn't himself and people could see through it," says Lynch, the starting cornerback for Phoenix. "Usually he'd come across as real. Now we felt like he was saying something just to feel like he said it. The team was saying, 'I don't believe this now, he's going way off the deep end.'"

It started becoming obvious, say the players, after the team's 42–35 loss to Tampa Bay in week five. Going into the Tampa game the Bears were undefeated (4-0), but then Ditka began unraveling like a cheap summer suit. The mood swings were not only wider than they had been at any time of his coaching career—ranging from rage to depression, from tirade to tears—but this time you got the feeling they were real, not some cartoon characterization. "He was like the monster

257

of the midway," recalls Lynch. "He was withdrawn, real mean, you couldn't go near him. That was the time he started crying a lot. To tell you the truth it was real sad. He actually went from crying in a meeting back to yelling. We just looked at each other, like, 'What's going on?' We thought he was cracking up."

"We were worried," says Singletary, "that he was having a nervous breakdown."

Indeed, a picture of Mike Ditka during this period would be painted in dark, disturbing colors. The images are similar to those of former president Richard Nixon during the final days of Watergate, the imperial president mumbling to portraits on the walls, lashing out at his subordinates and the press—a man losing touch with time and place. It was during this season, Ditka admitted, that for the first time in his life he was having trouble getting up and going to work. It was a time when each succeeding loss (the Bears would lose ten of their final twelve games and finish the season 6-10) seemed to multiply his misery by a thousand, each new injury (twenty-three different starters on defense) pulling him deeper and deeper into depression.

The first signs of Ditka's melancholy had actually begun to surface back in May 1989. During an interview with a sportswriter from the *Arlington Daily Herald,* he touched on the topic of old age, sounding worried and wistful, referring to the aging process as "a cruel SOB."

"It's harder on some than others," he said. "I have some friends who are older and in great shape. They play golf and do things like that. I hope I can do that when I'm that age. I don't want to get to the point where I have to live on one floor of the house or be in a wheelchair or something like that."

Ditka's lifestyle had been suddenly altered by the heart attack. Naps were now part of his daily routine. Fried foods were out. No more cigars or heavy drinking. Fewer speeches in San Diego one day and business deals in Florida the next. Some charities would have to wait. To help cut down on his time away from home, Mike and Diana had moved out of their rather standard four-bedroom ranch home in suburban Grayslake, a good half hour from Halas Hall, and into a million-dollar, custom-built mansion in the wooded North Shore enclave of Bannockburn, ten minutes from work. In training camp, Ditka said, there would be another concession to his ailing hip: "I may use a golf cart to go between drills. I get tired."

Subsequent press reports linked Ditka's emotional swings, particularly his depression, to an overreaction to the heart medicine he was taking. The blood thinner was undoubtedly at the root of the problem, but there was no discounting the impact of Ditka's frenetic lifestyle. Despite public pronouncements about reducing his travel schedule and easing off the commercial commitments, Ditka was still chasing the dollar. In the off-season he gave as many as four speeches a week, hopping a private jet or helicopter for a quick trip to Indianapolis or Washington, D.C., dashing in, dashing out. And if he wasn't doing commercials for banks or rental car companies or antifreeze (his price tag was now $200,000 for national campaigns), he was starring in health videos ("Straight from the Heart—A comprehensive video guide to a Heart Healthy lifestyle") or weighing the dozens of new business proposals that crossed his desk. And unlike Chicago's other marketing machine—Mr. Jordan—Ditka's only filter for all these proposals was his Girl Friday, Mary Albright, the crisp, silver-haired woman who takes his calls, types his letters, and protects his privacy. "Mary is all business," says Nova Lanktree of Burns Celebrity Service, which has booked Ditka for several commercials. "You cut to it very quick with Mary. Don't bother with the 'Hi, how are you?' It's 'Mary, I've got this deal.'" And while Albright would occasionally green-light minor changes in existing projects without her boss's approval, she hardly qualified as an experienced marketing executive or the kind of professional business counselor Vainisi had always pushed Ditka to use. Vainisi knew that Ditka abhorred agents and disliked taking advice from just about anybody this side of the pope. But the ex-accountant shuddered every time he thought of how Ditka diluted his stature with cheesy Grabowski videos or local limo ads, often relying on nothing more than gut reaction. "The world's worst businessman," says his business partner, Vainisi. "Mike makes his own review with his heart and his stomach. He doesn't have the time to give it the proper thought, or he chooses not to give it to professionals to evaluate."

That habit put the hurt on Ditka in the restaurant business in Dallas (remember Wolf Creek and the Hungry Hunter?). In the months to come, it was destined to cause him even more heartache.

Of course, in the early months of 1989, financial failure seemed out of the question. Over at Ditka's/City Lights, Shlaes was depositing $100,000 to $150,000 from American Express in the bank every two weeks. On weekends the wait for dinner was still two hours, and City Lights and the banquet business were booming. In '89, in fact, the restaurant/nightclub combination would gross a record $9.24 million; total sales from 1986 to 1989 would exceed $34.5 million. In 1986–88 the partnership had divided up profits of more than $1 million each year, a 12–14 percent return on investment, almost double what restaurant partnerships normally produced. By 1989, Pontillo's original $400,000 investment had earned him an additional $1 million. Ditka and the other investors had all tripled their money. In light of those figures the inevitable cry for spin-offs filled the air. Ditka listened and made his moves.

While Arlington International Racecourse was rebuilding from a devastating fire, Ditka's Trackside was formed and did business under a tent from August 1988 to July of '89. In the summer of 1989 the Trackside tent closed down as Ditka, Shlaes, and others opened up a second sports bar/restaurant on the ground floor of the fourteen-story Triangle Office Plaza on the city's northwest side near the airport. Ditka's O'Hare, as it was called, was managed by Ditka's golf buddy Ted Roberts. Meanwhile, out in Las Vegas, Nevada, Ditka, Shlaes, and Dodger manager Tommy Lasorda had signed a lease to open a 12,000-square-foot Ditka's-style restaurant and bar right on the Strip in a $30-million office complex called the Omni Plaza. The project fizzled, however, after an independent Japanese lendor discovered one of its U.S. representatives was embezzling funds.

All the better, since the NFL was leery of this project. "We were aware of the situation," says league spokesman Greg Aiello. "There would always be concerns about going into business in Las Vegas because of the gambling aspect. It would raise a red flag rather than, say, opening a restaurant in Chicago or New York."

No matter. Ditka was venturing into the fast-food business. "It was a way the regular fan could enjoy a piece of him," says David Hynes, the Chicago marketing executive who came up with the concept along with business partner Richard Schory. Their idea was for an upscale $2-million Chicago-style restaurant catering to family and kids. The decor would be a replica of an NFL stadium, complete with goalposts, "skyboxes," cheerleading waitresses, and a $100,000 "Ditka Vision" scoreboard entertainment center. The first "Ditka Dogs" restaurant would open in the fall of 1989 with ambitious plans for ten more restaurants within three years thanks to yet another syndication deal ($50,000 per unit) and possible tie-ins with the NFL Quarterback club in other league cities.

But Ditka's O'Hare, the Las Vegas venture, and the fast-food franchising were peanuts compared to the move into northwest Indiana.

Ditka's Merrillville.

The beginning of what local folks were calling "an entertainment revolution."

Merrillville, about fifty-five minutes southeast of Chicago, is a largely blue-collar Indiana city that Chicago commuters discovered back in 1987 as a quaint alternative to suburban living. Edward A. Kirk is one of Merrillville's major movers and shakers, a hotshot local businessman whose rags-to-riches story seemed pulled straight out of an Anthony Robbins "Personal Power" infomercial. A hard-charging, chain-smoking, fancy-dressing, yet fiercely private kind of guy, Kirk, now fifty-five, had turned a night-school degree and a $1,000 business stake into a local construction/business empire. Known to say things like, "Maybe it's more fun making kings than being one," he was also a political bigwig whose office complex looked like something out of a James Bond movie, with its expanse of perfectly paved asphalt parking lots (he owned an asphalt-paving company), the helicopter landing pads, and the Kirk name plastered everywhere. Away from the office, Kirk liked to relax at his 8,700-square-foot retreat just outside town where swans glided serenely on a man-made lake and gardeners tended ten acres of very secure grounds. Hank Stram, the former NFL coach and an Indiana native, had made the Ditka-Kirk introductions. And the two men, so similar in disposition and drive, had eventually decided the time was right to make Merrillville famous. "We're going to set the world on fire with this one," said Kirk.

Ditka, Kirk, Shlaes, and Chicago construction executive Bill Kent became general partners of the Merrillville project under an Indiana corporation called 7610 Broadway, Inc. The same four men, plus Rittenberg, also bought the real estate, a former bowling alley, for lease back to a limited partnership. The Ditka group eventually invested $60,000 each for working capital. The rest of the money arrived via a $250,000 local bank loan and the sale of limited-partnership units—at $45,000 apiece. Many of the limited partners were friends of Kirk's— local doctors and businessmen, along with several Chicago options traders who had missed out on the first Ditka restaurant opportunity. Some $2 million was eventually raised and used to renovate the Merri-bowl, a popular local landmark with its twenty-four lanes and proud history as the home of the best junior bowling team in the state, and an absolutely perfect location for an investment of this magnitude. The new Ditka's would be an anchor in a booming area of retail enterprises. The nearby Holiday Star Theater of Merrillville, a popular local attraction, had become the draw for a huge cluster of restaurants, office buildings, and hotels. South and east of Ditka's was an eye-popping strip of stores that included T.J. Maxx, Fretters, Sears, Toys "R" Us, and Indiana's version of Marshall Field's, an Ayers store. The crown jewel of the area was a new Wal-Mart, a company that rarely guesses wrong on a location. It was about one mile from Ditka's, leaving the restaurant in an ideal spot to take advantage of all this traffic.

On the outside the building was turned into a handsome 27,000-square-foot tan and concrete structure with GO FOR IT logos scripted across every black awning. A freshly paved megalot for parking (Kirk's asphalt company did the job) stretched on and on. Inside, the restaurant had seating for a thousand (an outdoor café sat eighty more). There were also ten separate rest rooms; a sixty-foot bar; a downstairs banquet room with seating for two hundred and forty; a gift shop; two dance floors; two changing rooms for brides; and chrome and etched glass all around. "It's like a hotel without rooms," Kirk told the Gary, Indiana *Post-Tribune*.

Rittenberg, naturally, was running the show. Rittenberg says he was reluctant to get involved, mainly because he didn't know Merrillville from Hooterville. "Why would I go to Merrillville? I don't like Merrillville," he says. "They said, 'Oh, it will be great out there. It will be super out there, this and that.'" What finally sold Rittenberg on the project was the proximity of the Star Theater. "So," he says, "we went out and did a Ditka's." For his efforts, J.R. Management Services, Inc. took its usual 5 percent off the top. (Ditka would receive $1,000 a week as a "royalty payment.") Also, according to the Merrillville investor prospectus, Rittenberg had other "varying interests" in the project. They included his piece of the lease, the right to sell or lease back equipment to the limited partnership at a profit, and the right to move members of his management team to "other nightclubs and restaurants from the Project" as he saw fit, meaning Merrillville employees could work at other Rittenberg projects if need be. The prospectus made it clear (if you bothered to read it) that there was no provision in the management contract to "prevent this cross utilization" of personnel.

Rittenberg and Kirk first promised an October 1988 opening. Then they promised November, December, January, and finally April of '89. When the restaurant finally opened its doors in June, the crowds were large, flooding in from all over the area despite still-incomplete construction and some immediate grumblings about the big-city drink and food prices and long waits for dinner. Local folks frowned at the valet parking stand and the attendants handing out paper towels in the washroom (who needed help to park their car or dry their hands?). Ditka missed the grand opening, but when he did arrive, it was often in spectacular fashion, at least by local standards, dropping from the sky in one of Kirk's helicopters. (In September 1988, Ditka and Kirk became partners in the aviation business, forming Ditka & Kirk Aviation, Inc. They purchased a King Air 90, an eight-seat turboprop jet for use by major Chicago corporations and music theaters all around the Midwest who needed to ferry rock groups such as The Who and the Rolling Stones to concert sites.)

As the summer concerts rolled on, training camp 1989 opened in Platteville with the Bears experiencing their first quarterback battle in years. McMahon was around just long enough to convince Ditka he couldn't cut it anymore and was shipped off to San Diego by the third week in August. That left Harbaugh and Tomczak under the wing of the Bears' new offensive coordinator—former quarterback coach Landry —recently promoted to replace Hughes. Hughes had been at the annual scouting-combine workouts for college seniors in Indianapolis back in February when McCaskey broke the news: "I'm making Landry the offensive coordinator." Ditka wasn't even at the workout, and when Hughes told him about the change, the head coach offered no resistance. "I figured loyalty goes one way, and that's it," says Hughes, adding, "I don't know why he didn't stand up for me. But all of a sudden I was assistant to the head coach and receivers coach." Hughes had been the offensive coordinator in Detroit in 1977 when Landry was the Lions quarterback. Hughes makes it plain he has nothing against Landry personally. He just doesn't believe Landry has the instincts or imagination, particularly when it comes to the running game, to put together an effective game plan. "It seemed like sort of a copy thing with him," Hughes says. "I think he gets everything sort of from somebody else's films."

From the beginning of training camp Ditka was caught in what Hughes now calls a clash between offensive coaches, a feud Hughes says threatened to erupt into fisticuffs. It started when Hughes was teaching receivers how to block. Landry, according to Hughes, told him to stop.

"It's a waste of time," he told Hughes.

"Waste of time?" said Hughes. "More than fifty percent of our players are blocking. These guys don't know how to block."

"I said it's a waste of time."

Two games into the exhibition season Hughes quit. "If I don't retire," he told Ditka, "I'm gonna punch Landry, and that wouldn't be the way I want to leave this business, because it's going to happen."

By early October 1989 the atmosphere around the locker room and

Halas Hall was charged with the same kind of choler. It began to surface right after the Bears absorbed that bitter 42–35 loss at Tampa Bay, after crawling out of a 28–7 hole. It was the Bears' first loss to the Bucs in twelve games and only the third in the previous twenty-one between the two division rivals. Certainly Ditka's depressive behavior brought on by the heart medication did not help. Neither did all the pressure of running from restaurant to commercial to restaurant and back again. Or how inexperienced defensive backs were making mistakes and costing games. On offense, Harbaugh and Tomczak, finally out from under the shadow of McMahon, were suffering through spectacularly uneven seasons. More than likely it was a combination of all those elements. Either way, it was obvious the Bears were now a team in transition, retooling, much like the Bears of 1982. But Ditka didn't see it that way. He could not cope.

He began threatening players in front of their teammates, challenging them to fights. "He ain't playing, he's not trying!" he screamed in the direction of starting cornerback Vestee Jackson, a fifth-year pro who had been worked over a bit by Bucs quarterback Vinny Testaverde. The normally soft-spoken Jackson suddenly screamed right back, telling Ditka he had given everything he could.

"Bullshit! Bullshit!" Ditka yelled, and began taking some menacing steps toward Jackson. Several players stepped in front of the coach. Jackson was so upset he went AWOL for a few days.

"That's when all the trouble started," says Lynch. "That's when we started going downhill."

The next Sunday at Soldier Field the plunge continued as Tomczak, in one of his habitual hair-pulling performances, completed 20 of 29 passes for 3 touchdowns and 4 interceptions. The Oilers won 33–28, with 14 points in the final quarter. Ditka rode to the edge of an emotional cliff, his tirades growing more abusive and desperate with each passing day. The veterans were sickened by his style of coaching. The younger players, meanwhile, were paralyzed on the field for fear of getting ripped. "A lot of people were getting threatened," says Lynch. " 'You'll be outta here, perform or you're gone.' You just worried about making a mistake. You're not playing your game. You just wish, man, I hope they don't throw it this way. Let me get by this game, so he won't be on your back."

Over the next five weeks, playing scared, the team took three more emotional beatings. The first was administered by the Cleveland Browns (27–7) on "Monday Night Football." Two weeks later, in the now infamous instant-replay game with the Packers, the Bears lost on the final play of the game. Trailing 13–7 the Pack had faced a fourth-and-14 from the Bears 14-yard line with time for one more play. Green Bay quarterback Don Majkowski scrambled out of the pocket—and he appeared to be over the line of scrimmage—before firing a TD pass to wide receiver Sterling Sharpe, who made a miraculous catch in the end zone as time expired. On the field an official ruled Majkowski had crossed the line of scrimmage, canceling the score. After further review, the replay official reversed the call for a touchdown and a Packer win. Ditka, who had gone a little crazy during that game, challenging one of his lineman to a fight, was disconsolate afterward. (He felt even worse after the league office later admitted the replay official did not possess the necessary "indisputable evidence" to overturn the call.)

Finally, just one week prior to the fateful Washington game, Tampa Bay beat Chicago again, this time 32–31 on a late field goal. For Ditka it was yet another tormenting loss to a team—like the Packers and Browns and Oilers—the Bears had easily put away in the past. His wild mood swings began to worry veterans such as Singletary and Dent. "It was scary in that sense you're dealing with a schizophrenic," says Singletary.

Adds Dent, "It's like anybody else. If you're rich for a long time and you go broke, you panic."

Ditka's behavior, however, drew little sympathy from the local press, particularly since they were absorbing the brunt of his burdens. After the second Tampa Bay loss, Ditka had lashed out at a TV reporter and writer, snapping, "If you're the Supreme Authority, fine! You're pontificating. If your job is to do a hatchet job on Jim [Harbaugh, who had had a rough day], do it. You're not going to write what I say, anyway." Glaring around the room, he said, "You're all going to editorialize and pontificate."

Tired of Ditka's imperial attitude, sportswriters pulled off the gloves and hammered away. The resultant portrait was what many had been afraid to write for years: an arrogant, mean-spirited, manipulative man—Coach Bully—who had worn out his welcome around town. The head coach was also taking a beating from the business press as marketing experts discussed how his constant shilling had backfired into an overexposed, money-hungry image. Ditka, they said, had been hurt by his refusal to hire competent outside counsel to screen potential endorsements and set long-term goals.

He certainly wasn't winning friends and influencing people in public either. "We never knew which Mike Ditka was coming in," says

Shlaes, who describes this period as a "very, very difficult one" for Ditka. More often than not, said Shlaes, Ditka either screamed at a waitress for service or sat coldly in a corner protected by a security guard. "I don't want anybody near me," Ditka would tell Shlaes upon arrival at the restaurant, "and I mean anybody."

In November during a luncheon appearance at Ditka's Merrillville, the coach drew a gasp from his audience when he grabbed a microphone and made a series of rambling, impromptu remarks obviously aimed at McCaskey and retirement. "Sometimes in life," he said, "honesty is appreciated, sometimes it's not. I've always tried to be honest from the day I got the job until now. There was a while when people appreciated . . . and now that we've had some success, people don't appreciate honesty so much anymore. You're supposed to tell them what they want to hear. Well, it won't be that way and I don't think they will have to worry about it very long. I'm not going to do this very much longer anyway. They can get somebody else and continue their own ways. And the Bears will continue to win because the blocks are in place."

At Merrillville, however, the blocks were beginning to crumble. The hallmarks of any successful restaurant are food and service. Merrillville had not lived up to its billing, and the drink prices were still rather stiff. Ditka's occasional visits by helicopter helped, but Rittenberg, the main man, wasn't a capable absentee manager. Rittenberg didn't have the luxury of a helicopter at his disposal, and he hated the two-hour round-trip drive; it was time away from the zillion other projects he had working: Ditka's downtown, O'Hare, Juke Boxes, and yet another Chicago restaurant called Les Violins. Rittenberg's pet project, however, was the construction of something called the Chicago Sports Hall of Fame.

To J.R., the Hall of Fame was a promotional dream come true, the chance to turn the vacant space next door to Ditka's/City Lights into a two-story tourist attraction. The hall would also offer additional banquet, kitchen, and storage space for Ditka's/City Lights, which was maxed out in all those departments. Rittenberg, who didn't put up a penny of his own money, proposed that Ditka's limited partnership take out a $1.5-million bank loan to finance the construction. To gain approval for the project Rittenberg needed the approval of two of the three general partners—Ditka, Shlaes, or Pontillo, the white-haired carefully coiffed direct-mail executive who had invested with George and Jimmy since the days of the original Juke Box Saturday Night on Lincoln Avenue. Pontillo was dead set against the Hall of Fame. So were many of the limited partners. "It wasn't necessary," Pontillo says. "It was just draining cash from our operation here. Jimmy didn't have any risk."

"Gene thought Jimmy was just trying to push up the gross to make more money for himself," says John May.

Shlaes, obviously, was a yes vote. That left Ditka to break the tie. At the time Ditka was tight with Rittenberg, so he listened as Rittenberg launched into his promotional spiel, how the hall would attract conventioneers, tourists, one sight feeding the other. Go ahead and build it, Ditka told him. The bank papers were signed. The partnership was not happy.

But Rittenberg was not finished. By now the Yes Man was riding high, earning upward of $600,000 a year, showing up in all the right columns, inundated with investors dying to delve into his next big deal. I'm the best, thought J.R. whose ego was now running neck and neck with Ditka's. *I can promote anything.* So when the opportunity to manage and promote a sports bar/restaurant in St. Louis with former Cardinals baseball manager Whitey Herzog came along, he grabbed it. Only this time, in his egotism and arrogance, Rittenberg broke two of his golden rules. He went out of his backyard and signed on the dotted line, guaranteeing several bank, construction, and personal loans for Whitey's restaurant. According to court documents, Rittenberg's St. Louis obligations eventually totaled at least $545,000, costing him some $15,000 a month to satisfy the loans.

On Sunday, November 26, 1989, as Chicago prepared to play Washington in RFK Stadium, the Bears were 6-5 and in desperate need of a win. On Wednesday, frigid temperatures had forced the Bears to abandon outside practice, setting off a search for some local college or high school gym, or whatever the Bears front office could find for an indoor practice. On this day it wasn't very good—a dimly lit *junior* high gym. Ditka was ready to strangle McCaskey. *A junior high school gym!* McCaskey was unfazed. He seemed to find strange comfort in these kind of conditions, conjuring up images of that old Bear mystique, how practicing in cold weather toughens a team up. It was also, several players noted, a helluva lot cheaper.

On Thursday the team practiced outside on a partially frozen field. The footing was terrible. The defensive backs were unable to practice Washington's intricate pass routes. It showed on Sunday. The Redskins' young quarterback, Mark Rypien, looked like Johnny Unitas, completing 30 of 47 passes for 401 yards and 4 touchdowns. "The worst showing a Ditka team has ever made," says Peter King, football writer for *Sports Illustrated,* who was in the stadium that day. King recalls sitting next to a Steelers scout by the name of Joe Mendes, who was watching Woolford drape himself all over Washington receivers Art Monk and Gary Clark, as Rypien, having the game of his life, hit one impossible pass after another. "I'll take that kind of coverage anytime," Mendes told King.

Not Ditka. His frustrations—the pathetic practice arrangements, all the last-minute losses, this putrid performance—boiled over after the game. He reduced Woolford to human rubble with an outrageous outburst. Then he took off on Lynch—"You don't deserve to be on this team!"—whom Ditka felt had messed up a kickoff return. The next morning on his WGN radio show his moods took another sharp shift; now Ditka sounded spacey and depressed when cohost Chuck Swirsky asked if Ditka really believed the season was over. "I didn't say I thought the season was over, did I?" replied Ditka. "Did I say that yesterday? What did I say, exactly—you tell me. I said we'd be lucky to win another game. I did say that. I remember saying that. Now, that doesn't mean I said the season's over. I haven't said anything about that. I said we'd be lucky to win another game. Now what does that mean? Seven and ten, seven and eleven, will get you in [the playoffs], whatever the record would be, I don't know." From there Ditka went off into an insecure rap, typically blaming everybody from the fans to the media to McCaskey for the terrible year. For a brief moment, Ditka even shouldered a bit of the blame before quickly couching that admission around a now-familiar threat of quitting, if, well, the Bears didn't want him anymore.

"I'll be honest with you, I don't see how we're gonna start playing any better. . . . I'll take the responsibility first. I say that maybe we were outcoached . . . and maybe it's time the organization does evaluate Mike Ditka, maybe it's time to tell him to hit the road. That doesn't bother me one bit. I think that's another thing the papers have been insinuating, so I think they ought to do it. If it's time to say, 'Hey, we need someone else in here, we need a different philosophy,' go ahead and get it. My whole job when I came here was to build this club, and I'll tell you what, gang, I did a helluva job. I built this football team exactly the way I wanted it. I did a few things lately that let it slip away from me because we weren't the same. We don't play Bear football in certain areas, and it bothers me, and that's my fault because I took too much for granted.

"I just know right now, even though the situation is not completely dismal, we have a lot people in this town, including the phony fans, including the media—it's the papers basically, and maybe one TV station—that have read doom all year, that have been negative all year. Well, fine, so they get what they deserve. Chicago gets what they deserve. The [Sun] Times and the Tribune get exactly what they deserve. That's what they want; that's why they advocate; that's what they preach; that's what they're getting. So why should anybody be disappointed except me.

". . . Do I think we need an indoor facility? I think we need it. I've always thought we needed it and I haven't backed off that. We don't have it. What do we do? We tried to make the best of a situation we had. Last week we didn't have a good practice on Wednesday. We were in a gymnasium with no lights . . . it seems like these things become a problem when you're not winning. When you're winning, you overlook them.

". . . I don't know if I'm burned out. I don't think I'm burned out in as much as I can't condone what I see, and if I can't condone what I see, I've got to blame myself a little bit for it, more than a little bit because I'm the coach."

So this was the man who sat and listened as Hilgenberg started to speak. A man who had tried to shift his persona so many times before, but whose life was now seemed as empty as one of the Aliquippa mills rotting along the banks of the Ohio River. In many ways Ditka was a modern-day George Bailey, the protagonist in Frank Capra's classic Christmas tale It's a Wonderful Life, a movie about a man who discovers his life isn't as hollow as he believes it to be. Oddly, Ditka had just watched the movie on TV.

Dent attended the chapel service that day. He still remembers thinking how Hilgenberg seemed to be speaking directly to Ditka. It was eerie the way Hilgenberg framed his life, the way he believed, as so many athletes do, that he could—and would—conquer the world, expressing feelings of immortality, the trappings of money and fame, the emptiness he felt inside. "You know," said Hilgenberg, "I've been searching all my life for the thing that was really going to make me happy. I've always been one of those guys who set goals, and once you get it, it doesn't mean that much to you. It was the chase that was more important than actually having it. I kept searching for the thing that would really make me satisfied.

"One day in 1977 we were playing the Bears. I had this set routine every Sunday. I would get up, shower and shave, go down to pregame meal, get taped, go over to the linebacker meeting, doing all the things you do for preparation. Then we'd [the team] drive over to the Met [Metropolitan Stadium]. As we would start to walk into the stadium, fans would recognize you. Out there tailgating, people yelling, 'Go for it, Wally. Go stick 'em. Do your thing.' I was a big tough linebacker at the time, the macho man. I remember walking in that gate, walking down the ramp, walking into the Vikings locker room, back in the far left-hand corner of the locker room, old number fifty-eight was hanging there. I went over and started putting that uniform on, piece by piece, kinda like a matador. I cut the sleeves off until they looked good, pulled the socks up, taped them, because I wanted to look good when I walked on that field. There were going to be forty-six thousand people in those stands, and as far as I was concerned, they were all going to be looking at me. That's kinda where I was coming from. I was into myself.

"I remember the game. It was a real tough game, physical, close, hard fought, right down to the wire [the Vikes won 22–16 in overtime]. After the gun went off, the excitement, the thrill of victory, took over. I ran off the field. At the Met there is no tunnel, so it got all jammed up, stuck there as players were running off the field. People were just cheering us everywhere. Forty-six thousand people on their feet cheering for us. It was the loudest cheer I had ever heard, anytime, anyplace. It was just incredible. You could actually feel the sound hit you and bounce off. I never felt sound before. It was an incredible feeling.

"Finally we ran into the locker room. Jumping up and down. Slapping each other on the back. Celebrating the victory. After we had celebrated for a while, we cooled down, got dressed, and went outside. My wife, Mary, was waiting for me. And she came up and threw her arms around me, kissed me, congratulated me. We started to leave the stadium that day, and as we got up this ramp to do what I normally did, which was go out and bask in the glory, sign autographs for a while or go to the first tailgate party I could find and bum of couple of scotches, I took a walk back into the stadium with my wife. To take one last look at the place. Where it all happened. Just minutes before it had been so bright, so alive, so exciting. But now it had taken on a great transition.

"The sun had gone down behind the roof, and it was getting dark in there. And it was empty. And it was cold. And it was a very lonely place. And I looked at that stadium and I said, 'This is just like my life.' Because when I'm out at the parties, the bars, the office, the locker room, I'm with the guys and we're slapping each other on the back and saying, 'We're doing our own thing.' It's like the stadium with forty-six thousand people cheering for me. But when I leave those places and I'm going home at night or I get home and I stand in front of that mirror and look inside myself, I realize that my life is just as cold, as empty, as lonely, as that stadium.

"Then I turned to my wife and shared that with her. I had always built this wall of protection. I kept my wife, my kids, everybody out there, with just me on the inside. When I told her that, she said, 'Wally, I've been telling you for six months what's missing in your life—Jesus Christ.' Six months before my wife had made a personal commitment to the Lord. For six months in our family I had fought it, rebelled against it. When she said that to me, I said, 'I'll think about it,' and I did."

Hilgenberg explained to the room how he thought about it for a full week, until the following Saturday night. Alone in his hotel room prior to an away game the next day, Hilgenberg pulled out the Bible that Mary had given him. He somehow turned to John 3:3, God's call to make a commitment to Jesus Christ. With his voice sounding like thunder in the still quiet of this room, Hilgenberg said a very simple sinner's prayer and accepted the Lord into his life.

"You know," he said on the morning of December 3, 1989, "I played in four Super Bowls and people always came up to me and asked when I was going to win the big one. I used to hate that question. But I said in December 1977, 'I won the big one.'

"You know you can win the Super Bowl in January and you're oh and oh in July, starting all over. The victory I'm talking about is the eternal victory that lasts forever. When our priorities are right, when we give Him first place, the other things are right.

"I know there are a lot of people who have that same empty feeling looking back at that stadium. If there is somebody who needs to make a commitment or recommitment in their life, today's the day. Today is the day of salvation. Today is the day to get on the winning team."

One by one Singletary, McCaskey, and some assistant coaches approached Hilgenberg and thanked him for his testimony. Ditka, on the other hand, turned and left the room, speaking to no one.

The schedule called for Ditka to address his entire squad soon after at a pregame meeting. No one was prepared for what transpired at that meeting. To a man the players were shocked and confused by the sight of their coach, this huge Goliath standing before them, grasping for words, crying, the bill for fifty years of a winner-take-all attitude suddenly come due. "He was pretty broken down, just saying he was going to make some changes," says Dent. "He basically apologized to the team for his ways. He was pretty choked up . . . he really couldn't talk that much. . . . A lot of guys were wondering what the hell was going on. It kinda blew a lot of people away. He was always being emotional. He had been that way before, but not in a soft way like that. Humble. I had never seen him that way before. It did surprise me. It knocked everyone for a loop."

Says Harbaugh, "He just said he had a lot to be thankful for and that he had kind of lost his priorities in a lot of ways. He said he wasn't going to throw tantrums anymore, and as long as you go out there and do your best, he wasn't going to get on anybody."

And even though the Bears lost that night to the Vikings, 27–16, and finished the season with three more defeats, yet another "new" Mike Ditka had emerged. A kinder, gentler man determined to find himself. Willing, for the first time, to shorten the distance between himself and his players, to deal with adversity in a more adult manner.

It was fortuitous timing since the bottom was about to drop out of his business empire.

IN JANUARY 1990 DITKA'S/CITY LIGHTS SUFFERED THROUGH ITS WORST month in history. January and February are notoriously bad times for Chicago restaurants given the wicked weather and predictable post-Christmas cutbacks. Ditka's had always bucked the spending trend by creating business around the success of the football team. But the Bears' abysmal 1989 season meant no playoffs and no playoff parties. There were other problems as well. Ditka's personal popularity was at an all-time low. Hot new spots such as Walter Payton's America's Bar, the China Club, and Shelter were siphoning off bar and banquet business, and the local economy was down. The result was a shocking 50 percent drop in January business.

The restaurant, which had been gearing up for a $10-million year, now faced a $7-million annual projection—a near break-even figure—but less than the restaurant/nightclub's first full year of operation. Pontillo saw the numbers and immediately pressured Rittenberg and Shlaes to cut the payroll by 25 percent, or over $700,000 of the expected $3-million shortfall. Both resisted. Rittenberg knew what Pontillo did not, that there were other variables besides the Bears, the fact that it looked like Anchorage, Alaska, outside and that the Convention Bureau had lost the big Housewares Show. Let's wait a month or two before doing anything drastic, Rittenberg argued. Shlaes agreed saying, "You look forward. You don't cut staff and overhead when you're at your peak. And we had some good employees, people who helped us build the business. We didn't want to let them go. So we tried to keep everyone together. It was a mistake. We should have cut overhead in January. We didn't start to cut overhead until March. Our losses were huge at that point."

The heavy bleeding slowed in the spring as Chicagoans left their health clubs and condos and started to sample the nightlife again. But the restaurant wasn't responding as it had in the past, and the numbers ran in the red through June. Rittenberg was still predicting a break-even year of about $7 million in sales (actually it would be $7.24 million, a slight loss), but the $2 million drop from 1989 would wipe out all profit distributions, much to the dismay of Ditka and Pontillo. Says Shlaes, "Mike and Gene became disgruntled because they weren't getting this money. Nobody figured the bottom was going to drop out of the business."

Maybe, but it was at this point, the principals agree, that ego and greed took over, fingers were pointed, and everyone started watching his back. The only disagreement was over whose ego was bigger and how greedy everyone got. Rittenberg charges Pontillo saw the dip in restaurant revenue as an "opportunity" to "knock the king off the hill," in essence rid the restaurant of Rittenberg's $450,000-a-year management contract. (Pontillo did not know Rittenberg was paying Ditka $104,000 a year.) "Nobody is going to get rid of the captain unless someone else wants to be captain," Rittenberg said.

Pontillo had a different take. Sitting in Ditka's bar one night, he pointed to the "colossal blunder" next door, the "monstrosity" now known as the Chicago Sports Hall of Fame, which Pontillo charges not only caused Ditka's/City Lights partnership to miss legitimate profit distributions, but also, because of a $30,000-a-month mortgage payment, drained the restaurant of much-needed cash at its most critical period. He also charges Rittenberg spent so much time in St. Louis and on his other enterprises that he ignored the home office. "I didn't feel he was minding the store," Pontillo says.

Not surprisingly, Shlaes refutes Pontillo's "minding the store" concerns. "He's the biggest lying son of a bitch there is," he said. "It's all greed. Gene Pontillo is a very, very greedy man who started to have problems in his own business and was depending on this for a living. Ditka was originally with Jimmy, and Gene slowly began to sway him."

As the war of words escalated, Rittenberg suddenly found himself swimming in deep financial water. Whitey's turned out to an abject failure despite big crowds and a prime location in the Powerhouse office building at Union Station. According to one of the restaurant principals, Whitey's grossed a respectable $2.5 million its first year, but for some reason was hemorrhaging money. It never saw year two. Today nobody is quite sure, as the principal noted, "where all the money went." Food and labor costs, said the source, were way out of line, and the manager Rittenberg put in charge of day-to-day operations proved to be much more of a fast-talking promoter than a businessman. Herzog did not return several calls requesting comment, but is known to be livid over the losses. Rittenberg claims he also took a financial beating—some $800,000. "I got murdered," he says. "I lost my ass."

As Whitey's was heading down the drain, in June 1990, just fifteen months after its doors opened, Ditka's Merrillville went bankrupt. It filed for bankruptcy protection under Chapter 11 and Rittenberg was fired. The partnership listed liabilities of $939,000 and assets of more than $1 million, tied mainly to the value of the land and restaurant furnishings. The Chapter 11 filing was supposedly just an attempt at reorganization, in this case ridding the partnership of Rittenberg and his burdensome contract, for which the absentee general manager had already been paid $103,823. Ed Kirk soon announced a new general manager had been hired, an ex–Radisson Hotel employee who would bring the menu and the drinks more in line with northwest Indiana pricing. Despite everything from country music nights to pasta lovers specials to concerts by Rare Earth, the restaurant never regained any of the excitement and the crowds of the first few months. It closed its doors for good on December 26, 1990. According to U.S. Bankruptcy Court records, more than $706,000 in unpaid bills (to unsecured creditors) had been left behind, as well as an obligation to Gainer Bank for more than $1 million, and a loss of at least $1.8 million to investors outside Ditka's group.

Given the St. Louis and Merrillville failures, it appears J.R.'s promotional luck had run out, not that, two years later, he showed much remorse. "I don't own the concepts," he said. "I could give a shit if Ditka's closes tomorrow. It's not my wife. Not my kid. I've had twenty different clubs. I don't fall in love with them. They come. They go. They cycle. Neighborhoods change."

Not down in Merrillville they didn't, or at least not as quickly. When talking about that property, Rittenberg blamed the poor middle management he hired, the distance he never wanted to travel, the payroll he never cared to cut. "Yeah," he admitted, "you can point the finger." Many people did. And time and time again that finger pointed right back at Rittenberg.

The original Merrillville bankruptcy petition charged that "J.R. Management depleted the operating capital necessary to operate the facility." Gordon Gouveia, attorney for Merrillville's unsecured creditors—companies and individuals that provided work, material, and supplies to construct and operate the restaurant but were never paid—points another finger. Both Gouveia and Kenneth Manning, an attorney representing the restaurant in its bankruptcy filings, said in interviews that Rittenberg was skimming money from Merrillville to prop up his other business ventures. Said Gouveia, "He came in and fleeced the place. There is a lot of money missing. A lot went into his pocket during the development of the property. There is a lot of concern about invoices involving Ditka's in Chicago and Whitey's in St. Louis. And I have talked with people who worked there during construction and installation. They all wonder why they spent so much money and still had used equipment and other cheap furniture all over."

Well into the spring of 1992, the question of where all the money went is still a subject of considerable debate among the limited partners. Despite its shaky run, Merrillville was hardly a financial failure. According to an affidavit Kirk filed with the Indiana Alcohol Beverage Commission, for a twelve-month period from August 1, 1989, until August 1, 1990, Merrillville had total sales of liquor and food of $3,185,390.30. A chart in the original Merrillville prospectus shows how if the restaurant grossed a figure of $3,048,500 in its first year, the cash flow before taxes was estimated to be $429,609. Several of Merrillville's forty limited partners are extremely curious how the restaurant could have grossed more than $3.1 million its first year—

and given the prospectus figures—not only failed to show a profit but ran up more than $700,000 in unpaid bills. "A very interesting set of numbers," said one angry investor.

Another concern of both the Ditka's/City Lights and Merrillville investors and management was Rittenberg's propensity to use employees of an existing restaurant to train employees at a new restaurant. The concern among various partnerships always centered on who was paying whom for what work.

Both John May and Barry Peterson, the longtime Rittenberg employees, admit they spent considerable time at Merrillville and several days at Whitey's, which had absolutely no connection to any Ditka partnership, while still being paid by Ditka's downtown. "I was spending more time away from Ditka's downtown than I was there," says May. "My check always came from downtown. I never got paid by any other place." Moreover, May says, the top ten payroll people downtown were spending "at least a third of their time in other places."

"It definitely got crazy," he says. "All these people were running all around opening places."

Peterson says he drove back and forth to Merrillville every day for six months. He bought all the nightclub equipment, installed it, and trained all the deejays. For that he was paid $600 a week from Ditka's on Ontario Street. "I never got any money from Merrillville," says Peterson. "All my checks were from Ditka's [downtown]. Same with St. Louis. I went to St. Louis for a couple of weeks prior to the opening. I still got my regular check from Ditka's."

Did Ditka's/City Lights ever receive funds for employee work outside that restaurant? "No, not at all," says Pontillo. "We were very unhappy about it. I don't think it was honest."

"There was a lot of commingling of funds," says Vainisi, an investor in both Ditka's/City Lights and Merrillville. "Rittenberg treated all of those [restaurants] as though they were his own businesses when, in fact, every one of them were separate and distinct partnerships.

"In my opinion he [Rittenberg] really ripped us off. He had no accountability for the money and he'd fast-talk you. That guy's a fucking thief."

Removing Rittenberg from Merrillville was one thing, but terminating his agreement with Ditka's downtown, Pontillo's desire, was something else entirely. "I had an ironclad contract," says J.R. "In order to get rid of me, they had to get a reason. And they brought up all kinds of things."

All through the summer Pontillo pressed his points to Ditka, whose support for Rittenberg was now wavering. Pontillo and Ditka had never been close ("They hated each other for three years," says Shlaes), but now, wedded by their mutual interest in restaurant profit, they warmed to one another. The battle lines were soon drawn: Rittenberg and Shlaes on one side; Ditka, Pontillo, Vainisi and Ditka's golf buddy Roberts on the other. In the late summer of 1990, Ditka fired the first real shot—ordering an audit of the Ontario Street books. Ditka was upset at the report. *"If I have to come down here with a fucking ladder, I'm taking my name down!"* he screamed during one partners meeting, his voice carrying down to the bar.

In early September, Shlaes says, serious allegations were made by the Ditka group based upon the audit. The group accused Shlaes and Rittenberg of everything from taking kickbacks from suppliers to stealing at least $250,000 in cash to finance gambling at casinos in Vegas. (Ditka's attorney, however, now says those charges were never made—and that Ditka was concerned about sloppy management and some dealings with other restaurants.)

Both Shlaes and Rittenberg deny all charges. "It was strange, strange, strange, strange," Shlaes says. "I never took any restaurant money. I never had any restaurant money to use. They don't know how many times I fought with purveyors to get better prices. It's all greed." Shlaes was so concerned about the seriousness of the charges, however, he immediately retained Bill Harte, one of the city's top trial lawyers. Shlaes remains extremely bitter about his final days at Ditka's. "We had a meeting the morning before I left for Europe," he says. "I was told everything was going to remain status quo. I said if it wasn't, I would stay. They said no, go ahead, everything will remain status quo, we won't discuss this anymore."

Three weeks later Shlaes returned home and was leafing through his mail when the former trader noticed an odd-sized envelope his wife, Gloria, had set aside.

"What's that?" asked Shlaes.

"Nothing, you'll look at it later," said his wife.

"No, what is it?"

What it was, he discovered, was a copy of a letter sent by Pontillo and Ditka to all the limited partners informing them that George Shlaes was no longer the managing general partner of Ditka's/City Lights, and that he was going back to the Options Exchange and was going to spend the remainder of his time building 59 West, Shlaes's new restaurant.

No one ever told you that you were fired? Shlaes was asked.

"No," he said.

Rittenberg described the meeting in which he was fired as "unpleasant" and "orchestrated." He denies any misappropriation of restaurant funds. "That was all bullshit, stupid innuendo," he says, "I didn't take one cent that didn't belong to me. I never even saw the audit. They wanted to know about $300,000 worth of missing pork chops. We were doing $45 million in business. That's like one percent. You think people don't steal? How in the fuck do I know where it went?

"Sure I go to Vegas. Do I drink? Yeah. Do I go around with girls? Yeah, I go around with girls. I'm not married. Do I do drugs? No. Do I steal? No. Do I gamble to excess? No."

Rittenberg, however, admits he has bet illegally on football and basketball games. "He's always gambling," says one associate. "Hundreds, fifties. He's a social gambler but definitely a gambler." As for the Vegas trips Rittenberg first said, "I've got a $20,000 line at Caesars, but I never used it." He later disclosed that the most he had ever lost at Caesars was $9,000.

But according to Las Vegas court records Rittenberg was sued by Caesars Palace for failure to pay $14,000 in gambling markers signed during two days of gambling on February 17 and 18, 1990. The markers were drawn on Rittenberg's checking account in Chicago and subsequently returned for insufficient funds. Caesars eventually filed suit in Clark County, Nevada, and won a judgment. The last public accounting of the debt listed Rittenberg as owing $20,845.31 for the original markers, interest, and attorneys' fees. According to three law enforcement sources, Rittenberg had gambled about ten times a year at Caesars since September 1988, and had his gambling credit suspended at Bally's Casino in September 1990. One of the sources describes Rittenberg as a "high roller" who was "dropping at least $20–$25,000" during the four or five times the source knew Rittenberg was in Vegas.

Even though Ditka apparently fired Rittenberg as soon as he discovered the alleged misappropriation of funds, his previous association with Rittenberg may have caused him—however unwittingly—to skate close to the edge of the NFL's "integrity of the game" rule regarding "associations with gamblers or gambling activities in a manner tending to bring discredit to the NFL." Any such associations, the rule states, "may result in severe penalties, up to and including a fine and/or suspension from the NFL for life."

League spokesman Greg Aiello said that while a coach or player is not obligated to monitor his business associates' private lives, he is still accountable to league rules regarding associating with gamblers. "It's definitely a concern," said Aiello of the Ditka-Rittenberg relationship.

"We would be concerned with any association involving gambling. People in our league are obligated to be aware of our rules and comply and protect themselves. Without judging anybody and not knowing the specifics, someone who incurs significant gambling debts, that would be something of a concern because of the threat of putting somebody in a compromising situation because of the gambling."

At the time of his firing, despite a rather expenseless lifestyle and earning more than $2 million from Ditka's restaurants the previous six years, Rittenberg was also wallowing in debt. In addition to the St. Louis losses and the Caesars judgment, court records reveal he owed more than $106,000 in back federal and state taxes, dating to 1987. He had also stopped paying employees of J.R. Management. Several valued people, such as May and Peterson, left in the summer of 1990 because Rittenberg could no longer pay bonuses to his top management people. "He wanted more hours and was paying less," said May. "It was the perfect time to leave because the shit hit the fan."

Yet sitting in the empty bar at 59 West in June of 1991 one morning, Rittenberg seems oblivious to all the accusations, and questions of character. Instead he strummed his same self-promotional tune, talking about two new restaurants he was opening, the Amazon rain forest concept he had running through his head, how, in this business, it all boiled down to opportunity and ego, and when it came to Ditka's/City Lights, ol' J.R. got beat. But in the end, he said, it would be Ditka and Pontillo who would lose.

"My only complaint in this whole scenario is they never came in and asked me anything. Ditka never said, 'Jim, why?' I'd have reasons for everything. . . . My only problem with Ditka was that people around him saw an opportunity and made him their ally to achieve their goals. I'm not saying he's dumb. They just laid out things that made sense to him. Everything gets turned around. They accomplished their goal. Ted Roberts runs O'Hare now. Kirk got the finger unpointed at him. Gene Pontillo, now he's the one who's going to get hurt because he thought he would step in and the place would make money by just cutting the payroll. He got rid of me, he got rid of four hundred thousand dollars, but it's like getting rid of Ditka and replacing him with four high school coaches.

"My projections were I could keep it [Ditka's downtown] at seven million dollars the next five years. They can't. Just the fact this place exists and is doing forty grand a week. Where would that forty grand have been? Ditka's Ontario. When the place did nine million dollars, the restaurant probably did four. Of that four million, they probably made five or six percent. So two hundred and forty grand. The place made a million dollars. The other seven hundred and sixty thousand dollars came from the nightclub, the banquets. They never understood that. They don't to this day understand it."

ON THE EVENING OF SEPTEMBER 25, 1991, WHAT THE WEDNESDAY-NIGHT crowd lined up outside WBBM-TV studios most understood was this: Da Bears were 4-0 and sooner or later Da Coach was going to show. Anxiously waiting for seats to the taping of the weekly "Mike Ditka Show," the night's studio audience was spread five across and ran deep down the block and around the corner. It was your basic all-white suit-and-dress crowd mixed with the die-hard Ditkaphiles (complete with Bears regalia, slicked hair, and aviator specs). At 6:35 P.M. a burgundy stretch limo stopped in front of the studio, setting off the requisite squeals and cheers. Ditka, the man of the people, exploded out of the car, tossed off a perfunctory wave, and was through the main entrance before Diana's hot-pink pumps hit the pavement. Thirty-five minutes later, after changing into a rather garish Capone-style suit, Ditka was on the set smiling out at his Arsenio-minded audience, which woofed and barked its delight. Hunkered down in the main control room, the show director said, "Okay, roll tape," and the cameras slowly pushed over the theme music toward Ditka and his longtime cohost and former Bears teammate Johnny Morris.

Forty minutes later, show credits rolled. In that short span the reasons why the Ditka show won a local Emmy in 1986 and still attracts a loyal Sunday-morning audience (the show airs at eleven A.M.) become self-evident. It is a fast-paced, highlight-happy, superbly produced thirty minutes of local TV, a Ditka love-in, to be sure, but an informative and entertaining half hour nonetheless. Ditka, who is paid a reported $150,000 a year for his efforts, played the part of the glib philosopher-coach to perfection. He joked about "becoming a tout at the racetrack" when he retired. He artfully diffused a question of judgment by saying, "I make a lot of indecisions, no question about that." He bashed the New York press ("They know nothing") while admitting he should have played his special guest, Tom Waddle, sooner ("I believed in Tom for a long time, but I didn't put him on the field before. That's my fault"). The studio audience lapped up every last bit of it.

Three seconds after Morris said good-night, Ditka hustled offstage. No sentimental handshakes or autographs, just a fevered march to his limo, which would carry him and Diana over to his restaurant, a regular Wednesday-night stop. Tonight, as always, Mike and Diana would dine with the guest Bear, in this case Waddle and his wife of four months, Cara. Waddle was a bit nervous about the prospect of dinner, talking about the "reverence" he had for Ditka as a player and coach. But the evening turned out splendidly. "They make you feel very comfortable," said Waddle a few days later. "It's really a great experience." During the course of dinner Waddle mentioned how he disliked all the sudden attention. Ditka just smiled and said, "Well, you keep playing the way you're playing and you're going to have to learn how to deal with it."

Prior to the '90 season these weekly dinners were about as close as Ditka got to his players. "Nobody could get next to him," says Dent. "You know, 'Iron Mike.' You couldn't hold a conversation with him. It was like a stone, no reaction." In the summer of 1990, Dent told the head coach in a private Halas Hall meeting it was time to come off the mountaintop. Dent had no idea what was happening at Merrillville or at the restaurant downtown—and neither did any other Bears. All Dent knew was the Hilgenberg talk had forged a dramatic new Ditka, and Dent was determined to keep it from fading back into the old. "It's time for the team to come together," he told Ditka. It was also, Dent argued, time for him to step out of the shadows and assume a leadership role on the ball club. In previous years, despite his stature as the Bears' all-time sack leader and the Super Bowl MVP, Dent had been overshadowed in the press and in the locker room by McMahon, Fridge, Singletary, Fencik, Payton, Hampton, and McMichael. "I've been in the back row for too long," Dent explained to Ditka. "Hampton's been here but people look for me to make things happen. But he's the leader. Well, leaders make things happen. You've got guys around here who ain't no leaders, and I'm no follower." It was time, said Dent, to make Anderson the leader of the offense and for Ditka to stop rolling guys in and out of the lineup. Set a team and stick with it, Dent told Ditka, and stop putting pressure on players, such as Tomczak, who can't handle it.

"Well," Ditka replied, "I'm gonna put some eggs in your basket."

"You won't be wrong in doing that," Dent said.

Ditka started dropping eggs in other baskets as well. He named Harbaugh his starting quarterback, then sat down for lively gin games with him, Anderson, and Roper on team plane flights. He invited Harbaugh, Anderson, and others out to Bob 'O' Link for golf. It seemed the latest New Mike Ditka—this was, after all, at least his third attempt at personal reform—had finally discovered his soul, learning there was more to life than black and white, than winning or losing. "I thought you were supposed to stay away from them," he told Al Michaels during a 1991 "Monday Night Football" halftime interview. "I didn't believe you could be a 'players' coach' and coach. I don't believe that anymore. I believe that's it's important that I communicate with them."

Of course, at the time, Ditka promised "never to blow up again." Of course, that lasted about five minutes—until the first day of training camp when he screamed at photographers who had drawn too close to his car to stick their cameras up their ass. He topped off the episode by belligerently pushing past a young boy asking for an autograph, telling the kid to "get the hell out of the way."

And religious awakening or not, he still acted small and unbelievably petty at times. He still bristled at any kind of criticism. He still crucified those who dared cross his path. Witness this telling exchange on Ditka's Monday-night WGN radio call-in show the day after the Bears had lost a tough 10–9 decision to the Redskins at RFK, just the Bears' third loss in thirteen starts.

"My call is about the media," the male voice began. "I get tired of hearing people like Pat [another caller] who sound like a jerk, kissing the coach's butt. Every single week it's a media confrontation. He's always mad at the media. He has to have it both ways. When the Bears are doing good, the coach will say, 'Ah, we're not doing that well, we haven't won anything yet.' If the media gets a bit negative, he gets mad at them. Dan Pompei asked a perfectly logical question: why play Harbaugh and Anderson in the fourth quarter of a no-win game against the Vikings, down by forty-odd points in the fourth quarter? [The game had occurred two weeks earlier, the Bears finally losing 41–13]. It was a perfectly logical question."

At this point Mike Pyle, Ditka's cohost, cut in, telling the caller to hang on for a response. As the caller kept talking, a voice could be heard in the background: "Big mouth, big mouth, take a break, big mouth!" It was Ditka. But the caller kept on, making an articulate argument for a full sixty seconds.

"You made your point, big mouth . . . take a gawl darn break. Inhale once in a while . . . inhale once in a while, will ya!"

The guy didn't stop.

"Mike, cut him off," Ditka ordered.

"Mr. Pyle?"

"Cut him off!"

"Can I say one last thing?" The voice was softer now, almost a coo.

Pyle cut him off, telling him to listen to his radio, the coach will answer your question. The coach answered all right. But said far more about himself in the process.

"He asked no question! All he is a big mouth. Here's a guy, he's typical of the small people in America who the only thing they can do is get on the telephone . . . this guy, probably, is a hundred-dollar-a-week guy. I guarantee you he is. He's a loser in life. And his only deal is to get up there and complain and cry because somebody else made it in life. That's exactly what this guy is. I'm sorry if I have to come on that way. But here's a big mouth, his mouth is going so fast that his brain isn't working." At which point Ditka goes on to explain the reason he kept Harbaugh and Anderson, his two most valuable offensive players, on the field in a blowout was because he was still trying to win the game. "If he doesn't understand that," Ditka sniffed, "that's tough." Ditka then went on to explain that in his opinion the real reason Pompei asked the question was to start a controversy over the quarterback situation. Of course that was not the reason at all, but Ditka was defending himself anyway. "You've got to understand the motive behind it," he lectured. "But this guy is too dumb to understand that. See, I've dealt with the media for thirty years. He has never had to deal with it. The only thing he wants to do is have his little animosity toward me. But he is a very small person to do that. He got his point across, I made mine. But I have the option of cutting him off; he doesn't have the option of cutting me off."

At this point Pyle defends the caller, saying he asked a legitimate question.

"He asked no question," snapped Ditka.

Yes, he did, answered Pyle, but you—

"I thought it was a silly question. Well, if you throw in the towel every time like he does . . . he's probably the kind of guy who every time he has a setback, he quits."

That same month, in November 1990, Ditka provided another look inside *his* soul, if you will. It happened at the Nikko Hotel downtown during the annual Ditka Foundation dinner. During the course of the evening some twelve hundred people showed up for the black-tie dinner or cocktail reception afterward, helping raise money for some of Ditka's favorite charities. As dinner was being served, businessman Ron Kushner noticed the coach standing in an alcove between the bar and the dining room. Ditka was alone, surveying the room. The look in his eyes, Kushner later said, was that of a child at Christmas, of wonderment, as if Ditka could not bring himself to believe a steel-town tough could one day bring all this high society together. Kushner walked over to his good friend and stood quietly for a moment or two before Ditka asked, "Do you think these people really like me?"

Kushner caught his breath for a second. He had never before heard the insecure side of Ditka. "Mike, you really don't give yourself enough credit. You're the guy who is responsible for this evening. You're the guy who is responsible for raising hundreds of thousands of dollars here, and we did it on forty-five days' notice. Don't you realize how important you are to all these things?"

Ditka turned and smiled the little-boy smile you see on Christmas morning. "Thanks," he said.

As one might expect, the 1990 Bears responded to their more sensitive, more accessible, slightly less confrontational coach. The mind games, petty threats, and intimidation tactics were replaced, more often, by a pat on the back or arm around the shoulder. The first real test came after the Bears won three straight to open the season, then lost 24–10, to the Raiders in Los Angeles. In years past Hurricane Ditka would have blown out the locker room. This time he praised a determined effort and moved on. Chicago responded by winning eleven regular-season games and another Central Division title. And even with Harbaugh sidelined with his separated shoulder, Chicago bumped off New Orleans, 16–6, before falling apart in the second half against the eventual Super Bowl champion New York Giants and losing the second-round playoff game, 31–3.

Now, as Dent stared out that picture window at Halas Hall, in late September 1991, he knew the next two weeks would be critical— games against Buffalo and Washington, the odds-on favorites to meet in

Super Bowl XXVI. "I told Mike last year I'm tired of other people walking into our spot," Dent said. "We'd just get there and get knocked off: '86, '87, '88, '90. Every team that knocked us off went ahead and won the championship. This is our time."

Against the Bills in Buffalo, however, the Bears played as if they were in another time zone. They committed 16 penalties (4 of which were refused), canceling two first-half touchdowns that could have pushed the visitors to a quick 14–0 lead. Instead it was 7–6 Buffalo at intermission. In the second half, Jim Kelly & Co. got hot and whipped Chicago, 35–20. It was obvious now that the mistakes that the Bears had overcome against Tampa Bay and both New Yorks would not slip by NFL powers such as Buffalo. "We had—I can't tell you how much miscommunication and errors," said Ditka. "The penalties . . . were enough to make you sick." So was the play of Waddle, who had his worst game as a pro, and that of left tackle Thomas, who got flagged for three penalties and who learned a serious lesson from All-Pro defensive end Bruce Smith. The proud and once-impregnable Bear defense took a beating (421 total yards), dropping to last in the NFC rankings. "To be last in anything is frustrating," said Singletary. "The most important thing is not to look at the stats now."

But Ditka was. On Monday following the Buffalo game the old Ditka crept back into Halas Hall once more. Repeatedly during the regular morning meeting he threatened possible lineup changes, directing his deepest digs at one player for being too "hardheaded" for his own good. "It's not just ability," Ditka said. "You have to have brains to play this game, and if you don't, I'll get someone else in there. I've run off all the other hardheaded quarterbacks around here. Take a look around. If you're going to be that way, you won't be around."

For five weeks now, ever since the opening win over Minnesota, Ditka had been harping on this "hardheaded" issue. Harbaugh had no idea why, other than some twisted motivational measure. It certainly could not have been the quarterback's performance. Entering the Bills game, Harbaugh had completed a heady 66 percent of his passes for a quarterback rating of 96.8, second in the NFC and third overall in the league. Others speculated that perhaps Ditka was sensing some McMahon-like commercial competition, given Harbaugh's "Monday Night Football" miracle against the Jets, his Hollywood looks, All-American image, and considerable charm. Ever since the Jets game Harbaugh's high-powered agent, Leigh Steinberg, had been fielding what he called "tons" of offers. Typically, Harbaugh wanted no part of the fame game. His lone local endorsement was a series of radio spots for Domino's Pizza. He told Steinberg to keep it that way and defer all commercials and endorsement possibilities until after the season. To Harbaugh the best thing about his hot streak was that a local children's home was able to sell twice as many tickets to its fund-raiser as they had a year earlier when he wasn't playing as well. "It's strange in a way that it makes a difference, but it's neat," said Harbaugh.

As for Ditka, Harbaugh held his anger. Sure, he thought, I made a couple of mistakes against Buffalo, but Harbaugh didn't like the reference about being dumb. "That's pretty personal," he said a few weeks after the Buffalo game. "They would be fighting words to anyone else."

Harbaugh decided to make a silent statement. He ignored Ditka in the halls and at practice Monday afternoon. On Wednesday, Ditka made it clear that if Harbaugh was staging a protest, he could not win. "Some of you guys think you can hold a grudge," he said. "Don't think it's going to hurt my feelings. It's been done before and it doesn't work."

On week six, the Bears faced the undefeated Redskins. "This will be a litmus test for us," Ditka said. If so, the Bears failed once again. Despite holding the 'Skins to a season-low 243 total yards in offense, the Bears got burned by big plays on both sides of the ball and lost 20–7. The offense, minus Muster, who was still out with a nagging hamstring injury, looked out of synch. Anderson gained 73 yards on 18 carries, but six games into the season, he had yet to collect a 100-yard game. Ditka, who had praised the passing attack two weeks earlier, now left little doubt he was tired of his team's averaging 40 passes a game, as the Bears had the last three weeks, more than any other team in the league. In contrast the Bears had not rushed the ball more than 33 times in any game, despite having a 41-2 record when they run more than 40 times. "We are doing other things right now," Ditka said. "When we have our minds made up we are going to run the ball and our minds made up we're going to run it forty times a game, we'll have a rushing attack as good as anyone." Harbaugh, who put it up 41 times, was intercepted 3 times, once by Wilber Marshall, who, in an emotional return to Soldier Field, left his mark with 11 tackles, 2 deflected passes, and his interception on the final play of the game. Chicago was now 4-2, a game behind the 5-1 Lions. After six games, the Bears now had a week off to get some rest and try to get healthy. Not that Ditka was sending any sympathy cards. "We'll practice regular this week," he said. "We might even scrimmage. We might as well hit ourselves since we're not hitting anybody else that hard."

On Monday after watching the films, Ditka changed his tune a bit: "I wish I could say I feel worse than I do. It's disappointing and disheartening but not hopeless. We were beaten on a couple of simple plays on defense, and on offense we had numerous opportunities. I'm still positive about this football team. We've got an opportunity to be a lot better and we will, I really believe that."

The off-week could not have come at a better time. Like Muster, Anderson had pulled a hamstring, an injury doomed to hamper his running the rest of the season. Things were even worse for Boso. His left ankle, repaired by surgery in December 1990, was still bothering him, but not as much as his left knee. It was scoped around minicamp in hopes it would be ready for the season. But it never really responded, forcing the tight end to submit to the needle to play. "It hurt when I just brought my foot down on the ground," he said.

Playing on the turf in Buffalo was a major mistake. "I knew something was wrong after that," Boso said. The joint constantly filled with fluid and the agony of every step told Boso it was trouble. He barely played against Washington and the following Monday went in for more arthroscopic surgery. The prognosis was for another four- or five-week layoff. The prognosis was wrong.

"How's it look?" When he asked the question, Boso was flat on his back on the operating table watching the doctor work through a TV monitor. His back was deadened from a spinal anesthetic. So was his heart when he heard the doctor's next words.

"Not good," said the doctor. "I'll talk to you after the surgery."

Later the doctor gave Boso the speech no football player wants to hear. *Your career is over, son. I advise you never to play again.* In Boso's case, his knee had a fourth-degree arthritic joint. The tibia and cartilage had been worn away to nothing from all the pounding they had taken. Six months after the surgery Boso was back home in Indianapolis, hoping not for a comeback but to be able to walk normally and, maybe, one day, play a little racquetball and hoops with Harbaugh. "Hopefully with some kind of surgery I'll get a little bit of mobility," Boso said. As it was now, his quadriceps muscle had totally atrophied after the surgery, and biking or rehab wouldn't make much difference. "It's mush," said Boso with an awful tone to his voice. "I just can't get the quad back to where it was." Ditka, he said, had recently called and said his good-byes. "He knew my career was over. He told me he really enjoyed coaching me, and if there was anything he could ever do, to let him know. He said don't hesitate to call, even at home."

After their week off, the slumping Bears went on the road to face Green Bay (1-5) in a Thursday-night game televised over Turner Network Television (TNT). The Packers were so feeble that with 7:36 to play they had just 87 yards in *total* offense. The game basically boiled down to the same old street fight, with Ditka determined to get his running game back on track. It helped that Muster was back. He teamed with Anderson, who later wound up on crutches after aggravating his hamstring injury—the latest on an ever-growing list of injured Bears. In the end, however, the Bears prevailed, 10–0. It wasn't pretty but it counted.

The visit to New Orleans on Sunday, October 27, was the first time since Super Bowl Sunday that the Bears had come back to The Big Easy. Beforehand, old reliables such as McMichael and Dent strolled the Superdome turf reliving a memorable moment or two, but unlike the rout six years earlier the line on this game made it look like anything but easy. The 7-0 Saints were the talk of the league, keyed by a helmet-busting defense led by a swarming set of All-Pro linebackers. The defense, ranked number one overall in the league, had allowed just 9.9 points per game, only 52 yards per game on the ground, and no touchdowns rushing. The Superdome was suddenly a mini–Mardi Gras with team owner Tom Benson, a car dealer, dancing along the sidelines and the NFL's newest battle cry, "Cha–Ching," the sound of a cash register ringing all over town, symbolizing how the Saints would "cash in" on this year's team.

Chicago looked limp by comparison. The dramatic wins over the Giants and Jets seemed so distant now, overshadowed by the humdrum offense, injuries, and inconsistent play. It was becoming increasingly clear just how much the Bears missed Covert. Thomas was proving incapable, in his first year, of making the mental and physical commitment necessary week after week. That left the critical left tackle spot in the hands of journeyman Ron Mattes, who was hurting (hamstring) and John Wojciechowski. To make matters worse, Chicago was playing inside a domed stadium for the first time all year. Make that doomed stadium, considering Ditka teams had lost five straight inside. Moreover, CBS was building up this one big, televising it nationally with John Madden and Pat Summerall on hand.

For those very reasons, Singletary began getting flashbacks to 1989. In those four early wins that year the defense had looked shaky, as the offense did now, and Ditka had worn the team out with his petty criticisms. Even the wins felt like losses. The last thing Singletary wanted now was Ditka calling players out, upsetting the delicate balance of a football team that had played its ever-loving heart out during the first seven games of the season. Not now. The veterans trusted Ditka again. The rookies were awed by his attitude and aura. He was getting more with less, approaching the peak of his coaching powers. "Last year, at this point, he would have screamed and shouted something he shouldn't have," said Singletary. "This year he didn't. He's fun. He's believable. He fires you up. You want to hear what he is going to say next. He's got it together."

To make sure Ditka kept it together Singletary privately and quietly told Ditka how pleased the team was with his new attitude, and any deviation, unexpected outburst, or job threats would prove counterproductive. "You're doing a good job," Singletary told Ditka in his office. "Hang in there with us. We're all family. Let's do it together." Ditka's reaction, according to the team captain, was "very positive."

It is at times like this, against all odds, going for the win, that Ditka seems to rise above every other coach in sport. He reaches back to his past and down into that iron will and molten fury, coming up with the wisdom and the words that send a tingle through your toes and feed some thunder to your heart. He did just that on Sunday in New Orleans. Butler and Singletary called it one of Ditka's greatest motivational speeches. "Top five, for sure," said Butler, who recalled how Ditka had hammered away about New Orleans mouthing off about the Bears squeaking by everybody, how the Saints were 7-0 and had been robbed in the playoffs by the Bears the year before. "A nation is watching you today," Ditka reminded his team. "New Orleans is talking like they're going to kick our ass. I don't think they respect the Bears. Do they know who and the fuck they're playing? *They're playing the Chicago Bears!*"

"He personally challenged us," Butler said. "That's Mike's greatest asset as a coach. He pulls things out of guys that nobody else can."

The Saints, as expected, buoyed by a mad-dog, sellout crowd of 68,591, came out flying. Linebackers Pat Swilling and Rickey Jackson were in the Bears backfield from almost the opening whistle, hammering away at Harbaugh. When the Bears QB made the mistake of trying to audible over the crazed crowd, Ditka was in his face on the sidelines. "You want to come out?" he screamed. "I'll take you out, if you want to come out." Harbaugh let it pass, but the way the Saints were playing it was not a bad idea. Late in the first quarter, New Orleans quarterback Bobby Hebert, who had a big day (291 yards and 2 touchdowns), read a Singletary blitz and found wide receiver Floyd Turner for 65 yards and a 7-0 lead. The Bears scratched back, barely, on two Butler field goals to trail 7-6 just before the half. Then as time expired, Morton Anderson matched the second-longest field goal in NFL history by blasting a cannon shot through the uprights from 60 yards away. The score read 10–6, but the crowd and the stats—Harbaugh had a total of 5 yards passing in the first thirty minutes, for example—said it was all New Orleans.

In the third quarter, the Bears parlayed a 37-yard pass-interference play involving Waddle to go up 13–10 as Muster, finally healthy again, banged home from 6 yards out. New Orleans countered late in the quarter when Turner caught another touchdown pass, this time from 8 yards out. It was now 17–13 New Orleans.

Ditka had seen enough. "You're out," he told Harbaugh. "P. T. [Peter Tom Willis] is in." Harbaugh had other ideas. Instead of sulking off or even slipping away for a drink (or some smelling salts), he kept his helmet on and stood right next to the coach, whispering in his ear.

"Give me another chance," he said.

"No," said Ditka. "It's not your fault, but we gotta make something happen. I've gotta try something."

"I'll make something happen. Give me a chance."

"No."

Two plays later the head coach spoke again. Something had changed his mind. "I want you to go back in."

For the rest of the third quarter and all but the last two minutes of the fourth, it looked like the wrong move. Just before the two-minute warning, the Saints faced third and 1 on their own 40-yard line. On the previous play Ditka had called his defense to the sideline, barked out some encouragement, then watched Saints running back Dalton Hilliard go up the gut for 8 yards. The Bears were out of time-outs. If the Saints made a first down, the game was over. It was here that the Fridge came up with the defensive play of the game, stuffing Hilliard for no gain. When Saints punter Tommy Barnhardt shanked his kick, the Bears had the ball on their own 48-yard line, with 1:54 to play, the same exact time left on the game clock as in the game against the Jets.

A slight hush fell over the crowd as Harbaugh leaned into the huddle. At this point he had thrown 11 straight incompletions and was just 2 for 19 for 16 yards passing. The Saints had sacked him 3 times, intercepted him twice, and knocked down 10 passes.

The huddle was silent, attentive. Harbaugh flashed on the Jets game for a second or two, the same sensation was running through his bones. "We're gonna win it," he told the men around him. "Sixty-eight-X-option, on two."

It was a play designed for Wendell Davis, the Bears acrobatic wideout from LSU. Now in his fourth year, the former college All-American was making fans forget about Willie Gault. The option part of the play allowed Davis to go post or corner, depending on coverage. This time he took the post and Harbaugh, given time to set and throw, drilled the ball to him for a 27-yard gain, down to the New Orleans 25. It was Harbaugh's first completed pass of the second half.

"Ninety-three trap," Harbaugh yelled in the huddle. This was a bread-and-butter play, Anderson on a dash up the middle. It went for 7 yards. "Hot Left eighty-two," barked Harbaugh. It was Anderson again, on a swing pass this time, the play he had scored on to tie the Jets game. It went for 6 yards, down to the 12, and when Anderson scooted out of bounds, it gave Harbaugh a chance to hustle over to the sideline. Harbaugh was thinking about calling a fullback draw to Muster, but then Landry made a decision. "Thirteen Wing Jet," he said.

Great call, thought Harbaugh. It was the third time in the game the Bears had tried the pass play, and even though one pass was intercepted and the other deflected, the play did two things: it worked well against the zone pass defense the Saints were using, and it made Waddle a primary receiver. While careful not to favor Waddle publicly over his other receivers, Harbaugh loved the wide receiver's work ethic, the way he never complained that a pass was too high or too low, how he "just did everything he could" to catch the football.

As Waddle heard the call and moved toward the line of scrimmage, he thought for an instant how times had changed. A year earlier in this situation he would have been afraid. Now he felt like he did back at Moeller and BC; he was the star receiver who wanted the ball. At the line of scrimmage he immediately noticed Vince Buck, the Saints cornerback, was playing loose, back in a zone. Perfect, thought Waddle. I won't get jammed.

This time, as Harbaugh pulled away from center, he got some protection. He looked first to Davis on a fly, then for Dennis Gentry on a deeper post. By that time Waddle had slid diagonally across the field into an open seam. Harbaugh hit him in stride and Waddle did the rest, slipping past two defenders before slicing into the end zone. Butler's extra point gave the Bears a 20–17 lead with 54 seconds to play. And that's exactly the way it ended after Johnny Bailey made a big hit on the ensuing kickoff, and McMichael, working a stunt, slammed Hebert to the turf on third down. As players from both sides walked off the field, a choking silence settled over the Superdome. "I don't think you can play a game any tougher or intense than this game was played today," praised CBS analyst Madden.

Ditka certainly seemed to agree. He was in emotional overdrive after the game. In a burst of postgame commentary that made all the cable sports shows, Ditka rattled on, red faced and neck bulging, as if he had fought the fight himself, which, in a way, he had. "This is what it's all about," he crowed. "Man, this is what football is all about—people getting the snot knocked out of them. I don't care what the score was. If they beat us, it's still a good football game. People were *hitting* each other. That's what it's all about."

Ditka seemed to have finally found a soul mate in Harbaugh, whose hard head kept him in the game. "God bless the kid," Ditka said. "I got mad at him a couple of times . . . but good Lord, he's trying to make plays out there. I mean, he's playing for his life."

Now, it seemed, after this improbable win, the Bears, 6-2 halfway through the toughest part of their schedule, had a new life of their own. "I don't know what this game proves," said Ditka, who played as big a part of it as anybody. "Maybe it proves we can play with the best."

THE FIELD MUSEUM OF NATURAL HISTORY AND ADJACENT SHEDD AQUARIUM are just two of Chicago's endless architectural wonders, rising up along the lake in the shadow of Soldier Field. In November 1991 the Field featured an exhibit titled "Into The Wild," which is exactly where the Bears and the Lions were headed on the first Sunday of the month. Eight weeks into the NFL season Chicago and Detroit were tied atop the conference with 6-2 records. It would be the 114th meeting of these two bitter Midwest rivals, but the first time since 1956 that they had met this late in the season with first place on the line. Under Ditka, Chicago had turned the NFC Central into something of a one-team show, winning more than 75 percent of its games. (Only one other team, Minnesota, had better than a .500 record in conference games since 1982).

Detroit, off to its best start since 1962, lived and died on the legs of

All-Pro Barry Sanders, in much the same way it seemed the Bears were riding the right arm of Harbaugh, who inexplicably caught more criticism from his coach. Now Ditka was complaining that Harbaugh needed to throw the ball *more*, to show greater courage and risk passes into tighter spots. Look at Troy Aikman, Ditka said, referring to the Dallas Cowboys' strapping third-year pro with a Nolan Ryan arm. He's not afraid to let it fly, Ditka said. "People aren't always going to be open," he told Harbaugh. "You've got to zip it in there." As usual Harbaugh had something to say. Yeah, you can zip it in there all you want, he told Ditka, but sometimes the ball comes back the other way, like it did for Aikman against the Lions, 96 yards.

On Friday, just before the Lions flew into town, so did the first snow of the season, a light dusting warning Chicagoans of the mean season to come. The snow was nothing, however, compared to the howling wind that screamed across the Halas Hall practice field. It left bystanders understanding what life on the arctic circle must be like. Dressed more like bank robbers than football players, various Bears left the locker room in ski masks and wool caps, screaming, "Ooooh! Aaaah! Yaaaaaw!" as they met moody Mother Nature head-on. Still, the field was ringed with about a hundred hardy souls, half of whom had flown or bused in from Aliquippa on their annual Bears pilgrimage. CBS commentator Madden was there too. The network seemed to have adopted the Bears; the Lions game would be the fifth time this season that Summerall and Madden would call a game.

Not ten minutes away from Halas Hall, cutouts of ghosts, goblins, and witches swayed from the trees in front of a fine two-story Cape Cod house. A brown-haired woman with large, librarian glasses answered the door. The house was quiet save for the sound of the barking cocker spaniel in her arms. "Not today," said Lucy Bell. "It's not a very good day. Yesterday was Becky's birthday."

For Lucy and Stephen Bell, November 1 had always been a day of sunshine and good cheer. Their daughter, Becky, was born on November 1, 1979. She was growing up to be a smallish yet spunky child with a face full of freckles who sang in the church choir. The Bells moved to Lake Forest from St. Louis when Becky was about six. She had a hard time switching her fan loyalty from the Kansas City Chiefs, but then she met Casey Covert (son of Jim) in one of her classes, and because Lake Forest was a Bears town, Becky switched her allegiance. She adored sports. Tennis, soccer, swimming, high-jumping, ice-skating, you name it, Becky tried it. But soccer was special. "Soccer was her life," Lucy Bell once said. That was, of course, all before Becky broke a leg playing soccer and the doctors operated and discovered a malignant tumor. In the summer of 1989, Becky lost that leg to the cancer. She lost her hair, too, from the radiation treatments, but Becky was a fighter and she took to wearing caps. Her favorite cap had CHAMPION written across the front.

It was through a Lake Forest friend that Mike Ditka found out about Becky. On November 11, 1990, he made sure one of Becky's wishes came true when he organized a special visit to Soldier Field for Becky and her family for her first Bears game. At the time Becky was in a lot of pain and weighed less than fifty pounds, but she loved the game. "She was so excited," her mother said. On Wednesday, November 14, Ditka went over to the pediatric center for the terminally ill at Rush Presbyterian Medical Center with a personalized game ball from the Atlanta Falcons game. Rev. Michael O'Connell, an associate pastor at the Church of St. Mary in Lake Forest, which serves some 2,200 families in the surrounding communities, was at Becky's side. St. Mary's was Becky's church, and O'Connell, whose bright, boyish face and horn-rimmed glasses give him the look of a college student, was holding a vigil. "Mike [Ditka] came in that evening," O'Connell recalled during an interview in the sitting room of his rectory one afternoon. "He brought the ball. Becky was pretty much at peace. They talked about God's love. They talked about the Bears. She really loved the Bears. And the Bears' most important man cared for her and about her."

"I hadn't seen her smile like that in months. She was in so much pain," Lucy Bell said at the time. "It was so touching."

The following evening, Becky saw another wish come true when Harbaugh, Jim Morrissey, and Ron Rivera visited her hospital room. Nine hours later Becky died. She was eleven years old. On Sunday, Ditka broke down and cried at the postgame press conference in Denver when talking about Becky. On Monday he was back in Lake Forest seated right in the middle of St. Mary's Church for Becky's funeral mass. Hundreds of other mourners packed the church, many of them children from Becky's fourth-grade class and their parents. "Well-meaning people may try to offer comfort by telling you there is a reason," O'Connell said at the beginning of his homily. "It is all part of a plan. I admire their faith—I think. In all honesty, I don't believe it's part of a plan. I can discern no reason in Becky's all-too-early death. It is unfair. Grossly unfair.

". . . I am sure a big part of Becky's determination to win is found in her love of sports. In various sports in which Becky excelled, she learned to strive for victory and she learned to handle loss. Most significant, she learned that for a woman determined to win, there are no defeats. Only setbacks. There will come another time. Another game. This conviction may have been confirmed for Becky by observing her precious Chicago Bears and their coach, Mike Ditka, who was so good to Becky."

When O'Connell had closed the Bible and the last recessional hymn had been sung, Ditka slipped away from the crowd. "What impressed me," O'Connell said almost a year later, "is he wasn't taking any limelight. He was there as a mourner, a friend. He didn't want to inappropriately divert attention from the family." O'Connell leaned forward an inch or two on his sitting-room couch. "I guess I always knew he was a good football coach. But now I saw him as a marvelous human being. I didn't know much about him as a person. That said a lot to me about the quality of his humanity."

That afternoon, at his regular Monday press conference, Ditka explained his feelings for the young cancer victim. "I know there are a lot of people in this world who are sick and have illnesses, but this is the one that touched me because it became important for me to do what I could do through prayer and through trying to encourage her. . . . I'm telling you what she went through was incredible. Her whole deal at the end was her family and the Chicago Bears. That's what made her feel so good. They buried Becky this morning. She'll be okay."

Ditka has been quietly devoted to children's causes as far back as his senior year in college. While playing in the East-West All-Star game in San Francisco, he visited the Shrine hospital, and the faces of the crippled children never left him. Today he regularly visits the Misericordia home. And he never just stops, presses a little flesh, and leaves. "Every time he comes here," says development director Jerry Lyne, "he says, 'I want to see the kids.'" And see them he does, walking slowly from ward to ward, greeting many of the smiling faces by name as they huddle around his hugs, grabbing for any part of the man they can.

In 1989, to further his commitment to kids, Ditka formed The Ditka Foundation, a public charity whose stated purpose was to "make grants to charitable and educational organizations," in this case, about a dozen different groups, including everything from Misericordia to the pediatric AIDS program at Children's Memorial Hospital in Chicago to $2,000 for a school in Platteville to build a wheelchair ramp.

Over the years Ditka fund-raising events have ranged from a hysterical Ditka celebrity roast in Las Vegas in March 1990 to more sedate annual outings such as the Mike Ditka Golf Classic, a skeet shoot, and glitzy black-tie Ditka Foundation dinner. In a striking testament to Ditka's local popularity, some 1,200 Chicagoans flew to Las Vegas for the roast, joining 750 others who paid $125 a ticket to hear the likes of Buddy Hackett, Jerry Lewis, Rich Little, and Norm Crosby cut the coach to ribbons. Ditka's golf tournament, one of the top charity events of its kind in the state, regularly attracts 155 heavy hitters and celebs, who pay up to $6,000 a fivesome, including Ditka, who, unlike so many other foundation leaders, insists on paying his own way. "He pays to golf with himself, to hunt with himself," says Ditka Foundation director Kathe Clements. The foundation's dinner is its major fund-raising event of the year. In 1989, it was called "Friday Night Live" and featured comedian Steve Martin. The 1990 version, held at the Nikko, was called "Evolution of Dance" and reportedly took three days to decorate. In October 1991, the third dinner, titled "Baby, You Can Drive My Car," was held in the ten-thousand-square-foot service department of Chicago's exclusive car dealers (a Ditka commercial client). The door prize was a $100,000 1992 Mercedes 500SL roadster.

The foundation's day-to-day activities are run by Clements, whose company supervises several Chicago charities. Clements is the wife of former Notre Dame quarterback Tom Clements, a former Chicago lawyer now back on the coaching staff of his alma mater. According to a letter to Ditka dated April 24, 1989, Kathe Clements stated her goal was to raise between $500,000 and $1 million annually on the Ditka Foundation dinner, of which, the letter said, her company would receive "a fee equal to 20 percent of the gross revenues generated by the Event." Yet according to forms filed with the State of Illinois, from 1989 to 1991, the foundation received $1.2 million in "gross contributions, gifts, grants" while reporting at least $880,000 in fund-raising expenses. At the end of 1991, the foundation showed $200,800 in reserve funds, meaning that just $320,800 of the $1.2 million would eventually find its way to charity. In 1989, for example, according to foundation records, it spent $330,000 to raise a reported $400,000. According to similar records, the foundation spent $225,000 and $325,000 to raise $400,000 in both 1990 and 1991, respectively.

The National Charities Information Bureau (NCIB), a New York City–based watchdog organization, which sets standards for foundations and public charities across the country, stipulates that, at the bare minimum, at least 60 percent of monies raised should be directed to programs. Established charities such as the American Cancer Society (seventy-six cents per every dollar to charity) and the local United Way chapters in Chicago (eighty-two to ninety-three cents) average much higher than the sixty-cent minimum. After reviewing Ditka Foundation documents, an NCIB official calculated the Foundation is sending less than twelve cents of every dollar raised to charity. "It's absolutely outrageous," said Dan Langdan, the NCIB director of public information. "The fund-raising expenses are absolutely ridiculous."

Clements passionately defends the foundation's work and disputes the twelve-cent figure, estimating a thirty-cent return on every dollar donated. She sees the high cost of fund-raising as typical for a new foundation. "All foundations struggle the first few years," she says. "It is very, very difficult to get started. It usually takes four or five years to reach your potential." Clements cites the inability of previous board members to live up to fund-raising commitments and the need for splashy social events to attract heavyweight contributors in the competitive Chicago charity scene as other reasons for the high fund-raising figures. This year, says Clements, new board members and streamlined operations should improve the donations and giving-figure dramatically. As an example she cites the February 1992 skeet shoot, which raised $50,000 while spending just $4,200, and the May golf tournament, which she estimated would send $185,000 of the $250,000 raised to charity. "Finally, we're on a roll this year," she said.

Langdan disagrees. "People would be better off making a direct contribution to a charity rather than give it to the Ditka foundation," he says. "That way, your money will go to the kids instead of the caterer."

Ditka's passion for charity contains more than a dash of irony since he can be so ungrateful and intolerant of others. For instance, a few years ago Ditka's limo broke down on the way—another irony—to a charity function. A local TV news crew noticed the car trouble, stopped, and went so far as to drive Ditka and Diana to the event. Diana overwhelmed the crew with thanks. "Mike never said a word," recalled one of the TV crew. "He just got out of the van and walked off. I guess he just expected it."

But where the irony takes root is when Ditka's passion for children's causes is contrasted against his strained relationship with his own kids. "I think in a weird way he thinks he's making up for [lost time] by doing that," Megan Ditka says. "He feels like he's redeeming himself. While I'm wondering why he doesn't pick up the phone and say, 'How are you?' rather than giving ten thousand dollars to charity.

"It used to bother me," she says softly. "I'm slowly not letting it anymore. It's taken me a while. All my life."

Matt sees his father's actions as equally ironic. "I see he does that for a lot of children. He'll attach himself to Becky Bell." It is after midnight at Ditka's downtown and Matt has just finished his shift as restaurant manager. He sits in a back booth for almost an hour, sifting through a wide variety of emotions about his dad. Matt played some pretty good football in high school, wore his dad's famous number 89 proudly his senior year. It was a big deal, Matt remembers, when his dad found the time to show up for a football game—twice during Matt's high school career. "I didn't expect him to go and I kind of didn't want him to go because I was way too nervous when he was there," says Matt, who played tight end. "But one game I do remember him going to for sure. I remember he was there for the first half. He left at halftime. I had no catches. I'm not sure why he left, I just know he left. After that I had four catches and a touchdown."

Matt fiddles with a napkin. His head hangs down a bit and he speaks in a hurried hush. "I really can't picture back to one moment when we were both really happy. I'm sure there were times, but it's just that one doesn't stand out. . . . I blame myself in part. I also blame him because there have been times I have tried to communicate and he hasn't wanted to. . . . I'm never going to have the father-son thing that's typical, so I just go with it. I'm not going to regret it that much. Well, I do regret it. That's a stupid statement, but it's not going to change it, so I just go with it."

Matt Ditka is asked a simple question. Just who is your father? He stops for a moment or two, fiddling a bit more. "I don't think I can answer that," he says. "I really don't think I can answer that. Thinking about it right now, I don't know how to, I don't know what to say. I have no idea."

Today close friends say Ditka would trade almost anything to replace time lost with his children. But the cold facts are that time can never be replaced. In life, as Ditka might say, it boils down to a matter of choices. Not right, not wrong, just choices. In his case, for better or worse, children and family were near the bottom of his list, and he has paid a stiff price for those priorities. The wife of one longtime friend remembers how envious Ditka was of her family ties, telling her, "You know, you have something I will just never have."

"This is a very sophisticated man," she says. "He has changed his life a lot in the last thirty years. But this is the one part of his life he has been unable to change." He has tried, however, as so many parents do, to bridge the gap with money. Megan admits while she always sought out her mom for "anything emotional," her dad bailed her out of plenty of financial jams. In recent years Ditka has brought Matt and Mike into the golf club and obtained fancy cars for his kids, much to the concern of friends such as Vainisi.

"What the fuck do you screw around with this shit for?" Vainisi asked Ditka one day. "Why do you give them all that crap? All you're doing is spoiling them."

"You know why I do it," said Ditka.

Today Vainisi says, quite simply it is a payback. "He always will give them money and things, but he can't give of himself. He doesn't designate the time to give of himself. That's his way of making himself feel good about the situation: 'Well, I gave them a car so I don't have to worry until the next car comes along'. . . . This is just something he's going to have to work out on his own time. Maybe as the kids get a little bit older, they'll be a little bit more understanding, too, and come together more at that point. There is an effort on both sides, but there's a wall in the middle that has to come down, and in time it probably will."

What has helped bring the family together, friends say, was the arrival of a granddaughter, little Lauren, born to Mike and Debbie Ditka three years ago. In the fall of '91, a three-by-four-foot photo entitled "Grandpa and Me" fairly leaped out of photographer Norman Phillips's studio window in downtown Highland Park. It was Ditka and then two-year-old Lauren, snuggled close to her grandpa, his left arm hugging her tight, index finger tickling the corner of her mouth. So enchanted is Ditka of his granddaughter and the picture, he reportedly took shots of McMahon, Halas, and McCaskey off his office wall to make space for the Phillips photo.

By nine-thirty A.M. on the first Sunday of November the parking lots surrounding Soldier Field smell of burning charcoal and smoked sausage. Men haul hunting gear and Gore-Tex suits from the trunks of their cars to ward off the nasty wind. Outside the main entrance, RVs and campers are lined up like members of a marching band, the rites and rituals of Chicago Bear football unfolding once more. In front of the Field Museum a rugged touch-football game is in full stride. Fans sporting every kind of Bear wear—hats, jackets, earmuffs, socks— gather in groups outside the stadium. Inside venerable Soldier Field the grounds crew peels away the tarp, revealing frozen grass covered with shards of ice. Mongo, alias McMichael, walks the field alone, checking the footing. The wind, gusting to thirty-two miles per hour, whips hard from the southwest, driving the temperature into the twenties and sending the windchill plunging to minus ten. The swirling winds have left the flags at the north end of the field limp, while the flags at the south end are rippling away. The bitter cold has shaved the crowd to 57,281 (nearly 10,000 no-shows), but before they can freeze to their seats, Butler stakes his team to a 3–0 lead over Detroit. Then, without warning, Chicago slips into the same soporific offensive state last seen against Washington. When Harbaugh resists throwing into coverage and takes a sack instead on third and 7 from the Lions 30, he and Ditka get into it. From the press box or stands, Harbaugh looks a little like a Chicago cop out in the middle of State Street, gesturing wildly as he walks off the field. From afar Harbaugh could have been upset with himself or a wide receiver. That, however, is not the case.

"Throw the fucking ball in there!" Ditka screams, his words hitting Harbaugh before he reaches the hash mark. *"Throw the fucking ball!"*

Tired of this blatant second-guessing, Harbaugh unloads right back. "It wasn't open!" he yells.

"Throw it!"

"It wasn't open!"

"Just throw it! Just throw the fucking ball!"

"Fuck you! It's not open!"

"Fuck *you!*" roars Ditka. "You're outta the game."

"Fuck you!"

(Later, after detailing the exchange, Harbaugh said, "I just got fed up with him. If I think I'm in the right, I'm going to do that. I mean, it's his right to coach any way he wants, but today I thought I was right . . . so"—he smiles—"fuck 'im.")

After the Harbaugh-Ditka debate, Sanders, with the quickest feet in football, bounces off tacklers making some of the most spectacular 6- and 7-yard runs of the year. The Lions finally break through early in the second quarter with an 80-yard drive for a 7–3 edge. Lions kicker Eddie Murray adds a 31-yard field goal just before the half, and the home crowd boos its Bears into the locker room.

Just before the third quarter ends, Harbaugh takes his team 83 yards in just 6 plays, the final 22 yards coming on a beautiful touch pass to Davis in the end zone. Then with three minutes left, off a nifty scramble, Harbaugh seals a 20–10 win with an 8-yard scoring strike to Davis again.

The only real sad sight is Ditka, his face a frozen mask, limping off the field flanked by two industrial-size security guards. Just before he enters the home-team tunnel, he plays to the hue and cry of the crowd with a mindless flash of the thumb. Inside the tunnel, away from prying eyes, Ditka's gimpy gait instantly deepens. Twice in ten seconds he reaches back and rubs the frozen joint where his buttock and hip fuse together. Rubbing a little blood and life back into his bones. "We played hard," he tells the assembled press a few moments later. "I don't think we're a great football team right now. But we played hard."

He praises Davis and Waddle and Wojo, Mangum and Woolford. Somebody asks about Harbaugh. "He hung in there and made some throws," says Ditka. "He was tough."

Inside the locker room the media mob shifts from Davis to Singletary to Carrier to Thayer to Waddle before settling outside the stall marked No. 4. They wait patiently until he appears. The interviews run constantly for nearly thirty minutes as the next great Bear quarterback—a winner in the mold of a McMahon or Luckman— reflects on his day.

Soon only two athletes remain. One of them is Singletary, a football Yoda, the voice of wisdom in this locker room and beyond. "He's coming," he says, looking proudly across the room at the other athlete, the No. 4 still taped above his locker. "He's coming."

On Monday, Ditka seemed to forget all about how "hardheaded" and tentative his quarterback could be. It is obvious that Harbaugh's willingness to stand his ground, his ability to produce under pressure, has won the head coach over, at least for now. "You can have all the fancy-Dan quarterbacks," Ditka said of Harbaugh. "Patton would have been proud of him. Schwarzkopf would have loved him. He might be America's quarterback."

Still riding the high on Monday afternoon, Harbaugh went a giant step further: "If we can just dedicate ourselves the next month, we can have this thing sewed up by Thanksgiving. We can be riding home on that plane, coming home Thanksgiving Day from Detroit knowing we pretty much got the Central Division wrapped up. At home, you're talking Indianapolis and Miami, two games we should win, and then we got to go to Detroit on Thanksgiving Day. I'm starting to get the feeling now, if we can get our running game going and our passing game working, get them all going at the same time, we won't lose another game. We'll go right through the next eight games and nobody will touch us."

In retrospect Harbaugh's prophecy proved as false as a campaign promise. The team flew home from Detroit on Thanksgiving Day not on a high but with an overriding anger. In the blink of an eye— actually, the snap of a ball—the Bears season of promise had suddenly come crashing to earth. And there would be no need for an in-depth investigation or overwrought analysis. The answers were obvious. They had only themselves to blame.

I think it all goes back to the Miami game. We had every right to win that game. But when it came right down to it, I think everybody waited for the next guy to make the big play.

Bears guard Tom Thayer

IN AN AVERAGE NFL WEEKEND PLAYERS PERFORM HUNDREDS OF TINY TECH-niques, many of them taught and monitored like the readings of a rocket launch. There are jab steps, drive blocks, crossovers, pivots, and spins. It was one such movement—a hip rotation—that grabbed a remarkably resilient and courageous football team and flipped it upside down. One play. One bad snap. And an entire season went haywire. "Tragic," Ditka would later call it.

Entering the Miami game on November 24, the high-flying Bears certainly had no reason to suspect trouble. They were 9-2, winners of five in a row, a major surprise given preseason predictions. Better yet, the tender hamstrings of Anderson and Muster had sufficiently healed to the point where, for the first time all year, they looked like the league's best one-two punch, which is exactly what they were. Muster was the key. In the words of Ed King, the former Bears scout, Muster, a fourth-year pro out of Stanford, "destroyed the stereotype" of the NFL fullback. At 6'4", 231 pounds with a shuffly style of running, Muster looked more like a tight end than a running back. But he had deceptive speed, and the pile moved whenever he took on tacklers. And nobody blocked any better or had better hands. Muster, simply, brought a new dimension to the Bears offensive scheme.

Oh, you could do without him if you had to, as the Bears did, but when he was in the lineup, the Bears were as balanced and versatile as any offensive team in the league. Defenses no longer keyed on Anderson. If they did, they had to deal with Muster's crushing blocks or his battering-ram runs or Harbaugh's faking into his backs' bellies and firing play-action passes downfield. And if all else failed, there was always Muster, the quiet, laid-back Californian, Harbaugh's security blanket, floating out in the flat or curling over the middle, turning second and 6s into first and 10s.

On the road against Minnesota on "Monday Night Football" on November 11, Chicago found this offensive rhythm for the first time all year. The Vikes (5-5) could have tightened the NFC Central race with a win, and they came out fighting, running off an 80-yard drive to lead 7–0. But Chicago just kept pounding away. Keying the 34–17 victory was a season-high 191 yards on the ground (81 by Anderson, 56 from Muster) and long touchdown drives featuring the kind of run-pass ratio Ditka and Landry had dreamed about. The defense, spearheaded by McMichael, in the midst of an All-Pro–like year, was relentless.

The next week, against the 1-9 Indianapolis Colts, Muster had a career day as the Bears turned a 10–10 halftime score into a smothering 31–17 laughter. Muster ran the ball 15 times for 101 yards, a career high, caught 6 passes for 44 yards, and scored twice. Harbaugh threw for 287 yards and 2 TDS, his 32 attempts giving him 328 for the season, the most ever by a Ditka quarterback, breaking McMahon's mark of 313 in 1985. But the significance of those numbers was this: the 32 passing attempts had been perfectly balanced by 32 runs. The Bears were peaking at the perfect time. New Orleans had lost to San Diego on a late field goal. The Saints were now 9-2, the same as Chicago, but in the all-important fight for home-field advantage and a playoff bye, the Bears had the edge now, given their comeback win in New Orleans. "For the first time in a long time, we feel we're approaching that level we've been searching for," Harbaugh said. "There is not a team in the league we can't beat if we have that type of balance on offense."

Out in Las Vegas, Patty Harris and Sean Rowland felt much the same way. They were leaders of a Las Vegas Hilton betting group known as the Baccarat 8. Eleven weeks earlier, the group had chipped in $10 apiece and picked one winner off the NFL schedule. Ten weeks—and ten wins later—that $80 pool had doubled and doubled and redoubled into $103,107. The group steadfastly resisted cashing in, shooting instead for a dream payoff of $1.63 million at the end of the sixteen-game season. Three previous times during the streak Harris and

Rowland had bet the Bears and won. Now, with the Bears, 7½-point favorites over the Miami Dolphins, they went with Chicago once more. Why not? Miami was just 5-6. The Bears were at home. It was not a divisional or even a conference game. And it seemed as if the last time the Dolphins had won a game in cold weather in November, Richard Nixon was president.

Midway through the fourth quarter the Baccarat 8 was well on its way to becoming $103,107 richer. In four-degree weather with snow piled up around the sidelines, the Bears were cruising along, leading 13–6, lined up for a 24-yard chip shot by Butler. The score would have been worse had the Bears not lost Muster in the first half with an injury, the *left* hamstring this time, after he had gained 54 yards on just 8 carries and caught 6 passes. At that point Ditka's game plan went out the window. He was forced to use Anderson, nowhere near 100 percent after re-straining his hamstring against Minnesota two weeks earlier. Still, Butler would kick the field goal, the Bears would lead 16–6, and more than likely, the Vegas group would cover the spread and double their money. Simple.

Suddenly the football gods, who had blessed the Bears all year, went a little crazy. Harbaugh fumbled Hilgenberg's perfect snap—"I just missed it," he said later—forcing Butler to stutter-step into the ball. His 24-yard attempt wobbled far short.

No matter (except in Vegas, where they were pulling their hair out). With 2:13 remaining the Bears still led by 7. The team's long snapper, Jerry Fontenot, settled over the ball on a fourth down and 2 at the Bears 42-yard line. The third-year lineman would have been a long shot to make the team were it not for his deep-snapping talents, and the last thing both Ditka and Kazor told him before coming on the field was to make sure he got off a good snap into the swirling sixteen-mile-per-hour wind. One good punt, they were thinking, the defense holds, and the game is over. The Bears would be 10-2 and sitting in the catbird seat. Fontenot did a little mental calculus and figured the wind would knock the ball down a bit, so instead of just snapping the ball back to Buford as he had all day, perfect every time, he rolled his hips a little higher than usual and extended his legs for a bit more lift   too much. The football sailed five feet over Buford's head. As Ditka, the Bears, and the Soldier Field crowd watched in slack-jawed horror, Buford chased the bouncing ball, grabbing it at the 15-yard line. Under heavy pressure while being pursued from behind, Buford tried one of those desperate sideswipe kicks. Forget it. A Dolphin got a piece of the ball and a teammate recovered on the Bears 4-yard line—a loss of 38 yards on a single play. The clock now said 2:01 left. Two plays and ten seconds later, quarterback Dan Marino, never one to waste an opportunity such as this, fired a 2-yard touchdown pass to tight end Ferrell Edmunds to tie the score.

The Bears nearly won it at the end of regulation, but Butler, burdened with a bum hip and bad karma, came up short on his 50-yard field goal with time running out. In overtime the snow picked up, the temperature dropped. The Dolphins won the toss. Marino wasted no time marching his team to the Bears 36. There he faded back and lofted a long pass along the right sideline where Woolford was running stride for stride with wide receiver Mark Clayton. Slipping on the turf, Clayton did a classic Chevy Chase pratfall, falling flat on his back, the perfect—and only—place to clutch Marino's dying pass. Woolford had been called for pass interference but it didn't matter. Miami had the ball first down on the Bears 5-yard line. Seconds later, after a 27-yard field goal, the Dolphins had more than that—they had an upset win.

"We gave it away," a shaken Ditka said after the game, echoing his locker room speech to his team. "Life is about challenges. If you're going to get beat, you want to get beat when you're in the other guy's face. We weren't."

The locker room was a morgue. Thayer put it best, saying, "Our season is in turmoil." McMichael, who had cursed his way to the locker room, looked ready to rip the head off something or somebody. "Everything," said Fontenot, "was fine until that one snap." Nobody needed to recite the significance of this loss and how suddenly the Bears' fortunes had shifted. Gone was all the huff and puff about postseason play and how wonderfully efficient and effective this football team had become. Now, instead of going into Detroit on Thanksgiving Day with a two-game cushion with four to play, the suddenly bruised and battered Bears would be once again fighting for first place against an entirely different Lions team. "This was a classic example of a team effort to lose a football game," said Ditka. "We had a number of opportunities to do what we had to do, and they beat us. We don't have too much time to feel sorry for ourselves."

Ditka certainly was not. An edginess had crept back into his attitude. Part of the reason was injuries. Muster was out for at least two weeks with his hamstring. Van Horne's shoulder looked bad. Thornton had a foot problem. Bortz was sidelined with a strained abdominal muscle. As for the press, the head coach was backing into his bunker again. The short week and a short fuse had Ditka whining about meeting the media on Monday. "I don't know what I can possibly tell you guys," he said when he did finally talk. "Ask your questions now because I'm not talking the rest of the week."

Ditka's attitude was understandable. The sands had shifted. Now the Bears faced a daunting task of quickly forgetting the unforgettable and finding a way to overcome some long odds. The Lions (8-4), hot off an impressive 34–14 win at Minnesota, were undefeated (6-0) at home, were playing on national TV on Thanksgiving Day, and had a shot at tying Chicago for the Central Division lead. That in itself was plenty. But now the Lions were being driven by something more profound, more personal. On November 17 in a game against the Los Angeles Rams, one of the team's starting guards, Mike Utley, a 6'6", 290-pounder, was paralyzed from the chest down when he suffered a severe spinal-cord injury while blocking on a pass play. The popular Utley, "Ut" to his teammates, a free-spirited sort who loved heavy metal music, had lost his balance while attempting a cut block on an onrushing defensive lineman. He pitched forward and landed on his head while his body was still moving forward. The resultant force snapped Utley's head back and compressed his neck on impact with the artificial turf. His sixth cervical vertebra was fractured causing extensive soft-tissue damage. Yet even as the stricken Utley was being carried off the field, he gave his teammates the thumbs-up sign and encouraged them to "finish the job."

"That's unbelievable courage," said middle linebacker Chris Spielman. "It's hard for us to fathom that kind of courage."

The Lions, a young, talented team learning what it takes to win in the NFL, were stirred and united as never before. "Mike has made this team more focused, more together, more thankful," said center Kevin Glover. That feeling soon spread throughout one of this country's great sports cities. The Lions, long the kings of the Detroit sports scene, had seen their crown passed to the Tigers, Pistons, and even the Red Wings in recent years. Now, on Thanksgiving Day, 1991, there was an opportunity, as one local columnist wrote, to "reclaim the dignity" of football seasons past. This was nothing less than the biggest football game in Detroit in twenty years.

Nobody had to tell Ditka any of this. He told his team straight up: we're playing for the Central Division title. The Bears came in prepared, no question. Vince Tobin and second-year defensive-backs coach Zaven Yaralian, a rising star in the league, devised a masterful defensive plan. The Lions played what is called a run-and-shoot offense, employing four wide receivers and one running back. Many teams defend against it by putting pressure on the quarterback or replacing linebackers with extra defensive backs. That, in turn, gave Sanders room to operate, to dodge and dart to daylight, while slipping more tackles than any back in the league. The Bears, just as they had earlier in the year, countered by bunching seven defenders along the line of scrimmage while employing an umbrella zone in the defensive backfield. The idea was for ends Dent and Armstrong to shorten their rush, to drive forward a couple of steps then pinch in and hold their ground. That would force Sanders back into the middle of the field. The Bears cornerbacks and safeties would play mostly zone pass coverage, hoping to force Detroit quarterback Erik Kramer into holding on to the ball longer than he wanted. The only real weakness of the coverage was, if Kramer was sharp, he could hit the short outs into the vacant flat areas about eight yards off the line of scrimmage. He had failed to do so in the first game against Chicago, and the Bears were banking they could exploit his inexperience again.

The Lions, meanwhile, had ideas of their own. The secret to stopping the Bears, particularly with Muster missing (as he would be), was shutting off the run and forcing Harbaugh to throw. Statistics showed the Bears were 2-5 in games in which they threw more than 40 passes and 42-2 in games in which they ran more than 40 times. Ironically, the Lions defense would be a hybrid of Buddy Ryan's 46, utilizing plenty of single coverage at the corners and heavy stunts and blitzes up front.

More than 78,000 fans delayed their turkey dinners to jam into the Silverdome, the biggest Lions crowd in seven years. For the second straight week every Lion wore a T-shirt underneath his jersey that read THUMBS UP. Signs supporting Utley were everywhere (MIKE, WE MISS YOU). Hanging from Kramer's pants was a towel that read SEIZE THE DAY. The Silverdome crowd grew quiet as Lions offensive tackle Lomas Brown, a respected vet, told Utley over national TV how "we're praying and pulling for you."

In the face of all this emotion, the Bears responded with a spectacular effort. It was a savage game straight out of the sixties. The only big mistake the Bears defense made all day came on the second play of the game when Kramer went over the middle for 28 yards down to the visitors' 19-yard line (a 44-yard kickoff return had put the Lions in great field position). But the Bears stiffened and Detroit settled for a 3–0 lead. Now it was Chicago's turn. Harbaugh said he felt great before the game, sharp and focused, despite playing in front of family and friends. Right out of the chute he hit Davis for 19 yards. The Bears were soon forced to punt, but caught an immediate break when Mo Douglass recovered a muffed punt at the Lions 14. On second down, the first sense of how this day would play seeped through. Hilgenberg was matched up against the Lions 300-pound nose guard Jerry Ball, who had manhandled the All-Pro center back in Chicago. Perhaps Hilgenberg lost concentration or tried to be a little too quick. Either way, his snap barely grazed the ends of Harbaugh's fingers. Spielman recovered. One blown opportunity.

On the next Bears series, after the defense completely stuffed Kramer and Detroit, Harbaugh had a third and 6 from the Lions 46. He broke clear on a scramble for 9 yards and a first down before feeling pressure and tucking the ball away. But a Lion linebacker popped the ball loose for another fumble. Two drives now and no points. And as so often happens, the opposing team came to life and scored; this time it was Kramer on a 9-yard pass to wide receiver Robert Clark. Detroit now led 10–0.

Early in the second quarter Harbaugh took over again. Twelve times in a 14-play drive he either passed or ran the ball, overthrowing a sure TD pass to Anderson by two inches inside the Lions 10. A Butler 3 (from 27 yards) made it 10–3. But the Bears' frustrations were mounting. One official had already warned the coach to tell Dent, fired up and having a hellacious game, to lay off the refs. But on a controversial sideline pass, Dent got in the side judge's ear again and Ditka exploded for the first time all year, right there on CBS.

He and Dent had had their problems in the past. A few years back Ditka had taken to calling Dent "Robert," as if to say he had forgotten all about his Super Bowl MVP. When the press asked why Dent suddenly had a spot in Ditka's doghouse, the defensive end replied, "I'm no dog and I got my own house, so I don't know what you're talking about." But as Dent told Ditka at the time, "a man is what he stands for and what he stands for is his name. If you don't call me by my name, you don't get my attention." This time, Ditka was calling Dent several names, none printable in a family newspaper, and when Dent yelled back, Ditka went off. No sooner had Singletary tried to mediate the matter then Ditka wheeled on his captain and screamed some more. Singletary, to his credit, put a smirk on his face and walked away. Three minutes later, with time running out in the half, Butler kicked another 3 to cut Detroit's lead to 10–6.

The rest of the game was like waiting all day in line at the DMV, only to discover your needed another document: total frustration. Kramer did not complete a pass from the beginning of the second quarter until there were two minutes left in the third, and overall, he was just 9 of 27 for 108 yards. Sanders was limited to 62 yards on 19 carries. Up in the press box Bear defensive assistants were whispering, "Just one score, one score," but every time the Bears got close, somebody turned it over, most often Harbaugh, who was suffering his worst game of the season—a dizzying spell of interceptions, fumbles, poor judgment, and bad luck. After a deflected pass turned interception gave the Lions a

13–6 lead (Murray banged it in off the upright from 50 yards, another omen), the game turned for good on the very next series. The Bears drove almost 80 yards in 11 plays as Harbaugh got in synch with Davis and Waddle, who was putting on another fearless All-Pro show that moved Madden, up in the TV booth, to compare Waddle to his childhood hero, Biletnikoff. Hitting 6 straight passes, 3 to Waddle, Harbaugh maneuvered down to the Lions 5, and finally, it was fourth down and 1 from the 1. During a time-out, Ditka, Landry, running backs coach Johnny Roland, and Kazor all yelled at each other. That kind of confusion was reflected in Harbaugh's rollout effort. Under pressure, he faded back a bit then lobbed a desperate, pathetic pass to Anderson, who had already stepped out of bounds and was thus ineligible.

On the next series, Butler missed from the 37. Ditka was grinding his gum and looking absolutely evil. Who could blame him? Chicago had been inside the Detroit 20-yard line six times and had just 6 points to show for it. A third Harbaugh interception led to Detroit's final 3 points.

The Bears had outgained the Lions 319–208, more than doubled them in passing yards (244–108), and had outgained them 147 to 47 in the second half. Ditka was so upset after the game that one assistant feared he would suffer another heart attack. All the born-again, love-thy-neighbor, Mellow Mike hyperbole was buried beneath a torrent of frustration and anger. "We gave the game away!" he shouted. "Gave the game away!"

What made the loss even more galling was not only had it signaled a shift of power in the NFC Central but the Bears had been beaten at their own game. The Lions had played Bears football, a tough, tenacious, team-above-all effort that forced mistakes and overcame statistics. It wasn't pretty. But to the group of young Lions it was a major step up. They were contenders now. Dignity had been reclaimed.

Outside the Bears locker room the assembled press was already making mental bets as to how Ditka would react. Could he control himself? Would he erupt? Standing on little platform, red necked, veins bulging, eyes ablaze, he mocked one reporter dumb enough to ask if the turnovers had hurt his team—"Yeah, they hurt like crazy. I cried a couple of times, all right?" Then he took off on an eight-minute tirade. "This was as much of a gift as last week. What did they do to us? Nothing. We did it to ourselves. The plays were there to be made. My God, we had people as open as they'll ever be in the history of this sport. There will be *nobody* as open as the people we had today." From there he went on to question "outside interests," another veiled slug at

Harbaugh, formerly America's quarterback, who had few if any outside interests, but had now suffered the slings and arrows of having gone 119 minutes and 16 seconds, nearly two entire games, without engineering a touchdown.

What could easily have been an 11-2 season was now 9-4. The Bears still held the division lead, but only slightly, on a tiebreaker formula based on fewer divisional losses. The locker room was tense. The bus ride to Oakland County Airport and the plane ride home were worse — a passel of silent thoughts and short curses. You could blame the injuries. You could blame the turnovers. You could argue about tiebreakers and Dent and Ditka screaming at each other. You could argue that Harbaugh, who had a hand in 53 of the Bears' 70 offensive plays, had failed at a most critical moment. "Jim tried to be a leader," said Singletary. "He wanted to do the right thing. But the sign of a leader is someone who takes control when things are bad, who gets the job done when the heat was on."

With three weeks left in the season, it appeared the Bears were ready to burst into flames.

DOUG GREEN HOLDS OUT HIS ARM LIKE A MEMBER OF THE SCHOOL SAFETY patrol, then draws it down with emphasis. "You're crossing the invisible line," says Green, with a grin. It is Friday, December 6, two days before the Green Bay game, and Green, a member of the Bears public relations staff, escorts me toward the training room, normally an off-limits area of Halas Hall, at the behest of the athlete stretched out on a training room table. It is Harbaugh. His brown hair is mussed a bit from the just-completed practice, but he looks cool in his navy blue

Bears turtleneck and sweats. I ask about his right foot, encased, as it is, in an inflatable sleeve. The foot is receiving some sort of electrical stimulation. "It's fine," he says, leaning back against a glass partition. Nearby, three Bears joke around in their underwear, a sharp contrast to the mood earlier in the week when, Harbaugh admits, "it was like a morgue around here." His previous weekend, he admitted, was one of total depression—lying low at home and wondering what might have been. But after a couple of holiday TV viewings of *It's a Wonderful Life,* the all-purpose pick-me-up, Harbaugh had rebounded. "That brought me back," he said, breaking into a grin.

Harbaugh was on the hot seat this week—no doubt about it. Once again, in the ephemeral world of pro sports, it was put-up-or-shut-up time. After the debacle in Detroit, Harbaugh's quarterback rating had slipped to a paltry 70.0, eleventh out of fourteen quarterbacks in the NFC, and the raves about his leadership and lion-sized heart had been replaced by rips about his character and consistency. His interception total was up to 15 versus only 12 touchdown passes, and the Bears offense was working on 22 straight possessions without a touchdown. In an effort to take the pressure off Harbaugh, Ditka held a private chat with the young quarterback, telling him straight up, he was the man no matter what happened. Then Ditka went public, admitting he had put too much pressure on Harbaugh. "He does things as competitively as anyone I've ever seen," Ditka had said, offering his highest praise. "He's trying to win you football games by making plays, and you gotta like that. He made a mistake. The fumbles hurt. That can happen to anybody."

But not three weeks in a row. Not if the Bears wanted to win the division title, retain the second seed in the NFC playoffs, and retain the home-field edge. Nobody cared if the left side of the offensive line looked lost without Covert and Bortz (Wojo was holding his own at tackle, having permanently replaced Thomas) or if starting tight end James Thornton could barely walk, or if Anderson and Muster had one decent hamstring between them. This was Harbaugh's team now, just the way he'd wanted it way back in June when he'd talked about doing it between the white lines, making big plays, not taking a backseat to anybody. He had stepped up and assumed control, and even though he made mistakes, it was frightening to think where the Bears would have been without him. But those nine early wins now took a backseat to the two latest losses, and a crossroads of his career. "It's all coming down this week," he said. "You don't want to lose three games in a row. If we lose, then what? We've got to beat Tampa Bay [the following week]. That would give us five losses going out to play the 49ers, which is going to be a ballbuster. Ten and six. I don't know if ten and six gets us in the playoffs."

Harbaugh slipped the sleeve off his bare foot. "Everything we've done has been great, but it doesn't mean anything. The whole season comes down to now. It's all right now. Whether we have a good season or not is going to come down to the next three weeks."

The story line for the Green Bay game was not just about the Bears staying alive in the playoff hunt. No, there would be an added twist this time around Mike Tomczak's homecoming . . . and his grudge match against Harbaugh.

Some three weeks earlier a feature story in the *Arlington Heights* (Ill.) *Daily Herald* had quoted Harbaugh describing an incident during the 1989 preseason that portrayed "T-zak," as Tomczak was known around Chicago, as devious and a backstabber. The incident allegedly took place during a Chicago–San Diego game shortly after McMahon was traded to the Chargers. Harbaugh charged that Tomczak, after flashing him a play from the sidelines, had then relayed the same play across the field to McMahon, who had just happened to be standing next to the San Diego defensive coordinator.

On Monday October 27, about ten days before the story broke in the *Daily Herald,* Harbaugh had been asked about a Tomczak statement after the first Green Bay game. Tomczak had said he respected Harbaugh as a quarterback, "but that's where it ends." Why the animosity? Harbaugh was asked. It seemed out of left field. "No, it wasn't out of left field," he replied, describing the 1989 incident in detail. "I mean, I knew he really didn't like me. When he and McMahon were here, I was never part of that clique, and you know, I lost all respect for Mike Tomczak as a person and a teammate during one game in the preseason. . . . It happened sure as I'm sitting here. I went up to Tomczak after the series and I said something. He said, 'Oh, I'm really sorry about that. It only happened once.' You know, I didn't say anything to Ditka or anybody else or the press or anything like that, but I said this guy is not a good teammate and you gotta watch yourself around people like that. I never ever did anything to that level. I mean, when he was in there, I was always, I was always trying, I was always pulling for him. I always wanted the team to do well.

"Then after he left here last year I said, 'well, maybe it's just the type of situation we're in, you know, one guy getting put in one week, another guy the next week, it's like you're fighting for your job.' I was willing to give it another chance. Then he goes to Green Bay and makes that statement. Fine. I'm not going to lose any sleep over not being friends with Mike Tomczak."

Harbaugh's description of the sideline caper in the *Daily Herald* was picked up by the major Chicago papers and the Associated Press, eventually spilling over into the Bears' "Monday Night Football" game against Minnesota. In an ABC Sports interview, Tomczak labeled the accusation "absolutely false" and threatened to sue Harbaugh for libel. Harbaugh told him to bring it on. McMahon tried to stay above the fray, declining comment. "But he told everybody here it happened," said Harbaugh, leaning against the glass.

So with T-zak coming to town the controversy began anew. Friday morning, WLUP's delightfully demented deejay Kevin Matthews called it "a hoot," doing his level best to fan the flames. "What's the big deal?" he cried. "Let's get Mac on the phone and see who he has his money on."

The best Matthews and his equally wacky staff could do was Nancy McMahon, which actually was plenty good. Ever the dutiful sporting wife, Nancy lamented how the entire episode had been "blown out of proportion."

"The whole thing is stupid," she said. "It was two years ago. Don't you think Jim knew the plays?"

"Well," pushed Matthews, "who does Jim want to win on Sunday, T-zak or Harbaugh?"

On this issue, Mrs. McMahon showed no equivocation: "If it's between T-zak and Harbaugh, you go with T-zak."

At four-thirty P.M. the following day, the baby-faced Tomczak strolled into lobby of the downtown Westin Hotel with the rest of his Packer teammates. He wore jeans and cowboy boots with headphones wrapped around his neck, swaggering in the style of a quarterback on a roll, which indeed he was. The previous Sunday in a heartbreaking 35–31 loss to Atlanta he had thrown for 276 yards and 3 touchdowns, bringing some much-needed life into the moribund (3-10) Packers. Only two reporters were present for the homecoming, one the ex-Bear took great pains to downplay. He insisted he wasn't going to let himself get "too emotionally anxious." He was here not to "make friends" but "win a football game." He stiffened however, when Howard Sudberry of WBBM-TV cut to the heart of the matter: "Because the Bears got rid of you, does it make this game any more special?"

Tomczak took a quick breath or two before answering. "It's not that the team got rid of me," he said evenly. Another breath. "They gave me the opportunity to go elsewhere. It was my decision."

If so, it was made with the knowledge that the Bears had yanked the official welcome mat from under his feet, Ditka making it clear Harbaugh was The Man, and Willis, the sharpshooting quarterback out of Florida State, was waiting in the wings. So the former Ohio State star who had won some big games for the Bears during his six seasons in his hometown went Plan B and signed with the lowly Packers, where he was promptly buried behind Don Majkowski and Blair Kiel. Tomczak rode the bench until mid-October before mopping up, ironically, in a game against the Bears. A week later, based on that performance, he moved up to number two. When Majkowski pulled a hamstring the first week in November against the Jets, Tomczak took over and hit 8 of 11 passes and his first Packer TD pass. The next week he threw for a career high 317 yards and two scores against a tough Buffalo Bills defense. The next two weeks he ran more hot than cold—and when Tomczak was hot, he could play with any quarterback in the league. But in Chicago he had never seemed to fit. A free agent pickup in '85, he was destined to be the understudy, never the star. He always waited until McMahon got hurt, stepping onstage, stepping off, fighting Steve Fuller, then Doug Flutie, then Harbaugh for playing time.

Tomczak's biggest problems were trying to force plays on the field and trying to avoid a hit ("He doesn't like to take a sack," said one Bears assistant coach). He habitually threw into coverage. The resultant interceptions (47 in his Chicago career versus 33 touchdown passes) perplexed and often enraged Ditka, leading to some memorable Sunday-night highlights. Perhaps more important, Tomczak never proved to be the kind of quarterback Ditka wanted in his foxhole—the fiery, Timex type who took a licking and kept on ticking. Tomczak was too high-strung; his personality was more suited to the teddy bears he collected. He was too sensitive, too concerned, says his best friend, Thayer, "about what was said to him, around him, about him," especially by Ditka. "When Ditka would yell at him during a game, it was like hitting the lock button on a computer," says Singletary. "He would just freeze up."

So shaken was Tomczak that he later sought counsel from a sports psychologist, which did little to inspire widespread confidence among teammates. Says Dent, "When it's your turn, and you're in charge, you've got to perform no matter what. Anytime a guy has to go see a psychologist about a coach . . . c'mon, this is football. This is not somebody getting beat up at home or something, it's only a game."

What's worse, insiders say, Tomczak brought bitterness to his job the last two seasons, especially 1990, when it was obvious that Harbaugh was the future and Tomczak part of an almost forgotten past. So he took his talents and hang-ups north to Green Bay, to a talented yet aimless Packer team led by Lindy Infante, a far more forgiving head coach. Now T-zak was back. Would he be ready to knock the Bears out of the playoffs? To rub Harbaugh's nose in the dirt? Or better yet, punch him out? Chicago couldn't wait to see how the latest episode of the Harbaugh-Tomczak soap opera would play out.

Ditka did his best to downplay any feud. "I don't think you play people, you play the system," he said early in the week. Still, he couldn't resist a subtle psychological dig: "One thing about Mike, he'll throw the ball into a tight area." That he would, and to force some errors the Bears planned to blitz more than usual, to mix up coverages in hopes of picking off a pass or two, while on offense it was back, once more, to ball-control, in-your-face football. Said one Bears assistant, "We're going to hammer it and hammer it, and at the end we're going to win."

By game time the temperature had risen to a ridiculous fifty-seven degrees. After the Bears went quietly on their first possession, Tomczak jogged on the field to a chorus of boos. On third and 12 he short-hopped a pass to wideout Charles Wilson. The crowd cheered. The Bears took over on their own 27 and quickly scored.

Early in the second quarter, with the score 7–3, Harbaugh's arm got hit and the ball popped into the air. Cornerback Vinnie Clark intercepted and returned the ball 20 yards to the Bears 30. Tomczak took over, and with Dent in his face on a big third and 7 from the 27-yard line, shook him off and fired a bullet across his body for a first down. Another sharp pass put Green Bay on the Bears 1-yard line. Tomczak then made a superb play-action fake and found tight end Jackie Harris in the left corner of the end zone. Singletary, late on the tackle, rose to find Tomczak kneeling right beside him, pointing a finger in his face.

"Seven points, Singletary," taunted Tomczak. "Seven points."

"Oh, you sorry rascal," Singletary replied.

An uneasy silence settled over the crowd. Miami? Detroit? *Green Bay?*

The Bears bounced back, on a dazzling 8 yard scoring run by Muster. Three Packers had a shot at him, but Muster danced over one shoestring tackle, sidestepped another, and slammed through a third before diving between three defenders into the end zone.

The game turned on the next series. As the pregame scouting report on Tomczak held true. Off a stunt, Dent tore up the middle and into Tomczak's face. Instead of taking the sack, the quarterback short-armed a pass into the right flat — right into the hands of linebacker Jim Morrissey, who returned the ball to the Packers 20.

A knockout punch came on the very next play: Harbaugh to Davis, who made a poetic over-the-shoulder catch. It was 21–10 Chicago. The Packers closed to within 8, 21–13 at the half, before Harbaugh put the game away for good with a 35-yard third-quarter TD pass to Davis. Butler missed the extra point—hooked it off the left upright—leaving Ditka snapping and snarling as his kicker stepped across the sideline. The game ended with Chicago ahead 27–13, but not before Tomczak suffered the indignity of two fourth-quarter fumbles to match an earlier intentional-grounding call, drawing the jeers of scores of beer-swilling, pennant-waving Grabowskis.

The TV cameras were glued to Ditka's face as he limped toward the locker room, and there was every reason not to miss this shot. After twice failing, he had finally reached a coaching milestone: 100 regular-season victories in, this, his tenth season. There was a genuine smile, almost a grin this time, the thumbs-up sign bolder and more defiant than ever, as if he were sticking it to all the naysayers, the doubters, the losers in life. "I'm not trying to be idealistic or fool anybody, yeah, it meant a lot to me, to my pride," Ditka said in the press tent. "When I came here, people said I wouldn't stay here. And I stayed here for ten years and whether I tricked somebody or not, I'm proud of it. I'm proud for the kind of football we have played for ten years. Those who don't like that, I think they are very sorry people."

A man's voice came from the back of the tent, loud and boozy, yelling, "Coach, what are you planning to do with punt returns the rest of the year?"—a reference to yet another fumble by punt returner Johnny Bailey. Ditka cut him off, sharp and sarcastic, his voice rising with every word: "Yeah, we're going to work on it. You got any suggestions, help. Help us. You got something, let me know. You guys don't know how thankless [returning punts] is. What do you think? You got people putting tickets in, saying I want to go back and return punts? [Laughter.] Nobody wants to do it. He took his eyes off the ball. He made the most simple mistake. But I tell you, I'm not going to criticize him. I'm not going to crucify him. I had my one week, thank you very much. I'm done. I'm done. You guys do it! I don't want to do it [criticizing people] anymore!"

Somebody asked about Harbaugh, 16 of 25, 209 yards, and 2 touchdowns. Ditka continued to pound the press, even though the question had not an ounce of attitude in it: "I thought Harbaugh did a helluva job, gang. I'm sorry for all the people who don't. I think the guy played about as good as you can want him to play. I'm very happy with him."

Tomczak obviously was not. At the end of the game he and Harbaugh had met at midfield. Extending his hand, Harbaugh had offered to "bury the hatchet." His counterpart (22 of 39 for 215 yards, 1 TD, 1 INT) limply squeezed back. "He didn't even look me in the eye," said Harbaugh. Now in the Green Bay locker room Tomczak was wearing a black T-shirt and smart-alecky attitude. What had he said to Singletary? "Something inspirational," he said. "I can't remember. I think it was something by Theodore Roosevelt, 'The Man in the Arena.'"

What about Harbaugh? "Who?" said Tomczak, adding a few minutes later, "I really don't care what he thinks or what he does, you know." Over in the Bears den, Harbaugh was being swallowed up by cameras and microphones. Davis, Muster, and tight end Keith Jennings—the day's biggest surprise with 4 catches for 63 yards—got much the same treatment. Kevin Butler, meanwhile, seemed lost in the postgame excitement, too depressed to dress completely. His suit pants were pulled up just below his underwear; he dabbed at the cuts on his chin with a towel. Each red dot might well have represented a mark for his most miserable season. The holdout . . . the drunken-driving charge . . . a hip injury against Minnesota early in the year . . . the flubbed field goal against Miami that would have sealed a win . . . the 50-yarder off the upright in Detroit . . . the missed extra point today. When a reporter began to question Ditka during his press conference with the words "When you yelled at Butler," Ditka cut the guy off. "No, I didn't get mad at Butler, you got that all wrong, pardner," Ditka declared. "I asked him, I said, 'Hey, you got to make those, that's important.' I didn't get mad at him. He got mad at himself."

Butler was mad at himself all right, but he had been challenged by Ditka. "He told me, 'God damn, you can't miss out there. You're gonna cost a game doing that shit. You're going to kick yourself right out of here,'" a sentiment Butler did not necessarily dispute at that moment. "Something every week," he said, "if not on the field, off the field."

Soon the Bears locker room was almost empty. Just a couple of assistant equipment managers picking up towels, and Harbaugh cutting tape from his ankles.

He wadded up a ball of the tape and tossed it twenty feet in the air. It landed dead center in an open garbage can. It was that kind of day, a day in which Harbaugh broke the team's all-time record for passing attempts set by Vince Evans back in 1981. (The previous week he had eclipsed Billy Wade's twenty-nine-year-old record of 225 completions in a season.) But most important, in a make-or-break game, he had responded to the pressures—personal, professional, and otherwise.

Singletary knew if the Bears had dropped this game, the finger-pointing would have started, and Harbaugh knew most of the pointing would have been in his direction. "I answered some questions for myself," he said with pride. "You know I was feeling pressure because if we don't win, can you imagine right now, especially after the Tomczak thing?" He laughed a big friendly laugh. "I went out and had one of my best games." He tossed another wad of tape into the open can. "I'm proud of myself. I responded."

THE NEXT DAY, THE CITY, BY AND LARGE, HAD RESPONDED TOO. IT WAS BACK ON the Bears bandwagon. Granted, a 14-point win over Green Bay was not exactly an upset of the Redskins on the road, but the Bears, now 10-4, still held their tiebreaker edge on the Lions. Two more wins—the dysfunctional Tampa Bay Bucs (2-12) were at Soldier Field on Sunday —or any Detroit loss and the Bears were sitting pretty in the playoffs.

On Monday it was a strangely humble and reflective man who sat down to meet the press at Halas Hall. Winning 100 regular-season games in ten years had obviously touched Ditka deeper than even Sunday's postgame soliloquy suggested. Ditka's 100-50-0 record now ranked third best among NFL coaches with at least five years experience, placing him behind only Don Shula and Joe Gibbs. In celebration of the milestone McMichael, as close to a modern-day Ditka as there was on the team, had ordered up some quiet in the locker room. Standing nearby was the man who had cursed them all, challenged them, and ultimately brought a franchise—and a city—back to life. McMichael proudly passed Ditka the game ball. "I couldn't have done it without players like you," Ditka said as he looked around the room.

That same day, gazing out at a group of reporters, he admitted hitting the century mark in just ten years had "put to peace some questions I had when I first came into this business." Soon after, a voice in the back of the room wanted to know a bit about what price Ditka had paid for all those wins. Scott Smith, a news reporter for WFLD, the local Fox TV affiliate, had never covered the Bears or attended a Ditka press conference before. As fate would have it, he was working on a series on stress in the workplace and figured Ditka would make an interesting subject. He was right, and his line of questioning served to inspire an already meditative man.

"I think if you don't put stress on yourself to do the best you can, that you'll never do the best you can," Ditka said. "I think you have to put so much pressure on yourself to achieve. To have enough discipline in your life to get up early and practice hard, and do the things it takes to get to the top." Ditka was into it now. "If I'm answering your question or I may be missing it . . . I don't know there's any way you can avoid a certain amount of stress if you want to be the best. If you want to be a guy who floats through life with nobody bothering you and nobody recognizes you, then I don't think you'll have any stress. But I think there's a way to do that. You never create waves. You don't make decisions that are unpopular. Those kind of guys never have stress. But when you go out into the process of making decisions, popular or unpopular, and you have to get into the real life. You have to say, 'Hey, I want to be better than average. I don't want to be the guy who is the middle salesman. I want to be the guy at the top.' Then I think you have to put some pressure on. There's got to be some stress. How you handle it? I think a lot has to do with how you . . . how a lot of things fit into your life. How your spiritual life is. How a lot of other things are. There are a lot of things that can take the edge off stress. But I think there's a certain amount of stress in everybody's life.

"We don't want to put undue pressure on ourselves because we realize this is only a game of football. I mean, it's not the end of the world. Yet in our little corner of the world it becomes pretty significant. Because this is it, this is it for us. This is all we do. It's not like we're going to go out and build a bridge or be an architect of a building next week. Or defend somebody in court. This is what we do. This is it. So this has got to be important to us."

At the moment, it appeared, with the season on the line, Ditka was in the midst of a rather stressful situation with his franchise running back Neal Anderson. Ever since Anderson's hamstring injury back in the first week of October against Washington, coach and player had knocked heads over Anderson's availability. Ditka wanted Anderson to rest, to heal before playing again. Anderson wanted to play, a sentiment complicated, as Boso explained, by Anderson's reluctance to "ever admit that he's hurt. He always says he's one hundred percent, no matter what. If he's seventy-five percent, he'll tell you he's one hundred percent." But Ditka knew better. He sat Anderson against Indianapolis and Green Bay in hopes the halfback would be primed for the playoffs. But something was obviously wrong. The last time Anderson had showed his trademark burst of speed and was back in mid-September against the Giants. He had yet to record a 100-yard game. That led some to speculate Anderson's problem was not in his leg but his head. His father was still awaiting trial on the murder charges, sitting in a Graceville, Florida, jail. "We don't discuss this with anybody because this is something that doesn't really affect the Bears," said Laurita Waters, Anderson's sister. "It affects Neal. But usually he goes on with his job."

Anderson maintained he could separate family from football, but close friends weren't so sure. What they said was, when Anderson let his guard down, the pain and strain of his father's incarceration were obvious. Either way, Ditka and Anderson had stopped talking to each other, communicating, just like in the McMahon days, through their respective radio and TV shows.

A couple of other squabbles were brewing at the same time, the wrong time as far as the team's focus was concerned. Ditka and Dent were still at odds over the extra pounds the defensive end was carrying. And in some late-breaking news, it had been announced that McMichael had been fired from his analyst job on WMAQ's "Sports Sunday." Since being hired in 1990, McMichael, who teamed with sport anchor Mark Giangreco, had built a cult following for the ten-thirty P.M. highlights show, moving it to No. 1 in its time slot against snoozers starring Ditka and Anderson. McMichael was out of control at times, at least by television standards. He often showed up on the other side of sober, reveling in bizarre physical gags—smearing lipstick on Giangreco, for example—and off-color remarks. Chicagoans could not go to sleep without seeing what outrageous stunt or offensive remark McMichael would offer next. On the Sunday after the Packer game, however, he crossed the line, at least the one drawn by WMAQ's station manager, who deemed McMichael's use of a phony syringe on Giangreco, as a tasteless turn on AIDS testing, as too much.

Ditka, meanwhile, was hardly immune to personal crisis. Both

Ditka's/City Lights and Ditka's O'Hare restaurants were now the business equivalents of the Tampa Bay Bucs. In October, Ditka had been forced to funnel some heavy cash into the O'Hare restaurant and sports bar to keep the front door open, and not surprisingly, he was none too pleased about it. The word was that Ditka's subsequent harangue to the restaurant staff had measured a solid 7.0 on the Ditka Scale. "He was tearing the place apart," said a source familiar with the meeting. "He was yelling at everybody."

The downtown Ditka's was on the respirator as well, dull and deserted most of the time, as it was the Friday night before the Green Bay game. At seven-thirty less than fifty diners were in the place, scattered about a sea of empty tables covered with white linen cloths and placards noting how the house was proud to serve "wines specially selected by Mike Ditka." Around the horseshoe bar, nine middle-aged men—and one woman—slowly swirled their drinks and stared up at video screens, bordered now by Christmas lights. The atmosphere, however, was anything but festive.

After Rittenberg and Shlaes had been removed, Ditka and Pontillo had assumed control of the restaurant. Pontillo took over as the day-to-day manager, and just as Rittenberg had predicted, the direct-mail specialist began slashing staff in an effort to limit further losses, which had next to no impact on what was really killing the restaurant: the loss of banquet, party, and nightclub business. When Rittenberg left, not only did he take forty of Ditka's top banquet and business parties with him, but he and Shlaes opened up 59 West, just a five-minute walk away, which immediately sucked in some $2 million a year. Morale at Ditka's dipped to an all-time low. Key employees, watching their tips dwindle, quit almost every day. Pontillo compounded his problems with some personnel blunders, firing long time Rittenberg managers and hiring employees Rittenberg had fired. According to club employees, one of the biggest mistakes, perhaps, was the selection of male catering and nightclub managers whose personal style was the antithesis of Ditka's macho sports image. The next thing anyone knew the sports photos came down in City Lights and were replaced by rather tacky disco decor. The new managers, in turn, hired several men who presented a rather effeminate image. Suddenly City Lights had an altogether different feel and appeal—one diametrically opposed, at least symbolically, with the man on the marquee. "The place was just a disaster, that's all I can say," said one former employee who quit in the summer of 1990 but retained ties to the restaurant. Overall, sales slumped near the $4 million mark and cash flow became so tight Pontillo was forced to pump $100,000 of his own money into the restaurant in the fall of 1991 to meet a couple of payrolls.

Just four blocks away from Ditka's, a middle-aged man and a decidedly younger woman sat alone at the bar at 59 West. The man's back was turned, obscuring his face. He was in deep conversation with a foxy blonde. The man spun around. It was Rittenberg. In seconds he was weaving another golden web of words, whispering about the progress of his two new places, the "inflation fighters" he was so hot to promote. He was still selling the story that the collapse of Ditka's was "all about money," but he admitted he made some mistakes: "I had spread myself too thin," he said.

For some reason Rittenberg broke his cardinal rule and bought a reporter a beer before hustling off to check on a party in the adjacent nightclub and to order his date an appetizer. Back at the bar, he said, "Did I tell you that three weeks ago Ditka called George and asked us to come back?" Shlaes says he was contacted by Ditka's attorney who was inquiring about bringing Shlaes back to manage the restaurant while rehiring Rittenberg as the promoter. Ditka's attorney confirms the overture. Shlaes says he declined the offer because Pontillo would not allow an independent accountant to look at the books. Rittenberg now allows himself a short, satisfying laugh. It comes at the expense of a football coach who ignored his own allegations of mismanagment of funds and now wanted Shlaes and Rittenberg back. "We checked the books," said Rittenberg. "They're doing less than five million dollars, but I think it's still salvageable."

A few moments later he slides off to a Bulls game with his pretty date, looking like anything but a man on the brink of personal bankruptcy. By ten P.M. 59 West is packed and partying.

By four P.M. Sunday the locker room at Soldier Field had much the same feel. In a textbook display of Bears football, Chicago had methodically pounded Tampa Bay into the frozen turf, 27–0.

The Bears led 13–0 at halftime. In the second half Chicago just toyed with Tampa Bay, scoring twice more off key Harbaugh passes to Waddle and halfback Mark Green's slashing runs (he would run for a career-high 82 yards as a replacement for the injured Anderson). Butler finally got untracked, drilling two extra points after flubbing a 41-yard field goal attempt. Dent finished with three sacks and an interception. Everybody played. And for the ninth straight week the Bears defense held an opponent to 17 points or less. With the win, the Bears had clinched at least a wild-card spot in the playoffs.

"I feel like this is our year," Dent said after the game. "The road is paved. We've got the perfect opportunity. If we play like we did today, we'll be all right. I'm not afraid of Washington. Next week, we'll shoot for home-field advantage and try to get a bye. You want momentum going into the playoffs. We're starting to get momentum."

THEY DRIFTED THROUGH THE LOBBY OF THE SAN FRANCISCO AIRPORT WESTIN Hotel sporting the caps and jackets of their childhood team, Californians on the hunt for their favorite Bear, *any* Bear. The dozen or so devotees were soon posing proudly with the likes of Ron Rivera or Stan Thomas in front of a beautifully decorated Christmas tree. People just don't understand, thought Trace Armstrong as he watched the fans hustle and the cameras flash. He wasn't being cynical or superior-minded—just honest. He was thinking about how behind all the autographs, the K Mart photos, and the Mercedes money, athletes, particularly football players, pay a heavy price. "Guys like Hampton and Hilgy are probably going to walk away from this game permanently disabled," he whispered. "Cap Boso is a good friend of mine. He is twenty-eight years old. He'll probably never run again."

Armstrong, now in his third year, a 6'4", 260-pound defensive end, was considered the likely successor to Singletary as the future voice of this franchise, its leader in the locker room. A starter from his rookie year on, he had proved to be a straight-up, deep-thinking impact player whose college major (psychology at the University of Florida, where he earned All-American honors in football) seemed perfectly suited to life with Mike Ditka. But today Armstrong had other things on his mind —the Buffalo Bills–Detroit Lions game on Sunday, for one. Thanks to its top-ranked, no-huddle offense, the Bills had already clinched the AFC East and had guaranteed themselves home-field advantage throughout the playoffs. The game against Detroit meant nothing to Buffalo. It meant everything to Detroit. If the 11-4 Lions beat the 13-2 Bills, it would force the Bears to beat San Francisco on Monday night to win the division on the tiebreaker and earn the prized first-round bye.

Under normal circumstances, beating Buffalo at home—where the Bills were 7-0—would require an act of Congress. Buffalo's frenetic offense featured running back Thurman Thomas, the league's best all-purpose back (1,407 yards rushing, leading the NFL, plus 62 receptions), and quarterback Jim Kelly (six 300-yard passing days to his credit). But Sunday was anything but normal. Thomas, Kelly, and star wide receiver James Lofton never played a down—in direct defiance of the NFL edict warning teams that had clinched playoff positions not to let up. The Bills barely ran their famed no-huddle offense. Twice they were caught with twelve men on the field, and in overtime they blitzed linebackers to insure one-on-one coverage in the secondary. That led to a 21-yard Eddie Murray field goal and a 17–14 Lions win. Almost to a man the Bears coaches and players were appalled by what they called Buffalo's laydown against the Lions. "You would never see the great teams, like the Cowboys or the Steelers, do something like that," said Armstrong. "You would never see this franchise do something like that."

But Armstrong was not looking for excuses, although he could point to a couple. Since a sprain of a ligament in his right knee against the Jets, his pass rush had suffered. He had reluctantly moved inside on passing downs and let it affect his play. He had just 1½ sacks all season and spoke now only of the "discomfort," and the relief arthroscopic surgery would bring. And most recently, just after the McMichael firing at WMAQ, Armstrong had found himself embroiled in some petty locker room politics that served only to distract the team from its playoff push. WMAQ had wanted Armstrong to replace the lewd and crude McMichael on a trial basis, but Armstrong was warned off the job by McMichael and other veterans who wanted a show of solidarity. Things got sticky until Singletary stepped in and asked Armstrong, for the good of the team, to turn down the offer and make peace with McMichael. Armstrong did.

But injuries and TV shows were secondary now. Armstrong's focus was on the 49ers. "We have to win," he said. "We have to forge our own destiny." Past experience told Armstrong the bye week was absolutely critical if the Bears were to make a serious run at the Super Bowl: "Last year we played with the Giants emotionally in the first half, at least defensively, but they just felt physically stronger as the game went on." Armstrong was asked about Ditka. What kind of impact would he have on the team? The young end's voice turned up a notch. "We're professionals," he said coolly. "This is our livelihood. We've been doing this since we were young. You think we need a fifty-two-year-old man to tell us how important this game is?"

The fifty-two-year-old certainly knew. He knew that his Bears were a combined 44-10 in September and October the last seven years, but had died in December (14-12). Obvious answers of injury and the physical deterioration of a football team obscured a more psychological possibility—the team grew tired of playing for Ditka. His preachings and teachings and rantings and ravings only took him so far. Against a Gibbs or a Walsh, Ditka couldn't cut it. Ah, the 49ers. Ditka knew that more than any team in the league the Niners had the personnel and playbook to exploit Chicago's weakest defensive links. The pass rush was one big problem. Besides Armstrong's knee, Perry now weighed close to 390 pounds and lacked the lateral movement to spin or work around blocks. McMichael was worn down from weeks of double-teams, and Dent's twenty extra pounds had negated much of his explosive burst off the ball.

The second area of concern was cornerback Lemuel Stinson, the 5'9", 160-pounder now in his fourth season. He had made a name for himself in 1990 with brash, cocky predictions—and by backing them up on the field. Known as Lemonhead to his teammates, Stinson was leading the NFL in interceptions with 6 that season until blowing out his left knee in a game against Denver in November. In '91 he had failed to pick off a pass until the Washington game, and now, despite leading the team in interceptions (4) and passes defended (20), it was obvious he was a step slow in coverage. Early in the season Stinson's play had been timid and tentative, the death knell for any cornerback. Lately he had been acting cocky again, overcompensating, perhaps, because as one assistant coach noted, "he's not as good as he thinks he is." In certain situations, often without Stinson's knowledge, the Bears were rotating defenders into his area for extra protection, particularly against teams with tall, rangy wide receivers, and the 49ers had two of the best: John Taylor (6'1", 185) and Jerry Rice (6'2", 200).

Actually, under the best of circumstances Stinson would have been the primary target. The other corner, Donnell Woolford, was on the verge of an All-Pro year. At safeties the Bears had Mark Carrier, just named to his second straight Pro Bowl (along with Singletary and Hilgenberg), and Shaun Gayle, a vicious tackler, who would make the Pro Bowl as an alternate. Stinson was the weakest link. As Harbaugh diplomatically put it before the game, "We have some matchup problems."

Some of those problems were passing through Ditka's mind as he sat in a pregame chapel service staring intently as the impassioned pastor—"Life is a genesis!"—preached for nearly an hour. At two-thirty the grim-faced coach, clad in a leather Bears jacket, limped toward the team bus, a stack of cigars in one fist, a Gucci bag in the other. Trailing right behind was Diana in a full-length fur, dripping in diamond earrings. Seconds later, the bus rolled off to Candlestick Park, where crushed beer cans already hung from parking-lot Christmas trees. When the bus finally came through Gate A, Niner fans pointed with derisive joy. "The fucking Bears are here!" shouted one tailgater. "Hey, Chicago," yelled another, "eat shit!"

Of course, such warm holiday greetings should not have been unexpected. No two teams symbolized NFL football in the 1980s more than Chicago and Mike Ditka, and San Francisco and Bill Walsh. The cities and coaches were complete opposites: the urban, volcanic Ditka, the urbane, sophisticated Walsh; Ditka's blood-and-guts football philosophy the polar opposite of the finesse-passing attack scripted by Walsh, who was widely considered to be a silver-haired offensive genius. Both teams had made marvelous runs through the eighties with one striking difference: the 49ers had four Super Bowl trophies, the Bears just one. Twice Montana & Co. had knocked the Bears out of the playoffs on their way to an NFL title. Ditka always took great pains to proclaim how his team was as good or better than the Niners, when actually the records indicated that from 1982 through the Monday-night game, the Niners had won 108 regular-season games, Ditka and his Bears, 101.

Part of the rivalry was obviously also personal. Back in the 1984 playoffs Walsh—whom Ditka now blew off as the "gray-haired guy"—had inserted offensive guard Guy McIntyre into the backfield to block against the Bears during a 23–0 victory. The next year Ditka rubbed it right back in Walsh's face, putting Perry into the backfield at the end of game and twice giving him the ball in the latter stages of a 26–10 win. Since then, however, Chicago had played like patsys in three games at Candlestick Park. They had been outscored 95–3, including 41–0 in '87, in the infamous Gum Game. By halftime of that "Monday-Night" game, Tomczak, replacing an injured McMahon, had thrown 4 first-half interceptions and the hosts had recovered 2 fumbles on their way to a 20–0 lead. Striding off the field and approaching a locker room entrance where fans are just inches from the face of visiting players, Ditka got struck by some flying ice. He responded by firing his gum up into the crowd and, as later described in the police report, "flipped the bird with his left hand and exited the field." The gum, Exhibit A in this case, evidently struck a thirty-eight-old Napa, California, woman in the back of the head, leading to a rather, uh, sticky situation. The woman talked about filing formal charges. The gum alleged involved was confiscated and booked as evidence. Assault with a deadly gum wad? There was film at eleven and front-page pictures and stories. It all eventually blew over.

Four years later the rivalry was no less bitter despite Walsh's move into the NBC broadcast booth. Unlike the Bills, the 49ers had no plans to roll over and die. Victim of a sluggish start (losers of four of its first seven games), San Francisco had rallied behind journeyman quarterback Steve Bono to win its last five games to improve its record to 9-6. Still, it wasn't quite good enough, and for the first time in ten years the Niners failed to make the playoffs. This "Monday Night Football" game would be their postseason party, a chance to show the nation that the 49ers were back. A victory over the Bears, putting Chicago in *its* place, would make it all the more sweet.

But Bono would not start against the Bears. He had suffered a knee injury the previous week, making way for thirty-year-old Steve Young, earning a cool $2 million a year to back up Montana, who had ripped a tendon in the elbow of his throwing arm before the season started. In the wake of Montana's injury, Young had opened the season at quarterback for San Francisco, but was vilified for the poor start despite completing 64 percent of his passes and leading the NFC in passing efficiency. Then Young hurt a knee and Bono took over and looked brilliant before injuring *his* knee, much to the Bears' dismay. They feared Young far more than Bono. When healthy, the former BYU star was a dart-thrower in the mold of Kenny Stabler, but at 6'2", 200 pounds, far more mobile and willing to run. Yet instead of starting the game in a nickel package and daring the 49ers to go on the ground, the Bears misjudged Young's health and unwisely played it straight. Young was flawless in the opening drive: 9 plays, 76 yards, 4:57 of pure Niner magic for a TD. His first play was a dart to tight end Brent Jones, working on Singletary, followed by a 10-yard toss to Taylor, who ran free of Stinson. A run went nowhere. Next Young threw long for Rice, over Woolford. It was a sure 6, inches overthrown, but it sent a chilling message: *it was going to be a long night.* On third and 10 from his own 41, Young went back to Jones deep over the middle, two strides ahead of Singletary, 29 yards, down to the Bears 30. Simple. It all looked so simple. Young was in complete command, mixing the run with the pass with the scramble. On first and goal from the 2, Young rolled left and spotted tight end Jamie Williams on a drag pattern. Williams caught the pass—his first TD catch in four years. It was not a good sign for Chicago. Later Singletary, beaten on this play, too, said he sensed as much. "I knew the tight end was coming across," he said, "but somebody had to hit the guy, to give me some time." Nobody did.

A team can choose one of two options when the knife thrusts in so deep and so quickly, on "Monday Night," no less, with everything on the line: it can fold or strike back. Clearly this was not going to be a defensive struggle. The offense would have to respond. Earlier in the day, dressed as if he were back in college in Ann Arbor, in a ratty T-shirt and jeans, Harbaugh had talked about celebrating his twenty-seventh birthday in a big way, partying hard on the flight home. "I feel as good as I have all year," he said. "I'm ready." If so, now was the time to show it, and he did. On the first play he improvised around right end for 8 yards. Behind him in the backfield now were Anderson and Muster, starting together for the first time since the Miami game a month earlier. Harbaugh handed off to Anderson around the left end. He only got a yard but the burst was back. On third and 1, Muster took a short pitch and barreled for a first down. A little momentum was building. At third and 5 from his own 38 Harbaugh scrambled for 16 big yards. Down the field the Bears went, grinding it out, the backfield doing it all, ABC keying in on the action, cutting back to the sideline where Ditka was spitting up a storm.

The 49ers eventually stiffened. It was third and 7 from the San Francisco 17. "Thirteen Wing Jet," called Harbaugh in the huddle. It was the same play, the slick slant-in, Waddle used to beat New Orleans. And it worked to perfection this time, too, Waddle pulling in Harbaugh's pass at the Niner 6-yard line. Waddle was angling toward the end zone when he decided to switch the football from his right to left hand. Two steps away from the goal line and a tie game, 49er nickelback Kevin Lewis crashed in and yanked Waddle's arm. The ball fell free. Cornerback Don Griffin pounced on it. An eight-minute Bear drive had ended 3 yards short. "That was a key play, definitely," Harbaugh admitted after the game. "When a team is as high-powered as San Francisco, you've got to take advantage of opportunities to score points."

The Californians had taken a shot on the chin and staggered back a bit but were saved by the bell. In round two they began to counter-punch. With Rice working on Stinson and Young dashing about, San Francisco drove 97 yards in 10 plays for 14–0 lead. After the next series, the Bears were forced to punt, Buford's kick bounding out of bounds at the SF 31-yard line.

During a TV time-out Stinson practiced his backpedaling moves. It did no good. The 49ers, looking to break the game wide open, lined up Rice against Stinson, who froze and stumbled just a bit off a play-action fake. It was all Rice needed. He tore by and Young hit him in stride at the Chicago 33 as Stinson fell awkwardly to the turf. One play, ten seconds, 69 yards. It was now 21–0. With ten minutes left in the half, Young was now 11 of 12 for 204 yards and 3 touchdowns.

After that, the game slipped into the surreal. Young later scored on a 2-yard dive to make it 31–7. On the next series Harbaugh and the Bears had it first and 10 at the Niners 1-yard line, but then as Mark Green fumbled, the ball popped straight into the arms of Don Griffin, who dashed a team record 99 yards for a touchdown. The wheels were off completely now. Ditka barked at Harbaugh as he came off the field; the quarterback jawed back. Willis took over on the next series. His second pass was picked off and run back 20 yards to the Bears 2-yard line. After the next play it was 45–7. With eleven minutes left, ABC began running its annual end-of-the-season list of credits, everybody from cameramen to hairdressers. The final score was 52–14—the worst defeat ever for a Mike Ditka–coached team.

Walking off, Ditka never flinched. Near the entrance to the locker room fans tore into the Bears—"You suck!" "Chumps!"—in a fit of drunken courage. Harbaugh shouted something back. Another Bear flipped up his middle finger. Inside the locker room Ditka exploded. Players say he repeatedly smashed a table with his fist. "I thought he was going to break his hand," said one. "You play *scared!*" he yelled at his team, pounding the table. When the tirade was over, it was the job of Bears PR director Bryan Harlan to escort Ditka the thirty yards or so over to the press tent, which, at this point, Harlan remembers "was twenty-nine yards more than I wanted to go." Once inside the tent Ditka stood on a platform, a vaguely distant stare in his eyes, a chip on his shoulder.

"What about the performance?" someone said.

"Life goes on," Ditka replied by rote.

"What's next for the Bears?"

"Ah, we play Sunday."

"Mike, what did you tell the team afterward," Pompei asked.

"That's personal."

"Mike, what happened defensively?"

"Ah, those that have eyes, let them see. Those that have ears, let them hear."

"What are you going to work on for Sunday?"

[Heavy sarcasm.] "We're going to practice our baseball."

When Chicago TV reporter Brad Palmer inquired about what the loss meant for the team entering the playoffs, Ditka detonated. "Let me tell you something, Brad. It will mean we resurrect ourselves and we play

329

good next week or we get trounced in the first round of the playoffs. There's only two things it can mean . . . you rebound or you fall deeper. That's the way it is. That's life. So what do you want me to do? Expound on some theological explanation here?''

Would the Bears rebound? Would they fall back? The feeling in the locker room was one of uncertainty now. Harbaugh had nothing to be ashamed of (17 of 24, 212 yards and a touchdown), but Muster and Anderson had combined for just 19 yards on 11 carries. The offensive line was moribund; the starting defensive line had combined for a grand total of 4 tackles and no sacks. The look on McMichael's face told the story. Sandwiched between two empty lockers, he sat on a stool, naked to the waist. His arms were folded across a massive, welted chest. He had been shut out. No tackles. No sacks. Armstrong, who had talked about playing so big, instead had come up empty. No sacks. No tackles. Nothing. He dressed ever so slowly, knotting his tie to perfection. Then he walked into the silent night, to a bus full of teammates fighting the same dark demons.

AS THE PLANE FEW EAST, DITKA HELD HIS ANGER. OTHERS, UNABLE TO SLEEP, rolled the Monday-night massacre from their minds and looked ahead to the short week, including practice on Christmas Day, and finally, the prospect of facing the Dallas Cowboys in Sunday's wild-card game. The Cowboys were a load. Unlike Chicago, they were peaking at just the right time, winning their last five, 11–5 overall. Dallas was a quick-strike, ballhawking club nobody wanted to tackle in the first round of a single-elimination tournament. They brought the league's leading rusher, Emmett Smith (1,563 yards), the NFL's leader in receiving yards, Michael Irvin (1,523 on 93 catches), and big-play special teams to the playoff table, along with a nasty new attitude courtesy of third-year coach Jimmy Johnson, whose University of Miami teams had dominated the national polls and local police blotter from 1985 to '88.

"The big question is," said the Bears Zaven Yaralian shortly after the 49er loss, "how will we react?"

The answer to that question was now complicated by injuries, the most significant to outside linebacker John Roper, the enigmatic third-year pro in midst of a strong season (90 tackles, 8 sacks), who pulled a hamstring and hurt a calf against the 49ers. Also sidelined were Anthony Morgan, the flashy wideout from Tennessee (strained knee ligaments), and several key backup players. The loss to San Francisco also raised doubts as to whether Chicago could elevate its game when it counted. Maybe Armstrong was wrong. Maybe the team *did need* a fifty-two-year-old man to tell them how important this game was. So it was that many of the players, in their time of need, turned back to the one man, as Butler had noted, capable of bringing them all together and salvaging a season. "If we win this game," said Yaralian, "everything's changed." He was right. A win over Dallas meant a return trip to Detroit, a chance to wipe the smirk off Wayne Fontes's face, a face that had spent the vast majority of the fourth quarter on ABC-TV Monday night, live from a team party at the Pontiac Silverdome, smoking victory cigars and pompously mugging for the cameras. The winner of that game, if it happened, would then more than likely move on to RFK in the NFC Championship game against the Redskins, one win away from the Super Bowl.

Ditka knew it. "We're not even going to watch the films," he told an attentive squad during a short Christmas Day meeting. "Fucking forget it. It's over. There's nothing worth saving." What was worth saving was Ditka's distaste for what had happened out west. But there was no pounding of tables this time. He never threw a fit. His weapon during Dallas week was his voice, a blowtorch on butter. "You embarrassed me," he told them. "You embarrassed yourselves. You embarrassed this team, this organization, the city of Chicago. We didn't play Bears football. We didn't play the way we can play. You played *scared*. You were all intimidated by the 49ers."

This time he never pointed a finger or mentioned a name. Every single player and coach shared the blame, he said. Every team was equal now, he said. We are all zero and zero. Only twelve left. Do or Die. How bad do you want it?

Pubicly he was playing it cool—too cool for *Sun-Times* columnist Jay Mariotti, who dubbed him "Rev. Ditka" and "Idle Mike." But behind the scenes "Idle Mike" was actually more vocal and involved on the field than he had had been all year. He warned the defense about Smith, Irvin, and the Cowboys' massive offensive line: "Play like you did last week, and they'll score more than fifty-two." He set the challenge: "They're going to try and establish the run. We've got to be ready."

Rivera, the steady eight-year linebacking vet, who had started the first five games of the year before hurting his back lifting weights and losing his job to Morrissey, moved into Roper's spot. Rivera was an instinctive player, very capable, but he lacked Roper's speed. The Bears coaching staff expected Dallas to attack Rivera both on the ground and with the pass, utilizing Jay Novacek, a topflight tight end. The object, the coaches said, was to spring Smith to the outside. As for Irvin, who averaged 16.4 yards per catch, it would be Woolford's job to shadow him on almost every down. Sure, it was an affront to Stinson, but at this point said one assistant coach, "we've got to do it."

Some players, such as McMichael and Butler, street fighters from the start, were ready. But what about Harbaugh? On Friday the quarterback had showed up at practice looking like somebody out of a Wes Craven film, deathly ill from the flu. He was quickly checked into a local hospital for fluids and rest. Would he recover? What about the phlegmatic Mr. Perry, invisible on the pass rush? Or the not-so-special teams? Other than for Glen Kozlowski the punt and kickoff coverage players appeared to lack any spirit or substance.

Would the Bears run scared? Or return to their gutsy, glorious, blue-collar ways?

"Hey," said Butler, "we'll win."

Yaralian was not so sure. "I really don't know," he said. "I can't tell. If we play like we can, we'll win. If not . . ."

There was no need to finish the sentence.

In the end it was a day packed with frustration and pointed fingers as a season slipped away in the gathering gloom at Soldier Field. Ditka limped off the field for the final time, head down as if ashamed, after the 17–13 defeat. Harbaugh screamed at some fanatic to fuck off, and Van Horne pinned two taunting fans up against a wall outside the locker room. In the locker room Butler seethed and said, "This fucking team has no guts." Singletary spoke of "weeding out guys who don't want to work." Thayer stressed "finding some big-play people on offense and defense." Everyone agreed there had to be a greater commitment to sacrifice and discipline.

A Harbaugh fumble keyed the first Cowboy score, a 27-yard field goal. A blocked punt and an illegal-use-of-hands call on Dent, who should have known better, helped set up Dallas's first touchdown. Three times in the first half the Bears had the ball on third down or better on the Cowboys 2-yard line and could manage only 3 points, thanks in large part to some insipid and indecisive play-calling on the part of Ditka or Landry. (Remember what Hughes had said about both Landry and Ditka when it came to calling a game? Well, it showed against Dallas.) It did not help, either, that Muster sprained a knee in the second quarter and was lost for the day. Or that Anderson (13 carries, 34 yards) ran without much blocking or passion or purpose.

Despite all these lost opportunities, the Bears were within striking distance, 10–6, midway through the third quarter. Butler had booted two field goals, including a gutsy 43-yarder at the 8:26 mark of the third quarter to cut the lead to 4. Momentum had shifted. The crowd was back into the game. But instead of shutting down the Cowboys, Ditka's defense gave up the kind of ball-control, in-your-face drive (14 plays, 75 yards, 8:03 off the clock) made famous by Ditka's Bears six years earlier. For the first time all year a team held the ball against the Bears for 14 plays and scored a touchdown. It was now 17–6 Dallas.

Harbaugh responded by leading a long drive, sparked by a fourth-down pass off a fake punt and the dynamic running of Darren Lewis. He had been the forgotten back all year (15 carries, 38 yards), but he was thrust into a desperate situation given the injury to Muster and Anderson's apathetic performance. With Lewis in the lineup, Landry or Ditka, whoever was calling the plays, suddenly got creative. Misdirection and trap plays were now part of the scheme, and Lewis made the most of them, gaining 65 yards on just 9 tries. But on fourth and 3 from the Dallas 7 with seven minutes still remaining, Harbaugh, under pressure, missed Gentry in the end zone.

Two minutes later, after the defense did its job, Waddle took over. The former Boy on the Bubble was now the Man of the Hour. He caught 4 of his 9 passes (104 yards), making one circus catch after another. In two plays sure to show up on any highlight reel, Waddle snared a slant-in from Harbaugh, taking an Excedrin shot from Dallas safety Billy Bates at the 3. The diagnosis would later read a bruised sternum and slight concussion, but right now it looked more like a broken body. Waddle wobbled to the sidelines supported by team trainers. The stadium crowd of 62,594, having found a new hero, chanted, "Wad-dle, Wad-dle, Wad-dle." The team doctor stuck some smelling salts under the nose of the wide receiver, and one play later, after a

Harbaugh sack, Waddle trotted back in. "I didn't know where I was," he said later, but somehow, someway, he grabbed another slant-in pass from 6 yards out. Touchdown! It was 17–13 now. Do or die.

In the end, the defense did its job, as it had for much of the day, for much of the season. McMichael and Rivera stacked up Smith on a crucial third and 1 near midfield with two minutes to go. But then the final sad lines of the 1991 season were written, first by Dallas punter Mike Saxon, who boomed a 52-yard punt down to the Bears 4-yard line, and then, finally, by Harbaugh, who had coaxed out one first down before his desperate pass to Gentry was picked off by Bates.

So in the darkening skies of Soldier Field, Ditka and his Bears slumped to their final exit. Ditka was strangely serene as he walked toward the press tent. *Relief* was the word he would later use. *Resigned* might be a better term, the word Vainisi used in judging Ditka's preseason assessment of the Bears. Perhaps that is why, despite his motivational ploys earlier in the week, Ditka did so little on the sideline. Maybe he was resigned to the fact that this team was headed nowhere. Maybe that is why he never once, especially early in the game, tried to fire up some of his flat and listless players. Instead he stood there, hands dug deep into his leather jacket, and watched, a captain who'd jumped ship, leaving the players he had earlier praised as "his life and love" slowly slipping into the ocean. "Our guys played hard and they tried," he said afterward. "There was no lack of effort. [Dallas] won, that's all. If you want to fault somebody, I guess you can fault me. Don't fault those guys. They fought like heck." But in almost the very next breath Ditka was angling to spread the blame. Moving criticism off center, away from the coach, and into the front office. "We have overachievers," he said, "and sometimes you need people who are a little bit better than overachievers. We have some magnificent overachievers, and I love them. I'll play with them anytime because, hey, gang, it's the hand I'm dealt." Personnel boss Tobin gritted his teeth and answered that comment by saying, "I don't think we have overachievers. We have achievers. If that's what he thinks . . ."

Harbaugh felt much the same way. "Win eleven games with overachievers, I guess it's a heck of a coaching job."

On Monday, Ditka limped back into his "final, final" press conference of the season, the one in the basement at Halas Hall. This time he brought along another "new" attitude and some additional areas to place the blame. He charged the media with "dwelling on the negative" during the '91 season and said they got what they wanted. "The great satisfaction, if any satisfaction comes out of it, is we didn't disappoint the media," he said. "See, I've disappointed them all year, and the Bears have disappointed them because we've done so much better than all those experts said we would.

"But we finally made a few local people happy because they'd predicted we'd get beat, and we did get beat. So I have no sympathy at all towards the media."

It was time, he said, to explore every avenue to improve the team, and a franchise that had gone 2-5 in postseason play since the 1986 Super Bowl. He said he wasn't "threatening or warning or scaring anybody," but it was time to bring some discipline back into the organization. It was time for him and McCaskey and Tobin to sit down and rebuild some bridges. The season, he acknowledged, had turned on two events—the loss of Covert in training camp and the bad snap against Miami. There would be changes, he said, how many he was not about to guess. But one thing was for sure: the Mellow Mike business was over. With that, he detached the microphone from his multicolored sweater and stalked out of the room, a wounded Bear on the prowl. Halfway to the door he slowed his hobble for a split second and growled to no one in particular, "And I'll tell you another damn thing. If this hip keeps me off the golf course, I'm going to get it fixed."

Why not? It could be part of yet another New Ditka, who seems to pop up every few years. Wasn't he reborn in Dallas in 1977? Didn't he promise to mellow out in 1983? And what about the post–heart-attack declarations of civility and restraint in 1988? Or the humbled and spiritually uplifted man in 1990? The fact is that as much as Ditka shouts "I like who I am, I know who I am, I know where I come from," even after all these years, through all these adaptations, he seems anchorless in his beliefs. He's a Famous Tough Guy offering countless opinions on everything from politics to race to stress but seems void, on the most basic level, of a core set of values, rocks on which to rest in times of personal and professional tumult.

He seems unable to trust the kind of man he was for much of the 1990 and '91 seasons, when he often mixed motivation with compassion, and resisted the urge to threaten or bully his team into action. He remains a thin-skinned, self-righteous contradiction. He's a man who demands others "look in the mirror" to find themselves, yet was unable to face his reflection for fifty years and, when he did, broke down and cried. He's a man who, no matter what, is still welded to life in black and white, who worships the one religion preached in the Church of the Holy Winner.

He's a man who is, like all of us, a product of his environment, yet at the same time, is some sort of cultural aberration—at once the best and worst his town has produced. Because for all his Herculean efforts to stay out of a tunnel, Michael Keller Ditka seems destined now to be drawn into a different kind of darkness: a place where a singular obsession overshadows his fame, his fortune, and his moments of motivational brilliance and inspirational charity. A man with an addiction to victory that, sadly, leaves one wondering whether he will ever see the light.

EPILOGUE

On December 14, 1991, Frank Marocco's Aliquippa High Fighting Quips won the Pennsylvania AA football title. Aliquippa (13-2) upset defending state champion Hanover, 27–0, snapping the No. 1–ranked Hawkeyes's thirty-game win streak. "A tremendous win," said Marocco.

On January 9, 1992, just a week and a half after the Dallas defeat, Ditka made his first major move. Steve Kazor was shifted from special teams coach to tight ends and special assignments. Ditka took great pains to alter the perception that Kazor had been demoted, saying, "I really loved what Steve did," and praising Kazor's loyalty. "That's important," added Ditka. "There are a lot of guys who are loyal to a lot of other things, but he's loyal to me." Kazor was replaced by former New Orleans Saints wide receiver Dan Abramowicz, forty-six, a classic overachiever, whose coaching résumé showed only three years of experience, all in high school. But Ditka discounted it. He was hiring Abramowicz because he was a "gung ho" guy who would bring some passion and excitement to the staff. A nine-year pro, Abramowicz had impressed Ditka during a chapel-service speech when the Bears played the Saints in October '91. Ditka and Abramowicz stayed in touch, and Ditka, going with his gut, made the decision to bring the New Orleans Jesuit High School coach into the NFL. "I believe in emotion," said Abramowicz. "You can play with emotion on any level. How a coach behaves can determine how his players play . . . if you show an enthusiastic approach, the players will respond."

A week earlier, the Bears had patched another hole. They hired former Green Bay physical development coordinator Russ Riederer, thirty-four, to run their off-season fitness and conditioning program. "We will be significantly expanding what we ask our players to do in the off-season," said McCaskey.

Doug Flutie was named the Most Valuable Player in the Canadian Football League. Playing for the British Columbia Lions, Flutie set league records in passing attempts, completions, and yardage. He later signed a reported four-year $4-million-a-year contract with the Calgary Stampeders.

Tom Waddle, who caught 55 passes during the season, was named a member of the All-Madden team. In the off-season he emerged as the darling of the banquet and public-speaking circuit. The Bears PR offices were deluged with requests. Waddle's appearance fees doubled to $2,000. In all likelihood he would earn as much money in the off-season—$125,000—as he did during the season. "They all want to talk about the Dallas game," he said, adding how people always remark about his size. "'You're so small.' They always say that. It makes people happy to know you don't have to be large to accomplish something."

And what about Bob Waddle, Tom's inspiration? What was his proudest moment during the season? The New Orleans game? The 9 catches against Dallas? "The Buffalo game," he said. "Tom had a bad game. He didn't do well and lost his starting job. It was a turning point because he really grew up. He learned you can work hard and do everything in life and things are not always going to go your way. He learned you have to work that much harder and go on. He learned not to be a loser because of one game. From my side, that was very probably the proudest point I had for him this year."

On January 26, the *Sun-Times* ran the results of a fans poll. Waddle was rated the most popular Bear, with 99 percent of the fans voting to keep him on the team. By the same measure, 71 percent of the fans wanted Ditka to remain as coach; 61 percent supported Anderson. By far the lowest rating went to Perry. Only 39 percent of the voting fans wanted to keep him, a figure just two percentage points lower than the CEO Mike McCaskey (41 percent), whose accompanying comment read "Too cheap for Chi-town."

In their expanding effort to bring in better players, the Bears dipped into the Plan B free-agency pool for only the second time in the four years since the inception of the system. First the Bears signed speedy Richard Fain, a former Phoenix Cardinal cornerback who played for Yaralian at the University of Florida. Shortly thereafter long-snapper Mark Rodenhauser, an ex-Bear who was playing for San Diego, signed a free-agent deal. The same day Rodenhauser was signed the team announced an increase in the ticket price of selected seats to "offset the escalating costs of fielding a team." The 16,000 prime seats between the 10-yard lines were bumped up $5 to $35.

On February 9, in a bizarre incident, Bears tackle Stan Thomas was shot in the head and seriously wounded when a gunman riddled his car with bullets outside a San Diego bar. Thomas and two friends were reportedly involved in a confrontation with several people outside the bar around one A.M. Thomas was driving his car when a white Honda carrying three men suddenly cut him off, police said. A gunman leaned out the window and fired five shots at Thomas. One of the bullets struck the windshield and deflected, grazing Thomas's head, leaving fragments in his skull. After a forty-five minute operation, Thomas was listed in serious but stable condition. He recovered, dropped thirty pounds of weight, and added thirty pounds to his bench press. He is penciled in to start at left tackle for the Bears in 1992. But, he says, he will never forget that night. "I'm almost scared to death to drive anymore," he told Chicago sports radio czar Chet Coppock. "I have friends pick me up. Psychologically, it scares me. I don't go out anymore. I just sit at home. You keep asking yourself why, why?"

In January, Gene Pontillo was forced to inject another $100,000 into Ditka's/City Lights to meet the employee payroll. "We are having, quite frankly, tough times," said Pontillo.

On March 12, Ditka finally gave in to the pain and underwent surgery to replace his crumbled left hip. The hour-and-twenty-minute operation was deemed a success, but it forced Ditka to miss the NFL owners meetings in Phoenix. Instead, one week after his surgery, Ditka was seen hunkered down at Bob 'O' Link where, according to sources, he played sixteen straight hours of gin.

On March 13, according to court records, James J. Rittenberg filed for Chapter 7 personal bankruptcy. In a petition filed in U.S. Bankruptcy Court, Rittenberg claimed more than $1.5 million in liabilities and just $121,900 in personal assets, including his $120,000 Chicago apartment. The listed liabilities include more than a dozen different bank and personal loans and deliquent state and federal taxes of $106,000. Listed among the $1,900 in personal property was just $300 in clothes, $200 in office equipment consisting of "two desks and a chair," and $150 worth of "old and used records." True to form, Rittenberg was still promoting his two new restaurants—Mother Hubbard's and Timothy O'Toole's—and even popped up on a national TV talk show as the best "schmoozer" in Chicago.

In April, Merrillville creditors were notified they had until July 21,

1992, to inform the U.S. Bankruptcy Court in the Northern District of Indiana if they wished to share in "assets recovered" by the bankruptcy trustee. The amount recovered was $654.71. If each of the forty Merrillville limited partners decided to file a claim based on his original $45,000 investment, what remained of that investment would be $12.38. As of late May several investors were exploring options against Ditka, Kirk, and other general partners to recover funds far in excess of the listed amount.

On Friday night, April 24, Ditka's/City Lights closed its doors for the final time. The official word was "reorganization" but it's unlikely the restaurant/nightclub, which grossed more than $50 million in its six and a half years of operation, will ever open again, at least under the Ditka name. A sign posted at the adjacent Chicago Sports Hall of Fame stressed, incorrectly, that the restaurant and hall were "separate entities," when, in fact, it was the hall that helped ruin the restaurant. In small print on the sign, it was noted that any banquet inquiries should be addressed to 59 West, a last laugh for Rittenberg and Shlaes. On the heels of the demise of the downtown restaurant, speculation was that Ditka's O'Hare was not far behind. As for Ditka Dogs, the original hype of a huge stock offering and restaurants in ten NFL cities had been scaled way back. The concept still had not gone public and a second Ditka Dogs had yet to be built. Ditka, did, however, sign a $1.25-million commercial contract with Toyota that will pay him an estimated $250,000 per spot.

A week after Ditka's/City Lights closed, the Bears opened their 1992 minicamp at Halas Hall. Much like 1991, the weekend weather was idyllic, as players stretched in a languid breeze. At the end of the first practice the press, as usual, huddled around Ditka's cart. Ditka wasted little time in making news, blasting Perry for missing the camp in a contract dispute. Sticking by earlier threats, Ditka said Perry had better weigh 320 pounds or less come training camp or his career in Chicago was over. "You can book it," said Ditka. "Take it to the bank and cash it right now."

And how's that new hip, Mike? "It's about two-ninety off the tee," cracked Ditka.

But the real story was not a rebuilt hip or an overweight defensive tackle. As usual it was the coach. In March, McCaskey had talked about how very pleased he was with the "renewed sense of enthusiasm" he saw on Ditka's part, "a real sense of urgency about the coming season." Part of the reason, perhaps, was the NFC Central had undergone radical changes. Three new head coaches, all disciples of Walsh and the dreaded San Francisco attack, had been hired. There was Sam Wyche, formerly of Cincinnati, now in Tampa Bay. Walsh's offensive coordinator, Mike Holmgren, had been grabbed by Green Bay, and Dennis Green, late of Stanford, was the new man in Minnesota. The image of the NFC Central as the "Black and Blue" division was fading as fast as the Bears' ability to control the clock. That image was being replaced by the finesse-passing, cornerback-harassing "offense of the nineties." Ditka mocked the hype—"I'm scared to death"—and went about retooling his team in preparation for a tough regular-season schedule. In '92 the Bears will open at Soldier Field against the Lions, one of six playoff teams on the schedule. Six of Chicago's first nine games will be at home, and there will be three "Monday Night" games.

Ditka gave a preview of what was in store for 1992 during the team's first meeting at minicamp. To many it was more like 1982 all over again with Ditka assuming his role as the short-tempered drill sergeant, last seen in that desert boot camp in Scottsdale, Arizona. "He was one mean, ornery son of a bitch," reported one veteran. During roll call Ditka pretended not to hear the acknowledgments of Butler or Gayle, jumping all over the two veterans in an effort to intimidate and impress the rookies, while sending a message to everyone in the room that the days of Mellow Mike, the Compassionate Coach, were over. For good measure Ditka fined Harbaugh $50 for being a few minutes late to the meeting. Harbaugh, who set team records for passing attempts (478) and completions (275) in 1991, had just returned from Hawaii where he won an NFL-sponsored quarterback challenge competition against ten other quarterbacks. In the accuracy drill Harbaugh was perfect and took home $17,000.

On Friday, just before practice, Ditka stopped Butler and told him to wear the same practice jersey as everybody else. "First time he ever said anything about that in three years," said Butler. "Definite changes. Big changes."

Not that the kicker was against it: "It's something we have to do. It's definitely for the best."

Other veterans were not so sure. They found the entire minicamp scene troubling. They agreed there was a need for greater discipline but were worried that the "volunteer" four-day-a-week workouts, virtually mandatory since March, were going to burn the team out before the season started. And they found Ditka's attack on Butler and Gayle contrived and desperate, particularly when it came to Gayle, an All-Pro who was not only a deeply religious athlete but a consummate team player as well.

"You don't call Shaun Gayle a liar in minicamp," said one respected veteran.

Butler, who had been ripped just like Gayle, just shook his head and smiled. Everything changes and yet nothing changes.

"Stick around," he said, chuckling. "It's going to be a wild, wild year."

AUTHOR'S NOTE

Much like the foundation of a home or the offensive line of a football team, there is a backbone to this biography. It was, without question, the more than 200 interviews I conducted with members of Mike Ditka's family, relatives, friends, former teammates and coaches, business associates, members of the media, and dozens of current or former players he coached. The vast majority of these interviews were taped and often resulted in follow-up calls for greater detail or clarity. Some interviews, such as my visit with Jerry Vainisi in Dallas, ran for several hours; others—Harbaugh, Butler, and Singletary spring to mind—stretched out over several visits during the course of a season.

I traveled to Chicago on more than a dozen different occasions, with sidetrips to Aliquippa, Dallas, Denver, San Francisco, and Detroit. My personal reporting was often augmented with newspaper clippings, radio and television tapes, or documents obtained from the public record. These documents include business filings, bankruptcy proceedings, divorce papers, and court depositions. I also obtained material from private investors in Ditka's restaurants. My interviews and reporting are central to many of the conversations I reconstructed. When I did recreate a major scene or conversation, it was done only after interviewing at least one of the principals present.

Beyond my efforts, two superb, nationally known reporters provided me invaluable assistance. They are Lester Munson of Chicago and Don Yaeger of Tallahassee, Fla. Munson, a former reporter for *The National,* and now a special contributor for *Sports Illustrated,* did extensive digging into Ditka's business dealings, principally the Merrillville mess, from which I followed his leads. Yaeger, author of the critically acclaimed *Undue Process—The NCAA's Unjustice for All* and, most recently, *Shark Attack,* Jerry Tarkanian's battle with UNLV, located and interviewed Mike "Dirt Dobber" Stevenson and also went one-on-one with Dave Edwards, among his many contributions.

In addition to Munson and Yaeger, I often relied on the writings, interviews, and impressions of other reporters in print, radio, and television. Sometimes it was for a quote. Other times I extracted a mood or a moment. Whenever I felt it appropriate I cited the work of a particular author. But now I would like to give further credit where credit is due.

In Aliquippa: At the *Beaver County Times,* assistant sports editor Mike Bires, and staff Mike Prisuta and Jim Tripodi, with Prisuta's work proving particularly valuable.

In Pittsburgh: My eyes and ears around the University of Pittsburgh, Derrick Willis, assistant sports editor of the *Pitt News.* Willis's research of his newspapers files and follow-up interviews with the likes of Pitt baseball coach Bobby Lewis were first rate.

In Dallas: Former Cowboys public relations director Doug Todd, and sports columnists Skip Bayless and Frank Luksa either pointed me in the right direction or had the answers themselves.

In Chicago: First, a blanket thank you to the entire Bears press corps for welcoming me into their midst, while offering dozens of insights and anecdotes, which, in one form or the other, are reflected on almost every page of this book. Two reporters stand out, Fred Mitchel from *The Tribune* and Dan Pompei of the *Sun-Times,* who not only spent considerable time answering questions but whose newspaper stories from 1986 to '91 filled in innumerable blanks and helped frame larger themes. Other heartfelt thanks at *The Tribune* to columnist Bob Verdi, National Pro Football writer, and Ditka collaborator Don Pierson, columnist Mike "Odds & Ins" Conklin, and staff writers Paul Sullivan and Bob Sakamoto whose writings and insights proved particularly helpful. At the *Sun-Times,* columnist Jay Mariotti, beat writer and columnist Brian Hewitt, and staff writer Toni Ginetti deserve special mention.

Members of the Chicago media I would also like to thank for an able assist or insight include Joe Mooshil of the Associated Press, television journalist Jeannie Morris, Mark Giangreco of WMAQ-TV; producer Kiki Olivera of WBBM-TV; Chet Coppock and producer Jim Modelski of WLUP radio; and Tom Shaer, late of WMAQ and now WSCR radio, who dug up a couple of invaluable audio tapes. Jeff Nordlund of the *Arlington Heights Daily Herald,* Mike Doyle of the *Rockford Star,* Kelly

Quain of the *Southtown Economist,* and *Copley News Service* columnist Gene Seymour are owed a debt of gratitude. Outside the state, the writings of Valli Herman of *The Gary Post-Tribune* helped flesh out the Ditka's Merrillville operation; while Bill Utterback and Gerry Dulac of *The Pittsburgh Press* provided perspective on the coach.

Outside the media, a round of applause to David Barrett for making my stays in Chicago so enjoyable; David Hill Spencer for helping me understand; Hans Humphrey of NFL Alumni Association, who helped me track down many a former player; and Ron Howard of the Philadelphia Eagles for a few key phone numbers.

I also relied on several books for background information, perspective, and a pertinent quote or two. The books were *Ditka—An Autobiography* by Mike Ditka with Don Pierson; *Halas by Halas—The Autobiography of George Halas* by Halas with Gwen Morgan and Arthur Veysey; *McMahon!* by Jim McMahon with Bob Verdi; and *God's Coach* by Skip Bayless.

Given the dense nature of this book I would like to stress that serious efforts were made to insure the accuracy of everything reported. The fact-checking of names, dates, descriptions, dialogue, even 70-year-old railroad strikes were double- and sometimes triple-checked. That is not to say the book is 100 percent accurate, only that I hope it is, and I have spent hours attempting to insure its veracity. One of my great fears was dismissal or doubt cast over an entire project because of misspelled names or otherwise inaccurate reporting. That said, understand that there are often three sides to every story, particularly when it comes to Ditka's diverse restaurant dealings.

As for Ditka, after our heated exchange in August 1991—as described early on in the book—I must say he maintained a civil and profoundly professional attitude toward my presence at press conferences and around Halas Hall throughout the 1991 season. He answered questions in a public setting while quietly telling several family and personal friends he did not approve of the project, as was his right. Adhering to Ditka's wishes, the Bears organization, as expressed by team president and chief exceutive officer Mike McCaskey, was off limits. That policy effectively eliminated request for comments from Ed McCaskey, Ted Phillips, and Bill Tobin on topics relating specifically to them. The Bears organization, as a whole, however, treated me with every professional courtesy, and for that I am extremely grateful.

On a more personal note, I would like to acknowledge the fast fingers of Jackie Marucci, who transcribed so many of my tapes; the keen eye of copyeditor Steve Boldt; and the sharp ear of my gifted editor Doug Grad, who heard my writing voice, then willingly put in the time and effort necessary to fine-tune the manuscript. I also want to acknowledge Jack Romanos of Simon & Schuster for his belief in, and backing of, this book, and my agent, Basil Kane, who helped bring my idea to life. I would also like to express my love and gratitude to Albert and Virginia, my parents, who remain my inspiration.

Finally, to Martin Francis Dardis, who has taught me more life lessons than I can count, and to a former editor whose ethical standards and journalistic eye remain unmatched in my business. This book is a reflection of these two men. It is also a reflection of my belief, one often expressed by a coach named Ditka, that what the mind can conceive the heart can achieve.

Armen Keteyian
June 6, 1992
New Canaan, CT